Moritz Heck
Plurinational Afrobolivianity

Culture and Social Practice

Moritz Heck studied Social and Cultural Anthropology and Spanish at the University of Freiburg, Germany. He obtained his PhD at the University of Cologne as a member of the interdisciplinary a.r.t.e.s. Graduate School for the Humanities. His research interests include Afrodescendants in Latin America, indigeneity, race and ethnicity, as well as identity politics and social movements.

Moritz Heck

Plurinational Afrobolivianity

Afro-Indigenous Articulations and Interethnic Relations in the Yungas of Bolivia

[transcript]

Dissertation University of Cologne, Faculty of Arts and Humanities, 2019

Bibliographic information published by the Deutsche Nationalbibliothek
The Deutsche Nationalbibliothek lists this publication in the Deutsche Nationalbibliografie; detailed bibliographic data are available in the Internet at http://dnb.d-nb.de

Cover layout: Maria Arndt, Bielefeld
Cover illustration: »In the coca field«, Cala Cala 2014, photograph by Moritz Heck
Printed by Majuskel Medienproduktion GmbH, Wetzlar
Print-ISBN 978-3-8376-5056-3
PDF-ISBN 978-3-8394-5056-7
https://doi.org/10.14361/9783839450567

Contents

Para mis Agentes del Caos

List of Figures

List of Acronyms

ADEPCOCA Asociación Departamental de Productores de Coca

AFROCRUZ Organización Afroboliviana de Santa Cruz

CABOLS Comunidad Afroboliviana Santa Cruz

CADIC Centro Afroboliviano para el Desarrollo Integral y Comunitario

CEDEAFROB Asociación del Centro de Desarrollo Afroboliviano

CEPA Consejo Educativo del Pueblo Afroboliviano

CIDOB Confederación de Pueblos Indígenas de Bolivia

CIPCA Centro de Investigación y Promoción del Campesinado

CONAFRO Consejo Nacional Afroboliviano

CONALCAM Coordinadora Nacional por el Cambio

CONAMAQ Consejo Nacional de Ayllus y Markas del Qullasuyu

CNMCIOB-BS Confederación Nacional de Mujeres Campesinas Indígenas Originarias de Bolivia - Bartolina Sisa

CSCIOB Confederación Sindical de Comunidades Interculturales Originarios de Bolivia

CSUTCB Confederación Sindical Única de Trabajadores Campesinos de Bolivia

EGPP Escuela de Gestión Pública Plurinacional

FUNDAFRO-PAP Fundación de Afrodescendientes Pedro Andaverez Peralta

FUNPROEIB Andes Fundación para la Educación en Contextos de Multilingüismo y Pluriculturalidad

IDB Interamerican Development Bank

ILC-AFRO Instituto de Lengua y Cultura Afroboliviana

INE Instituto Nacional de Estadística

IPELC Instituto Plurinacional de Estudio de Lenguas y Culturas

MAS-IPSP Movimiento al Socialismo – Instrumento Político por la Soberanía de los Pueblos

MNR Movimiento Nacionalista Revolucionario

MOCUSABOL Movimiento Cultural Saya Afroboliviana

ORISABOL Organización Integral Saya Afroboliviana

PNTC Programa Nacional de Turismo Comunitario

Glossary of Spanish and Aymara Terms

Asamblea Constituyente: Constituent Assembly drafting the Bolivian Constitution of 2009

Asamblea Legislativa Plurinacional: Bolivia's legislature constisting of the Chamber of Deputies *(Cámara de Diputados)* and the Senate *(Cámara de Senadores)*

ayni: reciprocal system and practice of cooperation and exchange within a *comunidad*

cajas: *saya* drums

campesino/a: peasant

cocal: coca field

cocalero/a: coca farmer

comunario/a: member of a *comunidad*

comunidad: lit.: community. Term referring to social, territorial, political and economic units in the Yungas

cuancha: percussion instrument used in Afrobolivian *saya* made of *tacoara* trunks. It is played by rubbing a stick along notches cut into the trunk to produce a ratchet sound

cumplir función social: lit.: "(to) fulfill a social function". Meeting the expectations/obligations for belonging to a *comunidad*

ganyingo: smallest of the *saya* drums

hacienda: large agricultural estate

indio/a: (mostly) pejorative term for an indigenous person

jilacata: *hacienda* foreman, supervisor of the workforce

jornal/mink'a: wage paid for one day of work

k'ichiri: coca harvester, derived from amyara *k'ichir* - (to) harvest

liberto/a: freed slave

libreada: practice of measuring work obligations according to the weight of the harvested coca leaves

mauchi: Afrobolivian funerary rite of supposed African origin

mayordomo: *hacienda* administrator

mestizaje: racial and cultural mixture and ideologies thereof

mestizo/a: person of mixed (European-Indigenous) ancestry

mezcla: lit.: mixture. Term used to refer to a person of mixed ancestry

moreno/a: lit.: brown. Sometimes used euphemistically instead of *negro* but also used to describe Afrobolivians of a 'lighter' complexion

mulato/a: person of mixed (European-Black) ancestry

municipio: administrative division below departments and provinces, governed by an elected mayor *(alcalde)* and a municipal council *(concejo municipal)*

patrón/hacendado: *hacienda* owner

peón: person tied to a *hacienda* by labor obligations in exchange for land in usufruct

proceso de cambio: process of change (referring to the political reform project lead by the MAS party)

pueblo: people/town

saya: Afrobolivian cultural expression *(expresión cultural)* consisting of music, rhythm, dance and poetry.

sayañero: *peones* who received land entitlements *(sayañas)* during the Land Reform in 1953

sindicato (campesino): (peasant) union

taller: workshop

yungueño/a: person from the Yungas

zambo/a: person of mixed (African-Indigenous) ancestry

Acknowledgements

I owe the greatest debt of gratitude to the people of Cala Cala. Without their friendliness, patience and welcoming spirit, none of this would have been possible. They kindly shared their homes, their stories and their time, allowing me, albeit temporarily, to feel part of a truly exceptional community. ¡Muchas Gracias!

Research for this dissertation was made possible by a PhD grant from the *Studienstiftung des deutschen Volkes*. I am especially grateful for the generous support of my fieldwork in Bolivia. Additional funding for proofreading was provided by the *a.r.t.e.s. Graduate School for the Humanities* in Cologne.

Michaela Pelican was the kind of supervisor any PhD candidate can only hope for. I thank her for her patience and for personally and intellectually engaging with my work. Her personal dedication and her pragmatic advice in all phases of this project have been truly exceptional. I also thank Heike Drotbohm for her yearlong guidance since my very first steps as an anthropology student, and for her encouragement and support in the early stages of this project. Many thanks also go to Barbara Potthast who provided important contextualization and interdisciplinary input for my project. At the University of Cologne and the *a.r.t.e.s. Graduate School,* I would like to thank all fellow PhD students and colleagues who read and commented on parts of my work.

In Bolivia, I thank the staff at *CESU-UMSS* for allowing me to be part of their institution in Cochabamba during the preparatory stages of my field research. I thank all the people at *CONAFRO, CADIC, ILC-Afro, IPELC, MOCUSABOL, ORISABOL, Mauchi, Comunidad Afroboliviana Cochabamba, CABOLS, AfroCruz,* and *Unión Afro* for allowing me to participate in their meetings and activities, sharing documents, travels and many hours of their time with me. I am especially grateful to Martín Ballivián, Juan Angola, Jorge Medina, Edgar Vázquez, Sandy Pinto, Juan Carlos Ballivián, Mónica Rey and Vianka Vargas whose support and guidance have been crucial in many ways.

Most importantly, I thank my wife and children who have faithfully accompanied me throughout all those years. They endured my prolonged absences and many dissertation writing-induced mood swings, but nonetheless always provided the support and encouragement that made this book possible.

Note on the use of names

To protect my interlocutors' anonymity I have used pseudonyms for all individuals, except for public figures like activists, politicians, and authors who have publicly spoken or written about the topics I discuss.

I have not used a pseudonym for my field research site, since my discussion of local history and geography make the *comunidad* easily identifiable as Cala Cala/Nogalani.

Introduction

On a sunny day in April 2017 I accompanied Roberto Angola, an Afrobolivian[1] *cocalero* (coca farmer) from Cala Cala to the recently finished structure of the *Centro de Interpretación de la Hoja de Coca, Café de Altura y Cultura Afroboliviana*, a museum built within the territorial boundaries of the *comunidad*[2] *Nogalani*, in the Yungas of Bolivia.[3] Several people from Nogalani, "*los de arriba*" (lit. "the ones from above") as Roberto usually referred to them, were busy with preparations for the visit of a commission from La Paz, led by the vice minister of tourism. The purpose of the visit was the final inspection of a project that people had been engaged in for the

1 To refer to my interlocutors, throughout the book I mostly use the term Afrobolivian/*Afroboliviano/a* or the very common and colloquial *Afro*, since this is the term most Afrobolivians prefer. I use *blanco/a, negro/a, moreno/a, zambo/a*, 'black' and 'white,' as well as any other terms connoting phenotype and race only in direct quotations or in cases where I want to highlight that my interlocutors explicitly referred to an individual's phenotypical appearance or skin color. I use the term *Afrodescendiente*/Afrodescendant in the context of dealing with specific political discourses and self-positioning practices. In Bolivia, *Afrodescendiente* is a term mainly used in political and legal language and not in everyday conversation.

2 I speak of *comunidad* or *comunidades* to refer to a very specific type of collective in the Yungas, *la comunidad cocalera* or *campesina*, which exhibits many particularities that are of great importance to my discussion of Afrobolivianity (see chapter 3). I will only use the term "*comunidad Afroboliviana*" in direct quotes, since in Bolivia, there is only one example of a *comunidad* in the sense outlined above that can be described as Afrobolivian. For referring to abstract, contingent notions of (Afrobolivian) collectivity in particular localities or nationwide, I will therefore use the English term community. Differentiating terminologically between *comunidad* and community allows for the fleshing out of some important aspects of the relation between an ethnoracially articulated sense of community and other forms of collectivity and belonging. Afrobolivians from Cala Cala, for instance, often refer to themselves in collective terms as "*los Afros de Cala Cala*" (which I translate as "the Afrobolivian community of Cala Cala"); yet they also belong to a *comunidad* that transcends this ethnoracial collective (see chapters 3-5).

3 Cala Cala is a small conglomerate of houses located downhill from Nogalani. It was once a small estate *(estancia)* inhabited exclusively by Afrobolivians but has been a part of the *hacienda Nogalani* since the end of the 19th century. I will clarify the relation between Cala Cala and Nogalani in later chapters.

last four years. The minister and a team of experts (architects, lawyers, and accountants) had travelled the four hours from Bolivia's highland metropolis of La Paz to oversee the final stages of equipping the *Centro de Interpretación*.

As I arrived at the scene with Roberto, several people were busy mopping the floors, assembling different kinds of local produce (coca, tangerines, oranges and coffee) in representative bowls. Víctor, another Afrobolivian community leader, was carrying four *saya* drums into a corner of the museum and placed them on a podium underneath some photographs showing Afrobolivian *saya* musicians and dancers in their colorful dresses. The museum was already equipped with flat screen televisions attached to the walls, and with information panels on coca and coffee cultivation, as well as on aspects of Afrobolivian culture.

Suddenly, more people started entering the building and announced the arrival of the first members of the commission. From a luxurious Toyota Land Cruiser emerged *"el arquitecto,"* the architect responsible for the construction and equipping of the museum. He informed the crowd that the minister had been held up in Coroico, another village in the Bolivian Yungas, where he had inspected the completion of another *Centro de Interpretación*, but that he would arrive shortly. He ordered some of the men to help him carry the last pieces of equipment he had brought with him at the last moment. From the trunk of his car, they unloaded a male and a female mannequin and various bags of clothes and carried them into the museum. There, they set them up next to the drums, unpacked the clothes – that turned out to be Afrobolivian *saya* dress – and hastily dressed them. The two mannequins and the drums Víctor had placed in the corner were the main attraction of the exhibition on Afrobolivian culture in the museum. At the opposite side of the room stood another statue of a man with visibly 'black' features stretching out his hand and holding a coffee plant, wearing traditional clothing associated with the region.

The preparations were just finished when another luxurious 4x4 vehicle emerged on the steep road leading up to the area where the *Centro de Interpretación* had been built. This time, it was the vice minister, accompanied by a member of the *Asamblea Legislativa Plurinacional*, Bolivia's parliament. The assembled *comunarios* (members of the *comunidad*) lined up in front of the main entrance, greeted the vice minister with warm words, welcoming him to Nogalani and thanking him on behalf of all its members for making the construction of the museum possible. He responded equally enthusiastically, commenting on the stunning beauty of the climate and landscape of the Yungas, and expressing his satisfaction at how nicely the museum had turned out. He was then invited to take the first ever tour of the brand new museum. The basics of coca cultivation were explained to him and his companions, and they were offered a gift of dried coca leaves that the *comunarios* had prepared for them. They went on to the section explaining the cultivation of organic high altitude coffee, and the process of peeling, roasting and grinding the beans. Eventually, it was time to move on to the Afrobolivian section, where Roberto

Figure 1: Mannequins with saya dress and Cala Cala's saya drums (left) and the statue of an Afrobolivian coffee cultivator (right) in the Centro de Interpretación (photographs by the author)

was given the task of explaining the *saya* exhibits and introducing the commission to "Afrobolivian culture."

Roberto was visibly nervous that day, despite the fact that I knew him to be a very calm, confident man with an astonishing gift of self-reflection, leadership, spirit and eloquence. As he stood in front of the assembled community and the visitors from La Paz, he pointed at the *saya* drums and said:

> "I have known this since I can remember. So it's very old. I mean in comparison with the *saya* of today" (he now pointed to the pictures on the wall accompanying the exhibition of the drums) "that came up only later, right? In those moments. I am forty-four years old now and those drums must be from the 60s or 70s, look, right? So they are very old, but they still have their strength, right? Yes, I think that's it."[4]

---

4 *"Desde que yo tengo uso de razón, yo he conocido eso. Entonces es súper antiguo. O sea en comparación con la saya de hoy que recién salió después, ¿no es cierto? En estos momentos. Yo hasta ahora tengo 44 años y aproximadamente esos son de los años 70 o 60, mira, ¿nove? Entonces son súper antiguos, pero todavía siguen mostrando, digamos, su fortaleza, ¿no es cierto? Sí. Yo creo que eso nomás."*

Through his statement, Roberto linked the drums – a material representation of Afrobolivian culture – with his biography, highlighting how important they were for him since "they have been there since I can remember." For him, the drums say something about who he is and while they are indeed "very old," they maintain their strength *("fortaleza")* up to the present. He juxtaposed the drums people were looking at with "the *saya* of today" *("la saya de hoy")*, often a shorthand description for referring to Afrobolivian culture more generally. Through this juxtaposition he revealed a tension between what he considered important about being *Afroboliviano* and the representation of Afrobolivianity put forth through the museum. When I later spoke to the vice minister and some members of the delegation, they expressed a similar concern, but from the opposite perspective. The vice minister himself remarked apprehensively that the presentation of the *saya* drums needed to be "improved and deepened" *("mejorado y profundizado")*, failing to acknowledge that Roberto had intended just that: giving the display of 'Afrobolivian culture' a meaning beyond the museum, expressing what it means for people like him. For the delegation from La Paz, the exhibition was based on a representation and performance of Afrobolivianity that, from their perspective, Roberto was not able or willing to produce at that moment. The mutual disappointment was based on diverging concepts and ideas of what it means to be Afrobolivian – to different people, institutions and the state – and how Afrobolivianity ought to be expressed and represented.

As the guests of honor were led into the adjacent auditorium for lunch, I sat with Roberto and Víctor at the entrance to this remarkable building, chewing coca in complete silence. Roberto and Víctor seemed to be quite overwhelmed and as we sat, I thought about the first time people in Cala Cala had told me about the tourism project they were in the middle of developing. In 2014, nobody was talking about a museum and people were discussing only the remote possibility of being granted government funds to develop a small community-based tourism project. In fact, people in Cala Cala initially hadn't even thought of community tourism at all when they approached the *Mancomunidad de Municipios* – the regional confederation of municipal governments – in order to ask for funds to build a simple, one-room building where they could hold community meetings. The officer at the *Mancomunidad* had told them that he unfortunately did not have any funds available, but that the "office down the hall" *("la oficina al fondo")* had just received a multi-million dollar grant from the Interamerican Development Bank (IDB) to fund the *Programa Nacional de Turismo Comunitario* (PNTC, National Community Tourism Program) and that they should ask there. The people from Cala Cala took that lead and, four years and innumerable meetings later, we were sitting in front of a large museum during a visit by the vice minister of tourism, an outcome nobody in Cala Cala would have been able to foresee.

People in Cala Cala often emphasized how strange and surprising many of the developments and the eventual construction of the museum in Nogalani were to them – a generalized feeling people expressed and something that goes well beyond the 'professional puzzlement' of the ethnographer. Not only had the people of Cala Cala and Nogalani – a *comunidad* of only about 150 households – just inaugurated a museum project worth tens of thousands of US dollars while the high school right next to it was in a deplorable condition; it was also quite remarkable that Nogalani was singled out as the site of a *Centro de Interpretación de la Cultura Afroboliviana*. There are only eleven Afrobolivian households in the entire *comunidad* – as opposed to over 100 Aymara households. Of these eleven Afrobolivian households, only two were actively engaged in the tourism project.[5] And – as we have seen – even one of the most engaged individuals was not able to produce a representation of 'Afrobolivian culture' deemed adequate in the eyes of the vice minister and his commission. What is more, the 'Afrobolivian culture' depicted in the museum was just thirty years ago expected to be 'lost' in the near future and despite efforts at revitalization, it hardly played a role in Cala Cala's everyday life or its residents' sense of being Afrobolivian (see chapter 3).

I argue, however, that this situation, as unlikely as it might seem at first glance, is by no means a mere coincidence, as Roberto sometimes contemplated when he tried to make sense of the journey that led him and Cala Cala from the "office down the hall" to the doorstep of the finished museum. The *Centro de Interpretación* is just one material representation of a wider set of processes set in motion by Bolivia's proclaimed 're-founding'; it is an outcome of plurinational governance and development. The journey of Cala Cala's inhabitants from wanting to have a place to socialize to becoming engaged in a museum project based on 'Afrobolivian culture' is only one example of the processes this book will describe and analyze. Cala Cala's journey is deeply entangled with a particular political, cultural and social conjuncture – Bolivia's plurinational moment – where an "indigenous state" (Postero 2017) engages with its subjects through politics, law and development in novel ways. In this plurinational conjuncture, discourses of cultural diversity and indigenous rights dating back to the 1970s have reached a preliminary peak in importance. For Afrobolivians in Cala Cala, the discourses of plurinationality are most strongly felt when engaging the legal entitlements and novel avenues for political enfranchisement associated with the recognition of *el pueblo Afroboliviano* ("the Afrobolivian people") in Bolivia's 2009 Plurinational Constitution. Since then, the concept of *el pueblo Afroboliviano* has become a central pillar of Afrobolivian identity politics, as well as an important discursive device for framing demands vis-à-vis the state. Without going into much detail here (see chapter 9), it is important to introduce some

5 See chapter 3 for details on the number and composition of households in Cala Cala.

key features of the concept. On the one hand, addressing Afrobolivians as a *pueblo* implies the assumption that Afrobolivians all over the country share definable characteristics that unite them as a collectivity, while at the same time clearly differentiating them from other *pueblos*. In the language of the Constitution, those characteristics have to do with "cultural identity," "language," "historic tradition," "institutions," "territory" and "world view" (see Article 30 of the Bolivian Constitution of 2009). In the example of the opening vignette, those purportedly unique characteristics form the basis for an exhibition on Afrobolivian 'culture,' but the impact and the scope of the *pueblo* concept are not limited to museum projects. On the other hand, invoking *el pueblo Afroboliviano* leads to the assumption that Afrobolivian demands ought to be accommodated by the Plurinational State within the framework of collective rights also applied to indigenous groups in the 2009 Constitution. As will become clear throughout my study, both assumptions and their myriad ramifications are often problematic and subject to severe criticism. Yet they also serve as new reference points and provide an additional sphere of resonance for articulating Afrobolivian claims. Beyond formally granting Afrobolivians special collective rights equal to those of indigenous groups (*"pueblos indígena originario campesinos"*), constitutional recognition has meant a great deal of attention for the category *Afroboliviano* in national politics, as well as from international development actors and the media.[6] As a consequence of these developments, local notions of identity, community and belonging are changing. In the opening vignette, we have already encountered references to various collective identifications (*Afros*, *cocaleros*, *comunarios*, and *"los de arriba"*). These local terms relate in different ways to the broader categories *Afro(boliviano)* and Aymara, as well as to specific places in the local ethnographic context (Nogalani and Cala Cala). As will become clear in subsequent chapters, they furthermore specifically relate to concepts of indigeneity and blackness on a national and global scale.

Beyond hinting at the multiplicity of collective identifications in Cala Cala, this short episode introduces another important aspect of my argument, namely that the meanings of Afrobolivianity itself are contested. The depiction of Afrobolivianity in the exhibition heavily focuses on the aspect of 'Afrobolivian culture' expressed by the explicit reference to *"Cultura Afroboliviana"* in the museum's name, but also by the overarching importance *saya* is given in the exhibition's concept. Yet it is clear that Afrobolivianity is also related to ideas of race and racialized difference.

6 Article 31 of Bolivia's 2009 Constitutions reads: "The Afro-Bolivian people enjoy, in everything corresponding, the economic, social, political and cultural rights that are recognized in the Constitution for the nations and the rural native indigenous peoples." (*"El pueblo afroboliviano goza, en todo lo que corresponda, de los derechos económicos, sociales, políticos y culturales reconocidos en la Constitución para las naciones y pueblos indígena originario campesinos."*) Unless otherwise noted, the translated passages from the Constitution are from the English translation provided by www.constituteproject.org.

The phenotypical appearance of the Afrobolivian mannequins serves as a material expression of this very widespread racialized perspective on Afrobolivianity. The fact that the mannequins' phenotype was neither explicitly addressed during the planning stages of the project, nor mentioned in the information pertaining to the exhibition, serves as a reminder of the "absent presence of race" (Wade, Deister, et al. 2014) in Bolivia and Latin America more generally. Moreover, as Roberto's short statement quoted at the beginning vividly exemplifies, there are also local understandings of what it means to be *Afroboliviano*. Those understandings of Afrobolivianity are often rooted in individual biographies, local history and kinship relations and reflect a different perspective on processes of collective identification, difference and community, and on the place of Afrobolivianity in plurinational Bolivia.

In what remains of this introduction, I will sketch my theoretical approach to Afrobolivianity as developed through my long-term involvement with people in Cala Cala and my engagement with the literature on Afrodescendants and indigenous people in Latin America. I will then provide an overview of the structure of my argument and how this is reflected in the ethnographic chapters that follow. In the next chapter, I will outline my perspectives and my methodology, including a reflection on my roles in the field and some general comments on the danger of reification when studying categories of identification.

Theoretical framework

My study of Afrobolivianity is situated within the recently emerging field of studying indigeneity and *Afrodescendencia* in Latin America within a common analytical framework. Similar to most of the studies I will introduce in the following paragraphs, my project was from its inception designed to be situated at the intersection of different disciplinary and regional areas of interest. Therefore, instead of being able to draw from a well-established canon of theoretical approaches and concepts, the analytical tools, perspectives and interpretative stances come from a variety of sources. I take my main cues from theoretical approaches that have – in some way or another – paved the way for decentering established notions of certain areas of inquiry. My basic understanding of the politics of difference with regard to Afrodescendants in Latin America is derived from Peter Wade's work, which has shown the complex interrelations of race, ethnicity, and nation in Latin America (Wade 2009a; Wade 2009b; Wade 2010). From Wade's work I take the fundamental understanding that there are myriad conceptual overlaps between race and ethnicity, blackness, indigeneity, and mixture *(mestizaje)* in Latin America, but also important rifts, separations and contradictions. This is why I embrace his approach of maintaining the terminological distinction between race and ethnicity in Latin America in order to address empirical and conceptual entanglements as well as separations. At the same time, I follow Mark Anderson's proposal to use the term "ethnoracial" in order "to highlight how identity categories often entangle notions of biological and cultural differences" (Anderson 2009:29), whenever my ethnographic data shows that references to ethnicity (broadly understood by most of my interlocutors to refer to a group identity based on cultural characteristics) and race (equally broadly understood as a group identity based on physical appearance and/or perceived biological descent) are not neatly separable. Viewing race and ethnicity, as well as blackness and indigeneity as inextricably linked in Latin America, I draw on scholarship on blackness and indigeneity in an equal manner, highlighting the possible avenues of cross-fertilization of these strands of literature. In order to ground my analysis of blackness and indigeneity as they relate to Afrobolivians in social practice, I briefly introduce selected contributions from the anthropological study of ethnicity and processes of shaping collective identities. Subsequently, I summarize my approach to law as a decisive factor in re-shaping notions of identity, 'groupness' and boundaries, namely the notion of "legalizing identities" as developed by Jan Hoffmann French in her recent work on Brazil (French 2009). French's approach not only destabilizes common notions of blackness and indigeneity as separate modes of identification, but also fruitfully links debates on cultural change, legal recognition, political mobilization and the renegotiation of identities.

New perspectives on blackness and indigeneity in Latin America

In recent years, there has been an upsurge in publications dealing with indigenous people and Afrodescendants in Latin America within a single analytical framework. This has not always been the case. As Peter Wade (Wade 2010:24) has observed, the situation was marked by a fairly deep-seated divide between studies of black people and studies of indigenous peoples. Citing Colombia as an example, Wade contends that this divide in scholarship is at least in part a consequence of the fact that black and indigenous peoples have for the longest time occupied different spaces in Latin America's "structures of alterity": indigenous people as cultural others and black people – if not "invisible" (de Friedemann 1984) – as racial others. As a consequence of this divide, in Latin American Anthropology there are few examples of studies that treat indigenous people and Afrodescendants within a single framework and usually indigeneity and blackness are approached with fundamentally different theoretical tools. Indigenous people have been studied as ethnic groups, Afrodescendants as a racial group (Wade 2010). Studying indigenous people, anthropologists inquired into 'traditional forms' of social, political or religious life that have survived or have been modified by colonialism (de la Cadena and Starn 2007a). At least implicitly, notions of continuity and rootedness have played a part in this, albeit that tendency is increasingly being questioned and debated (Canessa 2007; da Cuña and De Almeida 2000). In its most radical form, critics of indigeneity have questioned not only the analytical value of the concept but have also disavowed it politically due to its essentialism and exclusionary tendencies (Kuper 2003). Black people in Latin America have been approached either from a more sociological perspective, inquiring into Latin American 'race relations' or racism, or from an anthropological approach, in which black people have been linked to notions of cultural survivals from Africa (Herskovits 1990) and concepts like diaspora, creolization and hybridity. Rather than continuities, these concepts focus on transnationalism, cultural innovation and hybrid identities (Dixon and Burdick 2012; Greene 2007a; Rossbach de Olmos and Drotbohm 2009; Whitten and Torres 1998; Yelvington 2006; cf. Gilroy 1993; and Hall 1997). Although this depiction of the divide seems rather schematic, it has only been overcome in recent years and in many aspects still persists today.

Afro-indigenous multiculturalisms

However, in recent years, historically oriented works have demonstrated the relative flexibility of categories and ensuing negotiations of belonging within the Spanish colonial *casta* system (Albiez-Wieck 2017), and have occasionally even focused explicitly on the relationship between 'native'/indigenous parts of the population and black slaves or former slaves (Gutiérrez Brockington 2006; O'Toole 2012; Restall 2005; Restall 2009). Those studies have decentered the notion of separate spaces of black and indigenous sociality and culture from colonial and early republican times until the present. From an anthropological perspective, an increasing number of scholars have targeted the ways Afrodescendant groups make sense of multicultural reforms and draw on indigeneity by tapping into transnational indigenism (Niezen 2003) and related politics of identity (Hooker 2005; Hooker 2008). In an article focusing on Peru, but with wider regional implications, Shane Greene has argued that we are increasingly confronted with situations where "states project a potential, if not in practice an actual, ethno-cultural and racial equivalence between Afro-descendent and indigenous populations in the region" (Greene 2007a:329). This situation he refers to as "Afro-Indigenous multiculturalisms." For Colombia, Peter Wade has pointed out the tendency of indianizing or indigenizing blackness through engagement with the multicultural state (Wade 1995; Wade 2006a; Wade 2009c), an approach taken up by various scholars (Ng'weno 2007; Restrepo 2004) rendering it more precisely as an ethnicization of blackness and emphasizing its inherent tendencies to fix, homogenize and ruralize black identity in the Pacific Region of Colombia (see also Rossbach de Olmos 2009). Thinking along the same general lines, Shane Greene (Greene 2007a) has introduced the notion of the "holy trinity of multicultural peoplehood," highlighting the influence that the reforms' legal and political definition of a certain type of collective subject *(un pueblo)* have on the political subjectivities of indigenous and Afrodescendant people. In a very interesting case study from Honduras, Mark Anderson develops his concept of "black indigenism" in order to make sense of the cultural politics of Garifuna activism in multicultural Honduras (Anderson 2009). A similar focus on Latin American multiculturalism also informs recent analyses of black social movements in Latin America and blackness more generally (Rahier 2012a; Rahier 2014). At the same time, those studies have shown that beyond references to indigeneity filtered through multicultural regimes of recognition, Afrodescendants draw on notions of diasporic routes (Greene 2007a) and global notions of blackness and *Afrodescendencia* in processes of negotiating identities, constructing belonging and also political alliances (Rahier 2012b; Wade 2009c). The crucial point is that blackness and indigeneity – and associated tropes of diaspora vs. roots, race vs. ethnicity, 'Indians' vs. black people – should not be seen as two opposing and incompatible modes of identity formation and political contestation, but rather as complementary elements of a process by which concepts like "black indigeneity" or "indigenous blackness" can become avenues into "partially disrupt[ing] a conceptual-political grid that links indigeneity with Indians and Blacks with displacement" (Anderson 2009:22). I will directly address the possibilities and limitations of articulating Afrobolivianity as black indigeneity in my discussion of the changing patterns of Afrobolivian mobilization in chapters 8 and 9, and the basic assumptions of the approaches outlined above run through my entire argument.

Afrobolivians and indigenous people in a *mestizo* nation

Beyond the realm of the political, the relationships between black and indigenous peoples have been targeted in studies of *mestizaje* in Latin America, both historically, as well as through ethnographic inquiry in contemporary settings (De la Cadena 2005; Gruzinksi 2002; Hale 2014; Hale 2015; Miller 2004; Rappaport 2014; Wade 2009b). For reasons of space, it is not possible to summarize the vast literature on *mestizaje* in its entirety. Suffice it to say here that there is a lively debate of the concept as "an elite-generated myth of national identity" (Hale 1996:2) in Latin America on the one hand and *mestizaje* as a lived experience on the other (for a recent contextualization see Wade 2005). As an ideological notion linked to nation-building processes, *mestizaje* has been widely criticized and famously dubbed an "all-inclusive ideology of exclusion" (Stutzman 1981) that although celebrating mixture and inclusion, privileges whiteness and denigrates and excludes blackness and indigeneity. As a lived experience, *mestizaje* has occasionally been celebrated as a "counterhegemonic claiming of intermediate identities that, by its very indeterminacy and flexibility, escapes the use of ethnic and racial categorizations for the purposes of social control" (Mallon 1996:171; see also De la Cadena 2000). Yet, as

Peter Wade has observed, *mestizaje* – albeit fundamentally about cultural and racial mixing – also plays a decisive part in reifying ethnic and racial categories such as black, white and indigenous as the original allegedly 'pure' ingredients of any mixture. This is all the more important since in recent years the rise of genomic research in Latin America has catapulted *mestizaje* yet again to the center of debates on the nation and its origin (Wade, Beltrán, et al. 2014; Wade 2017).

Mestizaje is important for the present study insofar as it is connected to "modern racial-colonial discourses [that] located the classic colonial triad (white, *mestizo*, Indian) at the center of debates about national identity and racial destiny" (Larson 2004:68). Within those debates in the Bolivian context, blackness often occupies a space at the margins of the "dynamic triad of racial hierarchy" (Larson 2004:68) and the nation. Consequently, most state-led initiatives of nation-building and parallel debates on national identity in academic circles have been simplified and reduced to the question "What to do with the Indians?" (*"¿Qué hacer con los Indios"?)* (Stefanoni 2010; see also Larson 2004) – leaving little space for debates on blackness.[7] My discussion of different notions of blackness in relation to mixture and indigeneity in Bolivia in chapter 6 reflects the important discursive role of *mestizaje* as an ideology, but also leaves room for the discussion of racial mixture within families and communities, and how it relates to the Afrobolivian population more generally.

Emerging Afrobolivianity: articulations, performances and translations

If we conceive of indigeneity and blackness as fundamentally entangled, it is possible to draw on recent developments in theorizing indigeneity and fruitfully engage with blackness through this analytical lens. I propose studying blackness parallel to indigeneity as a matter of becoming, following James Clifford's perspective on indigeneity as a matter of "becoming" in an age marked by globalization, decolonization and their entanglements (Clifford 2013). Similar proposals have been made from a variety of scholars from a variety of regional backgrounds (for an overview see Levi and Maybury-Lewis 2012; for Africa: Hodgson 2009; Hodgson 2011; Pelican 2009; for Latin America: Course 2011; Jackson 1991; Jackson 1995; French 2009; for Asia: Li 2000; Rycroft and Dasgupta 2011; Tyson 2010). Building on his earlier conceptualization of "indigenous diasporas" (Clifford 2007), Clifford proposes studying indigeneity as a matter of articulation, performance and translation (Clifford 2013:54f).

The notion of articulation provides us with a means to overcome the rather unfruitful divide between primordialist assumptions with regard to indigeneity on

7 The marginality of blackness in this regard – that seems to be even more pronounced in Bolivia than elsewhere in Latin America – has become an important aspect in Afrobolivian mobilization and has fueled the notions of 'invisibility' central to many activist narratives.

the one hand and the assertions that claims based on indigeneity can be comprehensively analyzed as a result of identity politics relying on "invented traditions" on the other (Clifford 2013:54). "Articulation offers," Clifford argues, "a nonreductive way to think about cultural transformation and the apparent coming and going of 'traditional' forms" avoiding "[a]ll-or-nothing, fatal-impact notions of change" (Clifford 2013:60). Consequently,

> "[i]n articulation theory, the whole question of authenticity is secondary, and the process of social and cultural persistence is political all the way back. It's assumed that cultural forms will always be made, unmade, and remade. Communities can and must reconfigure themselves, drawing selectively on remembered pasts. *The relevant question is whether, and how, they convince and coerce insiders and outsiders, often in power charged, unequal situations, to accept the autonomy of a 'we.'*" (Clifford 2013:61f emphasis added by the author)

Since articulation is concerned rather with possibilities than with prefigured patterns and certainties, the concept allows us to furthermore accommodate "cosmopolitan" (Goodale 2006) and "creole" (Halbmayer 2011) frames of reference for 21st century indigenous identities. Linked to emerging black indigeneities, this seems like a logical fit, as it accommodates not only the increasingly transnational dimensions of indigeneity but also allows for the integration in our analysis of Afrobolivianity of globally circulating discourses, images and practices associated with the African Diaspora and transnational notions of *'lo Afro'* in Latin America (Anderson 2009; Wade 1999; Wade 2009c). Furthermore, it allows us to also consider (black) indigeneity in relation to the concept of autochthony that – albeit originating in an Africanist context (Ceuppens and Geschiere 2005; Geschiere 2009; Geschiere and Jackson 2006) – can be fruitfully employed in comparative studies of indigeneity (Canessa 2018; Hodgson 2002; Pelican 2009; Zenker 2011). I address the articulated nature of Afrobolivianity and the varying references to indigeneity, autochthony, and diaspora throughout the book as a whole, but most directly in my discussion of the emerging Afrobolivian movement and its consolidation in chapters 8 and 9. Moreover, such references play a role in state-led efforts at cataloging and normalizing Afrobolivian culture analyzed in chapter 7. What is more, although most of my interlocutors reject explicit references to being indigenous, local notions of Afrobolivian identity circle around autochthony, for example when representing Afrobolivians as the 'original' (i.e. non-migrant) inhabitants of the Yungas (see chapters 3 to 5).

Related to the basic understanding of indigeneity as articulation, Clifford suggests focusing on two additional aspects of "becoming indigenous": heritage preservation and performance, as well as translation (Clifford 2013:252). This is all the more important in times and circumstances where "indigenous experiences [are] no longer exclusively rooted in village settings" (Clifford 2013:222) and these performances enable "new identifications and more formally expressed notions of 'culture' or 'tradition.'" In Bolivia, notions of Afrobolivian culture have been decidedly shaped by migration and the experiences of Afrobolivians in urban environments. What is more, Afrobolivianity has been formally introduced into the canon of Bolivia's intangible cultural heritage and many representations of Afrobolivianity as heritage lie in constant tension with the lived experience of Afrobolivians all over the country. This is also where translation becomes so important. Afrobolivianity transcends conceptual spaces and cannot be considered to be rooted in a particular place or within a clearly defined unchanging collective. Thus, articulations, (re-)identifications and contingent performances of Afrobolivianity need to be translated between different contexts and people – for example between generations or regions, or between mediatized representations of Afrobolivian culture and local cultural practice (cf. Clifford 2013:224). In my discussion of *saya* in chapter 7, I will highlight the importance of performance and the dynamics of formalization as heritage, as well as the seminal role translation plays in bridging different conceptual spaces and sectors of Afrobolivian society.

Articulated Afrobolivianity and interethnic relations

There are limitations to articulation theory, however. Clifford himself recognizes that the concept (also due to its particular conceptual genealogy from Gramsci through Hall [1986]) tends to focus on discourse and speech (Clifford 2013:59). Moreover, if "pushed to extremes it can take you to a point where every cultural form, every structure or restructuration, every connection and disconnection, has a radical contingency as if, at any moment, anything were possible." (Clifford 2013:63). This is of course not the case. The articulation of Afrobolivianity is – as much as that of any ethnic or ethnoracial category of identification – "circumscribed by the historically available materials" (Lentz 2006:5). Therefore, emerging "new modes of self-understanding must be anchored in existing social relations and ideas for them to be meaningful" (Lentz 2006:5). This aspect has been addressed in the study of ethnicity and indigenous groups in Bolivia for example by Xavier Albó, who pointed out "the 'Long Memory' of Ethnicity in Bolivia" (Albó 2008), i.e. the great historical depth of indigeneity and ethnicity in the country, and this history's profound impact on society in the present. My aim is thus to "explore both the […] 'invention' of ethnic categories, by multiple actors and with diverse interests, and the embeddedness of these new constructs in […] [already established] modes of social positioning and belonging" (Lentz 2006:7). Throughout my discussion I will show that certain aspects of Afrobolivianity are more difficult to articulate than others and that processes of translation can also fail or be rejected. This is the case, for example, between Afrobolivian organizations and the state, as well as between different parts of the Afrobolivian population dispersed throughout the country.

In order to ground my study of Afrobolivianity in social practice and to make sense of how notions of being *Afro* become meaningful in contexts of face-to-face interactions and local processes of identification, I wish to add some input from other scholars to Clifford's proposition, as well as certain insights from anthropological theorizing on (ethnic) groups, identities, boundaries, social integration and conflicts (Eidson et al. 2017; Elwert 2002; Jenkins 2008; Schlee 1997; Schlee 2004). Engaging this literature grounds the study of Afrobolivian articulations in social practice and also helps us grasp the practical limits of articulation. There are multiple reasons for my engagement of theories of ethnicity: I understand Afrobolivianity and indigeneity as articulated and relational identities "without guarantees" (de la Cadena and Starn 2007b; see also Postero 2013) that become most relevant in day-to-day settings when negotiating social, economic and political relations with people that are considered 'others.' In contexts of concrete social interactions the question is often in what sense Afrobolivians can be considered a "we-group" sharing specific networks of communication, social norms (especially in terms of a moral economy and practical solidarity) and certain institutions of conflict resolution (Elwert 2002). Furthermore, engaging Afrobolivianity as a "we-group process" (as understood by Elwert), points our attention to the possibility of identity switching – both for individuals (situational switching) and collectively (for example in the realm of political positioning). Thus, the we-group and/or its boundaries may be widened, narrowed, re-drawn or re-conceptualized. However, Günther Schlee (Schlee 2004) warns us of the fact that though malleable, identities and boundaries, as well as belongings, affiliations and alliances, are not entirely flexible. They have to make sense within the conceptual spaces of the societies they are embedded in. Thus it is not possible to simply 'invent' them: "Social identities cannot be made up at will, because they have to be plausible to others" (Schlee 2004:137) and it requires "virtuosi in identity manipulation" (Schlee 2004:137) in order to succeed in plausibly widening or narrowing group memberships or inter-group alliances intentionally. In fact, the very existence of the group may be questioned and instead, as Rogers Brubaker has proposed, we can focus on processes of "group-making" and the creation of "groupness" (Brubaker 2002; Brubaker 2009). What is more, reconfigurations of social identities can remain incomplete, contested and can be reshaped or undone. They may furthermore overlap, creating "cross-cutting ties" that in turn may serve to integrate society beyond ethnically or racially defined identities and collectives (Schlee 1997; Schlee 2004). Likewise Carola Lentz has suggested that since "ethnicity itself is not only fluid, but fluidly connected to [...] non-ethnic bases of identification and commonality" it is "necessary to broaden the perspective and explore much more than 'just' ethnicity" (Lentz 2006:3–4). In the case of Afrobolivians, this mainly concerns the identifications as *comunarios* and *cocaleros*, as well as regional identity as *Yungueños*.

I take up these issues in chapters 3 and 4 when discussing Cala Cala/Nogalani as marked fundamentally by two horizons of community (in emic terms *"Los Afros de Cala Cala"* vs. *"La comunidad cocalera"*) referring to different "dimensions of identification" (Schlee 2008) or "conceptual frame[s] of reference for purposes of identification" (Eidson et al. 2017). The two different we-groups produced through identification with one or the other frame are not mutually exclusive and my analysis of Cala Cala shows that switching between those horizons is possible – and indeed occurs quite frequently, both on the level of individuals, as well as in collective identifications and organizational contexts. Both horizons are options for summoning groupness in formalized representations of the community, as well as in practice.

What I have found to be of great importance in terms of the continuous interactions of different horizons of community in Cala Cala is the law, and more specifically the legal codification of the category *"Afroboliviano"* as one possible dimension or frame for collective identification. The legal codification, recognition and the ensuing political entitlements and economic possibilities associated with the category *"Afroboliviano"* provide a very powerful impetus to framing community, belonging and social boundaries in a specific way. I therefore engage a third strand of literature focusing on the proliferation of legal discourse and the law's entanglements with identity in order to account for this shift.

Laws, rights and subjectivities

Since the passing of the New Bolivian Constitution of 2009, laws, legal language, procedures and rights have played a crucial role for many people in plurinational Bolivia. I understand the legal recognition and recurring references to rights, as well as the logics of formalization and bureaucratization this entails, as an important emerging site of the articulation of Afrobolivianity. The salience of law and legal discourses is by no means limited to Bolivia or Latin America, but has been identified as a global phenomenon (Benda-Beckmann, Benda-Beckmann, and Eckert 2009; Benda-Beckmann, Benda-Beckmann, and Griffiths 2005; Benda-Beckmann, Benda-Beckmann, and Griffiths 2009; Comaroff and Comaroff 2009; de Sousa Santos 2002; Nader 2002). In a programmatic essay on their approach to an anthropology of law, governance and sovereignty, John and Jean Comaroff go as far as to assert that it "is impossible to approach the contemporary global order without close attention to law; to law especially in its polyvalent relation to governance" (Comaroff and Comaroff 2009:31f).

This trend has been widely noted in Latin America. From a political science perspective (Nolte and Schilling-Vacaflor 2012) it has been labelled as Constitutionalism (or New Constitutionalism), while anthropologists have studied the process through ethnography (Postero 2017; Schavelzon 2012). In Bolivia, the constitutional reform process has been interpreted as the culmination of a process of "natives making nation" (Canessa 2005) and celebrated as an important means of expanding citizenship to encompass more and more marginalized groups (Postero 2006). Legal recognition in the constitutional text has been interpreted as the end of 'invisibility' by Afrobolivians and has become an important point of departure for renegotiating notions of national belonging, further political mobilization and the claiming of rights. I will address the key features of Bolivia's Plurinational Constitution and their perceived transformative potential from the perspective of Afrobolivians in chapter 9, but will also point out important limitations (cf. Albro 2010a; Crabtree and Whitehead 2008; Farthing and Kohl 2014; Goodale and Postero 2013; Postero 2017; Schilling-Vacaflor, Brand, and Radhuber 2012).

Legal recognition has in many cases fostered a growing importance of law way beyond constitutions. In Latin America and globally, there is a marked trend whereby the focus of conflict resolution moves from political contexts to the courts, subsumed under the umbrella term of judicialization of politics. Judicialization, following a recent conceptualization (Huneeus, Couso, and Sieder 2010), involves two distinct but closely related aspects. On the one hand, the term can refer to the observation that courts have taken on a new, more pronounced political role, positioning themselves as the defenders of constitutions and rights and occupying the role of arbiters in a variety of policy conflicts. On the other hand, speaking of judicialization signals the increasing use of laws and legal discourse by various political actors more generally – equally including individual politicians and social movements (Huneeus, Couso, and Sieder 2010:8). Importantly, the judicialization of politics can emerge from a variety of sources, including the state itself ("from above"), marginalized actors ("from below") or transnational entities and organizations ("from abroad") (Sieder, Schjolden, and Angell 2005a:4; on "legalism from below," see also Eckert 2006; on the transnational dimension of "empires of law": Goodale 2007). Law, the claiming of rights and the appeal to courts can become a strategy for advancing counterhegemonic political struggles (de Sousa Santos and Cesar A. Rodríguez-Garavito 2005:4; see also: Comaroff and Comaroff 2009; Eckert 2006), a view differing significantly from more classic approaches in Marxist legal anthropology and sociology that saw law as fundamentally at the service of hegemony (for an overview see Spitzer 1983).

The "legal cultures" (Huneeus, Couso, and Sieder 2010:6) or "cultures of legality" (Comaroff and Comaroff 2009:34) this engenders refer to the fact that "shifting repertoires of ideas and behaviours relating to law, legal justice, and legal systems" (Huneeus, Couso, and Sieder 2010:4–5) begin to shape social interactions that occur far beyond the formal legal system. Law permeates the social world "from constitutions to the capillaries of the everyday" (Comaroff and Comaroff 2006:24). "Humanity," as Comaroff and Comaroff assert, "knows itself more than ever before by virtue of its rights." In the cases I will discuss in this book with regard to Afrobolivians, it is the latter aspect of judicialization and the often elusive yet pervasive presence of legal discourse that are most important.[8] Through as little as "rumours of rights" (Eckert 2012) law emerges as a "site of hope" for Afrobolivians parallel to collective political action and mobilizing. What is more, through judicialization, hopes and needs are shaped into claims, turning hope into expectation (Eckert 2012:157, 166).

The most striking example of this tendency is certainly the Afrobolivian campaign leading up to constitutional reform in 2009 (see chapter 9): "More than 500 years give us rights" *("Más de 500 años también nos dan derechos")* was the slogan Afrobolivian organizations used in their mobilizations, articulating the grievances of their constituency in terms of rights to be claimed from the state. In the aftermath of recognition, such discourses became even more important and in the most mundane settings of everyday life – for instance in the coca field – people nowadays speak of their rights and how claiming them might improve their situation.

Legalizing identity and plurinational ID-ology

Law, recognition and the invocation of rights not only exert influence on the way needs, grievances and hopes can be articulated, but they shape the ways people conceive of their collective identities, affiliations and belongings. Building on socio-legal studies that approach "law's role in eliciting apparently natural identities" (Collier, Maurer, and Suarez-Navaz 1996:2) Jan Hoffman French has developed the concept of "legalizing identities" (French 2009). Studying a community of Afro-indigenous descent in northeastern Brazil, French analyzes processes by which one part of the community "became black" though asserting their (legal) status as the descendants of a fugitive slave community *(quilombo)*, whereas another part of the community "became Indian" by claiming the (legal) status of an indigenous community. Her enormously fascinating study sheds light on processes by which two communities that share kin relations and a common regional history and identity as *sertanejo* (backlander) peasants and *vaqueiros* (cowboys) have come to identify and become legally recognized as ethnoracially distinct groups – although as she stresses, they "have always been deeply involved in each other's lives" (French 2009:xiv).

The concept of "legalizing identities" builds on scholarship on the multifarious relations between law and social movement activism on behalf of collectives that share a certain 'identity' (as women, indigenous people, Afrodescendants) (see for example: Handler 1978; McCann 1994; Merry 2006; Rajagopal 2003; Scheingold 2004). These studies tend to focus on activists, strategies and movement messages

8 I am only aware of one case (the *Tundiqui* controversy briefly discussed in chapter 8) where the resolution of a conflict was pursued through legal means by an Afrobolivian organization or individual and this remained an isolated exception.

related to "rights talk." However, as Sally Engle Merry (Merry 2003) has argued, the transformative potential of rights talk transcends the levels of organizations and activists as it is capable of engendering a "rights-defined identity" through "encounters with the new subjectivity defined within the discourses and practices of the law" (Merry 2003:346–347).[9] On an even more general level, it has been argued that law plays a fundamental role in shaping notions of "Modern Personhood" (Collier, Maurer, and Suarez-Navaz 1996). "Bourgeois law," (i.e. "the legal concepts and practices developed since the eighteenth century in Europe and its colonies that are presently spreading around the globe" [Collier, Maurer, and Suarez-Navaz 1996:1–2]), the authors argue, engenders "legal constructions of naturalized identities" (Collier, Maurer, and Suarez-Navaz 1996:3). They conclude that:

> "[to] the degree that bourgeois law presupposes subjects with different interests capable of articulating and contesting their concerns, it encourages subjects to come together and assert their rights: to claim that their equal rights have been denied them based on difference, to assert that their difference – in cultural heritage, for instance – obliges them to demand special rights, or even to design their own system of rights based on their difference. [...] Law and bourgeois legality [encourage] people to be 'free to find themselves' and thus to 'realize' the 'inner' qualities that distinguish them from others. The kinds of 'selves' they are free to find are the basis of identity politics today. (Collier, Maurer, and Suarez-Navaz 1996:21)

In French's conceptualization, the process of "legalizing identities" has different entangled dimensions that play out simultaneously (French 2009:13). Most importantly for the case at hand, she emphasizes how important it is that people are confronted with and experience "new or revised ethnoracial identities," for instance when they "invoke rights based on newly codified legal identities" (French 2009:13). At the same time, local cultural practices are reconfigured, often in order to become vehicles for expressing particular identities in the course of the recognition process. This leads to situations where meaning and boundaries of community, as well as the terms of belonging are called into question and may be reconfigured. What is more, and although particular identities may have only recently been assumed and/or throughout the process of recognition "extrapolated from (or read into) the law," they are nevertheless often regarded to have essentialized characteristics.[10] As French emphasizes, these components of "legalizing identities" are neither meant

9 Her example is concerned with women who have been victims of violence and their interactions with the police, prosecutors, judges, shelter workers and feminist advocates, but her general points are easily translatable to a wide range of encounters.

10 Another important aspect in French's example in Brazil has not been as important in Bolivia up to this moment. She argues that the meanings of the laws that are invoked through processes of recognition can also be reshaped when communities, legislators, and specialists – including anthropologists – negotiate the terms of recognition of "new identities." So, for

to be regarded as describing a necessary sequence of events, nor as an exhaustive list of all the processes playing a role in the transformation of ethnoracial identities (French 2009:12–13). We also have to be cautious not to overstate the role of law on the one hand, and on the other the 'novelty' of the identities that emerge through engagement with legal categories. After all, 'black' and 'Indian'/indigenous are very long-standing categorizations with deep histories in Latin America (Wade 2010). What "legalizing identities" thus helps elicit is the question of the salience of certain identities in certain contexts and moments – and what law has to do with it – but not their existence. In particular, my discussion of Cala Cala's tourism project in chapter 10 owes a great deal to French's approach. As will become clear, *Cala Caleños* built on a rather recent salience and importance of the legally recognized category *"Afroboliviano"* in pursuit of a specific project. Engaging the logics behind the category, however, has important consequences way beyond the specific project and entails a profound reconfiguration of identities, local histories and interethnic relations.

Although this book is mainly concerned with the processes that legal recognition of the specific category *"Afroboliviano"* has engendered in Bolivia, there is a more generalized corollary of the legal recognition and codification of categories of identity. Identity (Afrobolivian, indigenous or otherwise) has acquired an unprecedented force as both a strategic asset in political mobilization and as a means to secure attention and funding from the Bolivian state and international cooperation. I argue that the legal codification of categories of identity in general is the preliminary peak of a process that began almost half a decade ago, leading to the pervasive presence of "ID-ology" in contemporary Bolivia. With the term ID-ology, which I borrow from John and Jean Comaroff (Comaroff and Comaroff 2003; reprinted as part of Comaroff and Comaroff 2012), I refer to the tendency to represent social interaction (conflict as well as integration), politics and cultural practice mainly as matters of differing identities.[11] This process has its roots in the 1970s, when in-

example, the definition of what is now regarded a *Quilombo* in Brazil was significantly shaped by the recognition of specific communities under the *Quilombo* clause.

11 Writing about South Africa, the Comaroffs have mostly political contexts in mind in their discussion of the term ID-ology. They refer to a general characteristic of the postcolony that also applies to Bolivia, namely the fact that postcolonial states were not built on the basis of a culturally homogenous nation united through horizontal fraternity – as proposed by Benedict Anderson in his seminal work "Imagined Communities" (Anderson 2006 [1983]). Rather, postcolonial nations have been and are still marked by a "fractious heterogeneity" (Comaroff and Comaroff 2003:456) and "a terrain on which increasingly irreconcilable, fractal forms of political being […] seek to open up possibilities for themselves" (Comaroff and Comaroff 2003:447). Studying how conflicts are resolved under such circumstances, they discern a "displacement from the struggle between political visions to struggles in the name of interest and affect." "And interest and affect," they continue to argue, "congeal in identity […]" (Comaroff and Comaroff 2009:41).

digenous movements and intellectuals began questioning the promise of national integration through acculturation put forth by the Bolivian state after the National Revolution of 1952. They put culture, identity and indigeneity back on the political agenda and political discourse shifted from debating mainly ideological alternatives (Marxism, Trotskyism, Capitalism) to debating identities (Aymara, Quechua, white, *mestizo*, indigenous). Driven by internal and external influences (see chapter 2), the Bolivian state responded through multicultural reform, the propagation of indigenous rights, bilingual education and the acknowledgement of Bolivia's pluri-ethnic make-up. Beginning in the 1970s, indigenous politics came, by and large, to be reframed as identity politics. Social inequality, discrimination and exploitation were increasingly interpreted as matters of cultural difference, ethnic diversity and indigenous identity, overshadowing the class aspect of the conflicts in Bolivian society and making talk of identity a ubiquitous phenomenon. This logic is now laid down in written form in the Constitution and Bolivian-style plurinational ID-ology is marked by the fact that the question of identity is positioned at the forefront of debates on nationhood, citizenship, participation, entitlement and equality. ID-ology has been converted from an option in political discourse to the legally sanctioned backdrop of understanding political and social life in the country. This is not to say that ideological debates have been entirely silenced and alternative interpretations of social reality have vanished. What I want to point out is the fact that ID-ology, "the '–ology' of identity" (Comaroff and Comaroff 2009:41) now occupies a central position in the country, permeating not only political realms but also the "small spaces of [everyday] life" (Canessa 2012c).

The final question then is how – and to what extent – legally codified identities and the general framework of plurinational ID-ology inform everyday life and the dynamics of immediate, day-to-day interactions of individuals and small communities. In order to approach this issue I draw on Andrew Canessa's (Canessa 2012c) concept of "intimate indigeneities" to make sense of the intimate Afrobolivianities "in the small spaces of everyday life." Canessa urges us to

> "focu[s] on the question of what it means to be indigenous to indigenous people themselves, not only when they are running for office or marching in protest but especially when they are in the small spaces of their lives, when they are lamenting their lot, cooing with their babies, cooking in their kitchens, or talking to their husbands who are far away." (Canessa 2012c:2)

This by no means contradicts concerns with (political) articulations of indigeneity or Afrobolivianity, but rather complements them: Canessa explicitly describes his project as being concerned with "those intimate social interactions to examine how identities are formed and articulated on a day-to-day level" (Canessa 2012c:35) without losing sight of the fact that even the most intimate sites of social practice (in his example the kitchen) are not isolated from the "political and economic currents of the nation" (Canessa 2012c:2).

Overview of chapters

In Bolivia's current plurinational moment, processes of collective identification, political articulation and law converge in the unprecedented efforts to 're-found' the country and transform its society. I analyze Afrobolivianity as a collective identification articulated at the intersection of local communities, politics and the law. Studying Afrobolivian people's often contradictory and highly contingent engagement with legally codified categories of identity offers a privileged vantage point from which to analyze the social and political dynamics shaping the country as a whole. Over 500 years of colonial and republican history, half a century of Bolivian (identity) politics, 30 years of Afrobolivian cultural revitalization and the emerging logics of Bolivia's plurinational 21st century crystallize around such seemingly simple and intuitive acts as 'invoking rights as Afrobolivians.' My study of Afrobolivianity thus aims not only at filling an ethnographic lacuna by systematically addressing the experiences of Afrobolivians, but also contributes to a more thorough understanding of Bolivia's current political conjuncture, its historical and conceptual roots, as well as its emerging social consequences. My aim is to shed light on the social dimensions of recent legal and political reforms in Bolivia and the consequences these have for people.

Beyond Bolivia, I contribute to anthropological debates on indigeneity and blackness in Latin America by pointing out their deep entanglements and continuous interactions. Analyzing local discourses on Afrobolivian autochthony, shared culture and ethnic 'groupness' through the lens of Afro-indigenous articulations contributes to decentering the all-too-common association of indigeneity with 'autochthonous Indians' in Latin America. It furthermore calls into question the equally widespread assumption that blackness in Latin America is best understood in a transnational, de-territorialized framework. Afrobolivianity, the term I use for the specific Afro-indigenous articulation I am dealing with in this book, is as much a matter of roots, territory and autochthony as it is a matter of displacement, diaspora and globalized black culture. My study also aims at enriching debates on politico-legal reform and social transformation more generally, pointing out how and under what circumstances collective identifications and intergroup relations stabilize and change.

In chapter 1, *"Encountering Afrobolivianity,"* I introduce the field sites of my study and discuss my methodology and the multiplicity of perspectives on Afrobolivianity that characterize this book. I furthermore address the dangers of reification when studying categories of identification and briefly introduce some major organizational actors that will become important throughout the following chapters.

In chapter 2, entitled *"The Afrobolivian Presence in Bolivia, Then and Now,"* I shed light on relevant aspects of Afrobolivian history and situate it within the wider context of Bolivia's political and social history. On the one hand, I summarize the available literature on Afrobolivians from a variety of scholarly perspectives, while on the other hand I situate this literature within debates on Bolivian national identity and strategies of political integration.

Opening the ethnographic part of this study, chapter 3, *"'We are los Afros de Cala Cala',"* introduces Cala Cala, a small community in the province of *Nor Yungas* that was the main field site of this study. After briefly situating Cala Cala in the regional and historical context, I will shed light on the processes of articulating a collective identification based on ethnoracial affiliations in Cala Cala – in emic terms: *"los Afros de Cala Cala"* – and describe the practices through which belonging to this collective is enacted and becomes socially relevant. I will show how notions of community and collective identification as Afrobolivians are produced in a process of articulating kinship affiliations and networks, local history and translocal practices of sociality.

In chapter 4, entitled *"Cala Cala beyond 'lo Afro': Cumplir Función Social, Identidad Yungueña and the Comunidad Cocalera,"* I will introduce an alternative perspective on community and collective identification in Cala Cala. This perspective entails a notion of community that is on the one hand broader than *"los Afros de Cala Cala"* as it includes non-Afrobolivians, with whom *"los Afros de Cala Cala"* share economic, religious and political networks. On the other hand, it is also narrower, as it is limited to a territorially bounded community of social and economic practice, *"la comunidad cocalera,"* the community of coca farmers.

Chapter 5, *"The Changing Meanings of Ethnoracial Identifications in Cala Cala,"* builds on the preceding chapters and discusses how different categories of identification are employed in negotiating belonging and a sense of community. Although *"los Afros de Cala Cala"* and *"la comunidad cocalera"* are not mutually exclusive categories of identification and social practice, I argue that the growing salience of the legally codified category *"Afroboliviano"* has led to an emerging reconfiguration of intergroup relations, fostering ethnic stereotyping, as well as a reinterpretation of local history and relations in economic and political spheres.

At this point my study widens the scope of analysis and situates the discussion of Cala Cala's local particularities within nationally circulating discourses on race, ethnicity and culture and how they relate to conceptualizations of Afrobolivianity.

In chapter 6, *"What It Means to Be Afro: Afrobolivianity, Indigeneity and the African Diaspora in Bolivia,"* I argue that what it means to be *"Afro"* in Bolivia is as much a matter of race (thought to be expressed through phenotype and ancestry), as it is a matter of ethnicity (expressed through 'culture' and customs). As such, Afrobolivianity is not only a matter of being black, but a concept deeply entangled with notions of indigeneity and debates on *mestizaje* (understood as racial and cultural mixture of particular individuals as well as in terms of referring to a general aspect of society). Consequently, debates on Afrobolivianity mirror engagement with the rooted politics of place characteristic of the otherwise global movement of indigenism, as well as with the transnationally circulating ideas of the diasporic black public sphere.

Chapter 7, "*'We are Culture, not Color': Musicians, Technocrats and the (Re-)Making of 'Afrobolivian Culture',*" elaborates on some of the aspects discussed in the preceding chapter, highlighting the growing importance of conceptualizing Afrobolivianity beyond race and phenotype as a category of 'culture.' This ongoing shift is analyzed in the context of cultural performance and folklore, as well as with regard to recent efforts at cataloging Afrobolivian culture in the aftermath of legal recognition and political enfranchisement.

Chapter 8, "*'El Movimiento Afroboliviano': Cultural Revitalization, Citizenship and Development,*" summarizes the history of Afrobolivian activism from the 1980s until the early 21st century. Emerging as a movement of cultural revival linked to a specific dance – *la saya Afroboliviana* – *"el Movimiento Afro"* evolved from a local effort of a group of high school students to a nationally active conglomerate of individual and institutional actors navigating the realms of local politics, the national folklore and tourism industry, Bolivia's state multiculturalism, and international development.

Chapter 9, *"Rights, Recognition, and New Forms of Organization – The Judicialization of Afrobolivian Activism and the Rise of CONAFRO,"* explores more recent and emerging political developments. I argue that in the context of constitutional reform and in the aftermath of legal recognition, Afrobolivian activism is increasingly inspired by legal discourse and now heavily centers on the notion of *el pueblo Afroboliviano* as a collective subject of rights.

Chapter 10, *"Plurinational Afrobolivianity on the Ground and Built Identity Politics: La Casa Cultural Afro Cala Cala and the Centro de Interpretación de la Cultura Afroboliviana,"* eventually leads us back to Cala Cala. In 2014, people from Cala Cala began developing a small community tourism project based on "Afrobolivian culture." This project eventually culminated not only in the realization of the Afrobolivian cultural center envisioned by the community *(La Casa Cultural Afro Cala Cala)*, but also in the construction of a large museum dedicated to "Afrobolivian culture" *(Centro de Interpretación de la Cultura Afroboliviana)*. The exceptional developments surrounding this project help draw together the arguments made with regard to the local particularities of the community, as well as with regard to Afrobolivianity in plurinational Bolivia more generally.

Chapter 1: Encountering Afrobolivianity

Some remarks on the particularities of Afrobolivian demography and social geography

In order to contextualize my ethnographic approach to Afrobolivianity and to understand how different aspects of the following descriptions of Afrobolivian cultural practices, political activism and social relations relate to each other, it is important to sketch the circumstances in which Afrobolivians live in the country. According to the National Population Census of 2012, there are about 16,000 people who self-identify as *Afrobolivianos*. Unfortunately, to this date, the *Instituto Nacional de Estadistica (INE)* has not published any data referring to the distribution of the roughly 16,000 Afrobolivians within the country, which makes it difficult to establish a clear-cut panorama of the demographic distribution of those identifying as Afrobolivians. What is more, Afrobolivian organizations have questioned the numbers presented by INE, arguing that their own estimates concerning the number of Afrobolivians are nearly twice as high (about 30,000).

It is very common to distinguish between Afrobolivians living in rural and urban contexts, although the divide is not as clear-cut as one might suspect. Speaking of rural versus urban Afrobolivians is mostly a way of differentiating between Afrobolivians living in the Yungas (a region on the eastern slopes of the Andes characterized by steep semitropical valleys, see chapter 2 for details) and Afrobolivians living in the larger cities of Bolivia, mainly La Paz, Santa Cruz, Cochabamba and, to a lesser extent, in Bolivia's constitutional capital Sucre (see figure 2).

However, the rural-urban divide overshadows important internal differences with regard to the Afrobolivian population of the Yungas, as well as with regard to the different urban experiences of Afrobolivians. In the Yungas, there are basically four types of settlement, located along a continuum from rural to urban in the regional context, although all four are considered rural (*campo*) from the perspective of La Paz or Santa Cruz. These types are: *comunidades* (lit. communities, in this sense of the word this refers to social, territorial, political and economic units organized in *sindicatos* (unions) and retraceable to former *haciendas*), *pueblos* (towns), *pueblos nuevos* (new towns, emerging after the abolition of *haciendas* in the 1950s)

Figure 2: Map of Bolivia (elaborated based on the CIA Map Bolivia Administrative)

and the *zonas de colonización* (agricultural colonization areas in the lowlands). The 'traditional' *pueblos* of the Yungas – Coroico (2,319 inhabitants) and Coripata (1,238) in the Nor Yungas province, as well as Irupana (1,949) and Chulumani (2,028) in the Sud Yungas province – predate Bolivian national independence and were founded in colonial times.[1] Those towns are nucleated settlements grouped around a central square *(plaza)* dominated by the church and the administrative buildings and are still the administrative centers of the homonymous administrative units called *municipios* (municipalities). They are also economically important as sites of trade and transportation, commerce and services. Especially before the National Revolution in 1952 and from the perspective of the peasants living in *comunidades* – for the most part dispersed settlements without much infrastructure – the towns were

1 Population figures according to the latest census of 2012 (see: www.ine.gob.bo [25/09/2018]).

often already a space perceived as decidedly urban where most people do not make a living from working the land, but rather engage in trade or live off government salaries. To some extent, the traditional towns' importance has decreased through the foundation of the so-called *pueblos nuevos*, new peasant towns, emerging in the 1950s and 1960s in the aftermath of the land reform (Léons and Léons 1971). Especially in terms of trade and transportation, the new towns have gained a strong foothold in the Yungas and in some respects have even eclipsed traditional towns. The colonization zones around Caranavi (13,569 inhabitants) and Palos Blancos (5,478 inhabitants) have experienced rapid growth in population, receiving immigrants from the *altiplano*, as well as from the Yungas beginning in the 1960s (Loza and Méndez 1981). Thus what appears to be simply *los Yungas* or even more generically *el campo* (the countryside) when viewed from La Paz is in fact a highly heterogeneous space (see fig. 3).

In terms of Afrobolivian demography, there is also some variation: in Yungas *comunidades* and towns (old and new), Afrobolivians are usually a rather small minority, ranging from 5 to 15 percent of the population according to my estimates. In the colonization areas, albeit that there are no reliable numbers, the percentage of Afrobolivians seems to be even lower, and in all of Bolivia there is only one *comunidad* (Tocaña) and no town where Afrobolivians are the numerical majority. Therefore, the references to *"las comunidades Afrobolivianas en los Yungas"* ("the Afrobolivian *comunidades* in the Yungas") by Afrobolivian activists and also the Constitution are misleading. As will become clear in my discussion of Cala Cala, speaking of *"comunidad"* in the Yungas is (with the exception of Tocaña) not a reference to a strictly Afrobolivian collective (see chapters 3 and 4). Therefore, and this is especially important for my discussion of Afrobolivian political mobilization in chapters 8 and 9, there are also no exclusively Afrobolivian organizations in the Yungas that function as local actors in ethnic politics.

'Urban Afrobolivians' living in La Paz, Santa Cruz or Cochabamba are by no means a homogeneous group either. They can be distinguished, most importantly, by their migration history: there are recent migrants born and raised in the Yungas, as well as people whose parents or even grandparents migrated in the 1970s and people that settled in La Paz in the 1980s and recently moved to Santa Cruz. Moreover, it also makes a difference if people live in La Paz or in Santa Cruz. While La Paz is only a three to four hour bus ride away from most Yungas *comunidades* and *pueblos*, travelling to Santa Cruz means at least an additional twenty hours by bus and significant costs. Therefore, in La Paz there are many more individuals living intermittently in Yungas *pueblos* and *comunidades* and the urban La Paz, whereas migration to Santa Cruz usually involves a more thorough spatial separation from the Yungas.

Although there is, as we have seen, a lot of variation within the groups generally represented as rural and urban, there are also important categorical differen-

Figure 3: Map of towns and villages in the Yungas (© OpenStreet Map contributors; Terms: www.openstreetmap.org/copyright)

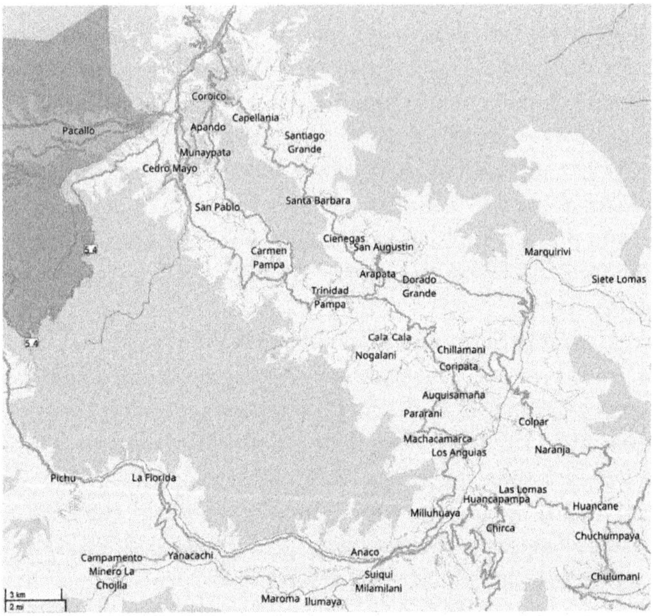

ces that explain the common juxtaposition of urban and rural Afrobolivians. Most strikingly, and very important in terms of how everyday life is experienced, Yungas residents are mainly peasants – producing coca, coffee, citrus fruit and rice. Some individuals in towns and *comunidades* have diversified their economic activities to include providing services like transportation, establishing little shops or engaging in mining enterprises. Yet their lives and social relations are shaped significantly by their peasant livelihood.[2] Urban residents, on the other hand, engage in a great number of different activities and are integrated into varying social networks of Afrobolivians and non-Afrobolivians alike. Some pursue high school and/or university education, some work in unskilled jobs, whereas others have achieved significant upward mobility and occupy qualified positions both in government offices and in private enterprises. The cities are also the center for a growing number of

2 Although the coca economy is marked by fairly particular dynamics (Léons and Sanabria 1997; Pellegrini Calderón 2016; Spedding 1994; Spedding 2004; Spedding and Llanos 1999) and hardly comparable to coffee and citrus fruit cultivation, from the perspective of most of my interlocutors, all this is eclipsed by the dichotomy of peasant vs. non-peasant.

professional activists/scholars with an Afrobolivian background. For most Afrobolivians the vast differences in lifestyle this divide entails eclipse all instances of internal differentiation and have become an important discursive device shaping their account of what being Afrobolivian means to them. Thus the juxtaposition of rural versus urban settings does occasionally shape certain arguments that I am making throughout this book. Yet I do not wish to imply that those settings are separate, unconnected spaces. In fact, it is the various connections among, between and beyond rural and urban communities and the networks that are spun by various actors that add an interesting level of complexity to negotiations of Afrobolivian collective identification and culture.

In order to illustrate the interconnectedness of contexts and the constant flow of people, concepts and discourses, it is revealing under which circumstances I first got to know Cala Cala, the place where I conducted the largest part of my fieldwork. Cala Cala is a former *estancia* (small agricultural estate) in the municipality of Coripata that was initially populated by Afrobolivian *peones* and was integrated into the larger *hacienda Nogalani* between the late 19th and early 20th century. Nogalani – one of the biggest coca producing estates in the Yungas – was inhabited by Aymara speaking *peones.* Since 1952, Cala Cala and Nogalani have formed a single *comunidad.* Although this entails many entanglements and a shared sense of community in many regards, *Cala Caleños* additionally express a very strong identification as an Afrobolivian collective, locally termed *"los Afros de Cala Cala."*

Arriving in Cala Cala

When I visited Cala Cala for the first time in 2014, I had already been engaged with different Afrobolivian organizations in La Paz, Cochabamba and Santa Cruz through several months of fieldwork as a graduate student in 2010 and 2012. I had also occasionally visited the Yungas before and was familiar with different settings of Afrobolivian reality. In 2014, before I came to Cala Cala and eventually decided that it would be a very productive field site for my study, I had spent some time in the provincial town of Coripata at the invitation of Martín Ballivián, an Afrobolivian activist and scholar whom I had met in Cochabamba in 2012. By the time of my visit, he was working in the public relations department at the municipal government of Coripata. He was always very eager to help with contacts and logistics for my research and established the contact in Cala Cala (where his mother was born) when I was in search of a rural field site for my dissertation project. On a Sunday afternoon we hired one of his friends to take us the approximately five kilometers to Cala Cala in his Toyota Minivan.

When we arrived in Cala Cala, Martín made the driver stop at certain houses and screamed out of the window that the 'meeting' he had told them about was going to start and that everybody was to gather at the small village church. After inviting the residents in this way, we headed for the church and waited. Little by little people flocked in from different sides of the community and shortly after, Martín started conducting the meeting with about six Afrobolivian men present. He introduced me very briefly and announced that I would be given a chance at a later point in the meeting to explain my request. He then went on to inform the community members of his plans to include them in a cooperative housing project he had started with some residents of Coripata and which he intended to extend to the rural community of Cala Cala. He urged them to come up with a possible location for the houses and start working on obtaining a legal title for some stretches of land or request permission from the local union *(sindicato)* to use land that was considered 'collective property.' He cautioned those present not to speak too openly about the plans, since he feared that if "the others" *("los otros")* heard about them, they could obstruct his plans for the Afrobolivian people *("los Afros")*.

The Cala Cala residents started debating how, where and under what circumstances they could obtain a stretch of land in order to apply for the funding to build their houses. There was, some argued, the piece of uncultivated land called *el Matuasi*, right next to the densely overgrown ruins of the former *hacienda* house, which "as everyone knows" *("como todos saben")* was land that belonged to "them" *("es de nosotros")*. Yet it had already been decided to build an Afrobolivian community cultural center *(Casa Cultural Afro Cala Cala)* with funding from the Interamerican Development Bank (IDB) there. The area of wasteland where the actual ruins of the former *hacienda* mansion were located would be an option, somebody argued. This idea, however, was met with general rejection. First of all, the ruins as physical remains of historical *hacienda* times were to be exploited as a tourist attraction in the *Casa Cultural* scheme; second, and even more importantly, "the ones from above" *("los de arriba")* would never give up such a large area of uncultivated land in the middle of the community. Martín proposed seeking out the offspring of the former *hacienda* owner, who was said to still own a legal title to at least some of the land surrounding the community. People nodded approvingly, yet nobody seemed to know how to go about approaching the family of the former landlords *(hacendados)* living in La Paz to ask them to sell or give up their land.

At this moment, Martín embarked on a passionate speech on how Afrobolivians have always been treated as "second class human beings" *("gente de segunda categoría")*, how the state and "the international community" *("la comunidad internacional")* "owes Afrobolivians" *("nos deben a los Afrobolivianos")* and how all this should be enough to demand both land and funding for building houses in rural Afrobolivian communities. He went on to lecture on "historical reparations" *("reparaciones históricas")* and how they should be implemented by the Bolivian government to remedy past injustices like "slavery" *("esclavitud")* and "exploitation" *("explotación")*. The community members mumbled approvingly and promised to see what could be done in order to obtain land for the housing project. They then shortly informed Martín about the progress of the IDB-financed *Casa Cultural* project and urged him to use his contacts at the municipal government *(alcaldía)* to speed up the issuing of an environmental certificate for the construction.

After all these issues had been discussed, it was my turn to explain my request to stay in the community and determine if it would be suitable as a field site for my study. I explained my request in the most general of terms, trying to avoid confronting the people with too much of my conceptual baggage at this stage. Martín, however, did not seem to share my reservations and 'clarified' that I was studying Afrobolivian communities and Afrobolivian 'culture' and was interested in visiting Cala Cala and getting to know its "traditions" *("tradiciones")*. If "traditions" was what I was interested in, said Víctor, one of the men there, then I should definitely visit and stay for the festivities on *Todos Santos*, and possibly there would also be a chance to witness a *saya* performance by the community members. He offered to let me stay at his house and we agreed to be in touch in order to settle the details for my visit, which turned out to be the beginning of my longer term engagement with the community. In order to get a first sense of the community, we took a short tour of the surroundings, passed by the ruins of the *hacienda* mansion, the *Matuasi* and some coca fields. Our driver urged us to leave shortly after, since he had other plans for the day, and the meeting was dismissed and everybody went their separate ways.

As we were about to leave, we came across Juan Angola Maconde, a renowned Afrobolivian historian and activist. Besides his scholarly writing and editing, and leading an NGO in La Paz, he is also a very active community leader in his home village Dorado Chico, a small Afrobolivian hamlet on the hillside opposite Cala Cala. He told us – slightly out of breath – that he had walked all the way from Dorado Chico to collect signatures pressing for direct representation of Afrobolivians in the municipal board (see chapter 5). He explained that only if Afrobolivians joined forces now and collectively pushed for it could they hope for their "constitutional rights" *("derechos constitucionales")* to be put into practice. Martín told him to look for the community members at their houses and we took our leave.

As I wrote down this episode in my fieldwork diary later that night, I did not understand even a fraction of the implications that many of the comments, categorizations, histories and concepts would reveal to me later, after months of intensive fieldwork in and around Cala Cala. It was clear to me, though, that within a few hours, I had witnessed and even become part of a variety of processes that – in some way or another – bring Cala Cala's residents into contact with different ideas, discourses and practices, as well as with economic, political, and legal resources that circulate locally, nationally and transnationally. From a single short episode, it was later possible to discern a variety of individual actors (community residents, regional administrative functionaries, urban activists, and anthropologists), organizations (*sindicato* [union], *alcaldía*, urban NGOs, transnational funding institutions [IDB], the Bolivian state) and their different projects (political mobilization, push for legal recognition, community development, and dissertation research). Along with actors and their projects appear certain discursive and conceptual formations (local concepts of community, difference and social groups, [international] development, community tourism, legal recognition, cultural difference, indigenous rights, slavery and reparation, discrimination and marginalization) as well as corresponding practices (holding meetings, writing applications, obtaining certificates, collecting signatures, mobilizing political favors, participant observation, and conducting interviews).

Researching Afrobolivianity in Cala Cala

My fieldwork in Cala Cala began with the episode described above and took place during two prolonged stays – one consisting of eight months between September 2014 and April 2015 and a second shorter stay of four months between February and May 2017. During this time, I participated in the daily activities of different households in Cala Cala, exploring life in the community through participant observation and innumerable informal conversations in a variety of contexts. I continuously visited the homes of all of Cala Cala's households, worked with them in the coca fields, shared public transportation to and from the *comunidad*, and met people in public gatherings like *sindicato* meetings, visits of technical or political commissions and the meetings accompanying the tourism project described in detail in chapter 10. The main research participants were members of two extended Cala Cala families with whom I lived and worked during my longer stays in the *comunidad*. They, in turn, introduced me to many other individuals and households in Cala Cala and numerous people from Nogalani, who occasionally also took me with them to their coca fields and with whom I participated in many public gatherings. Although I spent most of my days in the coca fields accompanied by groups of *comunarios* (varying in size and composition), I also met and engaged with people in other settings like the small store in the *comunidad*, the soccer field or the school courtyard.

To complement my findings from participant observation, I conducted a census of all the households in Cala Cala, gathering information on the number, age and gender of the residents, as well as on their relatives living elsewhere that maintain ties to Cala Cala. To corroborate the information on kinship I gathered through the census, I interviewed people in Cala Cala on the subject of their genealogy and drew up kinship diagrams in dialogue with them. The information gathered through those interviews was combined with insights concerning the history and demography of the *comunidad* that I gathered by analyzing administrative documents pertaining to the *hacienda Nogalani* (discontinuously covering the years between 1920 and 1965 approximately). Those documents were provided to me by Afrobolivian activist and scholar Martín Ballivián who obtained them from a Coripata-based lawyer in 2014, published some facsimiles in his publication *"Somos Afrobolivianas Afrobolivianos"* (Ballivián 2015) and in 2017 entrusted the documents to me for further analysis. As will become clear in chapter 3, kinship – and how it relates to local history – is an important dimension of community and belonging, as well as a decisive category of collective identification in Cala Cala.[3]

Spending time in Cala Cala and participating in the daily chores of its inhabitants meant engaging a series of topics beyond Afrobolivian 'culture', collective identifications or identity politics. During my stays in the *comunidad*, I learned a great deal about regional history and economy, peasant livelihood and the cultivation and marketing of coca leaves. Furthermore, I dealt with topics such as migration and translocal sociality, as well as with the functioning of local *sindicato* politics. This enabled me to approach Afrobolivianity and engage with my Afrobolivian interlocutors by way of their interconnections with other contexts and frames, as well as through cultural and social practices beyond those considered 'Afrobolivian.' It naturally also meant engaging the non-Afrobolivian parts of the population and their experiences, views and opinions (see below).

Roles and perspectives in the field

Having been introduced to Cala Cala by a locally well-known Afrobolivian activist (at that time also a municipal officer in Coripata) with kinship ties to the community, and – as we have seen in the episode above – being presented as someone who is interested in "Afrobolivian culture" and "local traditions" marked my initial role in the field to a great extent. I would have definitely been perceived and treated differently had I approached the community in another way. This became clear to me when I met Rolando, a non-Afrobolivian resident of Nogalani, who handled the e-mail correspondence of *ADEPCOCA (Asociación Departamental de Productores de Coca*, the regional coca growers' association). He told me that he had brought foreigners to the community that were interested in studying coca cultivation and who had approached him through ADEPCOCA. My presence in the community, on the other hand, was from the beginning framed in a way that gave the category *Afroboliviano*

3 It must be noted, however, that kinship is not the principal focus of this study, neither empirically nor theoretically. Therefore, I do not engage with the whole range of methodological, conceptual and theoretical literature on the subject, but limit myself to a few key points relevant for my study of community and collective identifications in Cala Cala (see chapter 3).

paramount importance.[4] Yet even in the very first encounter with *"los Afros de Cala Cala,"* local concepts of community, culture and tradition beyond *Afroboliviano* had already come to the fore when Víctor mentioned *Todos Santos* as an important local tradition. As I later learned (see chapter 4), this tradition is in no way framed as Afrobolivian.

Although my association with the Afrobolivian households in the community remained important in accounting for my presence until the end of my fieldwork, there were important developments that helped unsettle and change my initial role. The most important aspect was the fact that I worked with people in the coca fields day in, day out over the course of several months. The coca fields are not only the most important site of everyday social interaction, but also the context in which notions of community beyond ethnoracial categorizations are most salient. Through participating in the often arduous tasks of weeding the fields and harvesting the leaves, I got to know a great number of people not directly associated with *"los Afros de Cala Cala."* I thus not only learned a lot about the community beyond *"lo Afro,"* but was also less strongly associated exclusively with *"los Afros,"* especially since the conversations I had during the day circled almost exclusively around coca cultivation. Since everybody in Nogalani has a lot to say about coca (production, consumption, marketing and political implications) this opened up opportunities to engage in conversation with a wide range of people. My presence in the coca fields earned me several invitations to visit people's houses, join them for the monthly *sindicato* meeting, share transportation to and from Coripata and La Paz, and become more and more dissociated from the focus on Afrobolivians. Of course, there were also factors reinforcing my association with *"los Afros,"* most notably the fact that I lived with two particular Afrobolivian families for most of my time in Cala Cala.

It is important, however, to highlight the fact that there was not one single role that I occupied in Cala Cala, but rather roles (in the plural) that were subject to change over time and also between situations, depending on the specific topics, the range of interlocutors and the formality/informality of the context. While I researched the make-up and the history of the community, I spoke to Afrobolivians and Aymara alike. Other than the few specific Afrobolivian projects (some meetings in the context of the tourism project, for instance), the contexts of participant observation were often not specific to Afrobolivians and largely devoid of any ethnoracial separation. Although my ethnography clearly and willfully parts from an Afrobolivian perspective, the voices of self-identified Aymara or *mestizo* people

4 In Cala Cala and other Afrobolivian communities this is not uncommon. In fact, even though the discourse around the alleged 'invisibility' of Afrobolivians is still widespread, the Afrobolivian parts of the Yungas population have recently received far more anthropological and media attention than the Aymara populations of the region.

from Nogalani and elsewhere play a significant role in my study. They shape many of my arguments, since they are a fundamental part of public interactions, official meetings and the great majority of documents that I write about and reflect upon. Most notably, their input and perspective is crucial for my discussion of the shared sense of belonging and identification as *comunarios* or *cocaleros Yungueños* that applies to Afrobolivians and Aymara alike (see chapters 3-5 for details).

Researching Afrobolivianity beyond Cala Cala

Beyond Cala Cala, I researched Afrobolivianity in a variety of contexts in order to enrich the local perspective and in order to contextualize my findings. During various fieldwork stays in Bolivia (beginning in 2010 and 2012 as a graduate student, as well as during very frequent travels from Cala Cala in 2014/15 and in 2017), I conducted and recorded over thirty interviews with Afrobolivian individuals in the cities of La Paz, Cochabamba and Santa Cruz. I also spoke to Afrobolivians in various towns and *comunidades* all over the Yungas including Coroico, Coripata, Tocaña, Dorado Chico and Chillamani (Nor Yungas) and Irupana, Chulumani, Chicaloma and Palos Blancos (Sud Yungas), as well as in Caranavi. Many of those individuals were leading activists who hold (or held at the time of the interview) a leadership position in an Afrobolivian organization or government institution. Others were regular members of Afrobolivian organizations or people I met through personal contacts. Additionally, I visited and participated in dozens of workshops over the course of seven years (from 2010 to 2017) and I was part of innumerable gatherings of Afrobolivian organizations, covering a range from National Afrobolivian Congresses with dozens of participants to small informal gatherings with only a handful of attendees. Very importantly, during some of the workshops, I benefitted from the fact that people were already gathered in a formal space and setting to conduct focus group discussions and group interviews. Those techniques were especially relevant in unearthing the structures of activist discourse and the organizational logics of many of the Afrobolivian organizations I worked with.

Applying a multi-sited approach (Marcus 1995) and venturing through various different spaces of contemporary Afrobolivian experience was inspired by two interrelated factors: First of all, the general awareness of different regional and economic contexts among *Cala Caleños* themselves is very high. Every family in Cala Cala has kin all over Bolivia and people repeatedly told me about their relatives and friends in the cities. Many also directly suggested that I visit their relatives next time I travelled to La Paz, Cochabamba or Santa Cruz and mentioned me in conversations over the phone (*"Estamos en el cocal con Mauricio,"* "We are in the coca field with Mauricio").[5] This complements my earlier impressions while researching the activities of urban groups and organizations, when I was incessantly told that I had to journey to the Yungas in order to fully understand 'Afrobolivian culture' since "in the Yungas, there is another logic" *("ahí, la lógica es otra")*. For both rural and urban Afrobolivians, the other context is ever present and many of their experiences only make sense when bearing these relations in mind. Moreover, life in Cala Cala is in many ways characterized by constant travelling between the Yungas and La Paz. People mostly travel to sell coca on the market in La Paz, but take advantage of their trips to visit friends and family or engage in small-scale trade in fish, meat or other products (*chuño*, potatoes) not readily available in the Yungas. Through their travels, but also through the growing proliferation of mobile phones and internet access in Cala Cala, they engage in social practices transcending the geographical boundaries of Cala Cala, be it through doing business, sharing their leisure time with friends and family in La Paz or exchanging information and ideas in workshops and meetings with urban organizations. To account for those interactions and the practices linking Cala Cala with urban spaces of Afrobolivianity, I sometimes joined them on their travels, met their relatives all over the country and occasionally participated in the activities of urban organizations with them. Thus my commitment to mobility and a multi-sited ethnography of Afrobolivianity is grounded in my interlocutors' everyday experiences of mobility and translocal sociality.

However, my multi-sited approach was not only inspired by *Cala Caleños* everyday experiences of translocal sociality, but also by the crucial realization that the processes of articulating Afrobolivianity have transcended any given locality since their very beginning. Therefore, it is impossible to grasp the processes of articulation, translation and performance of Afrobolivianity from a localized perspective alone. Afrobolivianity cannot be 'rooted' in any single place, but emerges from journeys, encounters and mutual engagements of various actors in different contexts. This is true for the beginnings of the organized urban movement (see chapter 8) and the processes through which the concept of Afrobolivianity was shaped by discourses of plurinationality (see chapter 9). It is, however, also true for *Cala Caleños'* immediate engagement with Afrobolivianity.

Consider the case of Roberto, one of my main interlocutors in Cala Cala. He repeatedly told me how he started engaging with his Afrobolivianity as a young man of about twenty years, when activists and members of the newly founded *Movimiento Cultural Saya Afroboliviana (MOCUSABOL)* visited his community in the 1990s. He recalled them visiting Cala Cala in order to research and record Afrobolivian cultural practices and – very importantly – in order to foster community organizing

5 In Cala Cala, the Yungas and in most of the rest of Bolivia, I go by the Spanish version of my first name, "*Mauricio*".

based on a shared ethno-cultural identity as *Afrobolivianos*. His story resonates with that of many people in rural and urban contexts that emphasize the novelty of such developments in those years. One Afrobolivian interlocutor once stated very clearly: "Before, we knew nothing of the *saya*, we didn't know what Afrobolivian was".[6] Roberto added some very interesting detail pertaining to the second part of this quote. He repeatedly told me about his recollections of the first national meetings of Afrobolivian communities that took place in La Paz and El Alto prior to an audience with the Vice-President of the Republic in the early 1990s. As he recalled, it was the first time that he personally met people from *comunidades* further removed from Cala Cala geographically, experiencing belonging to a collectivity beyond his local *comunidad campesina*. He also found it very interesting that one of the main topics of those meetings was the question "What would we call ourselves?"[7] The term "*Afroboliviano*" already circulated among the participants of those meetings, but competed with other terminological options for naming and framing the emergent collectivity. Over the course of several years, "*Afroboliviano*" would displace the terms "*negro*" and "*moreno*" to become a fundamental pillar of discourses on identity, recognition and rights. Initially, however, the attendees of the gatherings in question agreed to stick to the commonly used term "*negro*," chanting in the Palace of the Republic: "*Señor Vice-Presidente, se hacen presentes los negros de Bolivia, pidiendo el reconocimiento*". I found it very intriguing how Roberto described the atmosphere of that event. For him personally, it was the first encounter with ideas and practices that he had not considered part of his everyday logics. He described the deliberations as extremely cautious and controversial, and attributed this to the fact that the different parties of the encounter did not have the conceptual tools to fully grasp what was happening. Therefore, it was necessary to establish a common ground for discussion and further action, beginning with the question of what this collectivity gathering for the first time that day could possibly be called. I do not want to overstate this point, since there are instances where Roberto did not express that sort of puzzlement, but instead emphasized the continuity of at least some sense of collectivity, belonging and awareness of Afrobolivianity prior to the revitalization efforts. I will argue throughout this book, however, that understanding the trajectory of the concept of Afrobolivianity means, in good part, tracing processes of imagining, articulating and performing a sense of community and identity that had hitherto not been imagined in that way. Within those processes, local communities are repeatedly invoked as the sources of Afrobolivianity, as the concrete places where its 'roots' can be found and located. Yet Afrobolivianity – even in its most localized forms – transcends local Afrobolivian communities, both geographically and conceptually. Therefore, my approach is guided by the conviction that

6 *"Antes no sabíamos de la saya, no sabíamos lo que era Afroboliviano."*

7 *"¿Cómo nos íbamos a llamar?"*

my ethnography of Cala Cala as a local community needs to be linked with a multi-sited ethnography of Afrobolivianity as a conceptual and political vantage point on questions of culture, collectivity and rights.

Panorama of Afrobolivian organizations

In many instances, Afrobolivian organizations and their political logics play a decisive role in shaping notions of Afrobolivianity, but also in providing and shaping the spaces of encounter, performance and debate. Therefore – and before closing this chapter on the various 'fieldsites' of my study – it is crucial to introduce at least a basic panorama of Afrobolivian organizations at this point (for a full discussion of organizational developments and the accompanying discursive dynamics see chapters 8 and 9).

The first Afrobolivian organizations, which emerged in the 1980s and were formally established during the 1990s, were first and foremost *saya* dance ensembles. They had a decidedly local scope and presence, limiting their activities to La Paz *(Movimiento Cultural Saya Afroboliviana MOCUSABOL, Organización Integral Saya Afroboliviana ORISABOL)*, Santa Cruz *(Comunidad Afroboliviana Santa Cruz CABOLS, Unión Afro Santa Cruz)* and Cochabamba *(Organización de Afrodescendientes Mauchi, Comunidad Afroboliviana Cochabamba)*, respectively. By far the most important and well-known organization until roughly fifteen years ago was MOCUSABOL. It was also the first organization to be formally established and influenced many of the other regional *saya* ensembles. Furthermore, MOCUSABOL was the first organization to start to transcend the mere performance of *saya* and begin lobbying for Afrobolivian interests in political contexts. In 2006, Jorge Medina, long-time president of MOCUSABOL, founded the *Centro Afroboliviano para el Desarrollo Integral y Comunitario CADIC* (Afrobolivian Center for Integral and Community Development), designed to be the "political and technical arm of MOCUSABOL" *("el brazo político y técnico de MOCUSABOL")*. CADIC is often characterized as an Afrobolivian NGO and it mainly organizes workshops with a wide range of topics funded by international development cooperation. Jorge Medina was also one of the leading figures of Afrobolivian mobilization during the Constituent Assembly 2006-2009 and was to become the first Afrobolivian member of the *Asamblea Plurinacional* in 2009.

In 2011, two years after constitutional recognition, a group of Afrobolivian activists – initially in hope of obtaining Medina's support, later in open competition with him – founded the *Consejo Nacional Afroboliviano CONAFRO* (National Afrobolivian Council), an organization that purports to transcend the localized efforts of former organizations and become a national representation of Afrobolivians (see chapter 9). CONAFRO's main interlocutor is not international cooperation, but the Bolivian state, mainly through its ministries and other institutions. There is one fundamental difference regarding CONAFRO: whereas MOCUSABOL never officially claimed to 'represent' a collective Afrobolivian subject and CADIC is run like an NGO, CONAFRO very clearly positions itself as the legitimate representation of all Afrobolivians. MOCUSABOL has members (some active, some passive, some with leadership positions), CADIC has a director and employees, whereas CONAFRO has an elected board of representatives and a constituency: *el pueblo Afroboliviano.*

Official recognition has furthermore led to the formation of state institutions pertaining specifically to Afrobolivians. Most importantly, those are the *Consejo Educativo del Pueblo Afroboliviano CEPA* (Educational Council of the *Pueblo Afroboliviano*) founded in 2011 alongside CONAFRO and the *Instituto de Lengua y Cultura Afro ILC-AFRO* (Institute of Afrobolivian Language and Culture) founded in 2013. They both depend politically and financially on the *Ministerio de Educación* (Ministry of Education). CEPA's main purpose is to foster and coordinate Afrobolivian engagement with the state in terms of educational reform. ILC-AFRO's purpose is broader, including the general tasks of researching, recovering and developing, diffusing and promoting, as well as teaching and normalizing Afrobolivian language and culture.[8] Both institutions are controlled by CONAFRO – either directly through formal integration in CONAFRO structures in the case of CEPA or by way of determining who will be appointed as an employee *(técnico)* in the case of ILC-AFRO. During the time of my fieldwork, the main task of both institutions – working closely together under the tutelage of the CONAFRO board of directors – was the coordination of the compilation and processing of the information that would be included on Afrobolivians in the new Bolivian public school curricula (see chapter 7). Besides this major project – spanning multiple years between compilation starting in 2012, ratification by the Ministry of Education in 2015 and the first attempts at implementation in 2018 – ILC-AFRO has coordinated some concise written compilations of Afrobolivian culture and history: a small leaflet on Afrobolivian funerary traditions and information on *haciendas* with Afrobolivian populations before the Agrarian Reform.[9] Before ILC-AFRO was formally established in 2013, the Ministry of Education published *"El Registro de Saberes, Conocimientos, Valores y Lengua"* of the *"Pueblo Afroboliviano,"* a sixty-six page booklet compiled by Juan Angola Maconde in 2010. Most recently, CONAFRO, CEPA and ILC-AFRO have joined forces with the Cochabamba-based NGO FUNPROEIB Andes to publish a full-length monograph entitled *"El Pueblo Afroboliviano. Historia, Cultura, Economía"* (Zambrana B. 2014). These publications are generally not known in detail by the wider public, circulating mainly among urban activists and within government institutions.

8 *"Es una institución que tiene como objetivo central: 1. La Investigación. 2. Recuperación y Desarrollo. 3. Difusión y Promoción. 4. Enseñanza y Normalización de la Lengua y la cultura del Pueblo Afroboliviano"* (https://www.facebook.com/ilcafroboliviano/ [19/06/18]).

9 See https://www.facebook.com/ilcafroboliviano/ [17/07/2018].

Ethnographic fieldwork in times of ID-ology

One fundamental question has accompanied me during the entirety of my engagement with Afrobolivianity, especially in the local context of Cala Cala: What part do I play, through my presence as a researcher, in the proliferation of the category of identification *"Afroboliviano"*? Coming back to the episode of my arrival to Cala Cala again, it is clear that there are – even with no foreign anthropologist present – more than a few actors that do the work of ID-ology. I was also, as I found out some weeks later, neither the first foreigner to spend time in Cala Cala, nor the first anthropologist to visit the community.[10] Moreover, the *Instituto de Lengua y Cultura Afroboliviana (ILC-AFRO)* – a government institution entrusted with the mission of documenting Afrobolivian culture (see chapter 7), had approached *Cala Caleños* in order to conduct research on the *hacienda* period in the village. While my presence as a researcher and my presumed interest in aspects of 'Afrobolivian identity' in Cala Cala had certainly not gone unnoticed, the experience of how my roles in the field changed, and with them the way I was approached and engaged in conversation by people in Cala Cala, gave me reason to believe that my presence was not an overly important factor. As is often the case – at least in my experience during fieldwork – the presence of the researcher becomes normalized to a certain extent quite quickly and people do not invest too much energy in acting a certain way or trying to pretend certain things are happening (or not) just for the sake of my presence. Of course, sometimes people verbally articulated very clear-cut distinctions explicitly addressing my (widely assumed) interest in *"lo Afro,"* but they did not seem to observe their own alleged rules for dealing with certain relationships afterwards. What is more, people often raised topics beyond ethnoracial identities and discussed competing alternative visions of the world and social relations in Cala Cala. While engaging the discourses of Afrobolivian identity politics and the possibility of highlighting *"lo Afro"* is always an option – regardless of the presence of an anthropologist – there are many occasions where *Cala Caleños* discuss questions of community, identity and belonging, referring to a wide range of interpretations and strategies for dealing with them. In fact, during the first weeks of my fieldwork in Cala Cala categorizations like *"Afroboliviano"* or "Aymara" played only a limited role and were hardly mentioned in everyday conversations. Without being prompted – and I avoided explicitly addressing matters of social categorization – people hardly resorted to ethnoracial categories when explaining

10 Cala Cala has received visitors from different parts of the world, mainly through the Catholic Church in Coripata which regularly sent foreign volunteers to work in the community. Moreover, an anthropology student from the United States spent some time in the community in the context of a Study Abroad Program in Bolivia (see: https://studyabroad.sit.edu/ [04/07/19]).

their notions of community, local history, 'culture' or 'tradition'. In contexts where specific categorizations were employed eventually – one of the clearest examples is the tourism project I will deal with at length in chapter 10 – but also in numerous other cases – *sindicato* meetings, informal conversations in the coca field and narratives of migration – I did not have the feeling that my presence altered people's ways of going about those deliberations. I was furthermore cautious not to get involved too tightly with one or another faction, opinion or strategy. Even on the occasions when I did become involved – actively or passively – as a referent for negotiating identity claims, categories and options, I regard my presence not simply as a distortion of the 'social reality' I am trying to understand, but as part of it. As an interlocutor I confronted people with my views, debated certain issues with them, answered their questions, gave them hints, assistance and critical feedback, depending on the situation. During these conversations people sometimes took me for an expert on subjects that I am not, giving my opinion more weight than it deserved. At other times, they easily dismissed my interpretations. In short, they very quickly treated me – for all I know and have been able to observe – as a slightly strange, sometimes appealing conversation partner that did not seem to exert such great influence on them as to constantly pretend to be something or somebody that one is not, concur with my opinions or interpretations, or care too much about my presence for that matter. Therefore I had the impression that I was able to carry out a productive kind of fieldwork that involved the establishment of meaningful relationships with a wide range of people.

In the next chapter I will discuss the existing literature on Afrobolivians and offer some important historical and political contextualization of the topics that I deal with in this book. I will also further situate my discussion of Afrobolivianity within ongoing scholarly debates on Bolivia. To that end, I first discuss the important trope of 'invisibility' with regard to Afrobolivianity and address the Yungas' place in Bolivia's cultural geography. Moreover, I will briefly situate Afrobolivianity in Bolivian colonial and republican history and sketch the implications of a set of profound social and political shifts in Bolivia and their relation to Afrobolivianity. With that I refer to the National Revolution and land reform in the 1950s, as well as Bolivia's turn towards multiculturalism and, most recently, plurinationality.

Chapter 2: The Afrobolivian Presence in Bolivia, Then and Now

In order to contextualize the ethnographic material presented in the following chapters, it is necessary to introduce some general aspects of Afrobolivian history. Moreover, it is crucial to sketch specific social, political and economic transformations in Bolivia and how they relate to the situation of Afrobolivians. This chapter serves a dual purpose. On the one hand it introduces the ethnographic and historical context of my study: the Yungas region and its role in the political and social history of Bolivia, as well as the Yungas' place in the "cultural geography" (Wade 2010:16) of the country. On the other hand, it summarizes the existing literature on Afrobolivians and delineates the state of the art. I begin with a critical examination of the discourse on 'invisibility' that is frequently deployed by Afrobolivian individuals and organizations, but also in some scholarly publications on the subject. I then sketch the regional context of the Yungas, and specifically how the topics of ethnicity and indigenous identity are approached with regard to the region. I continue with a brief examination of historically oriented work on Afrobolivians and then introduce early ethnographic accounts dealing with Afrobolivians and the Yungas. The next sections focus on political transformations in Bolivia since the 1980s, namely the country's shift towards multicultural politics and the recent turn to plurinationality within the so-called *"proceso de cambio"* ("process of change") led by Evo Morales and the party *Movimiento al Socialismo* (MAS, Movement towards Socialism).

"Are there black people in Bolivia?" Invisibility and beyond

As in other Latin American countries (de Friedemann 1984; see also: Minority Rights Group 1995), Afrobolivian activists and scholars have often decried the 'invisibility' of their people, their history, their culture and their contributions to the nation (Zambrana B. 2014). As I mentioned in the introduction, Afrobolivians have never been at the center of debates on Bolivian national culture, heritage or identity. They have consequently also received far less attention than indigenous people from politicians, intellectuals, in public culture or within debates in society at large. After the abolition of slavery in 1851 – and until the plurinational population census in 2012 – no official national statistics revealing the numbers of Afrobolivians were produced.

The 2012 National Population Census, for the first time in Bolivia's history, included the category *"Afroboliviano"* as an option for self-identification. This was seen as a milestone in Afrobolivian mobilization and interpreted as the long overdue recognition that Afrobolivians constitute a distinguishable collective within Bolivian society. Many Afrobolivian organizations engaged in a campaign aiming at motivating Afrobolivians all over the country to self-identify as such. When the results were released, however, most activists were highly disappointed to learn that only about 16,000 individuals across Bolivia had identified as "belonging to the *pueblo Afroboliviano*" (*"perteneciente al pueblo Afroboliviano"*). Activists' own estimates regularly cited figures of around 30,000 Afrobolivians in the country (occasionally up to 50,000).[1] In 2012, according to the *Instituto Nacional de Estadística (INE)* 16,329 people over the age of 15 years declared that they belong to the *"pueblo Afroboliviano."*[2] This amounts to about 0.15% of Bolivia's total population of 10 million. Afrobolivians are dispersed geographically throughout the whole country, although they are 'traditionally' associated with the Yungas region near Bolivia's highland metropolis La Paz.

Various publications assert that roughly thirty years ago it was fairly common for the Bolivian general public to be unaware of the existence of Afrobolivians at all (Angola Maconde 2001; Busdiecker 2007). Afrobolivian activists often cite the phrase "I didn't know there were black people in Bolivia" *("No sabía que había negros en Bolivia")* to exemplify the reaction they faced when identifying as Afrobolivians. Similarly, Afrobolivians assert that they are regularly identified as foreigners and are sometimes at great pains to assert their Bolivian nationality. By now at least, the generalized and extensive ignorance seems to have given way to a limited and stereotyped awareness that there are, in fact, "black people in Bolivia." It is rather uncommon to encounter people with no knowledge on black people

1 The inclusion of *"Afroboliviano"* in the National Population Census was a major topic when I first came to be engaged with Afrobolivian politics from 2010-2012. When I returned to Bolivia in 2014, the topic was hardly discussed among Afrobolivians anymore and the census data was seldom employed as a strategic means by Afrobolivian organizations. Many of my interlocutors told me that they worry that the numbers give the impression that Afrobolivians are only a very small group. In their view this might hamper political enfranchisement, rather than enhancing it as they hoped before Afrobolivians were officially counted. Some commentators even argue that the constant talk of being invisible and "ignored" *("ignorados")* has become the most powerful rhetorical tool for Afrobolivians in making political claims vis-à-vis the state (Spedding 2009:447).

2 Https://www.ine.gob.bo/ [16/07/2018].

in Bolivia whatsoever as *la saya Afroboliviana* has become such a fundamental part of the country's folkloric repertoire, represented in various forms in all kinds of media and present in the large *entradas* (parades) all over the country. What is more, in the 1990s, some Afrobolivian players were part of Bolivia's national soccer team that received a lot of attention for participating in the 1994 FIFA World Cup in the USA. When I talked to people in Bolivia about my project and mentioned Afrobolivians, the most frequent comments had to do with *saya* or *los Yungas* – and whether I had travelled there yet in order to go see them. 'Invisibility' has thus given way to a stereotyped depiction of Afrobolivians as *saya* dancers and inhabitants of a very specific region of the country (Busdiecker 2009a; Templeman 1998). Recently, the term *el pueblo Afroboliviano* ("the Afrobolivian people") has been legally acknowledged as a collective subject bearing "where appropriate" (*"en todo lo que corresponda"*), the same collective rights as indigenous groups (*"naciones y pueblos indígena originario campesinos,"* Article 31 of the New Constitution). Therefore, references to Afrobolivians have become rather frequent in government reports, in municipal action plans, in state-sponsored and/or NGO-led initiatives, as well as in legal documents that are in some way related to the constitutional provisions for indigenous people and other groups with special rights. Moreover – and I often had the impression that this was even more important than the special rights and the differentiated citizenship in Article 31 – Afrobolivians are mentioned in Article 3 of the Bolivian Constitution. It states:

> "The Bolivian nation is formed by all Bolivians, the native indigenous nations and peoples, and the inter-cultural and Afro-Bolivian communities that, together, constitute the Bolivian people."[3]

Being mentioned in such a foundational article of the Plurinational Constitution as an integral but distinct part of the Bolivian nation has afforded Afrobolivians a great deal of visibility and consequently serves as the basis for exceptional levels of pride among most Afrobolivian individuals. As a consequence of legal recognition and the ensuing political enfranchisement, Afrobolivian individuals have also been elected as representatives to national congress, regional parliaments and municipal councils, and some serve as public functionaries in ministries, vice-ministries and other government institutions. All this has led to a significant rise in visibility and public presence. 'Invisibility' thus doesn't fully capture the situation of Afrobolivians. It remains important as a motif of Afrobolivian political discourse, but has

3 In the Spanish original, Article 3 reads: *"La nación boliviana está conformada por la totalidad de las bolivianas y los bolivianos, las naciones y pueblos indígena originario campesinos, y las comunidades interculturales y afrobolivianas que en conjunto constituyen el pueblo boliviano."* Unless otherwise noted, the translated passages from the Constitutions are from the English translation provided by www.constituteproject.org.

given way to an – admittedly often stereotyped – partial visibility of Afrobolivians. Beyond the situation in politics and throughout Bolivian society at large, a partial and emerging visibility can also be identified in writings on Bolivian history and debates on the colonial origins of contemporary Bolivian society. Before I turn to publications dealing with the historical presence of Afrobolivians, it is important to sketch some particularities of the regional context of the Yungas in Bolivia and how this relates to Afrobolivians.

The regional context: the Yungas in Bolivia's cultural geography

In Bolivia, the term Yungas refers mostly to the steep semitropical valleys on the eastern slopes of the Andes, administratively divided into the provinces of Nor Yungas (North Yungas, capital Coroico), Sud Yungas (South Yungas, capital Chulumani) and Caranavi (capital Caranavi), which was separated from Nor Yungas province by decree in 1992. The region ranges in altitude between approximately 1,500 and 2,500 meters above sea level and is characterized by warm temperatures and a humid climate.[4] The Yungas are one of the centers of Bolivia's coca production and are also known for producing a variety of fruits and coffee (Klein 2003:5). They are situated geographically between Bolivia's *altiplano* (Andean high plateau) and the *amazonía* (Bolivian Amazon). For the context of this study, it is crucial to understand the Yungas' place in Bolivia's imagined "cultural geography." With that I refer to notions of "how cultural difference is spread over geographical space" (Wade 2010:16). In a crudely simplified account, Bolivia is often divided into the *altiplano* (associated with Aymara and Uru culture), the central valleys around Cochabamba and Sucre (associated with Quechua culture) and the Amazonian lowlands (associated with various indigenous groups of varying size, the largest being the Guaraní in the region around Santa Cruz). This highly schematic perspective is reflected in Bolivian school textbooks and government-sponsored tourism leaflets. It also informs a variety of political reforms, not least the distribution of special electoral districts for indigenous people *("circunscripciones especiales")* and the regionalized school curricula *("currículos regionalizados")* that are developed by the Ministry of Education (for details see chapters 7 and 9).

Within this classificatory scheme, the Yungas have until very recently not been associated with any particular ethnic group, indigenous language or culture. Although sometimes referred to as an "Aymara culture stronghold" (Klein 2003:52) due

4 More generally – beyond the provinces this study is concerned with – the term Yungas or Yunkas (derived from Aymara and Quechua *yunka* – hot) can also refer to an ecoregion including the regions of Huánuco y La Convención in Peru, as well as Inquisivi, Larecaja and Vandiola in Bolivia (Klein 2003; Spedding 1994).

to the influx of Aymara settlers beginning in the 16th century, the Yungas are not conceived of as the place where Aymara 'originally' belong or where 'Aymara culture' is to be found. This tension is reflected for example in the title of a publication from the 1970s headed "*Yungas: los 'otros' aymaras: Diagnóstico económico-socio-cultural de Sud Yungas*" (Equipo CIPCA 1976).[5] By addressing Aymara in the Yungas as "the other Aymara" *("los 'otros' aymaras")* the study discursively separates them from the Aymara population in the highlands, positing that the Aymara in the Yungas may speak the Aymara language, but do not exhibit 'Aymara cultural features' like in the highlands. In a similar fashion, in a more recent edited volume on "regional identities" *("identidades regionales")* (Arnold 2009) the Yungas are described as a region where "indigenous identity has not developed a lot, due to the multiethnic characteristics of the population since the distant past" (Arnold 2009:598 my translation).[6]

The multiethnic make-up of the Yungas is explained by the fact that since colonial times the region has been marked by a constant influx of migrants that intensified as the coca producing *haciendas* (large agricultural estates) kept expanding (Klein 2003:51–52). Chronic labor shortages on the countless coca *haciendas* of the region sparked the migration of mostly Aymara-speaking people from the highlands. The incessant demand for labor in the coca economy also explains why African slaves were brought to the region. According to some secondary sources (Bridikhina 1997:4–5), black slaves began to be brought to the Yungas in the 17th century, but official records referring to black slaves in the Yungas are only known from the 18th century onward (Léons 1972:287–288). The Afrobolivian and Aymara settlers displaced the various nomadic indigenous groups (Lecos and Mosetenes) that had populated the Yungas before, generically referred to as *chunchus* by people in the Yungas (Spedding 2009:432).

As I will detail in chapter 4, there is a strong discourse on *Yungueño* identity, yet this identity is conceived of mostly without reference to ethnicity or indigenous culture. Instead, coca production and the ensuing identification as *cocaleros* (coca growers) is seen as fundamental for constructing regional identity (Spedding 2009; Spedding and Colque 2003). The representation of the Yungas as a multi-ethnic society where indigenous ethnic identities only play a very limited role for collective identification has only recently been challenged. Interestingly, it was not the Aymara majority 'discovering their indigenous culture' or foregrounding their ethnic identity. The only ethnic group *(etnía*; or *pueblo* in the terminology of the Constitution) that is considered to be distinguishable in the Yungas is in fact *el pueblo Afroboliviano*. Although not 'indigenous' according to the prevailing common-sense

5 "Yungas: The 'other' Aymara: Economic-socio-cultural diagnostic of Sud Yungas."

6 *"[...] no se ha desarrollado mucho la identidad indígena, debido a las características multiétnicas de estas poblaciones desde tiempos remotos."*

definition of indigeneity in Bolivia that is related to pre-Columbian origins, Afrobolivian mobilization and official recognition by the state have led to the positioning of Afrobolivians as the most representative population of the Yungas in terms of identity and 'culture.'[7] This is, however, a very recent phenomenon and it is important to keep in mind that ethnic identity is generally regarded as secondary in the Yungas.

Afrobolivians in colonial and early republican society

Historical studies have since the 1960s unearthed a good deal of information on the presence of Afrobolivians in the country, focusing on a variety of aspects. Initially, historians set out to reconstruct black slavery in Bolivia (Crespo R. 1977; Portugal Ortiz 1977; Wolff 1964). These studies showed that due to its geographical location and the abundance of indigenous labor, slaves and slave labor did not play a fundamental role in the economy and society of the regions that would later become Bolivia. Bringing slaves to Potosí, Charcas (the contemporary Sucre) or La Paz through the ports of Callao and later Buenos Aires involved an arduous journey of several weeks through rough terrain and difficult climates, which made slaves a very expensive commodity in colonial Charcas. Colonial officials thus preferred to employ indigenous labor and black slaves were employed mostly in the households of rich urban families, as well as in the *Casa de la Moneda* – the colonial mint – in Potosí where they worked in the foundry.[8] Further studies have focused on slaves in urban contexts, mainly as domestic workers (Bridikhina 1995a; Bridikhina 1995b), and on slave labor in a wine-producing region in Chuquisaca (Aillón Soria 2005). More recently, and through a focus on social history, the relations of black slaves with other groups and the circumstances of their daily life in colonial society have been approached by a series of fascinating studies painting a vivid picture of colonial society that complicates one-dimensional accounts of colonial slavery. The authors point out instances of "negotiations of identities of the Afrodescendant population within the judicial system" *("negociación identitaria de la población afrodescendiente ante la justicia")* (Revilla Orías 2013a), as well as of the "adaptation, agency and fugitive action" of slaves (Gutiérrez Brockington 2000; see also Gutiérrez Brockington 2006). What is more, they shed light on a variety of Afro-indigenous encounters on

7 Accounting for this shift and its implications is a topic that runs throughout this book. Local concepts of Afrobolivian autochthony and the processes accounting for this shift will be analyzed in detail in chapters 3, 6, 8 and 9.

8 It is a common misconception in Bolivia that black slaves worked in the mines in Potosí. In fact, they were not employed as miners, but, allegedly because colonial officials valued their knowledge in the manipulation of metal, worked in small numbers in the colonial mint (Spedding 2009).

the level of individuals and families (Revilla Orías 2011; Revilla Orías 2015), destabilizing notions of the Spanish colonial *casta* system being characterized by rigid group boundaries (cf. Albiez-Wieck 2017; O'Toole 2012).[9]

Paola Revilla Orías (Revilla Orías 2014a) has furthermore studied the situation of slaves after Bolivia's formal declaration of Independence in 1825, pointing out that, the liberal ideals of the Independence Movement notwithstanding, slavery legally persisted in Bolivia until 1851. For the 19th and early 20th centuries, however, the historical records become increasingly scarce (Revilla Orías and Cajías de la Vega 2017:42). This also has to do with the fact that after the legal abolition of slavery, there was hardly any official language referring to Afrobolivians that would make it possible to consistently reconstruct the circumstances of their lives from historical documents (Revilla Orías 2014a:238). One of the few articles addressing the situation of former slaves in Bolivia during the second half of the 19th century analyzes the situation in the *haciendas* of the Yungas. According to Eugenia Bridikhina's findings, black slaves were employed only by the wealthiest *hacienda* owners *(hacendados)* of the Yungas, supplementing indigenous labor on the estates. After the abolition of slavery in 1851, and given the fact that alternative labor arrangements had long existed for the indigenous workers on the *hacienda*, the *libertos* (freed slaves) were quickly incorporated as *peones* on the *haciendas*. As *peones*, they received a small plot of land in usufruct in exchange for their labor on the *haciendas*' land (Bridikhina 1997). Bridikhina reports that, at least for some time after the abolition of slavery and on *haciendas* with a significant number of black *peones*, there was a specific position of authority reserved for black people called *capitán*. Their functions, similar to the indigenous *jilacatas*, were to serve as the representative of the *hacienda* owner in front of the *peones* and to coordinate the workforce at the will of the owner or the administrator *(mayordomo)*. According to a census of the Yungas dated 1883, black people (referred to as *morenos*, lit.: brown) made up an average of about 7-8 percent of the population in the province of Nor Yungas. Looking at smaller administrative units *(cantones)*, the highest concentration of *morenos* could be found in *cantón Mururata*, where they made up roughly 45 percent of the population. In absolute numbers, however, even in Mururata, only 324 *morenos* (out of a total of 734 inhabitants) were counted.[10] However, the fairly small numbers of former slaves notwithstanding, the Yungas were to become the only region in Bolivia with a discernible Afrobolivian presence until today. In all other places with a proven historical presence of Afrobolivians, they 'disappeared.' This process

9 For reasons of space, I cannot not detail any of this interesting work here. For a recent and timely overview see the work of Bolivian historians Paola Revilla Orías and Fernando Cajías (Revilla Orías and Cajías de la Vega 2017).

10 Bridikhina (1997) cites the following figures: *cantón Pacallo*, 56 *morenos* (total population 536), *cantón Mururata*, 324 *morenos* (total population 734), *cantón Coroico*, 130 *morenos* (total population 5,335), vice *cantón Coripata*, 315 *morenos* (total population 3,806).

is mostly explained with reference to migration and miscegenation (Aillón Soria 2005; Gutiérrez Brockington 2006). There are also no further accounts of Afrobolivian social organization or cultural practices – in the Yungas or elsewhere – until the second half of the 20th century when references to *la cultura negra* resurfaced in accounts limited to the Yungas (Pizarroso Cuenca 1977).

Before I focus on the situation of Afrobolivians in the Yungas in the 20th century, there is another body of historically oriented literature that has to be addressed. Important contributions in terms of reconstructing Afrobolivian history also came from within the Afrobolivian community, closely linked to the efforts to revitalize certain Afrobolivian cultural practices and mobilize politically (for details see chapter 8). Most important in this regard is the work of Juan Angola Maconde, an Afrobolivian economist (by training) and historian/ethnographer/linguist/activist (by vocation). His ethnographically and historically oriented contributions are explicitly positioned in order to overcome the 'invisibility' of Afrobolivians in Bolivian historiography and are often concerned with contributions *(aportes)* that Afrobolivians have made to Bolivian society and that have been neglected and obscured in 'official historiography' (Angola Maconde 2001; Angola Maconde 2010). In this context, Angola Maconde is mainly interested in highlighting the contributions Afrobolivians made to the Bolivian economy (as slaves and workers), but also their service as soldiers in various armed conflicts – for example in the rebellion of Tupac Katari in 1781, the wars for independence from Spain in the early 19th century and the Chaco War *(Guerra del Chaco)* in the 1930s (Angola Maconde 2001; Angola Maconde 2010).

Haciendas, the National Revolution and land reform in the Yungas

Unfortunately, the literature is mostly silent on the situation of Afrobolivians in the 19th and early 20th centuries. Therefore, it is hard to account for the 150 years between 1800 and 1950 in detail and we can only deduce how Afrobolivians lived from what we know from later sources. As Bridhikina's (1997) isolated account suggests, former slaves were swiftly integrated into the general workforce of the Yungas *haciendas* and lived there somewhat isolated form the rest of Bolivian society until the 1950s. With the exceptions of some accounts on Afrobolivian soldiers fighting in the Chaco War between Bolivia and Paraguay from 1932-1935 (Angola Maconde 2007), there are no hints at a significant presence of Afrobolivians beyond the Yungas.

In 1952, Bolivia witnessed one of the most profound social revolutions on the American continent, the *Revolución Nacional* (National Revolution) (Klein 2003:209). Backed mostly by peasant militias from the valleys around Cochabamba and miners from the *altiplano*, the *Movimiento Nacionalista Revolucionario (MNR)* seized power from a political and economic elite dominated by the mining oligarchy and large landowners. The mines were nationalized, universal suffrage was declared and the Revolution was followed by a large scale land reform in 1953 that dissolved the large land holdings of the *hacendado* elite in all regions of Bolivia, including the Yungas. Adopting the principle of *"la tierra es para quién la trabaja"* – "the land to those who work it" (de Mesa, Gisbert, and Mesa Gisbert 2008:513), the MNR's land reform freed the *peones* from their obligation to work on the estates of the landowners and distributed the parcels that had been occupied in usufruct to the peasants (Malloy and Thorn 1971). Afrobolivian and indigenous *peones* thus became small landowners and the former *haciendas* became *comunidades*, organized in peasant unions *(sindicatos)* under the tutelage of the MNR. The consequences of the revolution and land reform in the Yungas were enormous. The former *peones*, now small landowners, were freed from many of the obligations tying them to the rural estates – both physically and economically. The MNR also pushed for rural education, building schools and sending teachers to all *comunidades* – something the *hacendados* had always actively discouraged. Taken together, the land reform, rural education and political enfranchisement (through universal suffrage and *sindicato* organization) changed the face of the Yungas significantly (McEwen 1975a). The land reform furthermore laid the foundation for another development that came to be of paramount importance starting in the 1970s and 1980s: migration. As the plots of land distributed to each household were often not enough to support the households of all the children, many younger *Yungueños*, Afrobolivians and Aymara alike, migrated to the cities and to newly established areas of colonization in the lowlands, mainly Caranavi and Alto Beni (Léons and Léons 1971).

The post-Revolutionary developments and their impact on rural society in Bolivia received a good deal of scholarly attention and are thus a fairly well-studied subject (Kelley and Klein 1981; Malloy and Thorn 1971; Muratorio 1969; Pearse 1972; for the Yungas: Equipo CIPCA 1976; Equipo CIPCA 1977; Heath 1972; Léons 1966; Léons 1967; Léons 1972; Léons and Léons 1971). The focus of these studies is the impact of revolution and land reform on *peasants* and little attention has been paid to ethnic, cultural or racial differentiations beyond the dichotomy of white/*mestizo* landowner vs. indigenous/black peasant. With this focus on the class aspects of identity and social stratification, these studies mirror the Bolivian intellectual and political mainstream of the time that sought to incorporate indigenous people *(indios)* as citizens by way of their de-indianization, converting them into *campesinos* (peasants) (Stefanoni 2010). In fact, the use of the term *indio/a* was banned from official usage and the educational reform put great emphasis on inculcating the Spanish language and 'modern,' 'national' values to the people in the countryside (Luykx 1999).

The few studies that did make reference to Afrobolivians (referred to by that stage as *morenos/as, negros/as* or *negroes*, respectively), all emphasized that their class identity as peasants by far trumped their sense of ethnoracial belonging (Equipo

CIPCA 1976; Equipo CIPCA 1977; Léons 1966; Léons 1972). Studying the Sud Yungas town of Chicaloma, anthropologist William Léons (Léons 1972) describes the overarching tendency that the most relevant distinction within the community is that between peasants (*negros* [black people] and *indios* [indigenous]) and *mistis* (the Hispanic section consisting of *mestizos* and *blancos* [whites] who mostly worked in trade and as shopkeepers). To differences between *indios* and *negros* he only attributes a secondary role. Consequently, blackness and indigeneity are not analyzed in relation to each other, but much rather in terms of their relationship to *misti* identity and lifestyle. This view is also put forth by Alison Spedding in her more recent analyses of Sud Yungas communities (Spedding 1994). Cultural differences and social stratification, mainly expressed by the unequal distribution of political power and economic wealth, are approached by focusing on the distinction between *misti* and peasants, hardly discussing the relationship between *negro* and *indio* (see also: Equipo CIPCA 1976; Equipo CIPCA 1977). Although Léons (Léons 1972) mentions slight differences between *negros* and *indios* when it comes to land tenure and general income, he repeatedly stresses that the bigger and more significant cleavage is that separating those groups from the 'Hispanic section' that monopolized political influence, economic power and social prestige to a large extent.[11] Léons also stresses that acculturation is equally perceived as an important means to gain upward mobility by *indios* as well as *negros*. He reports that *negros* expressed little or no interest in cultural traits considered specifically Afrobolivian and even explicitly referred to *saya* as a "stupidity from the past" (*"una estupidez del pasado"* [Léons 1974:171]). Moreover, *negros* pursued accelerated acculturation through interracial marriage in order to "make the race disappear" (*"hacer perder la raza"* [Léons 1974:174]). He affirms that in light of the absolutely small numbers of *negros* in Chicaloma, interracial marriage, "would appear to be an effective [strategy]" and he speculates that in two or three generations, through marriage with non-black people, the offspring of "very dark grandparents" would be indistinguishable from the bulk of rural Bolivians (Léons 1972:176). In light of the reduced interest in Afrobolivian culture, the growing economic and political integration after the land reform and the declining importance of endogamy among *negros,* Léons concludes that *negros* in Chicaloma have been transformed from a "culturally, racially, and socially distinct" group into to a group that is now mainly defined by racialized difference (Léons 1972:284). Yet this racialized difference is highly visible and, interracial marriages notwithstanding, not as easily manipulable as dress, language or occupation, which he considers to

11 In the context of my fieldwork in Cala Cala and Nogalani between 2014 and 2017, references to *mistis* and/or *mestizos* did not play an important role in local accounts of social stratification and difference. In the local context, distinctions were made mainly between Afrobolivians (*"Afros"*) and Aymara and the terms *mestizo* or *misti* were not used to describe the society of the Yungas (for details see chapter 3).

be the main referents for the identification of *indios*. Thus he considers it unlikely that distinctions between *indios* and *negros* would completely disappear and give way to a social organization exclusively marked by vertical stratification (i.e. the difference between *mistis* and peasants).

From approximately the same time as Léons' account comes one of the few widely known publications on 'Afrobolivian culture' before the 1990s. Arturo Pizarroso Cuenca's *"La Cultura Negra in Bolivia"* (Pizarroso Cuenca 1977) neatly reflects the attitude of Bolivian intellectuals and politicians with regard to indigenous culture and processes of acculturation. Reflecting the spirit of the time that saw the disappearance of the 'traditional customs' of indigenous rural Bolivians as an inevitable – and necessary – step in the efforts to modernize the country, Pizarroso Cuenca describes Afrobolivian 'traditions' on the verge, as he sees it, of their obliteration. Yet acculturation and increasing interracial marriage did not produce results that were as straightforward as the author predicted. Despite acculturative pressures, interracial marriages and massive migration, Afrobolivian cultural and phenotypical differences did not disappear. The same is true for collective identification as Afrobolivians, which was not completely absorbed by peasant *(campesino)* affiliation. To the contrary, the 1980s saw an unprecedented upsurge in expressions of Afrobolivian 'culture' in a fundamentally changing political and intellectual climate.

Cultural revitalization and emerging ethnic politics in the multicultural age

The revolutionary MNR government was ousted from power in a military coup in 1964 and the peasant *sindicatos* were coopted by the government by way of the (in)famous *pacto militar-campesino* (military-peasant pact) that secured the power of the military in the countryside through a rigid system of vertical patronage and political clientelism (Klein 2003:223–225; de Mesa, Gisbert, and Mesa Gisbert 2008:534). Political opposition and unrest – including, among various protests and movements, the globally famous campaign of Ernesto "Ché" Guevara in Bolivia – were met with violence and repression (de Mesa, Gisbert, and Mesa Gisbert 2008:535–540). In the Yungas, as elsewhere in Bolivia, the emerging emancipatory politics were stifled by military rule and *mestizo* political brokers with ties to the ruling military were primarily in control of the fate of the population (for an excellent overview of Bolivian politics after 1952 see: Dunkerley 1984). The political climate changed only in the 1980s when, after almost twenty years of military rule, countless coups and an ever-growing involvement in the global drug industry, Bolivia formally returned to democracy. Plagued by foreign debts, hyperinflation, government corruption and a devastated economy, the governments in the 1980s and early 1990s took radical measures, applying a series of controversial political and economic reforms. Under pressure from the International Monetary Fund (IMF) and the World Bank, and initially advised by Jeffery Sachs, markets were liberalized, government spending was cut and the state-owned mining enterprises were privatized – with enormous consequences for large parts of the population (Gill 2000).

Accompanying the neoliberal restructuring of the economy, Bolivia adopted an important series of political reforms as well. In 1994, the Constitution was radically changed, declaring Bolivia to be "multiethnic" and "pluricultural," recognizing indigenous rights. The constitutional reform was accompanied by the *Ley de Participación Popular* (LPP), Bolivia's take on decentralization (Postero 2006) and educational reform, introducing bilingual education for indigenous groups and promoting respect for indigenous languages and values in the education system (Van Cott 2000). These reforms were meant to respond to the growing demands of indigenous groups claiming autonomy, land rights, respect for their cultures and languages, and an end to discrimination and disenfranchisement (Van Cott 2005).[12] They were also influenced by international developments such as the promulgation of ILO Convention 169, which Bolivia was one of the first countries to ratify in 1991.

Afrobolivians entered the scene of multicultural Bolivia through performance. Sparked by the efforts of a group of students and with the decisive support of certain key cultural and political brokers, the Afrobolivian dance and song genre *saya* became the vehicle for cultural revitalization and political mobilization (Busdiecker 2009b; Rossbach de Olmos 2007). I will detail this process and its implications in subsequent chapters. For the moment, suffice it to say that the 'rediscovery' of Afrobolivian culture and the popularity *saya* achieved in the 1990s and the early 2000s not only fundamentally altered they way Afrobolivians perceived of their 'culture,' identity, ethnoracial belonging and the general features of their "groupness" (Brubaker 2002), but also sparked an unprecedented rise in scholarly and media interest in Afrobolivians. Building on the pioneering work of ethnomusicologist Robert Templeman (Templeman 1995; Templeman 1998), who documented the circumstances of its revitalization, various studies have focused on different aspects of *saya*: its musical characteristics (Quispe 1994); its relation to Bolivian folklore and heritage (Bigenho 2002; Céspedes 1993; Rossbach de Olmos 2007; Sigl and Mendoza Salazar 2012); its role in Afrobolivian history (Sánchez Canedo 2010; Sánchez Canedo 2011); its role as a tool for communication (Rey 1998); and its importance for

12 For reasons of space, I cannot discuss the vast literature on indigenous mobilizations in Bolivia (for an overview see: Canessa 2005; for the period before the National Revolution in 1952: Gotkowitz 2008; for the postrevolutionary period: Dunkerley 1984; for the 1990s: Postero 2006; Ströbele-Gregor, Hoffman, and Holmes 1994; for comparative perspectives on Latin America: Jackson and Warren 2005; Postero and Zamosc 2004; Van Cott 2005; Yashar 2005).

political mobilization (Busdiecker 2009b; Komadina and Regalsky 2016; Lisocka-Jaegermann 2010; Rossbach de Olmos 2011), and as an expression of oral history (Ballivián 2014; Revilla Orías 2013b). *Saya* has also been the main subject of a series of audio-visual documentaries (Centro Pedagógico y Cultural "Simón I. Patiño" 1998a) and countless journalistic accounts – too many to cite even a fraction of them here.

The most ethnographically grounded full-length monograph on Afrobolivians from this period is the work of Sara Busdiecker (Busdiecker 2007), who has conducted ethnographic fieldwork in Tocaña, an Afrobolivian village in the Nor Yungas province. Tocaña is often represented – by Afrobolivian activists, as well as the media – as the most 'authentic,' 'traditional' and 'representative' Afrobolivian community. Nevertheless, Busdiecker asserts that even though Tocaña is often represented as the 'typical' Afrobolivian community, it is in fact in many regards rather atypical: it is the only *comunidad* in the Yungas where Afrobolivians are a demographic majority, which has consequences for the way blackness is perceived, represented and talked about on the one hand and for relations with non-Afrobolivians on the other (Busdiecker 2007:163). From the perspective of Tocaña, she argues that although Tocaña's residents display a great deal of socio-cultural similarities with non-Afrobolivians, there are important instances of them "being Bolivian differently" (Busdiecker 2007:88) by virtue of their blackness. She points out the seminal importance of *saya* for "performing blackness into the nation" (Busdiecker 2007:165) and has found expressive culture to be the aspect most commonly foregrounded by *Tocañeros* with regard to their blackness. *Saya*, as well as some other musical genres, is at the core of what people consider *"lo nuestro"* ("ours") and most important in determining what is distinctive about Afrobolivians (Busdiecker 2007:145). Moreover, certain marriage customs, locally known as *matrimonio negro*, and the funerary rite *mauchi* are cited as elements distinctive of Afrobolivians and although most of these cultural practices had already fallen out of use at the time of Busdiecker's research, they live on "in memory and oral history" and are part of *Tocañeros'* "narratives of blackness" (Busdiecker 2007:204). Her approach is characterized by embracing blackness as a relevant and consequential category of social differentiation in the Yungas quite uncritically. Moreover, she analytically separates the discourses of emerging ethnic politics and related state discourses on multicultural diversity from the local context by treating them in a separate chapter under the rubric of "representations of blacks and blackness arising from non-blacks" (Busdiecker 2007:230). This perspective is problematic since Tocaña has been an important hotspot of cultural revitalization and emerging Afrobolivian politics since the late 1980s and the rural community with the closest ties to the urban movement (see for example: Centro Pedagógico y Cultural "Simón I. Patiño" 1998a; Komadina and Regalsky 2016; Rey 1998; Templeman 1998). In my view, she gives nationally circulating discourses too little credit for the shifting local meanings of blackness in Tocaña. At the same time, she understates the importance of Tocaña's particularities as key references for the urban movement and the notions of Afrobolivian 'culture' it propagated (see my remarks on the Tocaña bias in chapter 7).

From multiculturalism to plurinationality

In an unprecedented election in 2005, Evo Morales and the *Movimiento al Socialismo* party (MAS) rose to power and set out to fundamentally change the country through what they refer to as *"el proceso de cambio"* (the process of change). Morales' election was preceded by years of civil unrest, violent repression and political turmoil (Kohl and Farthing 2006). Immediately after taking office in early 2006, the Morales government convened elections for a Constituent Assembly that started developing a new constitution in Sucre in mid-2006.[13] Through this constitutional reform, Bolivia was re-founded as the Plurinational State of Bolivia in 2009. As the sociologist and current Bolivian vice president, Álvaro García Linera (García Linera 2009:7), has argued, "it is not the same to define the state as plurinational as to define the society as pluricultural" *("No es lo mismo definir al Estado como plurinacional que a la sociedad como pluricultural")*. A plurinational state – according to García Linera – moves beyond the mere recognition of the diversity of society by making a "diversity of institutionalities and practices of the indigenous peasant world" *("una diversidad de institucionalidades y prácticas del mundo indígena campesino")* (García Linera 2009:13f) an important part of the "machine of political power" *("máquina de poder político")* (García Linera 2009:7). Whereas the "monocultural, monolingual, monoinstitutional" state – even in times when society was already officially acknowledged to be multicultural – only served the interests of non-indigenous national elites and transnational capital, the Plurinational State is represented as the institutional counterpart to a multicultural and pluri-ethnic society (García Linera 2008:13).

For Afrobolivians, the stakes in Bolivia's re-foundation process were high, as it represented a very immediate and palpable opportunity to push for legal recognition in a climate favorable to such claims (see chapter 9 for details). In the years leading up to 2005, Afrobolivians had achieved a certain degree of visibility, mainly by way of performance in folklore, but were still largely denied recognition in political and legal contexts. For example, Afrobolivian efforts to include *"Afroboliviano/a"* as a category for self-identification in Bolivia's 2001 population census were denied on the grounds that they did not constitute a legally recognized collective subject. Similarly – and despite the personal commitment of Vice President Victor Hugo

13 For reasons of space, it is not possible to detail here the political and economic crisis leading up to Morales' election in 2005. For an overview see Kohl and Farthing (2006) and Shultz and Draper (2009).

Cárdenas, who officially received Afrobolivians and listened to their demands in La Paz in 1994 – Afrobolivian activists felt excluded from spaces of political participation and decried ongoing discrimination and poor living conditions in most Afrobolivian communities.

Taking into consideration that Afrobolivian organizations had already begun adopting discourses centering on topics such as legal recognition as an ethnic group, it becomes clear why the political and social conjuncture of those years became so important. An Afrobolivian activist from Cochabamba once very neatly summarized two fundamental aspects and achievements of Afrobolivian mobilization during those times by saying:

> "With the Constituent Assembly, the results of this, after being there days, weeks, months in Sucre, fighting, it's that we have achieved that in the Constitution the terminology and the rights and all those things are included, right? I think that this was already a big step. And the second transcendental step for me particularly – because I know this fight from very close – was that Jorge [Medina] was able to be part of this new political conjuncture. Because that allows us visibility, in the eyes of the state, in the eyes of society, that is what we lack, you could say, the Afrobolivian community."[14]

As can be discerned from the quote above, the importance lies in the recognition of Afrobolivians and their rights within the Plurinational Constitution ("we achieved that the terminology and the rights are included"), as well as in the inclusion of concrete Afrobolivian actors in spaces of decision making within the Plurinational State ("that Jorge [Medina] was able to be part of this new political conjuncture"). From this perspective, the plurinational promise of recognition and empowerment seems to have been achieved for Afrobolivians – at least in the particular moment this statement was made in 2012.

However, this rather positive assessment of the plurinational conjuncture made by an individual activist, as well as Garcia Linera's remarks on plurinationality cited above, require some qualifications. As for Afrobolivian activists, not all share the optimistic view on recent political developments. As my analysis of activism in chapters 8 and 9 shows, there is considerable debate among Afrobolivian activists and within organizations concerning the general scope, as well as the specifics of Afrobolivian participation and empowerment in plurinational Bolivia. Secondly,

14 *"Ya con la asamblea constituyente los resultados de esto después de estar días, semanas, meses ahí en Sucre peleando, es que logramos que se incluya la, en la Constitución la terminología y los derechos y todas estas cosas, ¿no? Creo que eso ya era un paso grande, y el segundo paso transcendental para mí particularmente porque conozco muy de cerca toda esta pelea, es que Jorge [Medina] ha podido ser parte de esta nueva coyuntura política. Porque esto nos permite la visibilización, frente al Estado, frente a la sociedad, es lo que nos falta digamos, la comunidad afro."*

and with regard to the straightforward official rhetoric on plurinationality represented by Garcia Linera's statements, recent analyses of Bolivia's political conjuncture suggest that the situation is rather more complex and that the turn to plurinationality has produced contradictory results. Although Bolivia's plurinational model has been widely celebrated – much in the same vein as in the abovementioned statements – as being a fundamental step towards introducing indigenous values and logics in matters of governance, jurisprudence and economic policy (Acosta 2015; Escobar 2010; Schilling-Vacaflor, Brand, and Radhuber 2012) there are also various voices (Albro 2010a; Canessa 2012a; Postero 2017) pointing out the limitations and inherent contradictions of the MAS-led *proceso de cambio.*

Bret Gustafson (2009) offers a concise genealogical sketch of the concept of plurinationality (plurinationalism in his words) and traces it back to Ecuadorian indigenous movements from whence it "percolated upward from the grassroots" and "filtered downward through transnational movement debate" (Gustafson 2009:999) all over the Andes. He differentiates plurinationality from neoliberal multiculturalism, which, in his view, "sought to manage difference and call on the market to solve redistributive problems while depoliticizing deep historical inequalities". Plurinationality, on the other hand, "speaks of robust redistributive social rights rooted in a strong state alongside equally robust indigenous rights" (Gustafson 2009: 991). In Bolivia, plurinationality was first invoked in the 1980s by the largely Quechua and Aymara peasant unions and also influenced indigenous movements in the Bolivian lowlands. In the wake of demands for constitutional reform at the turn of the millennium, discourses of plurinationality soon became a fundamental part of the *Pacto de Unidad's* political agenda.[15] Eventually, plurinationality was also taken up by the MAS party as a part of their agenda and discursive repertoire. It is important to keep in mind, however, that the MAS party's discursive shift towards plurinationality was fairly recent (Gustafson 2009: 1003). That also might explain, among other factors, why the Plurinational Constitution that was eventually passed

15 The *Pacto de Unidad* (Pact of Unity) is an alliance of indigenous, peasant, and workers' organizations officially formed in 2004. It represents the core of *CONALCAM (Coordinadora Nacional por el Cambio)* a pro-government alliance of social movements. The composition of the *Pacto de Unidad* has varied over time, but since 2006 it has generally consisted of the following organizations: *Consejo Nacional de Ayllus y Markas del Qullasuyu (CONAMAQ)*, a federation of highland communities; the *Confederación de Pueblos Indígenas de Bolivia (CIDOB)*, a federation of lowland groups; the *Confederación Sindical de Colonizadores de Bolivia (CSCB)*, which has recently been renamed as *Confederación Sindical de Comunidades Interculturales Originarios de Bolivia - CSCIOB*, mostly highland peoples living in colonization zones in the lowlands; the *Confederación Sindical Única de Trabajadores Campesinos de Bolivia (CSUTCB)*, the peasant workers' federation, and the *Confederación Nacional de Mujeres Campesinas Indígenas Originarias de Bolivia – Bartolina Sisa (CNMCIOB-BS)*, the national federation of women peasant workers (for details see Postero 2017: chapter 2).

in 2009 under the leadership of MAS, fell short of the many more radical demands originally made by indigenous activists and other social movements in the years leading up to the *Asamblea Constituyente*. Nancy Postero (2017: 57-60) contends that the New Bolivian Constitution reflects the proposal made by the *Pacto de Unidad* only in terms of recognizing the plurality and diversity of Bolivian society. With regard to the possibility of indigenous autonomy, juridical pluralism and shared decision-making, however, she concludes that the Constitution approved in 2009 is much less progressive. Moreover, reconciling and balancing indigenous rights with state sovereignty and economic 'development' has not been an easy task in political practice. For example, the government's focus on 'development' and its extractivist economic policies have been objects of severe criticism for not respecting the rights of the indigenous communities the Constitution purports to protect. This contradiction became apparent and received great international attention in the context of the so-called TIPNIS controversy in 2011, sparked by the government's plan to build a highway through indigenous territory and the fierce resistance against those plans by indigenous movements (for details see Postero 2017). What is more, and although Gustafson (2009: 1001) urges us to view plurinationality as a "dynamic process of transforming relationships" rather than as a "congealed model" (Gustafson 2009: 994) of ethnic autonomy or federalism, much of the state's intervention in plurinationality's name has had the taste of rather "crude territorial, [...] political [and legal] fixing" (Gustafson 2009: 1001) of certain categories of identification. This tendency is exacerbated by the general conceptual perspective on indigeneity and ethnic difference that characterizes the New Bolivian Constitution. It has been criticized as too narrow and essentialist, privileging an imagined rural, pre-modern, collective indigenous subject and thus covering only a fraction of Bolivia's multiple and changing indigeneities (Albro 2006; 2007; 2010a; Canessa 2007; 2012a; 2018; Postero 2017).

Afrobolivians have received only very limited attention within these debates as scholars generally approach the multifaceted transformations observable in the country with a focus on indigenous people, both urban and rural (Albro 2010b; Lazar 2008; Postero 2017; Schavelzon 2012), or the growing importance of 'new middle classes' in the country (Pellegrini Calderón 2016; Shakow 2014). Afrobolivian communities and politics in plurinational Bolivia, as well as the transformations in the aftermath of recognition, have not been thoroughly studied to this date.[16] A few exceptions aside (Sturtevant 2013; 2017), recent contributions (beyond the works dedicated to Afrobolivian colonial history cited above) either summarize material

16 Significant recent contributions to the study of Afrobolivianity can be found the field of linguistics, where interest in Afrobolivian Spanish and its status as an Afro-Creole variant of Spanish has sparked considerable interest and debate (Lipski 2007; Lipski 2008; Lipski 2012; Pérez Inofuentes 2015; Sessarego 2011a; Sessarego 2011b; Sessarego 2014).

already presented earlier (Angola Maconde 2010) or are fundamentally descriptive and documentary in nature (Ballivián 2015; Zambrana B. 2014). They are furthermore, in my view, often uneasily positioned at the boundary between research and activism, often blurring ethnographic descriptions with evocative speculations on 'African roots' and Afrobolivian cultural particularities (Angola Maconde 2000; in this regard see especially: Ballivián 2014).

My discussion of plurinational Afrobolivianity takes up the topics of the debates sketched above and places special emphasis on the processes of "legalizing" (French 2009) Afrobolivian identity in the context of plurinational reforms. An important focus of my study are the effects that static, essentialist and collectivist conceptualizations of indigeneity (and hence also Afrobolivianity) engender in political practice and in everyday contexts. Throughout this study, I analyze how those conceptualizations are engaged politically and deployed strategically, but also how they are re-negotiated and resisted. In political and legal terms, the processes I am concerned with are most clearly expressed in the widespread use and propagation of the concept of *el pueblo Afroboliviano*. Speaking of a single *pueblo* insinuates boundedness, internal homogeneity and a very clear sense of collectivity (see chapter 9 for details). This approach to Afrobolivianity, which is characteristic of Bolivia's plurinational moment, represents a decidedly new take on the question of Afrobolivian collectivity and identity. The discursive invocation and legal recognition of a single collective subject that becomes the basis for political and social enfranchisement – *el pueblo Afroboliviano* – poses new challenges for Afrobolivian political activism, but also for individuals engaging with their Afrobolivianity. Finally, it urges us to inquire into the question of what it means to be a *pueblo* (in the sense of the Constitution) and what consequences the rise of this concept and the related perspective on society has for our understanding of Afrobolivianity. This is especially important in contrast to the focus of earlier studies that I have summarized in this chapter and their take on Afrobolivianity. As I have shown, studies in the 1960s and 1970s found the economic and political changes engendered by the National Revolution and land reform in the 1950s to be the main framework of political action and social transformation. During those times, Afrobolivians faced great acculturative pressures and their engagement with society was marked by efforts at blending in racially, as well as culturally. The 1980s saw an increasing flow of Afrobolivian migrants arriving in urban contexts, as well as Bolivia's return to democracy, an upswell of indigenous mobilization and Bolivia's turn to multiculturalism and neoliberal structural reforms. Afrobolivian music and dance, emerging patterns of political mobilization and the sometimes conflicting relationships between urban and rural Afrobolivians became major topics during those times. Most recently, plurinational constitutional reform and the legal recognition of a collective Afrobolivian subject have added decisive new features to the debate. As the following chapters and my ethnography of Cala Cala show, all of the abovementioned topics continue to be of great importance for the articulation of Afrobolivianity – a set of processes that draws on a wide variety of sources and differs across contexts.

Chapter 3: "We are los *Afros de Cala Cala*"[1]

Cala Cala is located in the *Departamento* of La Paz, Province of Nor Yungas, *Municipio* of Coripata at about twenty minutes by car, bus, or motorcycle from the town *(pueblo)* of Coripata and approximately the same distance from the *pueblos nuevos* of Arapata and Trinidad Pampa. In administrative contexts, Cala Cala is considered and treated as part of the much larger *comunidad Nogalani*, a unit of about 150 households and approximately 500 inhabitants.[2] Cala Cala's approximately 30 Afrobolivian inhabitants are distributed over eleven households. Nine of these Afrobolivian households are concentrated geographically in the 'lower parts' *(la parte de abajo)* of the *comunidad's* territory (i.e. closer to the river), one Afrobolivian household is located even further downhill on the shores of the river, and one is located in Bella Vista (see figs. 4 and 5). The Aymara households are grouped together in two geographical locations, referred to as *Bella Vista* or *Vaquería* and *Nogalani pueblo* (see fig. 4).

The distances between the different parts of the *comunidad* are short (approx. 1.5 kilometers between Nogalani and Bella Vista) and Cala Cala borders Bella Vista directly. What is now Cala Cala was once a small independent estate (referred to occasionally as *estancia Cala Cala*) populated by Afrobolivian slaves whose legal status changed to that of *peones* after the abolition of slavery in 1851. Later, Cala Cala became part of the *hacienda Nogalani*, a much larger estate inhabited by Aymara *peones*. I was not able to determine when exactly Cala Cala became a part of Nogalani but in a detailed listing of coca producing *haciendas* from 1902, Cala Cala is not mentioned explicitly and it can be assumed that it was by then already administered alongside Nogalani, one of the biggest coca producing *haciendas* in the Yungas at that time (Soux 1993:197). It certainly was part of the *hacienda Nogalani* by the 1920s, as a stash

1 *"Somos los Afros de Cala Cala."*

2 The *Plan de Desarrollo Municipal* 2001-2005 (Municipal Development Plan) cites the following figures for Nogalani: 508 inhabitants in 137 households. There is, however, a certain fluctuation. People in Nogalani repeatedly stated that there are "more than 150" *sindicato* members (*afiliados*, i.e. households) in the *comunidad*.

Figure 4: Map showing the locations of Cala Cala, Bella Vista and Nogalani (© OpenStreet Map contributors) Terms: www.openstreetmap.org/copyright.

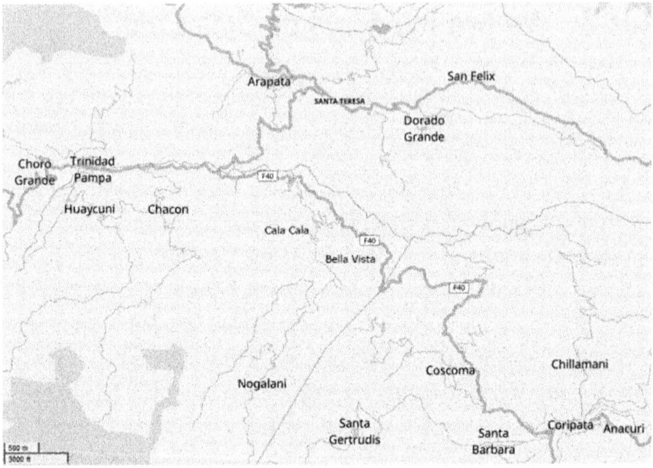

of the *hacienda's* administrative documents show.[3] However, there was a separate *casa de hacienda* in Cala Cala, including a *kachi* (an area used to dry coca leaves), offices for the administrator *(oficinas)* and two coca presses *(prensas de coca)* that were still functioning in the 1940s. This supports suggestions that Cala Cala was once independent since *oficinas*, *kachi* and *prensa de coca* are the fundamental equipment needed to produce and market coca leaves. The remnants of the buildings' outer walls remain visible and are referred to as *el Matuasi* by the inhabitants. There was another *casa de hacienda* in what is now referred to as *Nogalani pueblo*,[4] whereas the area referred to as Bella Vista/Vaquería – where the *comunidad's* school and soccer

3 The documents – mostly inventories of the *hacienda's* assets (including *peones*) and correspondence between the owner Jorge Cusicanqui and the administrators of the property, as well as the local and national authorities – were first shown to me in 2014 by a lawyer and self-taught historian in Coripata who claimed that he had obtained them from a descendant of the former owner. The lawyer then sold the documents to the Afrobolivian researcher Martín Ballivián who published facsimiles of certain parts in 2015 (Ballivián 2015). I obtained the original documents in 2017 from Martín Ballivián and they remain in my possession.

4 The term *pueblo* here is slightly misleading. Normally, *pueblo* is reserved for larger settlements like Coripata (with over 2000 inhabitants in almost 600 households) that are furthermore not entirely agricultural. What is expressed with the term *pueblo* here is rather the fact that *Nogalani pueblo* is a nucleated settlement grouped around a small *plaza* where the church and the *sindicato* headquarters are located as opposed to the pattern of dispersed settlement in Cala Cala.

field are located – has only been populated since the 1970s and before served as a place for pasturing animals (hence the name Vaquería, derived from pasturing cows *[vacas]* there).

Cala Cala's history and its incorporation into political and administrative units are quite particular. In what follows, I will analyze one specific aspect of the way *Cala Caleños* (inhabitants of Cala Cala) view their community (*"nuestra comunidad"*). This aspect comes to the fore when they use vocabulary such as *"los Afros de Cala Cala,"* or *"comunidad Afrobolivana Cala Cala"* – thus referencing ethnoracial identification and origins as the foundation of self-identification. Many people from Cala Cala very strongly express a sense of belonging to Cala Cala, despite the fact that they are deeply entangled with Nogalani historically, economically and politically (see chapter 4). *Cala Caleños* furthermore clearly stress that Cala Cala is a *"comunidad Afroboliviana,"* inhabited almost exclusively by Afrobolivians, whereas Nogalani's inhabitants are in their majority non-Afrobolivians (mostly referred to as *indígenas*, *Aymara* or *"gente del altiplano"* by people from Cala Cala).

Comparing the categories that *Cala Caleños* employ in order to describe individuals and groups in the local context to ethnographic accounts of the Yungas from the 1960s, shows one decisive difference. Whereas earlier accounts describe the Yungas as fundamentally marked by social differentiation between *mistis* (*mestizos* and *blancos*, see chapter 2) and peasants (the former *peones*, i.e. *indios* and *negros*), the category *misti* is absent from contemporary classificatory schemes. From the perspective of Afrobolivians in Cala Cala, the most salient boundary is that between Afrobolivians (*"los Afros de Cala Cala"*) and Aymara (also referred to as *indígenas* or *"gente del altiplano"*). Likewise, people from Nogalani refer to themselves as Aymara or *indígena*. That is, if they use an ethnic/cultural label in the first place and not just simply refer to themselves as *comunarios* or *cocaleros* (see chapter 4). This shift, marked by the declining importance of the category *misti* and the parallel rise of ethnoracial and 'cultural' categories of identification, stems from a variety of developments. On the one hand, the Yungas experienced profound transformations in the last fifty years that displaced *mistis* as the politically and economically dominant group. The landowning elite left the Yungas in the wake of the National Revolution and although many *mistis* remained important political brokers in the post-revolutionary period and also held on to many economic privileges in trade and transportation, their position vis-à-vis the former *peones* weakened steadily. This process was accelerated by the fact that the former *peones* pressed for their demands through the *sindicato* structure. What is more, many former *peones* sought economic opportunities beyond their *comunidades* (former *haciendas*) in the villages (*pueblos*) of the Yungas engaging in trade and transportation (hitherto *misti* privileges), as well as pursuing formal education in Spanish in rural schools. Those developments destabilized the boundary between *mistis* and peasants, as the latter had been defined mainly by their agricultural lifestyle and the fact that they did not speak Spanish. However, the blurring of the boundaries between *indios/negros* and *mistis* did not lead to the integration of Bolivian society within a 'modern' *mestizo* nation as the post-revolutionary politics had envisioned. Emerging in the 1970s, indigenous movements and later the *Movimiento Afroboliviano* (see chapter 8) challenged the ideology of *mestizaje* (Stutzman 1981) and began mobilizing a growing constituency on the bases of ethnic and cultural identity (cf. Scheuzger 2007). With the advent of multicultural politics in the decade of the 1990s and plurinational reform in the 21st century, indigenous and Afrobolivian identity politics became an increasingly important frame of reference also in the Yungas. In my view, one of the effects of those developments is the partial restructuring of classificatory schemes in Cala Cala – and the Yungas more broadly. When *Cala Caleños* intend to describe differences in their social environment that matter for them beyond the overarching similarities as *cocaleros* and *Yungueños* (see chapter 4), they address the boundary between Afrobolivians and *indígenas*, rather than that between peasants and *mistis*.

Being *Afro* in Cala Cala

The notion of identity and collectivity as Afrobolivians is, in Cala Cala, rooted in various interrelated dimensions. The most immediately observable difference between Cala Cala and the rest of Nogalani is the phenotypical appearance of its inhabitants, who are in their majority identifiable as *negros/Afrobolivianos*. However, according to Alison Spedding (Spedding 2013), being *negro/Afroboliviano* in the Yungas does not say much about a person:

> In the province [Sud Yungas], this [being *negro/Afroboliviano*] means little more than saying 'he is tall' or 'he is fat'; that is to say, it's a physical characteristic that helps distinguish or identify the person without adding or withdrawing virtue in any other respect [...]" (Spedding 2013:189, my translation).[5]

Spedding is arguably one of the most prolific authors with regard to the Yungas. She is, in Bolivia and internationally, considered an authority, especially on the coca economy and the Yungas, where she has worked from the 1980s until today. With regard to Afrobolivians, she has maintained a firm position, arguing against the salience of *Afroboliviano/a* as a category of identity and sociocultural differentiation in the Yungas from her earliest publications on the subject (Spedding 1995) until very recently (see for example Spedding 2009; Spedding 2013). She grounds

5 *"En la provincia [Sud Yungas] esto [ser negro/afroboliviano] no significa mucho más que decir 'es alto' o 'es gordo', o sea, es una característica física que ayuda a distinguir o identificar a la persona sin añadir o quitarles valor en cualquier otro aspecto [...]."*

her assertion in two observations. She maintains that the "cultural expressions" (*"expresiones culturales"*) that are generally associated with Afrobolivians (mainly the dance *saya*) are of no further significance for collective identifications and social organization in the Yungas (Spedding 2009:446). For her, the topic of Afrobolivians in the Yungas is a question of race, which she equates with phenotype.[6] As the quote above shows, however, she does not consider phenotypical variation a meaningful referent for collective identification or social differentiation.

Contrary to this assertion, I argue that being Afrobolivian in Cala Cala is more than a mere physical characteristic without social consequences. In fact, the physical appearance of an individual is in most cases considered of secondary importance for belonging to *"los Afros de Cala Cala."* I approach the term *"los Afros de Cala Cala"* as a "process of collective identification" in which different categories of identification and changing frames of reference for those categories become relevant. Speaking of "identification" rather than of "identity" takes into account that it is only through the actors' engagement with certain categories that they are "activated" and become the bases of a collective identity (Eidson et al. 2017:341; cf. Brubaker and Cooper 2000). Analyzing the emic concept of *"los Afros de Cala Cala"* as a "[process] under the appearance of [a] stable entit[y]" (Elwert 1995) not only helps avoid the "common sense groupism" (Brubaker 2002) that has frequently been criticized, but also enables my analysis to examine dynamics of "re-identification," understood as "alterations in the actors' orientation, attitude, and behavior with reference to selected categories of identification" (Eidson et al. 2017:342).

Most importantly for *Cala Caleños*, being *Afro* is tied to a notion of shared history and to how this history relates to networks of kinship in the present – cognate and affinal ties, as well as *compadrazgo* (godparenthood [Foster 1953; Mintz and Wolf 1950; Van Vleet 2008]). My approach to kinship in Cala Cala follows Krista Van Vleet's proposal (2008) taking into account that 'being related as kin' "is not solely about the genealogical relationships between people but about the practices of connection – and disconnection – through which people maintain and contest the emotional, social, political, and material parameters of their daily lives" (Van Vleet 2008:25). She argues that rather than focusing on "some essential biological relationship or on static social structures," it is important to track how "relatedness emerges among individuals who have differing life experiences and move within and between communities" (Van Vleet 2008:2). The narrative and practice-centered approach to kinship she proposes is based on the concept of "relatedness" first introduced to the anthropological study of kinship by Janet Carsten (2000). Instead of focusing solely on formal aspects of kinship and genealogical connections, the aim

6 In the Spanish original the passsage reads: *"[En] el tema afroboliviano [...] definitivamente se trata de un problema de raza, es decir, de fenotipo"* (Spedding 2009:447).

is to understand "the ethnographic particularities of being related in a specific cultural context without presupposing what constitutes kinship" (Carsten 2000:4–5). In her study of a rural village in Bolivia, Van Vleet identified "everyday talk [...] and especially the telling and retelling of stories" (Van Vleet 2008:2) as an important arena for negotiating notions of relatedness through contested narratives. Such narratives are common among *Cala Caleños*. A sense of shared history is expressed, for example, in the fact that people take considerable pride in pointing out the existence of a *casa de hacienda* in the community or the fact that in the registers of the municipality of Coripata, Cala Cala is occasionally listed as an independent *comunidad* because of its former status as an independent *estancia*. They deploy these facts in narrative representations of Cala Cala's history in order to highlight the historical continuity of their status as a separate community. The local history of Cala Cala is discoursively linked to notions of kinship and the social networks it entails in the present by representing Cala Cala's current inhabitants and their relatives as being linked to a handful of Afrobolivian ancestors *("los abuelos Afros")* who inhabited the *estancia Cala Cala* (later incorporated into the *hacienda Nogalani)* in the period before the Agrarian Reform in 1953. The connection to *"los abuelos Afros"* is important in formal terms since it secures access to land within the *comunidad*, but also central to narratives of belonging and the identification as *"los Afros de Cala Cala."* What is more, kinship has also long linked Afrobolivians from Cala Cala with Afrobolivians from other *comunidades* in the Yungas and more recently has been the basis for establishing and maintaining connections to the growing parts of the Afrobolivian population in Bolivia's major cities. Although less common in comparison to narratives of local Afrobolivian history and kinship, specific 'cultural elements' are occasionally invoked by people in Cala Cala in order to define their Afrobolivianity. I agree with Spedding's critical approach that problematizes the often taken-for-granted salience of 'cultural elements' for notions of Afrobolivianity. I argue, however, that 'cultural elements' are not entirely inconsequential. Although *saya*, for example, might have fallen out of practice for decades and is not usually performed in Cala Cala, it is invoked in discursive articulations of Afrobolivianity. As will become clear in my discussion of the changing tides of *"lo Afro,"* *saya* and 'Afrobolivian culture' more generally are important discursive spheres of resonance for debates on Afrobolivian history and collective identification.[7]

The chapter is structured as follows: First, I will introduce Cala Cala in its most basic geographic and demographic dimensions. I will then discuss the importance of understanding Cala Cala fundamentally as a group of relatives that can be traced back to the inhabitants of the *estancia/hacienda (peones)* that became the owners of the land (called *sayañeros)* through the process of land reform starting in 1953,

7 See also my discussion of *saya* in chapter 7 and of Cala Cala's tourism project in chapter 10.

and the historical backbone of the contemporary community.[8] Moreover, kinship networks are also key to understanding Cala Cala's entanglements with the growing urban population of Afrobolivians and they are a fundamental link that ties local concepts of belonging to nationally circulating ideas of collectivity and identity as *el pueblo Afroboliviano.* I will end the chapter with a brief contextualization of the notion of "*los Afros de Cala Cala,*" since in addition to identifying as *Afrobolivianos*, *Cala Caleños* also express a strong sense of *cocalero* identity and are embedded in social relations transcending "*los Afros de Cala Cala.*"

Geographical aspects of community in Cala Cala

Cala Cala is a small but dispersed settlement consisting of eighteen houses (some of them unoccupied) in the core area of settlement. There are two households that people consider part of Cala Cala, although their houses are located beyond the geographical boundaries associated with Cala Cala: one household in Bella Vista and one whose house lies at the river shore close to the road to Arapata/Coripata. Incuding those two, Cala Cala is home to eleven households belonging to six families. With the term house I refer to the material buildings, whereas household designates units of cohabitation and economic activity. Most households in Cala Cala consist of an adult couple with their children who live together in one house. However, there are also cases where (unmarried) siblings live together and form a household and one case of a widow living with her unmarried children. In economic terms, it is very important that the household is the unit that administers the coca fields and is the basis for exchanging labor. With the term family, I refer to a group of individuals tracing back kinship to the same 'original inhabitant' of Cala Cala and houses, households and families overlap in different ways (see below).

Approximately thirty people live permanently in Cala Cala. That I can only give approximate numbers of inhabitants has to do with the fact that some people live in Cala Cala only temporarily and that during the four years (from 2014-2018) that I have known the community some people have left, while others have returned to Cala Cala or have recently established residence there. Cala Cala does not have a central square and its houses are scattered along a winding dirt road. The only public building is a small, one-room chapel that is rarely used and only rudimentarily taken care of. Cala Cala's geographical boundaries are neither visibly marked nor

8 The word *sayañero* is derived from the land entitlements (called *sayañas*) the former *peones* received through the Agrarian Reform. It has no connection to the word *saya* referring to the Afrobolivian music and dance genre. The origins of the word *saya* are unknown (see chapter 7). It is sometimes said to derive from the Latin "*saga*" or alternatively from the Kikongo "*nsaya*" (Rey 1998: 100-102).

established in any formal way. However, there is tacit agreement among its inhabitants concerning which houses "belong to Cala Cala." It is furthermore known – and very strictly observed – where the boundaries between Cala Cala's *cocales* (coca fields) and those of other *comunidades* lie. Figure 5 shows the location of the eighteen houses (occupied and unoccupied), the small church and the area known as *el Matuasi* where the *casa de hacienda* was located and where the *Casa Cultural Afro Cala Cala* was built recently.

Figure 5: The distribution of houses and households in Cala Cala

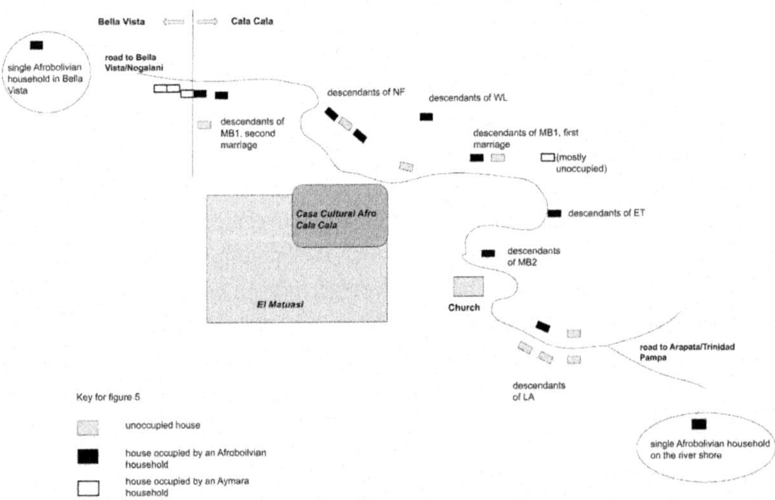

Each house (or group of houses) is associated with a certain extended family that can be traced back to the times of the *hacienda* and more specifically to the individuals that made up the last generation of *peones* living and working in Cala Cala, who became *sayañeros* by receiving land through the 1953 Agrarian Reform and being founding members of the *sindicato* established during the same period. There are the houses of the families Angola, who are the descendants of the *sayañero* Lorenzo Angola (LA), Ballivián 1 (descendants of Manuel Ballivián 1ro [MB1]), Ballivián 2 (descendants of Manuel Ballivián 2do [MB2]), Flores (descendants of Nicanor Flores [NF]), Landaveri (descendants of Waldo Landaveri [WL]) and Torrez (descendants of Eustaquio Torrez [ET]). As can be discerned from figure 5, many of the houses are not permanently occupied and, normally, of each *sayañero* family, only one descendant and his/her household actually lives in the community, works the land and is full member of the *sindicato*. The part of the community where the offspring of *peón* LA live, for example, consists of five houses, four of which are permanently unoccupied. One house is permanently occupied by Roberto Angola (a grandson of *sayañero* LA) and his family and one is occassionally used for visits by Roberto's nephew (ZS). Most extended families live under similar conditions. There are various houses that have been built in close proximity, of which only one is inhabited permanently, while the others serve for occasional visits or are abandoned.

Since the houses are dispersed and there is no central meeting place, *Cala Caleños* mostly socialize in the coca fields or meet on the way to their agricultural plots rather than gathering at a central square or visiting each other's houses. The house – and especially the interior – is considered private space and if there are visits, people normally gather on the patio in front of the house. People spend most of their time in the fields and only very limited amounts of time in their houses. Hence the preferred space of social interaction is the coca fields.

The spatial make-up and the location of the community occasionally plays a role when distinguishing Afrobolivian from Aymara households. I mentioned at the outset that Cala Cala was once an independent *estancia* and even after being integrated into the much bigger *hacienda Nogalani* and later the *comunidad* of the same name, it was still treated as a somewhat independent unit. This also meant that Cala Cala had its own *casa de hacienda (el Matuasi)*. The *estancia* Cala Cala was inhabited by a majority of Afrobolivian *peones* whose houses were concentrated around the *Matuasi*. Since Cala Cala's inhabitants of today are the direct offspring of these former *peones*, the history of the two *haciendas* and the fact that they were inhabited by Afrobolivians and Aymara respectively, is reflected in the location of their houses. The last house that is considered to be part of Cala Cala directly neighbors (literally wall to wall) a house that is said to belong to the more recent settlement of Bella Vista. For an outsider, the geographical boundary is therefore all but invisible; for *Cala Caleños*, however, it is by no means meaningless and it is widely known where 'their community' ends and where Bella Vista begins. In the same vein, none of Cala Cala's inhabitants considered an Aymara household that had built a house and wanted to establish a permanent residence within the geographical space associated with Cala Cala as part of the community. They were considered "people from Nogalani" even though they were intermittently living in Cala Cala (geographically) on a piece of land that nobody denied was rightfully theirs since many inhabitants of Nogalani have *cocales* and small plots of land in the hills around the houses of Cala Cala. When prompted to list the households considered to be part of Cala Cala, most people consistently singled out this Aymara household that they did not consider as much part of the community as the Afrobolivian households. In the same vein, people mentioned a single Afrobolivian household located geographically in Bella Vista as belonging to Cala Cala, although somewhat less integrated into the community due to its geographical location. The settlement patterns thus reflect Cala Cala's history and are often invoked in narratives on Cala Cala's status as a separate 'Afrobolivian community.'

"The Afrobolivian grandfathers" (*"los abuelos afros"*): From *peones* to *sayañeros*

In order to make sense of Cala Cala as a community, it is important to understand how the households and families there are related and how the collective they refer to as "*los Afros de Cala Cala*" can be traced back to the *sayañeros*, i.e. the former *peones* that received land entitlements through the process of the Agrarian Reform beginning in 1953. Additionally, my discussion takes into account the situation of Cala Cala in the years prior to the reform, when it was part of the *hacienda Nogalani*. This is rooted in the fact that although the Bolivian National Revolution of 1952 and the ensuing land reform that began in 1953 are generally considered among the most radical social and political shifts on the continent, various studies of ex-*hacienda* communities in the Yungas have emphasized that it is important to take into consideration that the *hacienda* – as an economic, social and political institution – can have a profound influence even on post-revolution *comunidades* (Heath 1972). What is more, the balance between pre-reform continuities and the changes brought about by the revolution varies significantly from case to case depending, among other factors, on the size of the *hacienda*, the amount of land available for distribution, the number of *peones*, as well as the relations between former *peones* and owners (Léons 1967).[9] It is also important to keep in mind that the land reform was not accomplished immediately on all *haciendas* and there are cases in the Yungas where as late as 1964 – over ten years after the Law of Agrarian Reform was issued – the process of distribution and titling had still not been completed (Léons 1967:695).

The *hacienda Nogalani* – and with it Cala Cala – was declared *latifundio* according to the Law of Agrarian Reform (Equipo CIPCA 1977:192).[10] This means that all the land of the *hacienda* was legally subject to expropriation.[11] From Cala Cala, six

9 I limit my discussion here to Cala Cala and Nogalani, for further information, case studies and discussion see Kelley and Klein (1981); Malloy and Thorn (1971); McEwen (1975).

10 The law established different provisions for different kinds and sizes of properties, distinguishing between small holdings, medium holdings, agricultural enterprises and large holdings (*latifundio*). Only in the latter case, was the property subject to expropriation. The complicated process of deciding what category applied to a property involved the *sindicatos*, local Agrarian Tribunals, *hacienda* owners and the National Agrarian Reform Council (Léons 1967).

11 In practice, however, *hacienda* owners were often granted the plots of land that had been under cultivation for the *hacienda* (i.e. not cultivated in usufruct by *peones*) before the reform. This was also the case in Nogalani/Cala Cala. As the documents from the period following

households received *sayañas* and the heads of these households, the *sayañeros*, are considered the founding members of the "*comunidad Cala Cala.*" Being related to a *sayañero* also has very practical consequences since it is the most effective way to access cultivable land in Cala Cala and is thus of great economic importance. Figure 6 below shows the relations of one particular household with the original six *sayañeros* of Cala Cala.

Figure 6: Household with ties to all of the six sayañero families.

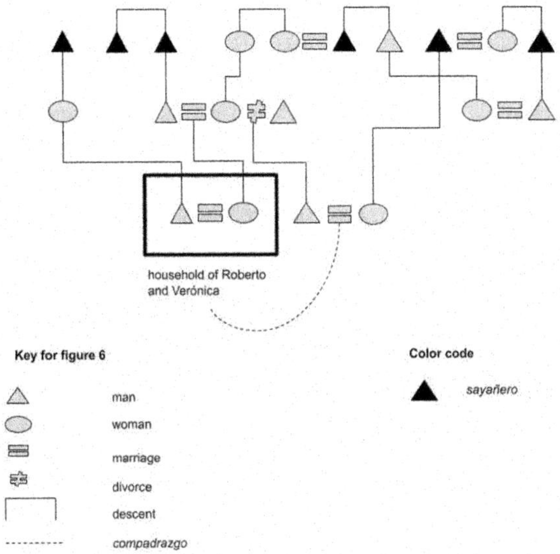

In this particular household two grandchildren of *sayañeros* are married to each other, husband Roberto being the grandson of *sayañero* LA and his wife Verónica being the granddaughter of *sayañero* MB1. Mostly through affinal ties, the household of Roberto and Verónica is furthermore related to the four remaining *sayañeros*. MB2, another of the *sayañeros*, was Verónica's grandfather's brother. Verónica's maternal grandmother is *sayañero* NF's sister-in-law. Verónica's mother, in turn,

the issuing of the Law of Agrarian Reform suggest, Nogalani's owner Jorge Cusicanqui was awarded certain parts of the estate referred to as *cocales de hacienda* and the administrative documents detail agreements between Cuscanqui and the former *peones* whom he now paid to work on the *cocales de hacienda*. Eventually, however, Cusicanqui abandoned his efforts at retaining control of the land and, as many other *patrones*, issued no further claims to land.

has a son from an earlier relationship who is married to the daughter of WL, another *sayañero* from Cala Cala. WL's daughter and her husband (Verónica's half-brother) are furthermore linked to Roberto and Verónica by ritual kinship as *compadres* for being their *padrinos de matrimonio* (lit.: godparents of marriage). WL was married to the sister of ET, the last remaining *sayañero* from Cala Cala. So even though the proximity of the relationships varies and they span generations, what is clear is the profound entanglement of the people from Cala Cala through kinship. Similar connections can be established for each individual/household in Cala Cala. What is important for the purpose of my discussion is the fact that to a great extent, *"los Afros de Cala Cala"* are a group of families related through cognate and affinal ties, as well as through *compadrazgo.* Everybody in Cala Cala is aware of these connections and the various kinship ties link *Cala Caleños* very firmly and closely together. All adult inhabitants – even though they might not be able to reproduce the precise genealogy of all the families in Cala Cala – are able to point out their relations to other Afrobolivian inhabitants of the *comunidad* and the networks that link the households and families in the village. Roberto, for example, was able to produce a fairly detailed account of his ancestors in the Angola line and although he was not able to produce a full list of all the siblings of his grandfather – some of whom left Cala Cala a long time ago – he was still aware of the fact that he was somehow related to people since their parents are 'cousins' *(primos)* of his mother. Together with his wife, he was also able to compile many details on the Balliviáns, and since Verónica's half-brother is married to a descendant of WL, also many details on the Landaveri family. The same is true for other individuals who by naming their matri- and patrilineal ancestors and affinal kin in many cases encompass the whole community. Being related as kin also entails expectations and practices of solidarity and material support among *"los Afros de Cala Cala"* and thus creates spaces of interaction and exchange among *Cala Caleños* that differ from the ties established with the wider *comunidad* mostly in economic and political contexts (see chapter 4).

There is also a historical dimension to this and the ties I described above are invoked in many narratives concerning the history and origins of Cala Cala as an 'Afrobolivian community.' Various interlocutors from Cala Cala mentioned to me that *"los abuelos"* (lit. "the grandfathers," i.e. the Afrobolivian *peones* of Cala Cala) had little to do with the Aymara *peones* from Nogalani. Some people also mentioned that the owners and administrators of the *hacienda* discouraged close relationships between the Aymara *peones* of Nogalani and the Afrobolivian *peones* of Cala Cala. Judging from the records of the *hacienda* administration, it was also neatly documented and closely observed which *cocales* were associated with Cala Cala and Nogalani, and therefore cultivated by Afrobolivians or Aymara respectively. Closer relationships thus developed only when Afrobolivians and Aymara started cooperating in the *sindicato campesino,* their children started going to the same schools and some Aymara households from Nogalani obtained pieces of land within the territory associated with Cala Cala in the wake of the revolution. A similar tendency for the Yungas as a region has been pointed out by Dwight Heath, who states that "campesinos on a particular ex-hacienda were often linked to each other only as distant neighbours and former co-workers" and "leadership and organization were minimal until the syndicates emerged as an effective institution" (Heath 1972:82). Given the geographical distances and the administrative boundary between the areas of settlement and coca cultivation in Nogalani and Cala Cala, it is therefore comprehensible that Cala Cala's *peones* had little to do with the *peones* from Nogalani. The entanglements were limited to specific contexts and only in the wake of the revolution and subsequent land reform, and most notably through the formation of a joint *sindicato campesino* in the 1950s, did relations between the former *peones* become more direct and gradually come to encompass more and more aspects of everyday interactions.

A further interesting aspect is the changing demography of Nogalani, as compared to the relative stability of Cala Cala. The number of households of what is now the *comunidad Nogalani* (including the former *hacienda Nogalani*, the former *estancia Cala Cala* and the new area of settlement in Bella Vista) has more than doubled from 65 households in the late 1940s to about 150 households nowadays. The growth of the community has occurred almost exclusively among the Aymara households of Nogalani and Bella Vista, however. The number of Afrobolivian households in Cala Cala – after rising from six in the 1940s to thirteen in 1976 (Equipo CIPCA 1977:193) – decreased to eleven in 2017.

Figure 7: Number of Afrobolivian and Aymara households in Cala Cala/Nogalani

	1940s	1976 (unofficial census by CIPCA investigators)	2017
Afrobolivian households	6	13	11
Aymara households	65	107	150 (estimate)

Nogalani's growth is attributed to the migration of Aymara families from the *altiplano* into the *comunidad*. This migration was in part possible because of unequal distribution of land between Nogalani's and Cala Cala's former *peones*. It is not unusual in the Yungas that *peones* of one single ex-*hacienda* would receive *sayañas* of different sizes. The households were usually granted the amount of land they cultivated at the time of the reform. The amount of land under cultivation by a *peón's* household in turn depended on the household's capacity to work the land and specific arrangements with the patron. It was common for people to increase or reduce the amount of land under cultivation for the household – and with that also the number of days they had to work for the patron – depending on the specific circumstances of the household. So while a household consisting of a middle-aged couple with various unmarried children was able to cultivate a rather large share of land and still meet the work obligations for the patron, many people reduced the amount of land they had under cultivation as they grew older, as their children formed households of their own or as a consequence of the passing of one of the spouses, an injury, sickness or other imponderabilities. Consequently, if a *peón* household *"era de tres días"* at the time of the reform, i.e. working three days a week for the patron and accordingly farming a larger piece of land in usufruct than a household *"de dos días,"* the *sayaña* this household received through the Agrarian Reform was bigger. Moreover, as far as people from Cala Cala are concerned, people from Nogalani *("los de arriba")* took advantage of the absence of the *patrones* after the land reform was declared and in addition to the plots of land granted to them through officially sanctioned proceedings (i.e. the decisions of Agrarian Tribunals), took matters into their own hands and seized additional plots of land. This is corroborated by the *hacienda* documents: In an undated document presumably from after the land reform was declared, the administrator of the *hacienda* alerts the owner Jorge Cusicanqui of the fact that certain individuals have taken over *cocales de hacienda ("se han apoderado de cocales de hacienda")*. Although the documents indicate that various Afrobolivians from Cala Cala were also among the *peones* that took over land illegally, people in Cala Cala share the impression that some Aymara families from Nogalani got the better share of them through such actions.[12] What is more, some Aymara households allegedly sold this excess land to migrants from the *altiplano* over the years, facilitating the rapid increase of Aymara households in Bella Vista and Nogalani.

There is thus an important difference between many Aymara households in Nogalani and Bella Vista and the Afrobolivian households in Cala Cala. Whereas the former are, at least in part, not related to *sayañeros* and former *peones* of the *hacienda*, the latter can trace back direct links to *sayañeros* and *peones*. For Afrobolivians in Cala Cala, this serves as a means to position themselves as the autochthonous inhabitants of the *comunidad* with deep roots within the territory. These Afrobolivian narratives reflect elements of "discourses of autochthony" as described by Geschiere and Nyamnjoh (2000), namely the focus on priority in time and the status as "first comers" in order to substantiate claims vis-à-vis more recent immigrants (cf. Pelican 2009). A similar logic can be observed all over the region in discourses about legitimate *Yungueños ("Yungueños legítimos")*. This term usually refers to people whose ancestors – as far as common knowledge in the community goes – have

12 According to the documentation of the administrator, about half of the seventy households took over land; among them are four of the six Afrobolivian households from Cala Cala.

'always' lived in the Yungas and are not first or second generation migrants (Spedding and Colque 2003). Thus in Cala Cala, being *Afroboliviano* can be employed to claim the status of *Yungueño legítimo,* an autochthonous inhabitant of the region. This is also reflected in a specific denomination *Cala Caleños* use for people from Nogalani. They call them "people from the *altiplano*" (*"los del altiplano"*), thus highlighting their history of migration, as opposed to *"los Afros de Cala Cala"* who are represented as firmly rooted in the locality.

Kinship beyond Cala Cala: linking Afrobolivians throughout the Yungas

Besides linking households in Cala Cala with each other and establishing a link to the history of the community, kinship is also the basis for establishing connections with Afrobolivians in other Yungas *comunidades*. When I spoke with people about their families, they often mentioned where certain relatives were from, especially if they were from somewhere other than Cala Cala. Comparing the genealogical charts from Cala Cala with the glossary of families from neighboring Dorado Chico that has been compiled by Juan Angola Maconde (Angola Maconde 2008), it becomes clear that the Afrobolivian communities of the *municipio Coripata* (Cala Cala, Dorado Chico, Coscoma, Chillamani and the village of Coripata) are also closely linked through kinship and migratory movement between the communities. Although nowadays migratory flows tend to be directed towards the urban centers of the country, migration up to the 1970s was largely inter-community migration or, before 1952, migration between *haciendas*.

If we take Roberto's family for example, we see that his grandfather, LA, was married to a woman from Suapi, a *comunidad* in the municipality of Coroico. Coroico, the largest town and the capital of the Nor Yungas Province, is located about 30 kilometers away from Cala Cala. Although only a trip of about 45 minutes by car today, in the past this was a significant distance given the mountainous terrain and the lack of reliable transportation in the Yungas. His grandfather's brothers married and lived in the neighboring *comunidades* Dorado Chico and Coscoma respectively. His wife's grandfather (MB1) was married twice: first to a woman from the Torrez family from Cala Cala, then to a woman from Colpar, a *comunidad* with a small share of Afrobolivian population in the *municipio* of Chulumani in Sud Yungas. The intercommunity connections that can be observed in Roberto and Verónica's grandparents' generation are also present in their parents' generation. The spouses of Roberto's uncles and aunts are from Dorado Chico, Dorado Grande and Coscoma. Verónica's mother is from Dorado Chico and was married to a man from there before marrying Verónica's father. Her son from this first marriage (Verónica's older half-brother) is married to a woman from Cala Cala. One of the *peones* that would become a *sayañero* (NF) migrated to Cala Cala from Dorado Chico before the Agrarian Reform. Thus, *"los Afros de Cala Cala"* are not only related among themselves, but also related to many Afrobolivian families in various Yungas *comunidades*. These ties are less direct and also less relevant in daily settings and in many cases are not remembered with much detail. Yet a basic understanding of having 'relatives' in other Yungas *comunidades* is an important part of how *Cala Caleños* conceptualize an Afrobolivian collectivity beyond Cala Cala. This situation and many of the descriptions from my interlocutors resonate quite well with what Barbara Léons reports from her fieldwork in the 1960s in the region around Arapata – a town very close to Cala Cala and Dorado Chico:

> "Negroes tend to know or know of other Negro families over considerable distances. Intermarriage between Indians and Negroes is relatively infrequent and, as Negro communities are sometimes small and scattered, elaborate intermarriage networks have grown up linking rather far-flung Negro enclaves. Couples who have never previously seen one another will agree to marry on the basis of exchanged verbal or written messages between their families." (Léons 1972:187; see also Léons 1966)

A tendency many people from Cala Cala repeatedly spoke of points in a similar direction. When I asked them if they remember how and why certain people left the community or came to Cala Cala, people explained by saying things like: *"Cala Cala trae mujeres de Dorado Chico, Coscoma lleva mujeres de Cala Cala"* ("Cala Cala brings women from Dorado Chico, Coscoma takes women from Cala Cala"). From all the statements and additional information in other sources (particularly Angola Maconde 2008), it is not possible to identify a clear pattern of either the direction of the exchange, or the gender of the people involved, despite what the above-mentioned statement suggests. What is important is the general tendency that was observed by Léons and confirmed by comparing my data with the information on Dorado Chico presented by Juan Angola Maconde (2008). In recent years, however, interethnic marriages have become more common than in the 1960s and 1970s and are in fact the norm nowadays, especially among younger generations.

Translocal kinship: Cala Cala's urban 'diaspora'

In the sections above, I have pointed out that kinship is important in linking the residents of Cala Cala to each other and furthermore in connecting them to other *comunidades* with Afrobolivian populations in the Yungas. I now turn to a dimension of kinship with an ever-growing importance, both in terms of numbers and with regard to the discursive construction of *"los Afros de Cala Cala."* When drawing up genealogical charts with people in the community, one thing became strikingly obvious: the largest part of the youngest generation (generally people born from the

1990s onward) and in most cases also the majority of the adult residents' siblings (i.e. people born during the 1970s and 1980s) nowadays do not live in Cala Cala, but reside in cities, mostly in La Paz or Santa Cruz, some in Cochabamba, in other Bolivian cities, in Brazil, Argentina and Spain. Taking as an example the descendants of the *sayañero* MB1, who has been married twice, and whose offspring (including children, grandchildren and great-grandchildren) add up to forty-two individuals, we encounter a distribution of residence that is quite typical for many Afrobolivian families. Of the forty-two individuals that make up MB1's offspring, only six live in Cala Cala (one of his children, four grandchildren and one great-grandchild), three are deceased and the rest live in La Paz or Santa Cruz, as well as in Spain or in Brazil. A similar situation applies to the descendants of LA, to cite just one other concrete example. Of his over thirty great-grandchildren, only two have remained in the community, along with one grandchild and one of his children. The majority of his descendants lives in Santa Cruz and they very rarely – if at all – return to Cala Cala. Some of the youngest generation have in many cases never even been to Cala Cala and do not relate to a Yungas lifestyle in any way. "*Ya son Cambas*" ("they are Cambas [people from Santa Cruz]") is an expression heard very often in Cala Cala. Yet, at least in some cases, Cala Cala's inhabitants consider those people to be part of the collective they refer to as "*los Afros de Cala Cala*," even though they were neither born in Cala Cala, nor reside there. This became clear, for example, when representatives of a cooperative housing project visited Cala Cala in late 2014 and proposed to found a cooperative that would build houses in Cala Cala. The inhabitants counted and listed the "community members" in need of a house. Roberto counted his three daughters as 'members of the community,' even though, at that time, two of them lived in La Paz and one in Santa Cruz, and none of the three had expressed a desire to return to Cala Cala – neither in conversations with me, nor in exchanges with their father, as Roberto told me many times. Yet for this purpose they were considered to be part of the 'Afrobolivian community' of Cala Cala. Thus, beyond the immediate and tangible geographical location and the approximately thirty people that continuously live there, Cala Cala is most importantly a translocal group of relatives that can be traced back to half a dozen Afrobolivian *peones* who inhabited the *estancia de Cala Cala* in the first half of the 20th century.

The understanding of Cala Cala as a community that transcends the locality also applies to migrants and individuals with relatives or ancestors in Cala Cala. They often conceive of themselves as "people from Cala Cala," even if they have spent most of their life somewhere else.

As can be observed in figure 8, many urban residents do express adherence to certain *comunidades* in *saya* performances, but also in interviews and during discussions with other members of urban organizations. The photograph shows a *saya* outfit with references to Cala Cala and the urban group the musician belongs to – in this case a group called "*Ubuntu*" from Cochabamba. Many urban Afrobolivians

Figure 8: A saya dancer (left) in Cochabamba with a saya shirt expressing his connection to Cala Cala (photograph by the author).

emphasize that they join organizations and participate actively in their activities mostly because it enables them to be with their family. More often than not, participating in urban organizations can also revive kinship ties, as cousins who did not know each other in person previously meet and end up establishing closer ties within the frameworks of urban Afrobolivian organizations.

The changing tides of *"lo Afro"* in and beyond Cala Cala

Being *Afroboliviano* in Cala Cala, as well as being an Afrobolivian from Cala Cala means, as we have seen, more than 'being tall or fat' (see Spedding 2013 quoted at the outset of this chapter). Beyond being a description of an individual's physical characteristics, being *Afroboliviano* means belonging to a group of people that shares specific geographical roots, ties of kinship and a particular perspective on local history, yet with individual variation in terms of how important and salient one or the other factor might be. It also means being drawn into the discourses and regimes of plurinational recognition and representation in specific ways and through specific means (see chapter 10). What is more, according to most of my interlocutors from Cala Cala, being *Afroboliviano* nowadays means something different from what it meant in the past. And finally, very clearly, it means something different for people of different ages living in different situations.

One of the oldest residents of Cala Cala is Gerardo Angola. I was therefore often referred to him when asking about Cala Cala's history or when people considered their knowledge "of how things were before" insufficient. I visited him at his house, which lies in the lower outskirts of the community, multiple times, and his life story as well as the ways he commented on it were very instructive in helping to understand the changing tides of *"lo Afro"* in Cala Cala. Gerardo was born in 1947 as the third child of Lorenzo Angola (born 1902). He was one of the first children from Cala Cala that was able to go to school starting in 1953 and part of the first generation of people from the Yungas to come of age in the post-*hacienda* period.

No longer tied to the *hacienda* as a *peón* like his parents' generation, vastly different horizons were available to him and his peers (cf. Heath 1972). The geographical, occupational and social mobility his generation enjoyed was far superior to that of his parents' generation, as he repeatedly stated during our conversations. During his life, he has lived in Santa Cruz, La Paz and the Yungas and has worked as a coca farmer, motorcycle taxi driver and as a miner. He has four children living in Santa Cruz, Argentina, Colopampa (a village in the Sud Yungas province) and Coripata, and over a dozen grandchildren. Together with his wife, who recently passed away, he converted to Pentecostal Christianity. He regularly participates in pilgrimages and undergoes fasting alongside the *hermanos* (brothers in faith). He frequently travels to Coripata on his motorcycle or even further away, to Santa Cruz or Bolivia's Amazonian lowlands, to visit family and friends. He has sold all his land in Cala Cala and only occasionally works as a *jornalero* (day wage laborer, see chapter 4) in other people's fields.

The first time I visited Gerardo at his house, he showed me a photograph (fig. 9) and explained that these were *"los abuelos"* (the grandfathers) and that the picture must have been taken in the 1920s. He told me that he had found it in the rubble of a demolished house and salvaged it from being thrown away. As far as he is aware, it is the only visual remnant of this era in Cala Cala. He was able to identify two of the people in the picture, the brothers MB1 and MB2 (far left and second from the right). The picture was most likely taken in the context of a *saya* performance of some sort, since various people are holding instruments. As far as Gerardo is concerned, the brothers MB1 and MB2 were very important for the organization of Cala Cala's *saya*.[13] He said that *los abuelos* used to play *saya* on special occasions, for example at Afrobolivian weddings and during the procession of San Benito, the patron saint of the community. He also recalled that as a child he joined Afrobolivian men on travels to other *comunidades* in order to borrow the bells *(cascabeles)*

13 This was confirmed to me by Martin Ballivián who told me that many people in the Yungas knew his grandfather MB1 since he used to travel *"con la saya"* (i.e. for *saya* performances).

needed for *saya* performances (*"nos fletábamos los cascabeles"*). He had no further recollection of the *tiempo de hacienda* and in subsequent conversations we had, other topics became central.[14]

Figure 9: Picture of Afrobolivian peones and saya performers from Cala Cala (unknown photographer, estimated at 1920s, picture courtesy of Gerardo Angola).

When speaking of those other topics, he did so in a way that suggested that they were important to him personally. *Saya* and further related practices considered specifically Afrobolivian were something he always reported other people doing. "*Los abuelos bailaban saya*" ("the *abuelos* used to dance *saya*"), "*la gente de antes hacía...*" ("people before did..."). He hardly spoke about *saya* as something he and his age group or peers pursued with great vigor. Indeed, he specifically pointed out that his generation did not place too much importance on *saya*; he rather pointed out spatial and occupational mobility as the defining experiences of his life. He described migratory trajectories leading people to La Paz, Cochabamba and Santa Cruz, and thus out of the Yungas region. He explained this by pointing out the fact that the children and grandchildren of the *sayañeros* realized that the land parcels their parents had received were not going to be enough to support them all in the

14 His expectations that I must first and foremost be interested in *saya* and "how things were back in the day" is something very common and an expectation I have learned to live with.

future. Thus many left Cala Cala in order to look for other opportunities in other *comunidades* in the Yungas, in the zones of colonization in the lowlands and eventually in the urban centers. In this context, he said that interethnic marriages and unions became more frequent. As far as my research in Cala Cala, as well as the data presented in other sources, indicates, the rate of interethnic marriage was fairly low in the decades preceding the 1950s and 1960s (Angola Maconde 2008; Léons 1966; Léons 1972); it became much more frequent from the 1970s onward and William Léons reports from Chicaloma that it was even preferred among Afrobolivians there in order to make "the race disappear" *(hacer perder la raza)*. Roberto corroborated this information by quoting his mother (born 1942), who used to tell him that "black with black is not good" *("negro con negro, no está bien")* and that he should marry a non-black person.[15]

The mobility and the opportunities Gerardo described as being crucial for his and especially his children's generation, according to him, gave way to significant social and cultural changes: an increasing geographical dispersal of the Afrobolivian population, a fragmentation of the community and an increasing blurring of ethnoracial boundaries through interethnic unions, and the decreasing salience of cultural practices associated with Afrobolivians. Very importantly, Gerardo's narrative also reflects the resurgence of *saya* in the 1980s, which has become a central symbol of Afrobolivianity for younger generations and a fundamental pillar of contemporary Afrobolivian identity politics. Besides remembering how *"los abuelos"* used to play *saya*, Gerardo also remembered how, quite surprisingly for him, a young man from Coripata turned up and started to gather Afrobolivians with "coca, alcohol and cigarettes" *("con coca, alcohol y cigarro")*, in order to rehearse *saya*. Most likely, this happened in the context of a series of events that mark the first peak of Afrobolivian cultural revitalization and its entanglement with the Bolivian culture industry: the preparations for the *Festival Luz Mila Patiño*, a national folklore event in 1998 that placed Afrobolivian music center stage and included efforts to compile musical traditions later published in the nationally famous document *"El Tambor Mayor"* (Centro Pedagógico y Cultural "Simón I. Patiño" 1998a, see chapter 8). These efforts, however, were much more directed at the generation born in the 1970s and Gerardo did not personally relate to them.

Gerardo's narrative thus neatly mirrors the changing importance of *"lo Afro"* in Cala Cala. He was born during a time when Afrobolivian *peones* in Cala Cala were occasionally referred to as *"los morenos"* by the *hacienda* administration.[16] This

15 Roberto himself, on the other hand, repeatedly expressed the desire that his children marry other Afrobolivians. He fears that with the proliferation of interethnic unions and migration, 'Afrobolivian culture and identity' will be lost (see chapter 6).

16 *Moreno* (lit.: brown) was often used in the past to refer to Afrobolivians since it was considered more respectful than *negro*. In the *hacienda* documents I analyzed, there is on the one hand a note from the administrator that "the *moreno* I.F. is afraid of sleeping alone in the house,"

group of people maintained close ties to other Afrobolivian communities in the region and shared certain cultural practices like *saya*. Until the National Revolution and Agrarian Reform in the 1950s, interethnic marriage was rare among Afrobolivians and migration was common only between *haciendas* in the Yungas. Gerardo, born five years prior to the revolution, was part of a generation of Afrobolivians that grew up experiencing major social and political changes, both locally and nationally. Throughout these processes of change, being *Afroboliviano* temporarily lost much of its earlier significance. It was only some decades later in the 1980s and 1990s that *"lo Afro"* resurfaced, now in the shape of the ideas and discourses that migrants from urban settings brought to the Yungas. Their notion of what it meant to be *Afroboliviano* was shaped by their experiences in urban settings and subsequent mobilizations in multicultural politics. Being *Afroboliviano* resurfaced first in the realm of performance, music and folklore, and later as a way to claim recognition as a culturally defined collective (see chapters 7 and 8). According to Gerardo and others in Cala Cala, the idea that Afrobolivians should be considered different from the rest of society because of their 'culture' (more specifically because of their practice of *saya*) was not very common or salient from the 1950s onward. In Cala Cala's case, all inhabitants I spoke to agreed that it was only in the late 1990s, when they were prompted by urban residents who came to the community, that they started to play *saya* again. Even now, nobody in Cala Cala gave me the impression that *saya* (or 'culture' more generally) was a decisive feature when determining who belongs to *"los Afros de Cala Cala."* Being Afro in Cala Cala is mostly a matter of kinship and local genealogy. *Cala Caleños* do consider themselves different from *"los de arriba,"* whom they classify as *"los del altiplano," "los indígenas"* or *"los Aymaras,"* but they hardly frame this distinction in 'cultural' terms, referring to the *"elementos culturales"* that have become so important in urban discourse and in processes of recognition respectively.

From kinship ties to *"La Famiya Afro"*: kinship, ethnicity and collectivity

In Cala Cala, being *Afroboliviano* is a collective identification based primarily on kinship and local origins. Gerardo's narrative exemplifies that the salience of this identification has changed over time, becoming more relevant again since the 1990s. Additionally, however, a novel conceptualization of what it means to be *Afroboliviano* has become increasingly important as well. Beyond referring to kinship and

where he was supposed to take care of a shipment of coca. On the other hand, among the documents there is a transcription of a declaration in Coripata made by LA pertaining to a case of physical assault that happened in Cala Cala. LA declares that "G.G. wanted to hit the *moreno* B."

local origins as the fundamental aspects of *"los Afros de Cala Cala,"* ideas of *el pueblo Afroboliviano* as an ethnoracially and culturally defined collective on the national level have become increasingly important (see also chapter 9 on the political and legal implications of this term). One dimension of linking local perceptions of *"lo Afro"* with nationally circulating ideas of *el pueblo Afroboliviano* is highlighting *saya* as the 'cultural element' linking all Afrobolivians. Another dimension is the invocation of the term *"la famiya Afro"* (the Afro family). Recently, many Afrobolivian groups and individual activists have been deploying discourses of *"la famiya Afro"* as the basis for collective identification as Afrobolivians beyond the local level. The unusual spelling of *famiya* (as opposed to standard Spanish *familia*) is highly significant here. The intention is to signal that this concept originates in Afrobolivian society in the Yungas and *famiya* is thus spelled according to the rules of Afrobolivian Spanish *(la lengua Afro)*, a creole language associated with Afrobolivians in the Yungas.[17] Within those discourses, *el pueblo Afroboliviano* is metaphorically represented as a family, echoing constructivist interpretations arguing that ethnicity is based on ideas of metaphorical extended kinship (Eriksen 2010:87). Similarly, many interlocutors from Cala Cala stated that there is a special connection between Afrobolivians, positing that *'entre Afros'* (among Afros) there is a much higher level of tacit understanding and common goals than between Afrobolivians and non-Afrobolivians. Moreover, expressing adherence to the idea of *el pueblo Afroboliviano* in terms of belonging to a family gives this particular aspect of identification great emotional strength in the eyes of many individuals. On a conceptual level, it links notions of Afrobolivians as a political community and legal subjects with notions of kinship and family.

Representing *el pueblo Afroboliviano* as an overarching ethnoracial collective that encompasses all Afrobolivians nationally and as an extension of local and translocal kinship networks – *"la famiya Afro"* – relates to people's ideas of what fundamentally constitutes collective identity and belonging in the local context. Since kinship ties are highly relevant in matters of everyday importance like access to land in Cala Cala, they are much more important 'on the ground' than cultural differences *(saya)*. Thus, I argue, notions of translocal kinship and the modes of sociality that this encompasses are, in fact, a much more effective and affective link between strongly localized notions of community and the national context than the ubiquitous talk of 'Afrobolivian culture' (in particular *saya*) as a foundation for cohesion.

In many of the narratives I collected during my fieldwork, the fundamental role kinship plays for engaging practically with Afrobolivian collectivity was very obvious. Generally, people expressed that the most tangible way of engaging with the idea of *el pueblo Afroboliviano*, is through seeing it as an extension of kinship ties between families in the Yungas and nationally dispersed migrant communities.

17 See chapters 7 and 9 for details.

Similar notions were also repeatedly expressed in the narratives of migrants that founded the first Afrobolivian organizations in the cities, describing them as being rooted firmly in networks of kinship. It is important to note, however, that the *"famiya Afro"* discourse in recent mobilizations is characterized by an increasingly diffuse reference to kinship and occasionally also serves as a foundation for even wider discourses of Afrobolivian identity as part of a global Afro diaspora (see chapter 6). Whereas this diasporic approach appeals to ideas and discourses of collective belonging among certain sectors of the urban Afrobolivian population, it has little relevance in Cala Cala.

Kinship, in sum, is crucial to the construction and experience of Afrobolivianity in Cala Cala. It is a fundamental pillar of the efforts to secure access to land as the basis for peasant livelihood in the Yungas. It is furthermore deployed in Cala Cala as a way to substantiate local belonging via genealogy and history, shaping the very particular and localized notion of *"los Afros de Cala Cala."* It is important also as a dimension of translocal sociality – linking communities in the Yungas with each other and with the migrant communities in urban settings. Finally, kinship and the concept of *"la famiya Afro"* can become a mediating frame through which to relate local notions of what it means to be Afrobolivian with discourses of *el pueblo Afroboliviano* on a national scale.

Los "Afros de Cala Cala" in context: migration, intra-community conflict and cross-cutting ties

As much as ties of kinship are a source of cohesion and *"los Afros de Cala Cala"* are an important dimension of community in Cala Cala, it is crucial to contextualize and also point out the limits of this identification. Through overlapping identifications and cross-cutting ties (Schlee 1997; Schlee 2004), *"los Afros de Cala"* are embedded in social relationships beyond this particular collective identification in multiple ways. What is more, notions of community are not limited to the collective identification of *"los Afros de Cala Cala."* Individual *Cala Caleños*, as well as *"los Afros de Cala Cala"* as a whole, approach the topic of collective identity understood as "an activated category of perceived, felt and feigned likeness, distinction and solidarity among human actors" (Eidson et al. 2017:341) not only in terms of kinship, local origins or wider discourses on Afrobolivian identity, but also with reference to other categories, frames and discourses.

The migrant, non-resident members of *"los Afros de Cala Cala"* are a first example of this and Roberto's daughters are a case in point here. Even though they were born and raised in Cala Cala and only recently migrated to La Paz and Santa Cruz, Roberto's oldest daughter Sandra told me that she neither had close relationships with any of her kin in Santa Cruz nor participated in any of the Afrobolivian organizations in the city. Roberto laments the former very much, but from Sandra's perspective, neither her relatives nor the Afrobolivian community in Santa Cruz more generally *(la famiya Afro)* have immediate relevance in the setting of her everyday life. When I asked her why she didn't participate in any of the organizations, go to their meetings from time to time, or get in touch with her kin, she said: "They don't do anything anyhow" *("Igual no hacen nada")*. Interestingly, many urban Afrobolivians are equally short-spoken on the subject. They do not feel the need to further elaborate – and only do so when pressed by an anthropologist. When they do elaborate on the subject, they refer to the contexts of their everyday lives in the city, highlighting migration, struggles to make a living and desires to achieve upward social mobility. Sandra framed her belonging, personal aspirations and the obstacles she encountered without reference to *"los Afros de Cala Cala"* or Afrobolivianity. For her, being a migrant, a woman, and a working mother were more immediately relevant categorizations when describing her situation in Santa Cruz.

In Cala Cala, being related as kin is far from the only relevant collective affiliation and also not always a factor for cohesion. It regularly leads to conflict and to competing claims, especially with regard to land. The Agrarian Reform established the boundaries of the community both in terms of territory and in terms of people with legitimate claims to the territory. As the land controlled by the landlord was distributed to the *peones* that worked on the *hacienda* at the time of the reform, all claims to ownership of cultivable land must be made through reference to the original *sayañeros* and in many cases a large number of grandchildren and great-grandchildren lay claim to certain parts of the land originally allocated to their ancestors. It is important to note that in terms of land distribution, conflicts between close relatives claiming to be the legitimate heirs of certain parts of the land are much more frequent than quarrels between *Cala Caleños* and people from Nogalani or other 'outsiders.' These conflicts do exist to a certain extent – with the general tenor that Nogalani has gotten the better share of Cala Cala in terms of land rights – and are sometimes framed in ethnic terms (see chapter 5). But what far more frequently makes feelings run high is intrafamilial competition. There are no written documents, official measuring records or legal titles accessible to the people. The scarce records of the reform period are stored in some enigmatic archive at the *Instituto Nacional de la Reforma Agraria (INRA)*, and are beyond access. Thus most claims and counter-claims are based on the oral and customary transmission of inheritance procedures, agreements and boundaries, making the conflicts difficult to settle in a formal way, since beyond the family there is no register of the distribution of lands. In these instances, even though there might be a claim based on formal kinship relations with a *sayañero*, what determines one's ability to enforce certain claims against others is first and foremost an individual's or family's standing and alliances within the wider *comunidad*. The crucial point here is that in order to make claims and settle disputes, the *comunidad* that becomes relevant is not limited to *"los Afros de Cala Cala,"* but encompasses Cala Cala as a *comunidad cocalera*. *"Lo Afro"* is not the only relevant horizon of community in Cala Cala, not in terms of identification, and even less in terms of actual social relations, politics or conflict resolution. For example, whatever an individual's standing among *"los Afros de Cala Cala"* might be, it is nearly impossible for anybody not living in the *comunidad* to enforce claims against residents that "serve a social function" *(cumplen función social)*. In the next chapter, I will therefore address a horizon and practices of community that transcend *"los Afros de Cala Cala"* and that have to do with far-reaching entanglements of economy, politics, religion and notions of shared 'tradition.'

Chapter 4: Cala Cala beyond *"lo Afro"*

Cumplir Función Social, Identidad Yungueña and the Comunidad Cocalera

In the preceding chapter, I have shown how collective identification as Afrobolivians, locally expressed through the term *"los Afros de Cala,"* is an important horizon of community for the people in Cala Cala. In this chapter, I will introduce another horizon of community before discussing their entanglement and emerging political and legal constellations that change the relationship between those horizons. I will initially approach this alternative horizon of community through an analysis of the emic concept *"cumplir función social"* (lit.: "[to] fulfill/perform a social function"). *Cumplir función social* is derived from the community's organization in a peasant union *(sindicato)*, but the ideas associated with it transcend institutionalized contexts. I will then discuss the importance of discourses on regional identity *(identidad Yungueña)* for people in Cala Cala and outline the sources of this regional culture and the lifestyle associated with it. As will become clear, the particular landscape, history and the multiethnic makeup of its society due to migratory flows in and out of the Yungas are decisive factors here. Next, I will consider the fundamental role of the practice of cultivating coca and its impact on labor exchange, solidarity and cohesion in a *comunidad cocalera*. Finally, I will introduce the coca field as the main space of social interaction in Cala Cala, highlighting the consequences that this has for how competing perspectives on collective identifications are debated.

"Cumplir función social": becoming a member of the *comunidad* through practice

As I mentioned at the outset of the preceding chapter, Cala Cala is considered and treated as part of the *comunidad Nogalani* in administrative settings. This is due to the fact that they share a *sindicato campesino*. People's everyday usage of the term *"comunidad"* mirrors this broader understanding to a great extent. When I travelled with people from Cala Cala to the towns of Coripata, Arapata or Trinidad Pampa – for example in order to visit the market there – we sometimes met people and my companions from Cala Cala engaged them in conversation. When I asked who those people were, the answer was often something like this: This is Robustiano, he's from the *comunidad* (*"Es Robustiano, es de la comunidad"*). The meaning of *comunidad* and a shared sense of identity as *comunarios* (as the members of the *comunidad* are called in emic terms) in those contexts thus went beyond *"los Afros de Cala Cala."*

The *sindicatos campesinos* (peasant unions) to which this dimension of *comunidad* is closely related were established after the National Revolution in 1952 by the Government of the *Movimiento Nacionalista Revolucionario (MNR)* as a means to politically and economically organize the inhabitants of the former *haciendas* (see chapter 2). The *sindicato* as an institution is of crucial importance for a variety of reasons. In particular, the *sindicato* handles questions of land tenure and oversees compliance with the provisional land demarcations and rights established through the 1953 land reform. This is especially important since there has been no official measuring, demarcation and/or individual land titling since the reform in the 1950s and any claim to land or quarrels about boundaries and usage rights have to be negotiated within the *sindicato* structure. Furthermore, all matters of infrastructure (the community school, the construction and maintenance of roads, drinking water and electricity supply) are handled by the *sindicato* on behalf of the *comunidad*. The local *sindicato* and the regional *subcentrales* and *centrales* (consisting of various local *sindicatos*) are also important in terms of political representation on the regional and national levels and funding from the national and municipal governments is channeled through those institutions to the *comunidades*. Through the *sindicato*, the *comunidad* is also represented in the regional coca producers association (*Asociación Departamental de Productores de Coca ADEPCOCA*), an organization that handles all issues related to the commercialization of the coca leaf. ADEPCOCA issues the credentials *(carnet de productor)* that allow peasants to transport their coca harvest to La Paz and sell it on the only legal marketplace in La Paz that is also run by ADEPCOCA.

Yet the *sindicato* is not only important in terms of institutionalized relationships. As Caroline Conzelman (2007:193) has described for the case of Coroico (Nor Yungas), *sindicatos cocaleros* function as a "system for community governance" that transcends issues strictly related to politics, labor and land tenure to "encompass all issues related to communal life"; in many regards, "a *sindicato* functions as the community" (Conzelman 2007:169). All households in a *comunidad* must be members *(afiliados)* of the *sindicato*. To become a member, a household must first own land within the territory of the *comunidad*.[1] But the requirements for membership

1 Obtaining land in a Yungas *comunidad* is possible in a variety of ways including inheritance, purchase and some very particular local arrangements that are characterized by a combination of temporary usufruct rights with specific labor obligations towards the owner that can result in obtaining permanent access. For details see Spedding (1994:41–45).

do not end there. What is even more important is what people locally refer to as *"cumplir función social,"* performing a social function in the *comunidad*. Membership is thus never achieved permanently, but has to be continually reaffirmed through practice.

Cumplir función social is a complex concept. It includes meeting specific formal obligations towards the *sindicato*: attending monthly *sindicato* meetings, paying quotas for *sindicato* expenses, participating in communal works (concerning schools, roads, or potable water supply) and/or attending political rallies and protests organized by the *sindicato*. It also means assuming an office in the *sindicato* hierarchy from time to time. Attendance at the monthly meeting and the observance of obligations concerning communal works and rallies is controlled very strictly and any member who fails to comply with the requirement will inevitably have to pay a fine *(multa)*. Beyond these rather formal obligations, it is expected that no member disturbs the peace of the community, engages in illegal activities or makes the community look bad *("hacer quedar mal a la comunidad")* for getting into trouble in other *comunidades* or in the neighboring towns. People that do not observe these rules are not only in danger of being fined monetarily, but will also lose the support of the *sindicato* in cases where they need a conflict to be resolved within or beyond the *comunidad*. If a household fails to fulfill the social function that is expected, its members can become the object of public reprimand and scorn, monetary sanctions and eventually – in extreme cases – people are evicted from the *comunidad* and their land is confiscated by the *sindicato*. No household – or even the whole of Cala Cala – could therefore afford to withdraw from the *sindicato*. This would mean not only withdrawing from an institution, but relinquishing membership of a community of social, economic and political practice.

Since it is firmly rooted in the practices of *cumplir función social*, collective identification as *comunarios* is viewed as processual from an emic perspective and belonging has to be reaffirmed continuously. This also means that the boundaries of *comunario* identity are inchoate to a large degree. In this sense, this collective identification differs from the emic perspectives on *"los Afros de Cala Cala,"* who are often represented as constituting a more stable collective with clearer and less permeable boundaries. The processual and performative notion of *comunidad* expressed through *"cumplir función social"* functions in a different register and, in my view, this also explains why references to allegedly stable categories of identification like *Afroboliviano* or *Aymara* are regarded as secondary when debating membership as *comunarios*.

Local traditions and *identidad Yungueña* in Cala Cala

Beyond constituting a single community of practice mediated by the *sindicato* and the 'social functions' an individual or a household "performs," there is also a very strong sense of common history and tradition in Nogalani that is expressed in the celebration of religious holidays, community fiestas and ritualized contexts like burials of deceased members of the *comunidad*.

A few weeks into my fieldwork, I participated in the events surrounding the holiday of "*Todos Santos*" (All Saints' Day). As in other parts of Bolivia, one important part of this holiday is the visiting of *mesas*. *Mesas* (lit.: tables, see fig. 10) are set up by the relatives of deceased community members for the spirit of the dead that is said to visit the house on *Todos Santos*.

Figure 10: Comunarios sitting next to a mesa prepared for the spirit of a deceased family member in a house in Cala Cala (photograph by the author).

People prepare the *mesas* with the favorite food and drinks of the dead relatives and invite people from the *comunidad* to their houses to pray for the spirits in front of their *mesas*. Visitors are offered drinks, bread and coca and are received throughout the entire day (see Canessa [2012c:157–159] for a detailed description of *Todos Santos*). I accompanied Víctor on his tour of different houses and during our visits to *mesas* in Cala Cala, Bella Vista and Nogalani, people repeatedly started discussing 'traditions' of the community.[2] The *tradiciones* people were discussing were all common 'traditions' of the *comunidad* not particularly associated with either Aymara or *Afrobolivianos*. In the context of *Todos Santos*, interpreted by most people as one of the *comunidad's* most important 'traditions', it became apparent that an interest in this type of tradition was very widespread. On the one hand, people argued that the maintenance of these traditions was a fundamental part of defining the identity of the *comunidad*; on the other hand many contributions during the exchanges I witnessed echoed a seemingly nostalgic preoccupation with the fact that many of the local 'traditions' were in fact waning. "How might it have been before?" *("¿Cómo habrá sido antes?")* was the most vividly discussed question. People share the assumptions that many things must have been lost, that the ancestors *(los abuelos)* must have done things differently. Furthermore, the question of who could know how to revitalize what has been lost was of paramount importance.

After some drinks – praying at a *mesa* is always rewarded with alcohol, coca and bread – people start talking about legends. One narrative that caught my attention was a legend of *hacienda* gold that is said to be hidden in *tapados* (hidden deposits of gold also occasionally associated with Andean religious beliefs (Spedding 2014)). These *tapados* are reported to burn at certain times of the year, the blaze of the glowing gold being discernible from afar. Yet nobody has ever been able to find the gold. When you get too close, the villagers said, it disappears. One man reported that he witnessed foreigners *("gringos")* turning up near the village. They were carrying secret maps and were using metal detectors to look for the gold. Yet they were also not able to find it. Everybody present started to wonder who might know where the *hacendados* hid their fortunes. The general thrust of the story is a shared feeling of having been tricked out of their fair share of the riches of the *haciendas*: How could the fruits of the work of so many people have been taken away? Why do we suffer, when there was so much money? What do we have to do to change our lot? These nostalgic tales express the desires and questions belonging to all *comunarios*. Not once did anybody make reference to Afrobolivians, Aymara, or any other clearly defined ethnic collective. The frame of this kind of tale is a shared sense of *Yungueño* and *cocalero* identification. Like the narrative above, there are many others. They are about quasi-mythical creatures that roam the outskirts of the community *(el tigre wasqueador)*, stories about the *camino de la muerte* (the road that leads to the Yungas and is infamously known as the Road of Death due to the high number of fatal accidents) and the spirits of the deceased that wander at the side of the road. My point here is that these are shared traditions and myths of a

2 This was certainly at least in part triggered by the presence of 'the anthropologist' (a profession almost naturally associated with an interest in 'traditions' of the people in Bolivia).

Yungas *comunidad*, not of any ethnically defined group in particular. In many instances, history and traditions are framed as the common and shared history of the *comunidad* and all the people that live there.

Beyond debating common traditions and history, a sense of 'belonging together' as a *comunidad* is furthermore expressed in the practices of festivities like *Todos Santos* or the patron saint's *fiesta* of the *comunidad* and through other ritual practices like the wakes and burials of deceased *comunarios*. In those contexts, community solidarity and belonging are created and performed in practice. Similar to what Andrew Canessa describes for the village of Wila Kjarka, fiestas are "occasions when the whole community acts as one household sharing food, drink, and coca together." He argues that "it is thus through fiestas and the sharing of food, alcohol, and coca with each other and the spirits that the community and its identity is created and affirmed" (Canessa 2012c:123).

Another illustrative example of how Cala Cala and Nogalani are entangled as one single *comunidad* was a *velorio* (wake) for a recently deceased person that I attended while staying in Cala Cala (for a full discussion of a *velorio* in the Yungas see Spedding 1996:82–85). Roberto's wife had alerted us to the fact that a man from Nogalani had passed away and that the *velorio* was going to take place that same day in the house of the family of the deceased. When we arrived, a great number of people were already sitting in the room where the coffin was displayed, as well as on the patio and on the stairs outside. Family members distributed coca leaves, soda and *pasankalla* (toasted white maize, typical of the *altiplano*, particularly the region around Copacabana on Lake Titicaca) for the people attending the wake. Inside, an Afrobolivian woman from Cala Cala was praying with the closest family members of the deceased, speaking in Spanish and Aymara interchangeably. She was *de pollera* (wearing the typical skirt, shirt and bowler hat of the *chola paceña)* and Roberto told me that she was involved in one of the evangelical churches based in Nogalani as a pastor. He added that this woman was widely respected among the members of the *comunidad*. Most of the family of the deceased were also members of that church *("Tambíen son hermanos")* and Roberto explained to me that there had been quarrels about land among the children of the deceased man and that the *pastora* was trying to reconcile them in light of their father's death. Later, we sat with other members of the *comunidad*, chewing coca and drinking soft drinks – due to the fact that the evangelical *hermanos* rejected the consumption of alcohol, which would otherwise have been served during the *velorio* (cf. Spedding 1996).

During these conversations, I was approached by various members of the *comunidad* who volunteered to explain the tradition of a *velorio* to me.[3] The important

3 It was soon common knowledge that I was doing some kind of project on the community and without me ever specifying, people assumed that I must be interested in the 'traditions' of the community. I have found that this is a very common assumption people have when

point here is that they approached the subject from a perspective that regarded tradition as something related to the *comunidad* and the region, not to specific ethnoracial collectives. In their comments on traditions they rather focused on the fact that the growing presence of Pentecostal churches is having an impact on how certain traditions are performed. When I later spoke to Roberto about the *velorio*, he also mainly focused on the peculiar aspects of the ceremony due to the family being *hermanos*. During that day, the only instance when anyone made reference to a distinction between Aymara and Afrobolivians was when – at the sight of the Afrobolivian *pastora* reconciling mourning family members in Aymara – Roberto told me that he did not understand what she said, but that his mother was equally fluent in Aymara, as were many *Afros de antes*.[4]

What these examples show, I argue, is that there exists a common horizon of community, tradition, and history that is expressed and reaffirmed through practices during religious festivities and ritual occasions, as well as mirrored in people's comments on these occasions. Moreover, the sense of commonality and solidarity expressed in those contexts finds a discursive referent in the concept of *identidad Yungueña*. As in many other regions in Bolivia, the inhabitants of the Yungas share a very strong sense of regional identity and the local traditions I have described are an important part of this. Additional markers of this shared identity as *Yungueños* include the climatological features of the region, which are so vastly different from the cold, mountainous *altiplano* and the peaks of the Andes, as well as a shared sense of history and suffering (mostly at the hands of the land-owning elite) as *Yungueños* beyond local *comunidades* (Spedding and Colque 2003). Most important, however, is the region's close and intense relationship with the coca leaf: "For the zone of coca cultivation, there is one central element that defines regional identity: the very fact of being cocaleros" (Spedding and Llanos 1999:285, my translation).[5] The overarching identification as *cocaleros* is the cohesive factor in a region that has historically been associated with colonization and migration (Spedding 2009:441f). This is not to say that there are no references to ethnoracial identifications with regard to the Yungas. Inhabitants of the Yungas have been described as "*los otros Aymaras*," whose lifestyle and culture differs significantly from the Aymara groups in the highland regions of Bolivia, although they speak the same language and are thus often considered part of the same ethnic group (Equipo CIPCA 1976). Similarly,

dealing with foreigners in their community, especially foreigners who conduct some kind of research.

4 In practice, the loss of bilingualism on the part of Afrobolivians does not hinder communication with the wider community since practically all inhabitants nowadays speak Spanish. Until after the land reform, this was different, as many Aymara were monolingual Aymara speakers.

5 *"Para la zona cocalera, hay un elemento central que define la identidad regional: el mismo hecho de ser cocaleros."*

the hyphenated denomination *Afro-Yungueño* is quite common for describing Afrobolivian cultural traditions originating in the Yungas. However, ethnoracial differences are regarded as secondary. Echoing Alison Spedding's contributions (Spedding 1994; Spedding 2009; Spedding and Colque 2003), in a series of influential publications, Xavier Albó and his CIPCA research team have described the Yungas as a region fundamentally influenced by coca cultivation, characterizing, for example, the region around Coripata as a "land of anguish and coca plantations" *("tierra de angustia y cocales")* (Equipo CIPCA 1977).

Figure 11: Typical Yungas landscape with cocales in Cala Cala (photograph by the author).

Recently, Alessandra Pellegrini Calderón has emphasized the continuing importance of coca for the region and the particular stance *cocaleros Yungueños* take towards plurinational identity politics by positively rejecting the 'indigenous people slot' (Pellegrini Calderón 2016). Moreover, coca cultivation not only fundamentally influences *Yungueños'* economy, but has also become an important factor in endowing a particular regional political solidarity. Defending their right to coca cultivation has united *Yungueños* behind a common cause very firmly for generations and in mid-2017, just about a month after I left Cala Cala and Bolivia, tens of thousands of *cocaleros* from the Yungas were protesting against the government's new legislation on coca in the streets of La Paz. All this serves as a backdrop for a fairly strong discourse on *Yungueño* identity and culture firmly associated with coca cultivation. It is important to note that this perspective is not only put forth in scholarly publications; it is something people in Cala Cala and Nogalani – Afrobolivians and Aymara alike – express frequently. Coca, however, is not only important as the basis of regional identity and political solidarity. It is also of vital economic importance and cultivating coca is the activity that shapes nearly all contexts of everyday life.

The coca economy: cooperation, cohesion and the distribution of labor

The most important aspect of daily life in Cala Cala is coca cultivation. The necessities associated with coca production determine the terms of cooperation and social cohesion, and shape relationships between individuals, households and groups. Beyond merely economic aspects, being a *cocalero* entails engaging in social relationships that span the whole community and serve to constitute it as such. Most *comunidades* in the Yungas are not only communities in a geographical sense and because they share a history as a *hacienda*, they are first and foremost *comunidades cocaleras*. Being a *cocalero* – and thus forming part of a *comunidad cocalera* – means developing communal ties around what Alison Spedding has called the "coca field as a total social fact" (Spedding 1997). According to this notion, being a *cocalero* means more than engaging in a certain agricultural activity and encompasses values, beliefs and practices that span the whole spectrum of society. These assertions fit Juan Angola's interpretation of the role of coca for Afrobolivians. For Angola, it is mainly by way of integrating in the coca economy that they have "put down roots" *("en la coca se enraiga su Africanidad en el entorno Boliviano")* in Bolivia and in the Yungas social fabric (Angola Maconde 2003:3). Saying this goes beyond the symbolic and rather hollow identification with the coca leaf that has prevailed in the political arena in Bolivia in recent years (cf. Grisaffi 2010). From this perspective, the constitutive element of *Afro-Yungueño* lifestyle and a determining factor for everyday social practice is the *Yungeño* part of the hyphenated denomination. The 'Afro' part is definitive only to a lesser extent, despite the fact that it seems to become ever more prominent in the realm of political positioning. Being *Yungueño*, as we have seen, means to a great extent being *cocalero*. In what follows, I will briefly describe systems of labor exchange, since they fundamentally determine how people relate to each other and thus provide a good vantage point from which to discuss the salience (or lack thereof) of ethnoracial categories.

Growing coca and the social significance of the exchange of labor

Life in Cala Cala is determined by the rhythm of agricultural work and organized mainly within small households that are the basic units in social and economic respects. Most households depend almost exclusively on the cultivation of coca leaf for survival. A household generally consists of two generations (a couple and their children), occasionally of three generations (including the parents of one of the spouses). Even though it is not uncommon for children to participate in the agricultural chores, most of them nowadays spend the majority of their time in school, joining their parents for work in the afternoons or on the weekends. Days in the Yungas start early. Women generally get up before sunrise and prepare both breakfast and lunch for all members of the family. After a simple breakfast consisting of bread and tea or *sultana* (an infusion made of coffee cherries) the children leave for school. Adult members of the household prepare to leave for the coca fields where they spend the rest of the day. In some cases, people eat a bowl of soup or *almuerzo* (lit. "lunch," usually at least one source of carbohydrates like noodles, rice or *yuca* [manioc] with meat and vegetables) right before leaving; in other cases they just take their food with them. In the fields, they complete different tasks depending on the requirements of their or other people's crops (dig, weed, harvest, etc.). Normally, people stay in the fields the whole day and return to their houses at dusk. This makes the coca field the main site of interaction with members of the wider *comunidad*. Depending on the occasion and the tasks that have to be completed, the group of people working together in one field varies greatly, from working completely alone to being part of a larger group of about a dozen people.

The fundamental importance of organizing the Yungas workforce stems from the fact that growing coca in the Yungas is a very labor-intensive endeavor. Due to the landscape in the Yungas, the botany of the plant and the fact that the leaves are very fragile and only intact ones are eligible for traditional consumption, coca agriculture has not undergone much mechanization. Comparing accounts of early colonial sources describing coca cultivation with what one encounters in the Yungas nowadays, one does not find great differences in terms of planting and harvesting techniques or the implementation of technology (Spedding 2004). Being a *cocalero* remains an occupation that demands a lot of manual labor and relatively little technology. The large amount of labor required makes it necessary to establish mechanisms for exchanging labor between households within the *comunidad* since, at times, it is impossible for a single household to provide the workforce needed by itself. This occurs when a new coca field has to be planted, during the rainy season when the growth of weeds becomes excessive and the fields need to be taken care of regularly, and during times of harvest (up to four times a year). For each of these tasks, all *cocalero* households have to mobilize support from the *comunidad*. For example, the very complicated process of digging and terracing a new coca field requires the work of several men over several days. Weeding larger coca fields can also not be accomplished by a household alone. And especially when the leaves are being harvested, good timing and sufficient labor at a specific moment is of paramount importance. If the leaves are not harvested within a determined timeframe, the quality and/or quantity of the harvest decreases with grave economic consequences for the household. In coca production there is a division of labor according to gender. Women are generally *k'ichiri* (harvesters, *k'ichir* means [to] harvest in Aymara), whereas men most often dig and plant new fields and weed the existing *cocales*. At times, men also participate in the harvest though, and it is also known for women to occasionally weed a *cocal*.

Ayni

When I first arrived in the town of Coripata, I met two *cocaleros* from Cala Cala and Afrobolivian historian Juan Angola Maconde from the neighboring community of Dorado Chico. When I explained my interest in the community to them, Angola told me: "It is good that you are here. In Cala Cala, you will be able to experience *ayni* [reciprocal exchange of labor] between Afrobolivians and Aymara." He went on to emphasize that Afrobolivians and indigenous groups have been living together for centuries and that there has been a lot of exchange between the two groups. Cooperation and exchange is not limited to the coca economy but in the realm of everyday agricultural practice it is most salient and also most regular. *"Hacerse ayni"* is a fundamental economic necessity in a *cocalero* community and a practice that determines social relations within a *comunidad* to a great extent (see Spedding 1994).

Neither in Cala Cala nor in Dorado Chico (according to Juan Angola Maconde) did people make a distinction between Afrobolivians and Aymara when it came to the subject of discussing *ayni*. The families I lived with engaged in *ayni* exchange likewise with Afrobolivian and Aymara households. Both Roberto and Verónica went to work in other people's fields while I stayed with them and never expressed any reservations about working for somebody based on his ethnicity. Determining their willingness to accede to a plea for *ayni* were practical reasons, economic calculations or already existing obligations to reciprocate *ayni* they had received previously. Verónica sometimes only reluctantly agreed to work on somebody's harvest due to the fact that she considered the field poorly taken care of and too weed-infested, which meant that there was constant danger of overlooking a snake and getting bitten. Or she would hesitate to accept an offer to work for money and rather accept an offer to "win *ayni*" (*"ganarse ayni"*) since she would then be able to claim the payment of an *ayni* debt instead of trying to convince others to work for her as a *jornalero* when she had need of help (see below). On other occasions she would chose to work in a certain field because a friend of hers had already accepted an owner's offer and they would be able to work together all day, which she found enjoyable. This non-exhaustive list of reasons could be continued; the point is that this type of reasoning and deliberation is much more common than approaching the subject in ethnic terms. To put it bluntly, I never heard anyone saying: "I am not going to work in X or Y's field because he/she is of this or that ethnicity." The same is true for Roberto, her husband. When he was asked to help another member of the *comunidad* he pondered economic factors, personal preferences, and basic circumstances in order to determine what he was going to do. From what I observed in the *comunidad*, other households made similar choices and there were no open references to ethnicity or 'culture' in this regard. As far as the information I collected in Cala Cala goes, there is no differentiation based on ethnic categories in the realm of *ayni*. [6] There is also no ethnic dimension to specific tasks, no system of ethnic trades and no ethnic division of labor. Nor are sources of livelihood or certain lifestyles associated with certain ethnic groups (as is the case, for example, in the pastoralist-agriculturalist divide in parts of Africa (Pelican 2015)).

Jornales/mink'a

Besides *ayni*, there have always been other modalities of organizing the workforce in the Yungas. Hiring *mink'as* (in Aymara) or *jornaleros* was and is a very common procedure when a household is in need of extra labor. A *jornalero* is paid a specific sum of money *(un jornal)* for a day's work in other people's fields. Unlike *ayni*, *jornales* do not imply a reciprocal relationship and the salary has to be paid the same day. In the past, working as a *jornalero* was regarded as a disgrace. Young men having to earn a living as *jornaleros* were considered inferior since they neither had a coca plantation of their own nor were part of a household with enough work (i.e. *cocales*) to keep them occupied. What is more, their need to generate immediate cash income was seen as a sign of poverty and financial need (Spedding 2009:464; see also Spedding 1994). Likewise, hiring a *jornalero* was also the less desirable option for the hiring party. It was assumed that an *ayni*-giver would complete the assigned tasks more thoroughly, since he or she expected to receive *ayni* in return at some later date. A *jornalero*, the assumption goes, gains significantly less strategic advantage in completing the tasks to the ordering party's satisfaction and even has little moral obligation to do so. In recent years, however, a significant shift has been occurring in terms of the economic and moral evaluation of *jornaleros*. Some would even go as far as to say that most people nowadays prefer to hire *jornaleros* over participating in *ayni* networks, since being part of such networks implies incurring significant debts and social obligations. The same facets of *ayni* that had been prized as fundamental pillars of community solidarity and social cohesion nowadays seem to hamper individuals' entrepreneurial activities. Well-off households

6 There are, to be sure, accounts (Léons 1972; Rey 1998) that report differentiation in ethnic terms between Afrobolivians and Aymara in the context of *ayni* in the past. Afrobolivians in Chicaloma, for example, preferred to work in so called *juntas* (working groups) and were not as deeply entangled in the *ayni* networks of the Aymara segments of their community (Léons 1972). Similarly, Rey (1998) asserts that in the *comunidades* around Coroico, *ayni* exchange does not cross ethnic boundaries.

prefer to invest money over incurring *ayni* debts and therefore gladly hire *jornaleros* to avoid the obligation to reciprocate on the other households' terms in the future.

Faena

Another mode of organizing collective work is the so-called *faena*. It dates back to the times of the *hacienda* and was mostly practiced when a significant labor force was needed at one particular moment in time. It is also sometimes referred to as *trabajo festivo* (work party) and the organizers of the *faena* are required to provide the workers with food and (alcoholic) beverages (Spedding 1994:78). Beyond the merely economic aspect, *faenas* also have ritual dimensions. For example, when planting a new *cocal* or for its first harvest, a *faena* is organized to ritually establish the new field (Spedding 1994:79). This mirrors not only the difficulty and intensity inherent in this task, but also the fundamental importance that the planting of a new field covers in the lifecycle of individuals in a *cocalero* community. By planting their 'own' coca field that usually produces harvests for up to forty years and thus lasts for their whole working life, young males become 'men,' full members of the community and the head of their household. As far as my interlocutors in Cala Cala are concerned, *faena* is hardly ever practiced anymore. Roberto remembered participating in various *faenas*, yet they were always 'special occasions,' not an everyday affair, and nowadays are even rarer. During the *hacienda* period, many landowners prohibited *faenas* organized by their *peones* and tried to do away with this 'uncivilized' custom that frequently ended in a generalized intoxication of large groups of workers. Roberto mentioned *faenas* where the organizing party would dig in bottles of beer and alcohol *(trago)* in the ground at the end of the stretch of land that was to be prepared for planting, encouraging the diggers to advance swiftly and rewarding them with an extra share of alcohol if they completed their task. He also mentioned that in the past it was not uncommon for the Afrobolivian population of Cala Cala to hold *faenas* with the neighboring Afrobolivian community of Dorado Chico, which would not participate in the community's *ayni* networks. Yet, as he emphasized, there has not been such a *faena* in a long time, since preparing new coca fields nowadays is done under the modality of *contrato*, where a group of people are paid a fixed amount of money in order to complete a specific task.

Libreada

A significant change in the coca economy occurred by introducing the practice of *libreada*, a way of organizing the coca harvest that originates in the region of La Asunta, an area of colonization and mainly 'non-traditional' coca growing (according to Law 1008) (Spedding 2004:139ff). The term *libreada* refers to the practice of measuring work by the exact amount of *libras* (pounds) harvested. In Cala Cala, the *libreada* is employed both for *jornaleros* and for *ayni* exchange. Before, a day of *ayni* comprised six *mitis*, i.e. six rounds of filling a cloth *(mit'iña)* tied around the waist with coca leaves. Nowadays, each *k'ichiri* pours the harvested coca from the *mit'iña* into his or her individual plastic bag, which is weighed at the end of the day. The corresponding payment or the *ayni* debts repaid or obtained are then established according to the weight of the leaves. Thus, for example, a good *k'ichiri* might be able to repay an *ayni* of twenty pounds in half a day, even though the other person had to work for an entire day to harvest the same amount of leaves. Most *k'ichiri* see this as a change in their favor, since they are paid for the exact amount of coca harvested. Before, many people stated, they were often subject to abusive owners of coca fields that would demand larger *mitis* or an additional round in an effort to exploit the *k'ichiris* they hired. The *libreada* also means that each individual can decide the rhythm and intensity of working more freely. Even though it is frowned upon for a person to rest for overly long periods of time in the field or too often, it will all be settled by the weighing in of the harvested leaves, which determines the salary for the day. The *libreada* also enables a more flexible adjustment of payments for the *k'ichiri* since the amount of money paid for a pound changes with the market price for coca leaves. The salary of the workers thus corresponds with the fluctuation of prices, whereas before only the owners of the *cocal* and the merchants could benefit from fluctuation. Yet the distributive effect of this is limited. Since most *k'ichiri* are part of a household that owns coca fields of their own and at some point occupies the position of hiring party, the gain in flexibility as *k'ichiri* results in the obligation to follow the same rules as owner and hiring party.[7]

Beyond structuring days, years and lifecycles and determining how households relate to each other through the necessary exchange of labor and the networks of cooperation, solidarity and economic integration this engenders, the lifestyle associated with coca cultivation also marks the more mundane activities of everyday life. For example, rather than the houses or patios of particular households, the central plaza of a village, the church or *sindicato* building *(sede sindical)*, the coca field is the main site of socializing and communicating with people from the *comunidad*. The monthly *sindicato* meeting is often crammed with dozens of topics and does not allow for much casual encounter, and the visits people pay each other at their houses are quite infrequent, rather short and mostly guided by a clear objective like asking someone for help in the fields or buying/selling coca. The space for casual conversation and gossiping is therefore the coca field.

7 If anything, the *libreada* has strengthened the economic position of women within the household. Besides being traditionally responsible for the management of the household finances (a very common trope in Bolivia), women now also contribute a growing share of the cash income, since the *k'ichiris* are more often women and they usually outperform men in harvesting by far.

Debates in the coca field

The coca field as a *total social fact* as described by Alison Spedding is "a social nexus that unites [...] diverse elements and activities" (Spedding 1997:69) of *Yungueño* life. It is, very importantly for my discussion of how certain horizons of community become meaningful, the main site of communication within the *comunidad*. Given the fact that everyday life in Cala Cala – as well as in most other Yungas *comunidades* – revolves around the cultivation of coca, it is not surprising that most conversations happen while working in the field or during the short breaks from work called *aculli (acullicar* literally meaning [to] chew coca, *aculli* being the act of chewing coca or any break from work more generally). There are other occasions – *sindicato* meetings, *talleres*, informal gatherings or occasional visits to people's houses – but these are less frequent and less intense in comparison to the interactions in the coca field. People spend up to twelve hours a day in the fields. Most of the time they are at least accompanied by the members of their household and very often people work in groups of up to a dozen in a field. As the *k'ichiris* are expected to advance "*wachu wachu*" (row by row) synchronically, they are always close enough to each other to converse. Topics include discussing family affairs, gossiping about fellow *comunarios*, discussing business (coca prices, wages, travel costs), politics, organizational aspects and the weather. In short, the coca field is the primary context for interaction within the *comunidad* and for debating a variety of issues.

Always accompanying the work is the *radio cocalera,* a small portable radio that virtually all *cocaleros* own and that is therefore the most constant and everyday form of engagement with national and local news and politics in Cala Cala.

Most people I worked with regularly listened to Radio Yungas or Radio Coca, two local radio stations from Chulumani and Coripata. The programs transmitted by Radio Yungas and Radio Coca are a combination of local and national news, political debates, announcements by *sindicatos,* local branches of ADEPCOCA *(Asociación Departamental de Productores de Coca)* and the municipal governments, as well as occasional musical interludes. Even though most households nowadays own at least one TV, the radio remains the primary source of information, especially at the local level. National TV stations only rarely cover smaller local news and watching TV has a much more recreational aspect than listening to the radio. The radio provides the *Cala Caleños* with a wide range of vital information. Many *sindicatos* convene their meetings through the radio or announce communal workdays *(trabajos comunitarios)* through the medium. If a note or information "has been on radio Yungas" *("salió en radio Yungas"),* it is taken to be common knowledge, since it is widely assumed that in all households at least one member listens to the radio and can communicate the news. For example, if a household fails to participate in a compulsory event that has been announced on the radio, it cannot claim to be exempted from the corresponding *multa* (fine). The radio – besides the monthly *sindicato* meeting –

Figure 12: People working together in the coca field (photograph by the author).

is also the main arena for political debates in the Yungas. Before elections, political opponents debate on air: critics of certain representatives voice their concerns on the radio and the authorities are given the opportunity to respond to the allegations directly or on one of the following days. The local news section covers everything from politics, the current prices for coca on the Yungas markets and the Villa Fátima market in La Paz, to warnings about bush fires, road blockades or the very common landslides on the Nor and Sud Yungas road. More often than not, due to its immediacy and local scope, information from the radio directly feeds into what is perceived by people in the fields. One day, Roberto directed my attention to clouds of dust behind one of the mountain ranges to the south. It was very early in the morning and we had just arrived in the field and were chewing coca before starting to work. As the radio reported problems on the Sud Yungas road between Chulumani and Unduavi, Roberto told me: "See the dust behind the mountains? The trucks from Sud Yungas have to take a detour because the road is blocked." Whereas the connection between the news on the radio and what was happening locally was in this case quite obvious and discernable even for the recently arrived fieldworker with little knowledge of Yungas geography, further along into my fieldwork I realized that this was the case even in instances where the connections were not as

Figure 13: La radio cocalera (photograph by the author).

easily visible as the dust on the road. This mainly concerns issues of politics and the coca economy. Most people are personally acquainted with the representatives appearing on the radio and hearing their declarations and what happens *"en la radio"* is mostly of very immediate concern to the people. I am stressing this point because I take the immediacy of the radio broadcasts in terms of their relation to everyday activities and concerns to be of utmost importance.

In contrast to the topics with immediate relevance like those mentioned above – most notably anything that has do to with coca – there were also moments when people commented on radio broadcasts in a different way, expressing what I interpreted as a mixture of amusement, puzzlement and disbelief. In what follows, I will discuss two short examples that give an impression of how topics – law and politics on the one hand and Afrobolivian identity politics on the other – with less immediate relevance are debated.

Law and politics as seen from the coca field: *"hoy en día, todo es ley"*

As opposed to immediately relevant local news and radio debates among local leaders, the ubiquitous government messages concerning certain legal novelties and political initiatives are mostly perceived as 'very far away' and are commented on in a very different fashion to those relating to local Yungas affairs. Yet they also serve as starting points for discussion around the issues addressed in the broadcasts and are thus an interesting context for understanding what people think about certain topics. This became clear to me when one day we listened to a broadcast related to a new legal regulation concerning intra-family violence and aspects of gender violence in Bolivia. The parliament had just passed a law incorporating a system of local-level justice, officially attributing certain competences to the *sindicato* in cases of violence within the family. The radio spot (transmitted in Spanish and Aymara) alerted women to the importance of reporting abuse to the authorities and informed them that according to the new law, the first contact person is as of now the local *sindicato* authority.

In a mocking tone, one of the *cocaleros* stated: "Nowadays, everything is law" *("Hoy en día, todo es ley.")*. This statement sparked a discussion around the law on violence against women and the prevalence of legal regulations in recent times more generally. People agreed that they considered it a lost cause and that the law would certainly not be observed *("no se va cumplir")*. Intra-familial violence is widespread and fairly normalized in Yungas *comunidades* – as elsewhere in Bolivia (Montaño 2016; Spedding 1994). Yet intra-community conflict, as ubiquitous as it might be, is a subject generally muted in public conversation, where people seek to maintain an image of equality and unity among members of the *comunidad* and social convention prohibits the open expression of conflicts (Spedding 1994:180). This is also true for intra-marital conflict. The husband is the representative of the household in public and it would be a serious insult to his symbolic dominance and authority if his wife spoke publicly about being abused, especially in front of other men (Spedding 1994:186).[8] Having a woman report intra-familial violence to a *sindicato* official, in the eyes of the *comunarios*, would be unthinkable as a generalized rule. It caused serious amusement among both men and women participating in the conversation that such an approach would even be considered. Moreover, and beyond the specificities of the law, it was clear that they considered the attempt by the state to determine and readjust the jurisdictions of certain institutions (in this case the *sindicato* vs. the municipal courts and the police) as an interference in the affairs of the *comunidad*.[9] Given that the Yungas' experience with state intervention has mostly been in the context of coca eradication programs, it is not surprising

8 It is even expected that young couples fight quite a lot in the first years of their marriage and it is only considered disgraceful if spouses keep solving their conflicts with physically violent means after several years of marriage, when they should have 'learned to get along' (Spedding 1994:186).

9 Although the law suggests otherwise, it is in most cases the *sindicato* that solves intra-community conflicts in the first place.

that people in Cala Cala are very suspicious of any attempt by the state to interfere in their internal affairs.[10]

The radio broadcast – in this case a government-sponsored advertisement intended to inform the population on legal reform – served as a way into a discussion of legal and political affairs more generally. It is rare for people in the Yungas to be confronted with this type of information in television broadcasts and even less likely to be encountered through written sources like newspapers, which are almost completely absent from everyday life in the Yungas. Listening to the news is a thoroughly social affair, since most often people do it in the coca field alongside other people while they are working. This also means that broadcasts are often immediately discussed and contextualized within the interpretative framework of the *comunidad cocalera* and its logics. During these discussions, people often very clearly expressed how relevant the news are to the practices of their day-to-day lives. In my view, the opening statement (*"hoy en día, todo es ley"*) cited above and the ensuing discussion express a general weariness of legal reform, especially in contexts that many people do not deem to be the jurisdiction of the state, in this case family life in the broadest of senses.

Raíces Africanas and *Radio Afroboliviana*

Another interesting case in point is the well-known radio show *Raíces Africanas* (African Roots) that has been broadcasted for over fifteen years by different local radio stations throughout the Yungas every Friday between 7pm and 10pm. Its foundation in 2001 was supported by a series of workshops and *Raíces Africanas* was initially conceived in order to facilitate the exchange of information among dispersed parts of the Afrobolivian population in different *comunidades* in the Yungas. The program is conducted by Jorge Medina, an accomplished Afrobolivian activist, founder of the *Centro Afroboliviano para el Desarrollo Integral y Comunitario (CADIC)* and the first Afrobolivian to be elected to National Parliament in 2009.

According to many of my interlocutors, the program was quite popular in the first years after its foundation. For many people it was their first experience of engaging with the emerging Afrobolivian political movement and the process of cultural revitalization. It is also often cited as one of the main reasons Jorge Medina was able to gain such great popularity and become one of the most visible Afrobolivian leaders. According to its creators, *Raíces Africanas* and the recently founded online station *Radio Afroboliviana* serve as a means to spread information

10 This seems to be common in other parts of Bolivia as well, as the comments of anthropologist Nico Tassi suggest. He reports that rural authorities tend to view the Plurinational State like an NGO, applying protective strategies in order to prevent the state from interfering with their internal affairs (Tassi quoted in Soruco Sologruen 2012:20).

concerning "the development of Afrobolivian culture in the country, with a touch of entertainment and information."[11] *Radio Afroboliviana* is presented as a "tool for communication in the context of the *proceso de cambio* where the *naciones y pueblos indígena originario campesinos, y las comunidades interculturales y afrobolivianas* make up a substantial part of the entirety of Bolivian society."[12]

The radio being such a fundamental part of everyday life, I asked people in Cala Cala about the program and what they thought of its content. Most people told me that they were familiar with it but did not listen to it on a regular basis and they offered different explanations for this. On the one hand, they said that the widespread availability of mobile phones made it much easier to communicate with their kin and friends not living in Cala Cala and that the radio was not needed for that purpose anymore. Moreover, they considered the informational aspects of the show hardly relevant. Roberto once told me that Medina – in his eyes – *"solo habla payasadas"* ("he only clowns around"), when we listened to the show one Friday night at my request. Roberto expressed personal dissatisfaction with Jorge Medina as a political leader, but also displayed a general weariness with regard to Medina's discourse of "speaking to all Afrobolivian *comunidades* in the Yungas." For him, the relevant aspects of his sense of being *Afro* are his kin, whom he reaches by mobile phone, and the local context of Cala Cala that he feels is not represented by Medina's broadcasts. Consequently, on other Friday nights Roberto would watch TV or go to bed early. *Raíces Africanas* was nothing he would ever comment on or discuss without me asking. Other inhabitants of Cala Cala didn't attribute any particular importance to the program either. Not once did I have the impression that the radio show was in fact, as it proclaims, a communicational tool for dispersed Afrobolivians. The most common reaction to my questions concerning *Raíces Africanas* was a shrug of the shoulders and in many instances I had the impression that this was not only true for this particular show, but also for the ideas, organizations and people associated with it.

By contrast, the whole community was captivated by the radio broadcasts surrounding the ADEPCOCA-led mobilizations of *cocaleros Yungueños* in La Paz protesting against the *Ley General de la Coca* in various weeks in 2017. During that time, there was hardly another topic that was discussed in Cala Cala and it was quite obvious that most of the people considered the question of coca to be of very direct and paramount importance for their daily life and economic survival. Of course, the events preceding and following the passing of the *Ley General de la Coca*, were

11 *"El desarrollo de la cultura afroboliviana en el país, con un toque de entretenimiento e información."*

12 *"Herramienta de comunicación en el contexto del proceso de cambio que vivimos en Bolivia, donde las naciones y pueblos indígena originario campesinos, y las comunidades interculturales y afrobolivianas, constituimos parte sustancial del conjunto de la sociedad boliviana."* See http://www.radioafrobolivia.com/azuca_pal_cajue.html [18/01/18].

far from quotidian, yet even during times of less conflict the most mundane news concerning coca prices, the situation on the market or even the state of the road to La Paz received more attention than *Raíces Africanas*.

Plurinationality as *"discurso ajeno"*

The comments on and discussion of radio broadcasts is, in my view, a quite adequate indicator of how far and in what specific sense certain news, campaigns and information relate to people's more immediate concerns. Whereas broadcasts on coca, *sindicatos* and local politics are discussed in a way that make their immediate importance quite clear, matters like information campaigns on recently passed laws and regulations are perceived as much more remote and less immediately significant. This can, at least in part, also be explained by their more national scope. Yet, since a significant share of legal reform that is advertised in Yungas radio broadcasts is directed at rural residents and/or 'indigenous groups' allegedly inhabiting this territory, it is striking how little they seem to have in common with people's everyday concerns. They are at times the subject of mocking comments, hinting at their irrelevance and inflationary appearance, but are mostly just ignored and not further discussed. The impression I got from numerous conversations during work in the coca fields is that most legal efforts are interpreted as either irrelevant or as threatening to the long-established lifestyles of the *comunidad*. They are seen and commented on as outside the scope of community life or foreign to it *(ajenos)*. This impression changes to some extent when people (Afrobolivians and Aymara alike) are actively prompted to comment on the Constitution's provisions concerning *naciones y pueblos originarios*. In these instances, comments tend to be much more positive and the impact of certain laws is evaluated as being quite significant, as opposed to the reduced importance it is granted in more informal contexts.[13]

This situation makes it highly difficult to reach a clear-cut conclusion in terms of assessing the relevance of legal provisions, social movement discourse and identity politics in general. On the one hand, my data suggests that without being prompted specifically, people place little importance on these matters and in everyday affairs they hardly play a role. Yet, when asked, many of my interlocutors were able to offer quite nuanced views on these topics, hinting at the fact that certain aspects of identity politics do resonate with local perceptions of social categorization. I would thus suggest that we are dealing with a situation where reference to ethnic identity and related stereotypes is often just a step away, and can be activated by a particular situation, comment, piece of information or conflict. I interpret this

13 This is one of the instances showing that interviewing people on these matters produces highly biased accounts that differ greatly from the experiences of participant observation and informal conversations.

highly volatile situation as another hint at the often unfathomable yet pervasive presence – or availability – of ID-ology and "rights talk" (Merry 2003) as a model for interpreting and enacting social relations; a presence that has an impact far beyond the realm of concrete legal provisions, but is a part of a subtler legalization of identities and related social relations. Engaging with legal discourse and identity politics through radio broadcasts, and the ensuing discussions, is at the same time the most common and everyday genre of engagement and the most elusive. Engagement is less focused, less explicit and less directed than in formalized contexts, but the information, opinions and options presented therein become increasingly internalized and thus contribute a conceptual backdrop that the more formalized contexts (see below) can build on.

Mobilizing Cala Cala: ADEPCOCA and the *Ley General de la Coca*

The limited mobilizing potential of plurinational identity politics in Cala Cala became especially obvious when I witnessed the mobilizing potential of *cocalero* identity. As I pointed out in chapter 3, the local significance of the concept of *el pueblo Afroboliviano* – the central category of Afrobolivian political discourse in recent times – is rather elusive. Mobilizing *Cala Caleños* as *cocaleros*, on the other hand, has a completely different force and relevance. In early 2017, after years of deliberation, negotiation and – as many people in the Yungas remarked – deliberate procrastination, the MAS government set out to reform the legislation concerning the cultivation of coca, its trade and its illegal usage in cocaine production. Until then, the legislation pertaining to coca cultivation was still to a large extent based on the polemical Law 1008, passed by Bolivian legislators in 1988 under international pressure led by the USA in its 'war on drugs.' To replace Law 1008, the government drafted Law 906, the *Ley General de la Coca*. It was not only hotly debated throughout the country, but was also the center of attention in the Yungas during the first half of 2017. I arrived in Cala Cala in the middle of the most serious disputes just a few days after thousands of *cocaleros* from the Yungas had been protesting in La Paz against Law 906 and were violently repressed by the police. The issue people were concerned about most was the increase in the legal limits for coca cultivation in the Chapare region in Cochabamba (an Evo Morales stronghold) while maintaining the strict limits established in 1988 for the Yungas. ADEPCOCA and the people from the Yungas argued that if there were to be adjustments and/or increases of the legally permitted cultivation of coca, it should be the Yungas benefitting from this increase and not the Chapare. Throughout various weeks between mid-February and the end of March 2017, there was hardly another topic in Cala Cala than the new *Ley General de la Coca*. Negotiations and the eventual signing of a compromise by a government-friendly faction of the Yungas' leadership with the authorities –

and the subsequent rejection of this very same compromise by ADEPCOCA – lead to a series of debates, confrontations, conflicts and even open hostilities that have still not ceased today. For example, in June 2017, Cesar Cocarico, Minister of Rural Development, had to be evacuated from the town of Arapata by helicopter after a group of *cocaleros* attacked an event where the minster was speaking about the contents of Law 906. The media have reported a number of other smaller incidents all related to different issues regarding the law. Roberto and I spent hour after hour during the evening listening to Radio Yungas to remain updated on all aspects of the *Ley General de la Coca*. Roberto repeatedly prepared himself to travel to La Paz, since ADEPCOCA had determined that one third of its affiliated members *("se despliega un tercio de la base")* had to be mobilized at all times in order to maintain the protests in La Paz and all over the Yungas. This meant that all members took turns travelling to La Paz, participating in road blockades, public gatherings and marches. Travelling and participating in protest rallies is an important part of *cumplir función social* and although Roberto would of course have preferred to stay at home and work his fields, he was ready and willing to follow the instructions of ADEPCOCA in order to fight for their common cause. What I would like to illustrate with this example is the fact that hardly any topic moves Cala Cala as much as coca. This is in part rooted in coca's seminal economic importance but does not stop there. It was not only rational economic calculation that led people to mobilize against Law 906, but also a shared sense of a coca-related Yungas identity that they did not find adequately represented in the law and in the government's attitude more generally. ADEPCOCA mobilized people through a strongly regionalized sense of identity and belonging as *cocaleros Yungueños*. Beyond the economic importance of coca cultivation and its central role for conceptualizing regional identity, being a *cocalero* is thus also very importantly a political identity.

Chapter 5: The Changing Meanings of Ethnoracial Identifications in Cala Cala

The two preceding chapters have introduced what I call the different horizons of community in Cala Cala. With the word horizons, I refer to the local perspectives on different categories of identification, related frames of reference and ways of representing sameness and difference. By examining different contexts of social, economic and political relations, I have fleshed out two basic horizons of community. One is based chiefly on kinship, local origins and ethnoracial affiliation. The collective identification most salient within this horizon is called *"los Afros de Cala Cala"* in emic terms. The second basic horizon grounds community mostly in economic and ritual practice, as well as in political cooperation and emphasizes the importance of coca cultivation, regional identity, and festivities in the *comunidad*.

The two horizons in Cala Cala are not mutually exclusive. Following Eidson et al.'s recent contribution, they can be understood as relating to each other in syntagmatic and/or taxonomic ways (Eidson et al. 2017:343–344). This means that identifying oneself or others as *"Afro de Cala Cala"* does not preclude identification as a *comunario de Nogalani* and vice versa. Locally, there is no problem in situationally emphasizing one or the other horizon of community and people in Cala Cala generally do not conceive of *Afro* and *comunario* as representing conflicting collective identifications. Variable identification (or "re-identification") understood as "alterations in the actor's orientation, attitude, and behavior with reference to selected categories of identification" (Eidson et al. 2017:343) is thus unproblematic and occurs frequently. As I have shown in chapter 4, *sindicato* organization, the coca economy, and local festivities are framed within the horizon of the *comunidad cocalera*. At the same time, there are networks of solidarity and cooperation based on kinship and collective identification as *"los Afros de Cala Cala."*

There is, however, a second dimension to identity change that goes beyond situationally changing between horizons of community, emphasizing one or the other – or both simultaneously – at different times and in different circumstances. Eidson et al. (2017:343) refer to this process as "re-definition of categories of identification" (as opposed to re-identification). In Cala Cala's case, the category *Afro* is undergoing a process of re-definition through engaging with notions of *el pueblo Afroboliviano* (see chapters 8 and 9 for a detailed discussion of the process of articulating this concept). At the same time, basic assumptions concerning collective identification as a *comunidad cocalera* are also being transformed.

In this chapter, I argue that friction between horizons of community is most strongly expressed by people in Cala Cala when local social relations are interpreted within a conceptual framework privileging emerging legal and political discourses on Afroboilvianity over more local understandings of community. I have pointed out the general tendency to view plurinationality as *"discurso ajeno"* (foreign discourse) and have also addressed the limited significance of Afrobolivian identity politics in everyday contexts (expressed, for example, in the marginal importance of *Radio Afroboliviana* in Cala Cala). Yet the discourses of plurinational ID-ology and Afrobolivian particularities are not without consequences. As I will argue in the following sections, plurinational ID-ology on the one hand serves as a backdrop for deploying ethnoracial stereotypes in Cala Cala. On the other hand, the increasing political salience of Afrobolivianity significantly alters the strategic advantages of collective identification as *Afrobolivianos*. Together with a parallel weakening of the ties of solidarity and reciprocity that bind together Nogalani as a *comunidad cocalera*, this leads to a situation where the conceptual relationship between collective identifications, as well as their respective strategic advantages, are rapidly changing.

Analyzing contexts of complementarity and friction between different collective identifications also helps in avoiding a common problem of many of the publications that deal with Afrobolivians in the Yungas. Two main thrusts of argument – depending on the position of the researcher and the main focus of the study – can be identified here. On the one hand, in publications focusing on 'Afrobolivian identity,' contexts of cooperation and collective identification beyond the realm of the ethnoracial (i.e. Afrobolivian) are briefly recapped in a few pages before turning to 'Afrobolivian particularities' that take center stage for the argument. This perspective tends to downplay the fact that Afrobolivians engage in most of their day-to-day activities within contexts where it is indeed of hardly any consequence that they are Afrobolivian. On the other hand, scholars interested in the functioning of *comunidades cocaleras* in the Yungas – for the most part skeptical of claims to ethnic particularity by any group in the region as a whole and on the part of Afrobolivians specifically – downplay ethnoracial affiliations and privilege non-ethnic *sindicato* politics and the coca economy to such an extent that ethnoracial distinctions are rendered close to meaningless. I argue for a more nuanced view that neither overstates nor downplays the significance of ethnoracial classification and self-identification *a priori*, but rather inquires into the interdependencies of ethnoracially defined belongings and other affiliations. In what follows, I will first discuss how people talk about ethnoracial differences and the meanings people in Cala Cala ascribe to them. I will then sketch two parallel developments occurring in Cala Cala recently: on the one hand, the coca economy has been undergoing significant changes in recent years, transforming the relationships in the *comunidad Nogalani* in general. On the other hand, the revitalization of Afrobolivian culture originating in urban contexts and legal recognition of Afrobolivians in the Constitution has given ethnoracial differences new meanings. As a consequence, the relationship between the different horizons of community is shifting, both in institutional settings *(sindicato)*, as well as with regard to a sense of shared common history and tradition.

"No se juntan así nomás": ethnoracial identifications and individual social relations

As I showed in chapter 4, a large part of everyday activities in Cala Cala can be accounted for without reference to ethnic and/or racial distinctions. What is more, race, ethnicity and skin color are fairly muted themes in everyday conversations and one has to look for them very closely. The question then is in what sense and to what extent does being 'Afrobolivian' in Cala Cala have an impact on concrete social relationships between individuals and groups. When I once asked Roberto during a break in the coca field who he considered to be his best friends and why, he started to name a number of individuals and gave me short summaries of the histories of their friendship. I had met most of them and knew that they were all Afrobolivians. Since it was not at all uncommon to see him interact with Aymara on a daily basis and these exchanges – from my perspective – were marked by a great deal of familiarity and seemed fairly unstrained, I asked him if he thought that this (i.e. all the people he considered "friends" being Afrobolivian) was a coincidence or if he could think of any other reasons. He told me: "*Afros* and Aymara don't get together just like that." *("Afros y Aymaras, no se juntan así nomás.")*. The crux, I think, of this statement lies in the meaning of *"así nomás"* ("just like that"). As I have shown, there are a myriad of contexts in which Afrobolivians and Aymara do get/work together *(se juntan)*, be it the ever-present coca economy, religious ceremonies and *fiestas*, trade and transportation, political organization and matters of infrastructure that are discussed in the *sindicato* or the regional branch of ADEPCOCA. Yet, according to Roberto, if there is no economic, political or otherwise contextually predetermined occasion – and that is what I believe is meant by *"así nomás"* – Afrobolivians and Aymara do not get together. When I asked him what concrete contexts might be implied in this statement, he again referred to 'friendship' in a very general sense. He went on to detail that it was not common for an Aymara to simply stop by at his house to chat and chew coca as was the case with Afrobolivians. If Aymara did visit, he said, it was always because they had something else in mind, for example to ask for a favor or discuss past or future *sindicato* meetings. In the same vein, he also cited an occasion when he and I attended the *fiesta patronal* in Nogalani, sharing a table with other Afrobolivians and not mixing with the rest of the *fiesta* – unlike what happened during *Todos Santos* and the *velorio* described in the preceding chapter. He explained this particular situation and his general comments on friendship with reference to a set of character traits that, from his perspective, made it difficult to establish closer personal relationships between Afrobolivians and Aymara. Although Roberto attempted to make a very strong case for the generalized importance of ethnoracial identifications and differences, I find myself unable to fully subscribe to his view. Most of the time he only made this kind of comment in private settings and I was hardly able to detect any recurring contexts in which his alleged reservations against Aymara would have had tangible consequences. Moreover, concerning the topic of friendship and sociality, it must be remarked that casual visits to people's houses did not happen very often to begin with – neither between Afrobolivians, nor between Aymara. Most of time in the *comunidad* is dedicated to work – thus the importance of social interaction in the coca field – and scarce spare time is mostly spent with the members of one's household.

What is more, in concrete cases, conflicts were also not addressed with reference to ethnoracial identifications. For example, when I returned to Cala Cala in 2017, Roberto told me that he was in the middle of a court trial. He had gotten into a fight with a man originally from Dorado Chico, but intermittently living in Cala Cala for many years. According to Roberto, they had gotten into a fight that resulted in a physical struggle during which the man threatened to beat Roberto and his daughter visiting from Santa Cruz with a metal chain. After describing the details of the struggle, Roberto declared in outrage: "And he isn't even a *comunario*" (*"Y ni siquiera es comunario"*). The fact that the man was considered an 'outsider,' in Roberto's view, made the physical assault all the more serious. But the relevant collective identification in this case was *comunario*, not *Afroboliviano* or Aymara. In fact, Roberto never mentioned if the assailant was Aymara or Afrobolivian. I found out one day by coincidence when I asked Roberto how Gustavo was doing, an Afrobolivian man I had met in Cala Cala in 2014 and whom I hadn't seen there in 2017. It was only then that Roberto disclosed that Gustavo was in fact the man he had been fighting with.

"Es bien abierto por más Aymara que sea": ethnoracial stereotypes

Like Roberto, many people in Cala Cala employ a very subtle set of distinctions in order to position themselves as 'a different kind of people' vis-à-vis other groups in the *comunidad*. For example, when I asked people in Cala Cala about a person from Nogalani that I wanted to interview on a specific topic, one *Cala Caleño* told me: "You should go talk to him. He is nice, he is very open, even though he is Aymara" (*"Es bien abierto por más Aymara que sea"*). Similar to the situation in this example, differences in character between Afrobolivians and Aymara are often mentioned when trying to account for the distinctions between those groups in Nogalani. Although these differences are stereotyped to a great extent, they nevertheless have considerable impact on how people perceive of the social networks that surround them and use these widely accepted ascriptions as a basis for action in social contexts. Afrobolivians consider themselves to be cheerful *("alegre")* and open-minded *("abierto")* people, who have a more relaxed view on things *("relajado")*. Aymara on the other hand are said to be stubborn *("terco")* and closed-minded *("cerrado")*. From an Aymara point of view, this translates to Afrobolivians being somewhat lavish, not taking things as seriously as they should, whereas they consider themselves to be humble and serious people. As can be observed, the characterizations correspond to each other from both perspectives; the point of observation just determines if they are evaluated positively or negatively. What appears to be cheerfulness from an Afrobolivian perspective is seen as lavish behavior by Aymara. Accordingly, what Afrobolivians interpret as stubborn and closed-minded is for Aymara a positively evaluated seriousness vis-à-vis the imponderability of life.

Besides the *abierto-cerrado* dichotomy, there are other stereotyped ascriptions employed to characterize Afrobolivians and Aymara. A widely held belief – and one that is furthermore maintained by both groups in almost the same way – is that while Afrobolivians are lazy *("flojos")*, Aymara are hard-working *("trabajadores")*. For both groups this in part explains the different levels of economic success within the *comunidad*. In a decisively self-reflexive way, many Afrobolivians see the economic advancements of many Aymara families to be the outcome of their hard work and almost all-encompassing work ethic. I have not gathered sufficient statistical data to corroborate the accuracy of the impression that Aymara in Nogalani are indeed better off economically, but it is a widespread belief among the residents of Cala Cala. On the one hand, they self-critically represent this situation as an outcome of an Aymara virtue that Afrobolivians allegedly lack; on the other hand they relativize the desirability of such a life by pointing out that Aymara are ambitious *("ambiciosos")* to an extent that Afrobolivians do not approve of. Aymara households are of course far from homogenous in economic terms, displaying great variation in the amount of cultivated and uncultivated land, as well as in the amount of work force at their disposal (cf. the ethnographies of *cocalero* communities by Léons 1966; Léons 1998; Pellegrini Calderón 2016; Spedding 1994; Spedding 2004). The same goes for the Afrobolivian population in Cala Cala, where some households are better off than others. Additionally, as Alison Spedding (1994) has pointed out, discourses pitting hard-working individuals against lazy ones are also very common within the Aymara segments of the population and within *comunidades* comprised entirely of Aymara. That is, the topic is not reserved to *comunidades* in which Afrobolivians and Aymara live in close proximity. Spedding attributes the importance of such discourses to the importance of manual labor in the Yungas coca economy on the one hand, and the overarching ideology of equality in the Yungas on the other. She argues that economic inequalities, if they are admitted at all, must be legitimized through linking economic gain to hard work rather than to an unequal distribution of land and exploitative work arrangements (Spedding 1994:204–207). This trope is central to the moral universe of all *cocalero* communities. It is interesting to note, however, that the moral universe that Spedding describes for Aymara *comunidades*, obtains an ethnoracial dimension in *comunidades* with Afrobolivian presence, providing an additional (ethnoracial) frame of reference to discussions of virtue, integrity and standing in the *comunidad*.

A third and very important pair of characterizations remains to be discussed. Aymara are characterized as united *("unidos")* and together with their characterization as *cerrados* this makes it difficult for a non-Aymara individual to become close friends with them. Interestingly, the higher degree of unity that is ascribed to Aymara is framed in clearly ethnic terms. People repeatedly characterized Aymara as exhibiting a stronger sense of ethnic identity, whereas Afrobolivians lack a deeply-rooted commitment to their "race" *("raza")*. Afrobolivians are deemed more resentful *("resentidos")*, often letting personal animosities get in the way of ethnoracial solidarity. This assumption is especially important since it directly touches on the subject of ethnic identification and group cohesion. From the perspective of the people in Cala Cala, it is less a strong commitment to their ethnic identity on part of the Afrobolivians that prevents closer friendship from developing, but rather the relatively strong ethnic community spirit of the Aymara population, which excludes Afrobolivians. From the perspective of many people in Cala Cala, their ethnic solidarity – their "groupness" (Brubaker 2002) in a political sense – has enabled Aymara to furthermore act as a corporate entity in negotiations with the state and has enabled them to gain significant political and economic advantages over the Afrobolivian population. This 'folk' conceptualization of ethnicity and the conclusions that are subsequently drawn from it by many Afrobolivians is of course not unproblematic. On the one hand, the very question of whether an ethnic group can/should be considered a corporate entity – or even a group (cf. Brubaker 2002) – is highly contested. On the other hand, numerous studies have shown that there is a great level of factionalism among different parts of the Aymara population (see Albó [2016] on the question of Aymara factionalism). Yet most of my interlocutors emphasized that – in their view – what distinguishes Afrobolivians from Aymara most clearly is the fact that the former lack a sense of political groupness, while the latter not only exhibit a strong sense of ethnic identity as Aymara, but also manage to appear before the state and society (including Afrobolivians) as a corporate entity capable of achieving their collective goals. The alleged ethnic groupness and solidarity of Aymara from the perspective of Afrobolivians in Cala Cala is also not something I have been able to document in practice. Not only are there numerous conflicts between and within Aymara households, but the moments of greatest cooperation were always marked by solidarity as *comunarios* and *cocaleros* – thus including Afrobolivians – and not as Aymara linked to ethnic politics on the national level. It is very important, however, that from a local perspective, Afrobolivians lack a feeling of groupness in a political sense, explaining at least partially why it has been so difficult for ethno-political entrepreneurs to make the concept of an overarching *pueblo Afroboliviano* a meaningful frame of reference in Cala Cala.

It was only in very particular moments that the described stereotypes and discourses on ethnoracial differences did influence the way people approached each other and interpreted social reality through an ethnoracial lens. Before I address these instances, it is crucial to introduce two developments in Cala Cala: on the one hand, it is important to sketch recent trends towards the monetarization and individualization of the coca economy that transform how the members of the *comunidad Nogalani* relate to each other as *cocaleros*. On the other hand, it is vital to understand how Afrobolivian cultural revitalization and the discourses of plurinationality and recognition are reaching Cala Cala.

Economic individualization and the weakening of the *cocalero* community

One of my main arguments for the importance of viewing Cala Cala as a community beyond *"los Afros de Cala Cala"* is the paramount importance of the coca economy and its quite far-reaching consequences. Taking cues from ethnographies of *cocalero* communities in the Yungas (Léons 1966; Léons 1972; Pellegrini Calderón 2016; Spedding 1994; Spedding 2004), I have made the point that the coca economy and its sociocultural and political repercussions tie the *comunidad* together beyond economic calculation. Very importantly, the coca economy has great influence on how and under what circumstances households relate to each other. I have briefly introduced the practices of *libreada* and the growing importance of cash payments *(jornales)* as new ways of organizing the distribution of labor. Even though the effects of *libreada* and *jornales* on the distribution of wealth and economic benefits within the *comunidad* seem to be limited due to the fact that each household eventually occupies each of the roles in the networks of exchange, it does have a significant impact on group cohesion, solidarity and the importance of the idea of reciprocity. The *libreada*, and especially the growing proliferation of cash payments *(jornales)*, effectively undermine the reciprocal basis of *ayni* exchange networks and introduce more flexibility in the relationships between the households in their exchanges of labor. Those practices are so popular largely because they provide immediate cash returns, which are growing in importance since many daily necessities are no longer produced locally, but have to be bought on the market. While a household could do fairly well without cash income in the past, producing many subsistence crops on its own land and being able to survive until the next coca harvest could be sold on the market, it is now imperative to maintain a steady flow of cash income. Most households have focused on the production of coca almost exclusively, maintaining only a small number of fruit plantations that cannot support the needs of the family in terms of subsistence goods. Before, each household planted *yuca* (manioc) and *walusa* (a type of potato very common in the Yungas) for subsistence, a practice that has almost completely ceased to be of any importance in Cala Cala. Nowadays, the diet consists of rice and noodles that are bought on occasional trips to La Paz, in neighboring towns at the weekly market or in the small shops that have opened in the *comunidad* in recent years. What is more, most families also heavily depend on cash income for transportation (either hiring a car or buying gasoline) and most people have children in the cities that they regularly support with money.

The growing monetarization and liberalization of the coca economy has to some extent undermined the social fabric that had developed based on this economy in the past. It opens up spaces for individualization in economic and social terms and changes the value judgements associated with certain practices. Whereas in the past, working as a *jornalero* was considered a disgrace in the Yungas, I have met a number of individuals who work as *jornaleros* in the Yungas not as a last resort, but as a temporary strategy in order to progress economically and make some cash. Mostly young people work as *jornaleros* before they acquire a plot of land of their own. However, as we have seen in the case of Gerardo described in chapter 3, working as a *jornalero* can also become an option for elderly people who cannot sustain *cocales* of their own anymore. People who work as *jornaleros* enjoy a much greater level of independence since they are neither tied to a specific plot of land, nor face the obligations of *sindicato* membership. They do, in most cases, eventually aspire to acquire their own land and not work as *jornaleros* forever, but it gives them a certain amount of flexibility knowing that they could survive as *jornaleros*.

Yet flexibility and individualization are not the only outcomes of the transformation. The weakening of the ties associated with the expanded coca universe allows for new positionings to arise. These positionings are in part based on alternative collectivities that are emerging along the way. One tendency is the strengthening of the already important role of the household as the fundamental unit of agricultural production, consumption and solidarity. Given the decreasing importance of structures of support and solidarity spanning the whole *comunidad*, many people resort to their more immediate kin for support and identification. Additionally, in the case of the Afrobolivian parts of the population, the idea of solidarity as an ethnic group is also on the rise. In light of the experiences of fragmentation, economic self-interest and declining solidarity as a community of *cocaleros* – most clearly expressed through the logics of economic flexibility and individual/household self-interest in the practice of *libreada* – discourses about uniting as Afrobolivians become increasingly important. This also entails a de-localized perspective on community. Many younger members of the families live in the cities, so relying on kinship ties for financial or moral assistance very commonly means crossing the territorial and social borders of the *comunidad cocalera* localized in the Yungas. The networks spanning to urban areas have only emerged in recent decades, adding a de-territorialized dimension to the notion of a kin-based Afrobolivian community. As I have pointed out, the emerging sense of belonging to a translocal community of relatives from Cala Cala resonates to a certain extent with notions like *el pueblo Afroboliviano*. In my view, the transformation of systems of labor exchange – most notably the declining importance of *ayni* and the growing rationalization of exchange – is leading to a situation where the ethnoracial bases for imagining belonging are increasingly important as ties established through the *cocalero* community become less rigid.

Cultural revitalization and the ID-ological force of the Constitution

Parallel to the weakening of the ties associated with coca cultivation, another development deserves attention when trying to account for the changing meanings of ethnoracial identifications. By way of Afrobolivian political activism, and more recently as an outcome of official recognition, *"Afroboliviano"* has become an increasingly important category of self-identification in political contexts and the source of quite some attention from the media and international development. Although Cala Cala always played a very marginal role within the broader efforts at Afrobolivian cultural revitalization in the 1980s and 1990s, people do recall participating in a meeting held in Coripata in 1993 and some representatives from Cala Cala were also part of a visit by a group of Afrobolivian *saya* performers to the Presidential Palace in 1994. However, *Cala Caleños* generally agree that the revitalization of their *saya* group only gained momentum in 1998 when a team of researchers and *saya* performers associated with the *Centro Pedagógico Simón I. Patiño* came to Cala Cala in order to record *sayas* for a documentation project including a book and a CD (Centro Pedagógico y Cultural "Simón I. Patiño" 1998a). The visiting researchers and activists from La Paz motivated the people not only to partake in the process of documentation, retrieving their *saya* instruments and recording for the CD, but also meant engaging with the discourses on Afrobolivian cultural particularity of the urban movement. The ideas of cultural particularity and discourses on Afrobolivians as an ethnic group (*"etnía"*) and later as a *"pueblo"* championed by urban Afrobolivians fed into local concepts of Afrobolivianity as described in chapter 3. Yet rather than grounding Afrobolivianity in local history and kinship, the notions of Afrobolivianity put forth by the agents of cultural revitalization grounded *"lo Afro"* in culture, and mainly in the practice of *saya*. This not only prompted younger

Cala Caleños to play *saya* but also intensified Cala Cala's contact with the neighboring Afrobolivian communities of Dorado Chico and Coscoma, which were equally drawn into the project of revitalization by urban residents. As many *Cala Caleños* recall, the relationship between the three geographically close communities (Cala Cala, Dorado Chico and Coscoma) was not as close as it had been in earlier decades, even though it was still quite common to marry across community boundaries. The renewed interest in *saya*, and the growing momentum of discourses surrounding Afrobolivian cultural identity, however, sparked a series of opportunities to come into closer contact once more. This was not always conflict free. Roberto remembered *comunarios* from Dorado Chico demanding that Cala Cala give them their *saya* drums. The people from Dorado Chico argued that since they had been performing *saya* together with Cala Cala before and immediately after the Agrarian Reform, it was only fair that their community get at least a share of the instruments that had been salvaged. Cala Cala refused these demands, stressing its independence from Dorado Chico and the exclusive ownership of all instruments left in the community. In Cala Cala, people take considerable pride in emphasizing that Cala Cala is the only community with a proven history of *saya* dating back to before the Agrarian Reform, whereas the other Afrobolivian communities in the Municipio Coripata (Dorado Chico, Coscoma, Chillamani) have only recently founded new *saya* ensembles.

The aftermath of legal recognition: "We have to think about identity"

Legal recognition and political reform in the Yungas have built on those discourses of cultural particularity and have expanded their reach. Whereas the revitalization of *saya* was initially framed as the recuperation of 'tradition' mostly relevant in enhancing the repertoire of Bolivian national folklore, recent efforts at political reform at the municipal level carry the logics of *pueblos indígena originario campesinos* and *el pueblo Afroboliviano* to Cala Cala. One interesting example was a workshop explaining the government project of municipal reform *(autonomías municipales)* to local leaders that I attended in Coripata in 2014.

The workshop was held by two representatives from the *Escuela de Gestión Pública Plurinacional EGPP* (School of Plurinational Public Administration) who had arrived from La Paz that same morning, fairly typical 'experts' sporting the hiking gear many middle class *paceños* (urban La Paz residents) wear when travelling to the Yungas countryside (cf. Goodale 2009 for a similar description of the "experts" roaming the Bolivian countryside on certain occasions). The EGPP is an institution that depends on the *Ministerio de Educación* whose mission is to

> "contribute to the development, construction and consolidation of the new public administration of the Plurinational State through the formation and training of

> public servants, members of social organizations, leaders, and authorities of the *pueblos indígena originario campesinos.*" (www.egpp.gob.bo [30/05/17], my translation)[1]

Accordingly, workshop participants included the members of the *Consejo Municipal* (Municipal Board), the delegates designated by every *comunidad* for the committee, as well as some employees of the mayor's office *(alcaldía)*.

The first half of the workshop was an introduction to Bolivia's recent political history, especially the series of political upheavals that led to Evo Morales' watershed electoral victory in 2005 and the arduous process of constitutional reform from 2006 through to 2009 (for a recent, very well-balanced overview see Postero 2017). Aided by animated Powerpoint presentations, the EGPP representatives introduced the audience to the basics of constitutional theory *("¿Qué es una Constitución?")*, explained the ideological outlines of the *Movimiento al Socialismo (MAS)* reform project and summarized the contents of the New Bolivian Constitution that would become relevant for the second half of the workshop, which would be concerned with putting the constitutional principles into practice while elaborating the *Carta Orgánica Municipal*, a document serving as the legal basis for the municipality's autonomous government. The presentation they gave – including a Powerpoint projection packed with diagrams and bureaucratic terminology – seemed to be fairly standardized and also informed the audience about the ways that the EGPP goes about its task to

> "recover, generate, integrate and transfer intercultural, multilingual and decolonizing knowledge with regard to public administration [...] in order to support the construction of the Plurinational State." (www.egpp.gob.bo [30/05/2017], my translation)[2]

The lecture by the EGPP officials was an interesting mixture of political propaganda, legal theory and community organizing and in many regards exemplifies the intermingling of collective identifications, politics and law that this book is concerned with. Much emphasis was placed on the fact that the New Constitution was based on the values of pluralism, indigenous culture, communitarian organization, and interculturality. Very importantly, and *Cala Caleños* also attributed great value to this when I later asked them what they thought of the lecture, they reminded the audience of the fact that Bolivia was now a Plurinational State fundamentally based on the recognition of different *naciones y pueblos indígena originario campesinos*

1 *"Contribuye al desarrollo, construcción y consolidación de la nueva Gestión Pública del Estado Plurinacional, mediante formación y capacitación de las y los servidores públicos, miembros de organizaciones sociales, líderes, lideresas y autoridades de los pueblos indígena originario campesinos."*

2 *"Recupera, genera, integra y transfiere el conocimiento intercultural, plurilingüe y descolonizador, sobre la Gestión Pública [...] para coadyuvar a la construcción del Estado Plurinacional."*

and the *pueblo Afroboliviano.* By invoking the categories employed by the Constitution, the workshop is thus a striking example of one fundamental aspect described by Jan Hoffmann French as constituting the process of legalizing identities:

> "[T]here is the experience of new or revised ethnoracial identities in the lives of the people who invoke rights based on newly codified legal identities. As the new laws are invoked and the rights associated with or extrapolated from them are put into practice, people begin to revise their self-identifications to some extent as their designation by the larger society is also revised." (French 2009:13)

A decisive moment came when the EGPP representatives urged the assembled community leaders to think of an adequate preamble to their *Carta Orgánica,* one that captures and expresses the identity and essence of Coripata: *"Tenemos que pensar en la identidad"* – "We have to think about identity," was a slogan repeated multiple times during the presentation. Before elaborating specific regulations, they argued, it was important to determine what constitutes "the identity of Coripata and its people." From this essence, they insisted, the contents of the document should emerge. What is more, however, the *Carta Orgánica Municipal* would have the power to transform Coripata, to bring a desired identity to fruition and to produce the society that most aptly fits the essence of the region. As one of the EGPP officials repeatedly emphasized, the New Constitution and thus also the *Cartas Orgánicas Municipales* are supposed to restructure society and relations between people. This restructuring ought to happen according to the logics of the Plurinational Constitution. The relationship between society and social identity on the one hand and law on the other hand that is expressed through these statements is twofold: while law should emanate from social relationships and identities – expressing and representing them – it also has the capacity to change them or even bring social identities into existence (cf. French 2009). With their emphasis on the overarching and seemingly unquestionable salience of 'identity' as the starting point of any further deliberations, they soon placed matters of ethnic identity at center stage. Nobody seemed to question the basic assumption that the most important essence of human beings and any form of sociality is in fact 'identity.' The purpose of the preamble was to capture this essence, crystallize it into written form and proclaim it for all to read. This was one of the first – and by far not the only – instances in which I was reminded of the pervasive presence of identity politics in 21st century Bolivia and the proliferation of what I have described as plurinational ID-ology.

Taking the importance of coca for the region as a starting point, the EGPP speakers sparked the discussion by raising the following rhetorical question: Is there anything else besides coca that is important and should be mentioned in the preamble? After some deliberation, the present community representatives came up with further aspects. "Aymara culture" could be named as a fundamental pillar of Coripata's cultural history, one participant proposed, since most of the inhabitants of the town and neighboring *comunidades* speak Aymara and most families have a history of migration from Aymara communities in the highlands to the Yungas. One Afrobolivian representative from Dorado Chico argued, of course, that "Afrobolivian history and culture" (slavery, African cultures, Afrobolivian cultural expressions) should be part of the document, highlighting not only the notable Afrobolivian presence in Coripata since its foundation but also the fact that Afrobolivians were explicitly mentioned in the Constitution and could thus not be left out of a *Carta Orgánica* that purported to rely on the Constitution and its principles.

It was not only the representation of an Afrobolivian presence in Coripata that was at stake and the participants were less interested in the big picture of decolonization and indigenous emancipation the EGPP tried to conjure. Instead, they focused on concrete issues affecting their access to power, resources and political positions. The crucial point is this: access to political positions and economic funds was framed as corresponding to discrete ethnoracially defined groups, the *pueblos* the Constitution makes so much of. By way of being introduced to the idea of plurinationality and the logics of culturally distinct *naciones* and *pueblos* as the conceptual bases for how the Plurinational State addresses its subjects, participants were inspired to think about themselves and others in terms of ethnoracial differences (as Aymara and *Afroboliviano*), rather than approaching the reform as *cocaleros* that share a collective identification. In plurinational discourse the complementary horizons of community based on identifications such as *"los Afros de Cala Cala"* and *comunarios de Nogalani* are replaced by the collective identifications of *"Afrobolivianos"* and "Aymara." Since they are regarded as different *pueblos* by the Plurinational State, the categories of identification *Afroboliviano* and Aymara are not compatible and their relationship is seen as paradigmatic, i.e. incompatible and mutually exclusive, a matter of "either, or" (Eidson et al. 2017:344–345). Afrobolivians and Aymara were addressed and encouraged to speak to (and about) each other as 'different people' even though they are often neighbors, have known each other for decades, are occasionally related through affinal or ritual kinship ties and share almost their entire political, economic, and religious institutions. Local leaders engaged those discourses, for example, when referring to their struggle for the direct participation of 'their people' in order to represent 'their interests' and protect 'their culture and identity.' The local repercussions of this particular project (municipal autonomy) became apparent to me just a few days later: As I arrived in Cala Cala for the first time (recall the episode I described in chapter 1), I met Juan Angola Maconde breathlessly collecting signatures to press for direct representation of Afrobolivians on the municipal board. Juan Angola was the representative for the *comunidad* Dorado Chico in the municipal reform project and very practically carried the logics of the workshops to local communities, highlighting the importance of rallying around ethnoracial identification behind the category *Afroboliviano* to achieve greater political influence within the municipality.[3]

Through projects like those described above – recording *saya* and restructuring municipal politics along ethnoracial identifications – being Afrobolivian has become an increasingly important factor when people speak about their sense of identity, belonging, community and political participation. In what remains of this chapter, I will discuss two concrete examples from Cala Cala where tangible consequences of plurinational ID-ology emerge in local settings.

The *sindicato* as an "Aymara affair"

Although the *sindicato* in *comunidades cocaleras* is often considered 'neutral' in ethnic terms and as guided mostly by the interests of a territorially and economically defined collective, many comments from Cala Cala suggest that we ought to reconsider this assumption. Although the *sindicato* is not structured according to or usually represented as a space that follows the logics of ethnoracial categorization, the workings and happenings within the *sindicato* are nevertheless increasingly interpreted under these premises from an Afrobolivian perspective. What is at stake is the very representation of the *sindicato* as a context that is not shaped by ethnoracial categorizations. From an Afrobolivian viewpoint, the Aymara majority in the *sindicato* is normalized to an extent that makes the *sindicato* look neutral in ethnic terms, when in fact it is an institution shaped mainly by Aymara concerns excluding specifically Afrobolivian sensitivities and demands. When making those claims, Afrobolivians resort to the ethnoracial stereotypes described above. Similar attitudes have been described by William Léons in his ethnography of the Sud Yungas town Chicaloma (Léons 1972). According to Léons, Afrobolivians there sought political participation not through the *sindicato* structure that they perceived as being "an Indian affair" but through the pursuit of positions in the municipal government. Léons explains this in part with reference to the language barrier – *sindicato* meetings were often held in Aymara – but also with a more generalized rejection of indigenous ways of organizing on the part of Afrobolivians. Instead of participating in the *sindicato*, Afrobolivians in Chicaloma organized in so-called

3 Juan Angola Maconde, one of the most well informed researchers and experts on Yungas society, details hybrid Afro-indigenous cultural practices in a variety of publications and has pointed out the existence of an *Afro-mestizo* culture in urban areas. Both these concepts run counter to the essentialist pigeonhole logics of the Plurinational Constitution. Yet, as a strategy, he embraces these logics, introduces them to his *comunidad* and motivates others to mobilize around an Afrobolivian identity conceived of in essentialist terms as something other than *cocalero* or Aymara identity and 'culture,' not something that is commonly *Yungueño* (see also my remarks on the invisibility of Afro-Aymaras in chapter 6).

juntas (working groups). In recent years, these parallel Afrobolivian and Aymara institutions seem to have disappeared in Chicaloma, as Charles Sturtevant's (2013) ethnography of the town suggests. In Cala Cala, nobody mentioned parallel institutions and according to my interlocutors *"los Afros de Cala Cala"* have always been engaged in the *sindicato*. Yet people occasionally expressed a feeling of being left out of complete participation in the *sindicato*. Many Afrobolivians framed this problem of participation in explicitly ethnoracial terms and attributed the problems in the *sindicato* to what they considered a specific Aymara 'mentality' and their exclusion as racial discrimination.

A frequent topic of conversation, therefore, involved the question of whether close cooperation or a certain distance should be the guiding principle in negotiating relations between Nogalani and Cala Cala. The households in Cala Cala that I spent most time in represent somewhat different opinions on that question. Whereas Roberto maintains a position that is very critical of Cala Cala's close association with Nogalani, Víctor, a highly respected individual in the *comunidad* and one of the leaders of the Afrobolivian community, stresses the importance of cooperation. They also differ in their opinions on the type of relationship Cala Cala and Nogalani actually maintain. Roberto interprets the relationship with Nogalani as one of dependence (also due to racial discrimination) that Cala Cala has to overcome, whereas Víctor stresses the strategic importance of joining forces with the significantly bigger Nogalani and points out the historical continuities, the common struggle of both communities and the closely intertwined economies of the two parts of the *comunidad*.

The relation between Cala Cala and Nogalani in formal and institutionalized contexts was discussed in Cala Cala in the context of two initially unrelated but eventually intertwined developments. On the one hand, the *sindicato* leaders of Nogalani approached Cala Cala residents with the idea of forming a separate *sindicato campesino* for Cala Cala. The motivation behind this idea was the fact that Nogalani leaders aspire to claim the status of a *subcentral* (a federation of local *sindicatos*), which is only possible if a certain number of local *sindicatos* are affiliated. Therefore, splitting the *sindicato* of Nogalani into smaller parts (Cala Cala, Bella Vista and Nogalani) would enable its leaders to formally form a *subcentral* and thus enhance their power in negotiations with institutions higher up in the hierarchy of unions, the municipal government and other state institutions. From the perspective of leaders in Nogalani, the initiative was motivated by strategic considerations and had nothing to do with ethnoracial differences. In Cala Cala, however, the proposal was debated from a different perspective: At about the same time as *Cala Caleños* were approached by leaders from Nogalani with plans to split up the *sindicato*, Cala Cala was also in the process of participating in a Ministry of Tourism (*Viceministerio de Turismo)* program in order to benefit from a national project that aimed at fostering community tourism (see chapter 10). Cala Cala therefore had founded an

Asociación de Turismo in order to coordinate the negotiations with the representatives of the ministry and the funding party, the Interamerican Development Bank (IDB). The efforts of the *Viceministerio de Turismo* were based on singling out Cala Cala as an 'Afrobolivian community.' The parallel developments catapulted debates on Cala Cala's status as a separate entity to center stage. What is more, due to the explicitly ethnic dimension of the tourism project, they also stirred up discussions of Cala Cala's status as an 'Afrobolivian' community and the consequences this assertion should have for the relationship with Nogalani. Most hotly debated among *Cala Caleños* was the question of whether people from Nogalani – who had expressed interest in participating in the tourism project – should be allowed to be members of the *Asociación de Turismo* and on what terms. Many argued that they shouldn't, based on the fact that they were not Afrobolivian and were thus not qualified to participate in the realization of a project based on 'Afrobolivian culture.' Others seconded that position by pointing out that people from Nogalani had only become interested in 'Afrobolivian culture' after learning that money could be made from it. Other voices stressed the vital importance of cooperation not only because of strategic calculations, but also because of the long history of a shared *sindicato*, and they argued the case for the participation of people from Nogalani. Yet another faction supported a somewhat ambiguous position. They argued that if Nogalani's leaders got the impression that Cala Cala's residents would exclude them from the tourism project based on ethnic differences, they would never let Cala Cala form their own *sindicato* for fear of further weakening their position vis-à-vis Cala Cala – Nogalani's strategic intentions regarding becoming a *subcentral* notwithstanding. All this shows that the conceptual basis (i.e. which horizon of community is foregrounded) of formal political organization is by no means uncontested. In part due to the new salience of the category *Afroboliviano* (expressed through interest in developing Afrobolivian community tourism), but also because of strategic maneuvers by Nogalani's leaders that were based on political and economic calculations, the question of what horizon of community determines the make-up of formal organization is highly contested. Beyond the realm of institutionalized relationships, the relationship between Cala Cala and Nogalani, Afrobolivians and Aymara, and different horizons of community was debated in terms of local history.

Reinterpreting history and inequality through an Afrobolivian lens

In my earlier account of *Todos Santos*, as well as in my description of the *velorio* for a deceased community member, I emphasized the importance of common practices of the *comunidad cocalera* and related discourses on shared history, tradition and values that encompass the whole *comunidad*, not only Cala Cala explicitly. However, there is also an increasingly important 'Afrobolivian side' to history that people do put forth when referring to their understanding of the present with relation to the past. I have discussed the importance of tracing one's family back to what are considered the original inhabitants of Cala Cala, and have also pointed out the importance this has for claims to land, as well as for a local history. The identification of *"los Afros de Cala Cala,"* however, has undergone decisive transformations. This shift becomes apparent when comparing Gerardo Angola's comments on the meanings of *"lo Afro"* for his generation (roughly people born in the 1940s and 1950s), with the opinions expressed by people in the context of the reorganization of the *sindicato* and the tourism project. Not only is Afrobolivianity increasingly considered a category of cultural and ethnic difference, it is also summoned to explain a much wider range of phenomena. At one occasion, during a gathering of the tourism association in Cala Cala (see chapter 10), some Afrobolivian inhabitants of Cala Cala started discussing the inequalities with regard to land tenure in the *comunidad.* Interestingly, they framed this in terms of racism. They argued that the fact that Aymara from Nogalani *("los de arriba")* owned land within 'their jurisdiction' (i.e. the territory associated with Cala Cala), whereas *Afrobolivianos* from Cala Cala do not own parcels of land within the territory of Nogalani, was clearly a form of racial discrimination. Although there are various possible explanations for this situation, during the discussion people exclusively referred to ethnoracial distinctions and heavily relied on ethnoracial stereotypes. As the debates went on, they took a turn towards even more generalized characteristics of inter-ethnic relations as seen from the perspective of Cala Cala. In the end, people did not simply debate a concrete case of land distribution (as is the case when tracing specific parts of land to specific ancestors) but debated inter-ethnic relations more generally. The participants of the meeting reached the conclusion that "they" *("ellos," "los Aymaras")* had "always" *("siempre")* gotten the better of Afrobolivians and that Afrobolivians had been victims of discrimination.

Such ethnoracial interpretations of past and present leave unmentioned a variety of factors that might support an explanation completely devoid of any ethnoracial content (or at least one that complicates the clear-cut designations). First of all, it is not 'all of them,' but only a few Aymara from Nogalani that do in fact own land in Cala Cala. Secondly, this version of the story leaves out the important fact that Cala Cala had been incorporated into the jurisdiction of the *hacienda Nogalani* even before the revolution, being absorbed by a much bigger *hacienda* and administratively integrated into its structures on unequal terms. It ignores the complexity of the year-long negotiations between the institutions introduced by the Revolutionary Government, the landowners, *hacienda peones*, village and *sindicato* authorities and a variety of other actors that shaped the land reform process (for an overview of the very heterogeneous outcomes of the Agrarian Reform on land distribution in the Yungas see Léons 1967; and the case studies in McEwen 1975). Finally, representing *"los de arriba"* as usurpers of Cala Cala's land and Afrobolivians as victims masks the fact that – according to *hacienda* documents – both Aymara and Afrobolivians appropriated land that legally belonged to the patron even after the Agrarian Reform. With this in mind, the straightforward 'ethnoracial' view on history becomes increasingly volatile. Yet this way of thinking about the past is on the rise in assessing the community's history. Just as Jan Hoffman French (French 2009:16) has observed in Brazil, in the process of legalizing identities, not only can present-day social relations be re-interpreted and re-shaped, but past developments and struggles can also acquire new meaning.

Entangled horizons of community in Cala Cala

As I have argued throughout the preceding chapters, in Cala Cala there are different horizons of community and collective identification. In chapter 3, I introduced a first horizon that coalesces in the collective identification *"los Afros de Cala Cala"*. Belonging to *"los Afros de Cala Cala"* is fundamentally based on kinship and local origins. Yet, although discourses on *"los Afros de Cala Cala"* are mostly local in scope and heavily rely on references to specific individuals *("los abuelos Afros")*, the collectivity it refers to transcends the locality and includes Afrobolivian kin living in different urban centers of the country. References to *"los Afros de Cala Cala"* are important aspects when accounting for a local history as a separate community and the contemporary relationships between households and families in Cala Cala. They are furthermore crucial – and therefore conspicuously on the rise in certain contexts – in efforts to latch onto emerging plurinational discourses on culture and identity as part of the *pueblo Afroboliviano*.

In chapter 4, I discussed a second horizon of community – what I have referred to as *la comunidad cocalera Nogalani* of which Cala Cala is a part. Rooted mainly in *sindicato* organization and economic cooperation through coca production, belonging to *la comunidad cocalera* is achieved through specific practices, namely the emic concept of *cumplir función social* (performing a social function) and participation in systems of labor exchange. For the practices associated with performing a social function, as well as for arrangements concerning the distribution of labor, collective ethnoracial identifications are secondary. Moreover, there is a strong sense of regional identity and shared traditions as *cocaleros Yungueños* within the *comunidad* that serves as a discursive backdrop for strong collective identification as *comunarios*. Finally, being a *cocalero* is also a political identity, crucial for the mass mobilizations of *Yungueños* over several decades.

In Cala Cala, the two horizons are integrated mostly in a non-conflictual manner. I have proposed considering them as complementary ways of conceptualizing and organizing community, sameness and difference and not as conflicting frames of reference for collective identification. Their complementarity stems mostly from the fact that each of the horizons functions according to its own set of logics. Therefore, it is possible for individuals from Cala Cala, as well as for Cala Cala as a whole, to situationally switch between horizons of community and even to express commitment to Afrobolivian identity and to *comunario* identity simultaneously. The relationship between identification as *comunario* and as *Afroboliviano* only becomes problematic in specific contexts. These contexts are marked by processes of "re-definition of categories of identification" (Eidson et al. 2017:342). In the concrete context, the local meanings of being *Afro* are enhanced with the plurinational logic of *el pueblo Afroboliviano* and, at the same time, the hitherto non-ethnic categorization *comunario* is increasingly associated with the ethnic categorization Aymara, for example by viewing the *sindicato* as an 'Aymara affair.' Through this re-definition of both *Afro* and *comunario* identifications, complementary collective identifications suddenly appear as mutually exclusive, making variable identifications increasingly complicated. Although I have not gathered sufficient systematic data on this subject among Aymara households, my general impression, corroborated by Pellegrini Calderón (2016) and Spedding (2009), is that this is mostly relevant from an Afrobolivian perspective. Aymara in the Yungas deploy plurinational ID-ology to a much lesser extent and their understanding of *comunario* remains essentially inclusive and rooted in "performing a social function." For Afrobolivians, on the other hand, *comunario* is increasingly associated with Aymara and their response is to rally more strongly around the ethnoracial identification *Afroboliviano*. This tendency is furthermore strengthened by the experience of weakening reciprocal ties as a *comunidad cocalera*.

Under those circumstances stereotyped characterizations of ethnoracial 'others' emerge as a factor that influences certain aspects of institutionalized relationships between Afrobolivians and Aymara. It furthermore leads to the reinterpretation of certain aspects of local history and social inequality as rooted in ethnoracial differences. In most day-to-day social interactions, an individual's ethnoracial identity is seldom the reason for open conflict and generalized mistrust, and the overarching identification as *comunarios de Nogalani*, *cocaleros* and *Yungueños* provides sufficient grounds for cooperation and solidarity. Yet, and given the fact that ethnic categorizations play such a fundamental role in shaping the emerging political practices of the Plurinational State, hitherto subtle distinctions become increasingly salient and begin to shape the way people interpret and – as a consequence of this interpretation – orient their social relationships with each other.

This is not to say that previously stable categories and collective identifications are only now being transformed. As I have shown, identification as *Afros*, as well as identification as *comunarios* must be seen as processual. From the narratives I have collected in Cala Cala – recall my remarks on the life of Gerardo Angola – as well as through the scarce historical records and the *hacienda* documents, it is furthermore possible to trace various shifts and show how ethnoracial differentiations and their social consequences have been in constant flux. On the one hand, the Afrobolivian population was highly endogamous until the middle of the 20th century. Afrobolivians from various *haciendas* maintained close-knit networks of integration through marriage across communities. With the abolition of the *hacienda* and the formation of *comunidades* and *sindicatos*, the ties between dispersed Afrobolivian parts of the Yungas population weakened and Afrobolivians developed common institutions and practices with Aymara in *comunidades cocaleras*. What is more, the years after the revolution in 1952 were also the time when the Bolivian central government introduced a large-scale educational reform in the countryside, propagating the use of Spanish, national citizenship and the ideal of cultural *mestizaje* as Bolivia's way into the future: *Indios* and Afrobolivians were to become *campesinos* and citizens, and ethnoracial labels lost traction in political discourse for a while. From the perspective of most of Cala Cala's residents, the period after the revolution and land reform was marked by the declining importance of a collective identification as *Afros* and a 'loss' of Afrobolivian culture. Important factors were the assimilationist policies of the educational reform, political and economic integration with the Aymara majority, as well as massive migration and dispersion of the Afrobolivian population throughout the country. It was only in the 1990s, after a constitutional reform and a multicultural law of education had been passed, that the tides began to turn. Afrobolivians in Cala Cala began engaging with the ideas of cultural diversity, multiculturalism and Afrobolivian mobilization through their contact with urban migrants. This engagement reshaped the way Afrobolivian culture was conceived of, articulated and discursively framed. In 2018, yet another constitutional reform later, Afrobolivians are negotiating their place in plurinational Bolivia.

Making sense of the changes with regard to what it means to be *Afro* in Cala Cala is, however, not only related to plurinational ID-ology. Although many state-sponsored campaigns and many contexts of Afrobolivian engagement with the state, the development industry and wider society suggest that ethnicity and collective racialized identity are the main frames of reference and also the routes to a vision of Bolivia's future, analyzing Cala Cala's situation points to the importance of other interpretations. For example, discourses of cultural particularity and the growing political salience of ethnoracial identifications go hand in hand with increasing rates of interethnic marriage. Ever more localized definitions of identity and belonging cannot mask massive migration and the dispersal of Afrobolivians from Cala Cala. Contrary to the ubiquitous talk of salvaging 'genuine local culture,' Cala Cala has furthermore entered an age of unprecedented exposure to globalized mass media and communication, as not only radio and television, but also mobile phones and internet access have reached the community. It is thus vital to not lose track of a great range of multidirectional processes that shape the way people make sense of their place in history and society, as well as the way they position themselves vis-à-vis topics of community, diversity and difference.

In order to contextualize Cala Cala's particularities, the following chapters will widen the scope of analysis to include discourses on Afrobolivianity circulating nationally in political, legal and mass media contexts.

Chapter 6: What It Means to Be *Afro*

Afrobolivianity, Indigeneity and the African Diaspora in Bolivia

In the preceding chapters, I have examined the meaning of the emic categorization *"los Afros de Cala Cala"* and have analyzed the relationship of this particular construct with other possible frames of reference for collective identification. As I have shown in chapter 5, local notions of what it means to be *"Afro,"* as well as notions of being *comunario* are undergoing important changes. On the one hand, the transformation of collective identifications in Cala Cala is shaped by local particularities such as the history and demography of Cala Cala and Nogalani, as well as by regional developments such as the changing dynamics of the coca economy. On the other hand, however, there are a number of developments that cannot be explained from the local perspective alone, but require a broadened conceptual focus. The workshop I described towards the end of chapter 5 is a clear example of this. In such contexts, specific discursive approaches to 'identity' in general and to Afrobolivianity and indigeneity in particular are experienced and negotiated.

In the following chapter, I approach Afrobolivianity as an articulation that is constantly "made, unmade, and remade" (Clifford 2013:61–62). Following Eduardo Restrepo's perspective on blackness in Colombia, my discussion of Afrobolivianity "does not start with the assumption of historical constants, anthropological universals or generalizations that would give a 'master coherence'" to Afrobolivianity (Restrepo 2008:16). What I will flesh out are "contingent articulations" of Afrobolivianity marked by "contradictory trends" (Clifford 2013:30) and how these articulations are shaped by their conceptual location in the "fraught borderland between 'indigenous' and 'diasporic' affiliations and identities" (Clifford 2013:52).

Following Shane Greene's approach to Afro-indigenous multiculturalisms, I argue that we need to take into account and interrogate the ramifications of the fact that "contemporary states project a potential, if not in practice an actual, ethnocultural and racial equivalence between Afro-descendent and indigenous populations in the region." (Greene 2007a:329). Such an approach furthermore presses us to "think beyond the apparent dichotomy of the indigenous as an essentially immovable (rooted) identity and the African diasporic as an essentially movable (uprooted/routed) identity" (Greene 2007a:333). Analyzing the interplay of indigenous and diasporic affiliations and identifications with regard to Afrobolivianity means also discussing the relationship between race and ethnicity in Latin America and how they relate to indigenous people and Afrobolivians respectively (Wade 2010). I aim at complicating the often-cited picture of black race and Indian ethnicity in Latin America, taking cues from various contributions that have shown the fragility of the exclusive association of *indígenas* with ethnicity and Afro-Latin Americans with race in Latin America (Anderson 2009; Canessa 2012c; Greene 2009; O'Toole 2012; Wade 1999; Wade 2013; Weismantel 2001). As will become clear through the ethnographic examples in this chapter, racialized images of Afrobolivianity coexist with notions of a culturally defined Afrobolivian ethnicity.

"Yo soy doble Afro-indígena, pero me siento afro"

The close entanglements of Afrobolivianity with indigeneity, as well as with matters of culture, race and ethnicity were neatly expressed in a comment during the biannual *Consejo Nacional Afroboliviano (CONAFRO)* congress held in La Paz in September 2014 where I participated in the proceedings of a working group on Afrobolivian language *(la lengua Afro[boliviana])*. The working group's task was to elaborate an overview of the status quo concerning the use and distribution of *la lengua afro,* a creole variant of Spanish that developed in the Bolivian Yungas (for details see Lipski 2008; Perez 2015; and Sessarego 2014). One participant of the roundtable was a woman of about fifty years of age from the Sud Yungas province. When she was asked by the CONAFRO member who coordinated the working group to share her knowledge of the *lengua afro* and comment on her experiences related to its use – and Afrobolivian 'culture' more generally – she said that she did not have any knowledge of the language, nor recall any 'cultural element' *(elemento cultural)* that she considered valuable for the discussion. She went on to say: *"Yo soy doble Afro-indígena, pero me siento Afro. He vivido con los indígenas toda mi vida y casi no he podido captarme con mi raza"* ("I am double Afro-indigenous, but I feel *Afro*. I have lived among indigenous people for all my life and have almost not been able to get in touch with my race").

The particular individual quoted above, of course, could have meant any number of things with her statement and I was at that moment unable to ask her for further details, and therefore it is impossible to know which of the following interpretations would have fitted her intentions best. But let us consider the options: By speaking of herself as *"doble Afro-indígena"* she introduces two basic and well known categories of social differentiation in Latin America – blackness and indigeneity – in joint fashion. From her statement alone, it is hard to discern how she conceptualizes the relationship between the two categories and also what exactly she means by blackness *(Afro)* and what by indigeneity *(indígena)*. We can assume from the context – her statement was part of her response to being asked to contribute knowledge on language and 'culture' – that both blackness and indigeneity have something to do with those topics for her.[1] We can furthermore assume that language and 'culture' are not all there is to blackness (and presumably also indigeneity), otherwise it would not be possible to be *Afro-indígena* without any knowledge of *Afro* language and/or 'culture.' The only hint that she gives in her statement is her reference to race towards the end of the quote *("[...] no he podido captarme con mi raza")*, which, in turn, leaves it open what she means by *"raza"* (see below).

As far as the relationship between *Afro* and *indígena* goes, her assertion that she is *"doble Afro-indígena"* could be interpreted as referring to a creolized/hybrid/mixed category that blends blackness and indigeneity racially (similar to the colonial term *zambo* [black/indigenous mixture]) and/or culturally; or she considers the possibility of being both *Afro* and *indígena* at the same time or interchangeably. Blackness and indigeneity would thus remain separate modes of identification at a conceptual level; they could, however, become relevant for one and the same individual at different times or in different contexts. Related to the question of context, one final aspect I want to briefly highlight is the juxtaposition of being *("soy Afro-indígena")* and feeling *("me siento Afro")*. Her reference to being Afro-indigenous could be interpreted as implying that this is stable and unchangeable, whereas feeling *Afro* is more a matter of context, disposition and maybe even choice.[2] From the above statement alone, this interpretation would be fairly courageous, yet it fits neatly with countless more explicit statements that exhibit the same structure (being vs. feeling or something more indeterminate). One young Afrobolivian man I know very well and have spent a lot of time with in the last few years, for example, once introduced himself to an audience of university students with the words: *"Soy zambo, mezcla, pero me identifico como Afrodescendiente"* ("I am *zambo*, mixture, but I identify as Afrodescendant"). Here, a mixed racial identity *(zambo)* is juxtaposed with a conscious self-positioning "as Afrodescendant." This is all the more telling since *Afrodescendiente* (even more than *Afro[boliviano]*) is the denomination most clearly associated with political discourse and diasporic identity politics. With this in mind, and considering that the statement we're concerned with was directed at a CONAFRO representative at an official political event clearly framed as *"Afro,"* I argue that *"feeling Afro"* here refers to a rather conscious act of self-positioning.

1 That would still leave us with the questions of what concepts of 'culture' might be relevant here. Her usage of the term *"elementos culturales"* points in a rather specific direction, though (see my remarks in chapter 7).

2 This interpretation put aside the rather philosophical question of whether "being" can be considered a more stable state than "feeling."

This short statement thus leads the way to a series of questions that this chapter is concerned with. By closely examining possible interpretations of the hyphenated denomination *Afro-indígena* and by contextualizing the references to race *("raza")* and culture *("cultura")* in the above-quoted statement, I aim to shed light on the articulation of Afrobolivianity. As Mark Anderson (Anderson 2007:407) reminds us:

> "When attempting to assess emerging paradigms of Afro-Indigenous multiculturalism, we need to pay particular attention to multiple, shifting meanings of the relational categories separated by the hyphen. Ultimately, we should critically analyze the way that hyphen marks similarities and differences, disjunctions and articulations, and leave open the possibility that the terms modify each other so that we might speak of 'indigenous blackness' or 'Afroindigeneity'."

Following this lead, I first will discuss Afrobolivianity in relation to indigeneity, as well as in relation to the African Diaspora. I will then address the relationship between race and ethnicity in Latin America (Wade 2010), as well as the location of Afrobolivianity in the wider context of Bolivia's "political economies of identity" (Healy and Paulson 2000). In my discussion of a series of ethnographic vignettes, I will show that Afrobolivianity cannot be understood without taking into consideration discourses on phenotype, racial purity and admixture. *Mestizaje* – racial and cultural mixture – as both an ideology and a "lived experience" (Wade 2005) is an important contextual reference for the articulation of Afrobolivianity and the contradictions engendered by the "Longue Durée of Racial Fixity and the Transformative Conjunctures of Racial Blending" (Whitten 2007) have to be taken into account. This is true even in light of repeated declarations by varying Afrobolivian organizations and individuals that they strive for an exclusively cultural understanding of Afrobolivianity. Contrary to the widely repeated narrative that *"El negro no es un color, es una saya"* ("Black is not a color, it is a *saya* [culture]") (Mendoza Salazar 1992), I will show the ongoing importance of phenotypical appearance and racial ancestry that lie at the core of Afrobolivian discourses on identity.

Articulating Afrobolivianity: *"lo Afro"* and *"lo indígena"* in Bolivia

In processes of self-identification and categorization, certain images of Afrobolivianity and indigeneity are negotiated and employed as references. These images of blackness stem from a variety of sources and differ greatly in terms of content and the evaluation of Afrobolivians' 'culture.' They are furthermore deployed by a variety of actors in different circumstances and with more or less conscious and/or strategic calculations. As Sara Busdiecker (2007:230f) rightfully observes, the talk of invisibility and the constant claim by Afrobolivians that they have been neglected altogether by the state, the media and the academy has served to obscure a variety of images and representations of black people and blackness circulating in Bolivia, albeit, admittedly, somewhat beneath the surface (Busdiecker 2003). These representations and images of blackness circulate in the realms of folklore (and studies thereof), music, literature (scholarly and fictional), media (newspapers, magazines and television, in recent times also the internet) and in state discourse. By now, international political fora, declarations and campaigns – most recently for example the United Nations International Year (2011) and International Decade for People of African Descent (2015-2024) also play a significant role.[3] Moreover, images of blackness as a part of globalized consumer culture have entered Bolivian public imagination and have become an important reference point, particularly, but not only, for Afrobolivians.

Apart from scholarly circles and political activists, Bolivian people's knowledge about Afrobolivians and what they associate with them is fairly limited and can be grouped roughly around the topics of slavery, Africa, *saya*, and the Yungas.[4] Most people know that there were black slaves originating from Africa in Bolivia and some are able to reproduce the well-known narrative of how those slaves were brought to work in the mines of Potosí, how they could not stand the climate and were therefore taken to the Yungas, which is where they live today. In the eyes of most Bolivians, Afrobolivian culture is essentially *saya*, a dance that most Bolivians know from the important folkloric parades *(entradas)* throughout the country (*Carnaval* in Oruro, *Urkupiña* in Cochabamba and *Gran Poder* in La Paz) and from the media. Through its close association with *saya*, Afrobolivian culture is often reduced to folkloric expressions and happy and colorful dance performances attaining a festive character, conveying a joyful, happy and non-conflictual image. Finally, through its association with Africa, Afrobolivianity is represented as something foreign, culturally "out of place" in Bolivia (Busdiecker 2009a), even though the Afrobolivian presence in the country dates back to the earliest days of the colony. Beyond these basics, there is astonishingly little information regarding Afrobolivians that circulates in non-academic, non-specialist circles in Bolivia. Only occasionally do people offer a gendered perspective on blackness related to sexuality, remarking that having sex with a black woman is believed to have curative effects on rheumatism.[5] Finally, black people are often considered to be somehow 'good luck,' a belief that is most vividly expressed in a custom called "*suerte negrito*": when

3 See http://www.un.org/en/events/africandescentdecade/ [11/07/2017]

4 This is true even of people with university degrees and high levels of education. In the years since I started working with Afrobolivians, I have had countless conversations with Bolivians from all sectors of society, age groups, educational backgrounds, regions and political positions. There are vast differences with regard to many things, but their views on blackness are strikingly similar.

5 Spedding (1995:326) explains this with the fact that the color black is thought to have certain characteristics in Andean curative rituals that point in this direction.

seeing a black person on the street, people pinch each other and exclaim *"suerte negrito"* (lit.: lucky little black) for good luck.

Against the backdrop of those notions of Afrobolivianity, Afrobolivians themselves develop a very specific notion of Afrobolivianity that draws inspiration from "the language of global indigeneity" (Canessa 2012c:3; cf. Niezen 2003), as well as from discourses on diasporic blackness. In the next sections, I will outline those seemingly contradictory inspirations and show how they are employed in the articulation of Afrobolivianity.

Afrobolivians as the people of the Yungas

When expressing what it means to be *"Afro,"* many Afrobolivians at first basically resort to the same set of references and associations as non-black Bolivians. When asked specifically about what it is important to know about blackness in Bolivia culturally or historically, Afrobolivians most readily mention slavery, *saya* and the Yungas. Yet they add some specific elements and group them together in a particular fashion. They build on established and widely known associations of Afrobolivians with *saya* in order to highlight the cultural dimension of Afrobolivianity. However, Afrobolivians usually cite additional '*elementos culturales*' pertaining to Afroblivians beyond *saya,* most commonly other dance genres *(semba, baile de tierra),* the funeral rite *mauchi,* and the Afrobolivian monarchy (*el Rey Afroboliviano,* see chapter 7). They cite those elements to highlight the importance of Afrobolivian culture beyond *saya* in order to counteract the equation of Afrobolivian culture with folklore. More recently – and especially among urban residents engaged with CONAFRO and other organizations – the list has been enhanced to include *la lengua afro* (Afrobolivian Spanish), even though its status as a language remains contested, its history unclear and it has fallen out of use in all Afrobolivian communities (for different views in the debate on Afrobolivian Spanish see Lipski 2008; Pérez Inofuentes 2015; Sessarego 2011a). Afrobolivians also discursively elaborate the widespread association of Afrobolivianity with the Yungas. They point out the deep historical roots of Afrobolivian settlement in the Yungas, position the region as the sole origin of migratory trajectories and highlight how networks of kinship fundamentally tie all Afrobolivians to specific places in the Yungas up to the present (see chapter 3). Through such discursive maneuvers, the Yungas are increasingly framed as Afrobolivian "ancestral territory" *("territorio ancestral")* a terminology reminiscent of indigenous politics in Bolivia and elsewhere. Moreover, this invocation of the Yungas also builds on the discourses of Afrobolivian autochthony that I have described in chapter 3 as an important element of the notion of *"los Afros de Cala Cala"* as the original inhabitants of the *comunidad* (as opposed to "the people from the *altiplano*" – *"los del altiplano"*). By referring to factual or putative individual and collective origins in specific geographical locations, Afrobolivians, as Sara Busdiecker (2009a) has also comprehensively argued, construct and represent the Yungas as the place "where blackness resides." The Yungas thus are not only considered the "natural place" of blackness in Bolivia, but are also represented as the origin of Afrobolivian culture and collective identity: Afrobolivians are the "people of the Yungas" (Templeman 1998) and the Yungas is "the cradle of Afrobolivian culture." Those references to a specific place (the Yungas) and the rootedness of Afrobolivians in this particular place are very important in political discourse in order to substantiate claims that they are a *pueblo* similar to indigenous people, as I will detail in chapter 9. Yet references to distinctive cultural features *(saya, mauchi)* that are furthermore related to the collective spatial origins of Afrobolivians in a specific territory are an important aspect of the everyday articulations of Afrobolivianity as well. Additionally, the emerging references to linguistic particularity *(la lengua Afro)*, and specific Afrobolivian institutions *(el Rey Afroboliviano)* make the parallels to "the language of global indigeneity" (Canessa 2012c:3) even more striking.

This specific articulation of Afrobolivianity is not uncontested, nor should it be understood as constituting an exclusive frame of reference. As I have shown in my discussion of Cala Cala, the salience of 'cultural elements' for defining what it means to be *Afro* is not as straightforward as those discourses suggest. The generic references to the Yungas as the origin of a shared sense of identity and culture also overshadow the decidedly local focus of the collective identification *"los Afros de Cala Cala"* and the emphasis on Afrobolivian distinctiveness obscures the importance of shared cultural practices within the *comunidad cocalera*. What is more, the language of indigeneity is not the only inspiration shaping the contemporary articulation of Afrobolivianity. As will become clear in the next section, references to the African Diaspora are equally important when trying to make sense of what it means to be *"Afro"* in Bolivia.

Afrobolivians as part of the regional and global diaspora

In the introduction to the Afrobolivian *"currículo regionalizado"* (regionalized curriculum for public schools) authored by representatives of CEPA, ILC-AFRO and CONAFRO and published by the Ministry of Education *(Ministerio de Educación)*, this document is presented as an important step on the path towards an education that respects Afrobolivian students' "identity with cultural values and principles of their own."[6] The following paragraph of the document deals with the sources of these values and principles, referring to *"Afros"* and *"Afrodescendientes"* interchangeably and citing examples from different contexts and times, among others: Nelson Mandela, Frantz Fanon, Martin Luther King, Touissant Lubertu, Mohamad Ali, Mike Tyson, Pelé, Usain Bolt, Bob Marley, and Celia Cruz. Only after that does the document

6 *"Identidad con valores y principios culturales propios."*

mention "local values and contributions" *("valores y aportes locales")* and cite examples of Afrobolivian participation in the rebellion of Tupac Katari in 1781, in specific uprisings in the context of the Bolivian independence movement and in the Chaco War between Bolivia and Paraguay in the 1930s. It goes on to detail Afrobolivian contributions to agriculture, national cuisine, music, dance and soccer.

While we have to keep in mind that this document represents the outcome of a long process of negotiation and also a very particular perspective on Afrobolivianity (see chapter 7 on the elaboration of the curriculum), it is still striking to note the prominent place references to African, African-American and Afro-Latin American personalities occupy in this document, being placed even before references to well-known Afrobolivian personalities and contributions. This is particularly striking when compared to a short episode that Sara Busdiecker reports from her early days of fieldwork at the end of the 1990s. It should alert us to the significant changes in how people think and talk about blackness in Bolivia. Busdiecker reports having met two Afrobolivian women in a village near Coroico in the Yungas. The women asked her about where she came from and inquired into her ethnic, cultural, and national origins, but in particular – as she puts it – into her "*racial* origins" (Busdiecker 2007:6 italics in original). Her traveling companion clarified that she (Busdiecker) was a "black *gringa*" *("gringa negra")* to which she reports the women wondering: "Are there blacks like us in the United States? [...] I thought there were only blacks like us in Bolivia!" (Busdiecker 2007:5). I concur with Busdiecker in her interpretation that even though the women must have made some sort of diasporic connection between themselves and the researcher – having detected black phenotypical features in her appearance – they nevertheless "displayed some ignorance about her [Busdiecker's] [...] space [...] in that Diaspora," as she puts it. This episode is one very vivid example of the fact that at least until quite recently, Afrobolivians conceived of their blackness without any concrete relations to the diaspora and little, if any, reference to Africa.[7] Various accounts that I collected during fieldwork concur in asserting that until fairly recently – similar to what Tanya Golash-Boza (Golash-Boza 2012) has described in the case of Afro-Peruvians – Afrobolivians considered themselves black, without necessarily being 'African' or referencing Africa when defining blackness (see also Restrepo 2004). Only in the context of cultural revitalization and political mobilization did a clearer reference to diaspora and Africa emerge and, since there are organizations and individuals active in diasporic political and cultural networks, references to Africa, the global African Diaspora and regional Afro-Latino connections have become increasingly important. What is more, *Afrodescendiente* and *Afroboliviano* have replaced *negro* as the terminology of choice to refer to blackness in most political and legal contexts.

7 At the same time, it shows the pervasive importance of racial labels and phenotypical features when defining what is 'black' in Bolivia.

Yet in the first meetings of the emerging *Movimiento Afroboliviano* held in La Paz, it was not even clear what they would call themselves (*"cómo nos íbamos a llamar"*) and many participants recalled a good deal of debate concerning whether *Afroboliviano* should be the term of choice. Up until then they had referred to themselves simply as *negros* and *negras*. They also told me that at the meeting in question some Africans, presumably from Nigeria, were invited to explain the importance of their African roots to Afrobolivians.

Today, referring to 'Africa' as a source of 'culture' and identity is quite common among Afrobolivians, although it is most widespread among young urban Afrobolivians and less frequent and explicit in the Yungas. Initially, the major sources of references to Africa were the publications of Afrobolivian activists and scholars active in political mobilization. One example is Mónica Rey's (1998: 102) attempt to link the dance *saya* to Africa more firmly by establishing linguistic ties of the word *saya* to purported origins in the Kikongo language. Rey's assertion that the word *saya* stems from the Kikongo word *nsaya* meaning "working together under the leadership of a singer" (*"trabajo en equipo bajo el mando de un cantante"*), although unverified until the present day, has become common knowledge among Afrobolivians. It is not only cited in the context of accounting for the origins of *saya*, but is at times elaborated into a proto-philosophical approach to life purportedly unique to Afrobolivians (by virtue of their African-ness) – paralleling the processes of promoting *vivir bien* as indigenous philosophical wisdom (Ballivián 2014). Approaches linking Afrobolivians with Africa directly can also be found in Juan Angola Maconde's publication *"Raíces de un Pueblo. Cultura Afroboliviana"* (Angola Maconde 2000), a book that is frequently quoted as a primary source on Afrobolivian culture. The book starts with an overview of 'African culture,' presenting information on different types of houses, customs, dances, religion and marriage patterns in different parts of Africa. Its second part is an ethnography of Afrobolivian life in the Yungas. The divide between the content of parts one and two is vast, yet African culture and Afrobolivian lifestyles are symbolically grouped together as a logical succession of sorts.[8] Lately, some Afrobolivians have also declared themselves to be adherents of the spiritual and practical teachings associated with *Ubuntu* and a recently founded organization in Cochabamba has chosen the name *"Ubuntu – Organización de Afrodescendientes."* In La Paz, various Afrobolivians are members of the *Asociación Cultural Ifá Yoruba Boliviana Cubana*, an Afro-Cuban religious organization. According to the

8 The breach is not only apparent in terms of content and argumentation – the author does not even try to establish concrete linkages and identify possible explicit 'Africanisms' – but also in terms of the quality of the material presented. Part one is a clutter of information superficially stitched together with no apparent leitmotif besides the fact that all of the information somehow relates to the African continent. Part two, on the other hand, is a fine-grained ethnography with rich detail, displaying both well-founded knowledge of the region and analytical clarity.

founder and spiritual leader *("Babalawo")* of this organization, his Afrobolivian adherents seek his help to "connect to their ancestors and their original culture."

Another important dimension of engaging with diasporic narratives of identity and belonging are narratives that situate Afrobolivian history within the broader history of African slavery in Latin America. The explicit reference to slavery and the geographical origins of the Afrobolivian population in Africa are rather recent phenomena as well. In the few records of Afrobolivian oral history collected among senior members of Afrobolivian communities in the Yungas in the 1980s and 1990s, slavery *("esclavitud")* is mostly associated with the times of the *hacienda*, when Afrobolivians worked as *peones* for the landowners (Centro Pedagógico y Cultural "Simón I. Patiño" 1998b). Alison Spedding also cites various testimonies of Afrobolivians that assert that many people expressed the notion that Afrobolivians had "always" lived in Bolivia *("siempre habían vivido aquí")* (Spedding 2009:464). Only in the context of cultural revitalization, political mobilization and through engaging with transnational political networks have Afrobolivians adopted narratives of the transnational dimension of slavery and the African origins of slaves.[9] As Kevin Yelvington (2001:245) has remarked "[t]he past proves to be a dynamic resource for identity, seen in the considerable effort thrown into the commemorating of slavery [...]." This is expressed, for example, in Afrobolivian *saya* lyrics. One very popular *saya ("Honor y Gloria")* begins with the line: "Honor and Glory for the first *negros* that arrived in Bolivia. They died working in the *Cerro Rico* of Potosí."[10] Another *saya* links current struggles for equality explicitly with slavery, addressing the audience with the line: "It is not the time of slavery anymore. Why do you treat my people with such resentment?"[11]

Beyond referencing important political and intellectual personalities of the African Diaspora, a shared sense of diasporic history tied to slavery, as well as cultural, spiritual and geographical 'origins' in Africa, Afrobolivians engage *"lo Afro"* through novel practices of consumption. 'African' fashion and clothing (called *"camisas estilo dashiki"* by my interlocutors) has made its way to Bolivia and is now used by Afrobolivians in many contexts to highlight their cultural distinctiveness. For example, I witnessed many Afrobolivians wearing "*dashiki* style shirts" to an official reception at the *Casa de la Libertad*, a museum in Sucre dedicated to Bolivia's struggle for national independence, which hosted a temporary exhibition on Afrobolivian history at that time. Many Afrobolivian political leaders also wear this

9 This type of discourse has recently also become important in local settings, as my discussion of the tourism project in Cala Cala in chapter 10 exemplifies.

10 *"Honor y Gloria a los primeros negros que llegaron a Bolivia. Murieron trabajando al Cerro Rico de Potosí."*

11 *"Ya no es el tiempo de la esclavitud. ¿Porqué tratas a mi gente con tanto rencor?"*

kind of outfits on official occasions and for press conferences. Especially in political contexts, 'African' garments are beginning to displace *saya* clothes (white pants and shirt and a red neckerchief) as the outfit 'most representative' of Afrobolivians. Similarly, as figure 14 below shows, 'African' garments and iconography have also come to be considered part of Afrobolivian 'culture' in official representations. As we can see, they are displayed alongside *saya* garments in the section on Afrobolivians in the newly inaugurated *"Centro de las culturas indígenas y Afrobolivianas"* ("Center of indigenous and Afrobolivian cultures") in Santa Cruz.

Figure 14: The exhibition on Afrobolivians in the "Centro de las culturas indígenas y Afrobolivianas" in Santa Cruz (photograph by the author).

Yet, as Peter Wade (2009c:175) has observed in Colombia, very often the "'afro' element [...] is becoming increasingly distant from Africa itself and from ideas about 'real' Africanisms." Instead, referring to Africa, or Afro 'culture' more generally, allows people to engage with an increasingly "globalised, mass-mediated culture of blackness associated with certain images and styles – of music, bodily comportment, dress – and realised to a great degree through practices of consumption." In Bolivia, this can entail wearing your hair in dreadlocks or cornrows (bolivianized as *"wachus de coca,"* lit. rows of coca), listening to Bob Marley, or wearing Usain Bolt's T-Shirt collection in order to appropriate the aesthetics of globalized blackness through practices of consumption. This kind of globalized Afro consumer culture was limited to the younger generations in mostly urban settings until very recently. Through the proliferation of smartphones and internet access, it is now affecting younger people in the Yungas as well, as I have experienced among the few younger residents of Cala Cala.

In a territorial sense, references to 'Africa' and the wider African Diaspora always coexist and interact with references to the Yungas and the national context. Politically, it was crucial to stress roots in national contexts rather than displacement and diasporic affiliations, and rooted-ness has played a much more important role than belonging to the diaspora. This is why the Yungas, rather than 'Africa,' are seen as the 'ancestral territory' par excellence by Afrobolivians, making references to the Yungas much more common, elaborate and important than those linking Afrobolivians directly to Africa. Many people do, however, emphasize that what is sometimes referred to as the "African cultural matrix" ("*la matriz cultural Africana*"), is most authentically present in the Yungas, which does link Afrobolivianity to Africa, but always with the Yungas as a stepping stone. Interestingly, it is less the Afrobolivians still residing in the Yungas that make these claims, and more the first-, second- or even third-generation migrants in urban centers.

Both the discursive thrusts presented heretofore as being important for the articulation of Afrobolivianity presuppose that Afrobolivianity is chiefly a matter of territorial origins and culture and how they relate to each other. The task so far has been to show that Afrobolivianity is best understood as an articulation engaging the languages of indigeneity and diaspora simultaneously. Yet there is another important dimension of Afrobolivianity that needs to be addressed. I have already briefly hinted at the fact that being "*Afro*" is also often perceived as having something to do with race and in what follows I will discuss the importance of racialized notions of Afrobolivianity.

Racialized notions of Afrobolivianity

It has become a firmly established starting point of any social scientific inquiry into questions of identity that all social identities, among them ethnic and racial ones, are shaped and constructed in a dialectical relationship between categorization and self-identification – what Richard Jenkins has called the "internal and external moments of the dialectic of identification" (Jenkins 2000:7; see also Jenkins 2014). Although it has been argued "that ethnicity is generally more concerned with the identification of 'us,' while racism is more oriented to the categorization of 'them'" (Banton [1983: 106] quoted in Jenkins [2008:23]) – and, from this point of view, ethnicity could be considered rather a matter of group identification and self-positioning, whereas race could be considered more a matter of social categorization from outside the group, i.e. interpellation – Jenkins reminds us that this distinction is a rather weak one and only valid when heavily qualified since "group identification and social categorization are inextricably linked, logically, inasmuch as similarity entails difference [...] and processually, with respect to individual as well as collective identification" (Jenkins 2008:23).

With that in mind – and before addressing the relationship between race, ethnicity and indigeneity – I want to briefly comment on the relationship between self-positioning practices and external categorization with regard to Afrobolivians. It is important to note that black (*negro* and *negra*) individuals always stand out in Bolivia and that the narrative of 'invisibility' does not apply with regard to individual people. Almost every Afrobolivian individual I spoke to recalls some episode or situation in his or her life when he or she was "the only *negro/a*," always standing out and being looked at and treated differently. Black individuals are thus confronted very commonly and very directly with social situations in which they are externally classified and categorized by people on the sole basis of their physical appearance. Who is considered 'black' and on what grounds, obviously, depends on certain normative expectations of what 'blackness' ought to look like – both phenotypically and in terms of 'culture.' In Bolivia, these normative expectations date as far back as colonial imaginations and representations. Additionally, they stem from more contemporary images of blackness, disseminated through mass media and the growing number of self-representations created by Afrobolivians in recent years in different spaces (see Rossbach de Olmos 2007). The external categorization of mixed-looking people is more contingent on other factors and less clear. Here, clothing, social context and what the other person knows about the individual in question is very important for the question of how certain phenotypical traits are interpreted. Very interesting for me were the comments of friends (both Bolivian and otherwise) who occasionally, after having met someone I knew from my fieldwork, incredulously asked: "And this was supposed to be a *black* person, he/she doesn't look like it at all." Apparently, the individuals in question did not meet my interlocutors' normative expectations with regard to blackness.

Afrobolivian self-positioning practices must always be seen with relation to the above-mentioned expectations and normative assumptions, and it is important to keep in mind that even though who should be considered Afrobolivian might seem a straightforward issue, it is by no means a simple question. People constantly resist and relativize clear-cut designations and references to their or others phenotypical appearance – no matter if it is interpreted as denoting mixedness or purity. Thus, whenever phenotype becomes ambiguous, 'culture,' genealogy and geographical origins become important factors in external categorizations and self-positioning. My general aim is to complicate the often assumed natural correspondence of the phenotypical category *negro* with identification as *Afroboliviano.* Even *negro* and *negra* individuals can – depending on their stance towards Afrobolivian identity politics and on the specific social context of the categorization – embrace or reject different possible options (for example, *Afroboliviano* or black foreigner).[12] Mixed-looking individuals can make efforts to blend into non-black society or openly emphasize their blackness depending on the context, their decision or even their mood. With certain markers – especially hairstyle and certain styles of clothes, and of course through *saya* dancing – they can manipulate the framework determining their categorization. As much as they can visibly position themselves as Afrobolivian by emphasizing phenotypical aspects that they believe hint at blackness, these aspects might be easily de-emphasized as well, opening up possibilities of being categorized and positioning oneself as non-black. What is more, it is quite common for people to clearly state that they themselves or others are not *negros* or *negras*, but of course *Afroboliviano/a*. In this sense, they exhibit a strongly anti-essentialist view on Afrobolivian identity in racial terms, making *Afroboliviano* an inclusive category of identification with great mobilizing potential, although this is something that people do not always agree on.

Race and ethnicity in Latin America

There exists a long-standing and controversial theoretical debate concerned with the role of race and racism in Latin America, and its relationship to ethnicity (Wade 2008; Wade 2015). From an anthropological perspective, what becomes clear is that ideas of race and ethnicity are highly contingent on historical and social contexts and cannot be dealt with in a generalizing fashion on a global scale. For the purpose of this chapter, it is therefore important to point out certain basic notions concerning the situation in Latin America and Bolivia. For Peter Wade (Wade 2010:14) – and I follow his view as a very practical working definition for the Bolivian case – "races, racial categories and racial ideologies are [...] social constructions on the basis of phenotypical variation" combined with "ideas about innate difference" related to this phenotypical variation. As Wade correctly reminds us, it is not phenotypical features *per se* that are considered to connote racial difference, but rather "particular aspects of phenotypical variation that were worked into vital signifiers of difference during European colonial encounters with others" (Wade 2010:14). For black people in Bolivia and elsewhere, these features mostly refer to (a combination of) skin color, hair texture and facial features that have been worked into "racial signifiers" (Wade 2010:14) (see fig. 15). There are a number of terms and categorizations that connote blackness racially in Bolivia. It is common to hear people speak of *los negros* or *las negras*, sometimes also in the diminutive *los negritos*

12 Especially in Santa Cruz, it is not uncommon – as many interlocutors have confirmed – for black Bolivians to pretend to be Colombian, Brazilian, Cuban or Venezuelan, whereas others feel insulted if they are considered to be from 'elsewhere' and strongly emphasize their Bolivian nationality.

or *las negritas*. Mostly among themselves, Afrobolivians employ a number of complementary qualifications, speaking of *negros chiris* (referencing curly *[chiri]* hair), *negros netos* ('true' blacks), *negros retintos* (lit.: dark brown blacks), *negros carbón* (lit.: carbon [colored] blacks) and *negros negros* (basically the same as *negros carbón* or *negros netos*). All of these qualifications denote a 'blacker than average' appearance. To refer to people of mixed ancestry and generally 'lighter' complexion, there are also a number of terms like "*moreno/a*" (lit.: brown) – often also used euphemistically by non-Afrobolivians – and the denominations *mulato/a* (black and white mixture) and *zambo/a* (black and indigenous mixture). *Mulato* and *zambo* are categories hardly used by non-Afrobolivians: in general, talking about grades of blackness or mixedness is inappropriate for non-Afrobolivians and tends to be seen as racist by Afrobolivians. Among themselves and – after some time – also in conversations with me, however, Afrobolivians do not hesitate to use this kind of vocabulary.[13] Non-Afrobolivians are expected to use the denominations *Afro*, *Afroboliviano/a*, or *Afrodescendiente*. The colloquial "*Afro*" is very common among Afrobolivians, who also use the terms *Afroboliviano* and *Afrodescendiente*, although the latter is a more specifically political term that is used mostly by activists and in certain formalized interactions and documents.

Ethnicity, on the other hand, is mostly thought of as referring to cultural difference rather than phenotypical difference (Wade 2010:15). To this we might add the fact that ethnicity often invokes a language of place, as people use "location, or rather people's putative origin in certain places, to talk about difference and sameness" (Wade 2010:17). The distinction between ethnicity as defined through culture (and therefore seen often as less natural and more socially constructed) and race through phenotypical variation (and therefore biology) is of course less clear-cut than the above juxtaposition suggests. Ethnic difference (and with that cultural difference and indigeneity) is very often naturalized and biologized in much the same way as is racial difference. Additionally, we also have to keep in mind that – at least in the Bolivian case – indigenous phenotypical features are obviously an important element in the complicated realm of social differentiation. With regard to race, we are dealing with a similar situation. Race, albeit often regarded as relying on biology and objective differences in human nature, is by no means less socially constructed than other categories of social differentiation (Wade 2004). What is considered black or *Afro* in Bolivia today depends – at least in part – on social markers beyond phenotype. In short, ethnicity in Latin America is not clearly and comprehensively a simple matter of cultural difference; neither is race more

13 Except in conversations with a select few individuals I got to know very well over the course of the last few years, it would have been inappropriate for me to make distinctions between people on the basis of their phenotype and use this kind of terminology.

Figure 15: A 'typical' black person from Coripata (left) and a 'typical' image of an 'ethnic' Afrobolivian (right) (images courtesy of Municipio de Coripata/Martín Ballivián/ Ministerio de Educación).

natural/biological than ethnicity, nor does it function as a category of social differentiation unrelated to further social and cultural markers.

The distinction between race and ethnicity in the Latin American context is therefore not necessarily a radical one (Wade 2010:19). They overlap as analytical concepts and in practice, as they both involve a discourse about origins and certain essences related to these origins: in the case of race, aspects of phenotype that are transmitted through generations become cues for categorizing people; in the case of ethnicity, origins in a cultural geography become the basis for perceived cultural differences (Wade 2010:20). What is more, in the Colombian case, according to Wade, "if ethnicity invokes location in a cultural geography, it may be the case that the phenotypical traits used in racial discourse are distributed across that geography" (Wade 2010:20), and this has also been suggested for Bolivia (cf. Busdiecker 2009a).

Being such closely related concepts, distinguishing race and ethnicity in the Latin American context becomes a matter of accounting for differences in their historical genesis and social consequences rather than a radical conceptual distinction (Wade 2010:19). The necessity of accounting for the specificities of the social, political, and legal consequences of distinguishing between race and ethnicity emerges from the ways racial and ethnic categories have been applied to different populations in Latin America. Whereas Indians (now *indígenas*) have been viewed and classified mostly as an ethnic group on the basis of a distinct culture, Afro-Latin Americans have been considered a racialized group in most circumstances, based on variation in phenotypical appearance (see Wade 2010). This split has led to significant differences in a variety of ways. Starting in colonial times, being classified as black or indigenous had consequences in legal and political terms that influenced access to opportunities for black and indigenous people (O'Toole 2012). Blackness and indigeneity, conceived of as racialized and cultural difference respectively, have also occupied different discursive roles in debates on nation and 'national culture' in many Latin American countries (Rahier 2008; Wade 2009b). Moreover, until the present, multicultural schemes of recognition have perpetuated the legal and political boundaries between Afro-Latin Americans and indigenous peoples. For example, Juliet Hooker has argued that indigenous groups have had significantly higher success rates in terms of political and legal inclusion since Latin American multicultural regimes of recognition tend to privilege indigenous (cultural) difference over the claims of racialized Afro-Latin Americans (Hooker 2005; Hooker 2008).

In Bolivia, indigeneity has been the primary category of otherness and the 'Indian question' has been a prominent item on the political, legal and intellectual agenda for most of the country's history (Stefanoni 2010). This situation has not changed; if anything, the scope of debate on indigeneity has broadened and the intensity increased since the election of Evo Morales, the continent's 'first indigenous president' in 2005 (see, for example, Albro 2005; Canessa 2005; Canessa 2012c; Postero 2013; Postero 2017). For Afrobolivians, this has meant that engaging with indigeneity, as well as with indigenous forms of politics and the conceptual universe of indigenous rights (cf. Niezen 2003) has become a political necessity. They have had to deal with the central question of the sense in which and the circumstances under which a "relocation of blackness in structures of alterity" (Wade 2010:37) could be articulated in order to make Afrobolivian claims "legible" (Scott 1998) to the multicultural and plurinational state in Bolivia (see also Albro 2010a). As will become clear in my discussion of Afrobolivian activism, there are a lot of different variables that have to be taken into account when analyzing the way that this political articulation and Afrobolivian engagement with the logics of specific regimes of recognition take place.[14]In chapters 8 and 9 I will analyze Afrobolivian political activism as relying on a culturalization of blackness and an ensuing indigenization of black political identity (cf. Wade 2006a:13). This is most clearly expressed in the articulation of black collectivity as *el pueblo Afroboliviano*, since it

14 Various studies have shown how specific notions of blackness and indigeneity, as well as their respective positions in imaginaries of national history, identity and society vary from case to case (for an overview see for example Andrews 2004; Rahier 2012a; Whitten and Torres 1998).

(*"pueblo"*) can only be analyzed in close dialog with the concept of indigeneity, as it is directly derived from the concept of *"pueblos indígenas originarios campesinos"* guiding the plurinational logics of the present political conjuncture.

Although successful on a political level and increasingly propagated in legal documents, the question remains in what sense this political articulation of Afrobolivianity can transcend organizational rhetoric and spaces of political negotiation, and influence the way in which people conceive and represent their blackness in day-to-day contexts. As will become clear in the anecdotes in the next section, the articulation of Afrobolivian collectivity as a *pueblo* does create novel *"political* subjects and subjectivities" (Restrepo 2004:711 emphasis added), and "a novel assemblage of memories and identities" (Restrepo 2004:711). Racialized difference, however, also remains an important reference when Afrobolivianity is debated and negotiated.

Negotiating Afrobolivianity

After introducing the key elements of the articulation of Afrobolivianity, as well as addressing the question of how race and ethnicity relate to each other in Bolivia with regard to Afrobolivianity and indigeneity, I will now turn to discussing concrete examples of how, when and under what circumstances such questions are debated by Afrobolivian individuals. The three episodes I will discuss have some recurring themes, yet point us in different directions or introduce different perspectives on certain matters. The first example is concerned with a rural perspective on urban Afrobolivianity, dealing with the question of how processes of racial mixture might relate to a sense of groupness among Afrobolivians. The second and third examples stem from urban contexts. These, in turn, address questions of race and cultural authenticity, while at the same time alerting us to the flexibility and malleability of racial and cultural identities in Bolivia. Although situated in rural and urban contexts, they nevertheless share the same conceptual horizon and are situated within a common frame of meaning, highlighting once again the close interconnections between urban and rural Afrobolivians in the articulation of Afrobolivianity.

Mamanis negros y Angolas indígenas: migration, kinship and the perceived perils of racial mixture

The following narrative was recounted in Cala Cala and aptly illustrates a common view many people hold on questions of migration, racial mixture and the ensuing consequences for Afrobolivian culture and identification with an Afrobolivian collective. One day, several months into my fieldwork, I asked Roberto, one of my main research participants from Cala Cala, to draw a family tree of his relatives in order to make sense of the various kinship ties that many members of the wider Afrobolivian community share (see chapter 3). He named his mother's siblings, members of his wife's family (parents and siblings), and was also able to produce a list of numerous descendants of his and his wife's parents' siblings. He emphasized, however, that many of these individuals had never lived in the community and had hardly ever visited the Yungas. What is more, Roberto has also not frequently travelled to more distant cities such as Santa Cruz or Cochabamba in order to establish personal contacts and closer ties with many of his relatives.[15] While he lamented the fact that "his family" is dispersed throughout the whole country on a general level, there was one aspect of the dispersion that especially troubled him. He told me that his oldest daughter had a child with an "indigenous man from Potosí" and that his grandchild was certainly not the only *"Angola indígena"* to be found in Bolivia.

"Angola" is a very typical Afrobolivian last name, and with the term *"Angola indígena"* he referred to a person of mixed Afrobolivian/indigenous ancestry. He also used the expression "*Mamani negro*" on that occasion: *Mamani*, in much the same way as *Angola* for Afrobolivians, is a last name very much associated with indigeneity in Bolivia, making the *Mamani negro* a person of mixed indigenous/Afrobolivian ancestry. From his perspective, the 'problem' with the countless *Angolas indígenas* and *Mamanis negros* is that they have few personal ties to the communities in the Yungas and also little "love for their color"; they rather privilege their indigenous heritage over the Afrobolivian side. Roberto interpreted this as a serious threat to the Afrobolivian community as a whole, since he argued that mixed ancestry most often meant that Afrobolivian cultural heritage would be downplayed or even openly neglected. It is interesting to note the conflation of race and culture in Roberto's statements. "Having little love for their color" to him means the same as neglecting or downplaying Afrobolivian cultural heritage. It also seemed to be 'natural' to him that strong identification as Afrobolivian would be hindered by racial admixture, as he thought of the Afrobolivian cultural essence being diluted much in the same way that "Afrobolivian blood" was diluted through racial mixture. Thus, for him, having lost touch with the offspring of his uncles was not only a matter of personal dissatisfaction, but was interpreted as saying something about the Afrobolivian community more generally. In his view, migration, as well as cultural and racial mixture, is clearly a threat to Afrobolivian groupness and culture.

Judging from this account, it could be argued that racial mixture as such poses a threat to Afrobolivian culture and should therefore be avoided. And, in fact, similar

15 As we have seen in chapter 3, the lack of close personal relationships with many urban residents did not prevent Roberto and others from including some of them within the notion of "*los Afros de Cala Cala*" in other contexts.

points have been made at least implicitly by a number of Afrobolivian interlocutors of mine who stressed that it is in some sense a political and even ethical necessity to marry another Afrobolivian in order to preserve their culture. Yet the relation between racial mixture, culture and Afrobolivian identity is not as straightforward as the above statement suggests. This became obvious to me when Roberto spoke about his own mixed racial ancestry. I found him on his porch one day early in the morning burning a pile of papers in a small bonfire. He told me that he had been taking advantage of the bad weather that prevented him from working in the coca fields to clean up his room. He had found some old papers that he didn't think he would need anymore. He went on to show me different pictures (that he did not intend to burn), but my attention was caught by a yellowed piece of paper on the pile of disposable documents ready for burning. I was intrigued by the official heading displaying the credentials of the municipality of Coripata and asked if I was allowed to see it. He showed the document to me and it turned out to be an original copy of his birth certificate from 1972. As I was skimming through the data, one line immediately made me curious. Besides the expected information on date and place of birth and further administrative data, one line specified Roberto's *race ("raza")*. I was surprised as I had not known that Bolivian authorities recorded racial identification in birth certificates at that time. The handwritten information states that Roberto's race is *"nigra"* (the 'i' instead of 'e' possibly indicating that an Aymara native speaker authored the certificate). I asked him if he would mind giving the document to me and not burning it. At first he seemed surprised at the fact that I would be interested in such a document, but gladly agreed to give it to me as a present. When he expressed his surprise at why I would want the document I told him that I found it interesting that the civil registry authorities would specify someone's *raza* on such an occasion. This was the cue for him to explain his interpretation of the certificate. He told me that he thought the registry official must have written *"negra"* because he must have seen his mother, whom Roberto spoke of as being *"negra,"* and therefore designated the child as black. In fact, Roberto stated, he is *"mezcla"* (lit.: mixture) because his father (whose data is not specified in the certificate due to the fact that he never formally acknowledged paternity) was an indigenous man *("indígena")*. He went on to point out that his mixedness was something that could be easily deduced from his physical appearance, especially from his skin color and his hair texture. Yet, as he made clear, he strongly identifies as *"Afroboliviano": "Ya soy mezcla, pero Afroboliviano."* For him, identifying as Afrobolivian is rooted in his feelings *(sentimientos)*, and his heart *(corazón)* as he told me, tapping his chest with his hand. He made it very clear that he did not consider his physical appearance or any type or degree of race mixture to be a significant factor in how he himself feels about his belonging to the collective subject of Afrobolivians. This, of course, runs counter to the opinions and doubts he had expressed when referring to the numerous *Mamanis negros* and *Angolas indígenas.*

Interestingly, Roberto told me on another occasion that he had been confronted by a fellow community member from Cala Cala with the allegation that he was not "truly *negro*" and thus not entitled to speak on behalf of the *"Afros de Cala Cala"* or on matters of Afrobolivian culture.

What is clear from this example is that Afrobolivianity is thought of and talked about in racial terms, the efforts to emphasize cultural aspects of blackness notwithstanding. Being Afrobolivian in the above-mentioned example is clearly about phenotype – i.e. about being *negro* – and genealogical ancestry – i.e. about being *mezcla* or not. Moreover, we get a glimpse of the widespread belief that mixed or mixed-looking individuals are more inclined to disregard their Afrobolivian heritage than *negros/as* and are considered less authentic in cultural terms. Beyond racial markers, self-identification and adherence to certain cultural practices also play a role: Roberto does foreground individual *sentimiento* and *corazón* as the basis for his self-positioning as Afrobolivian, yet it is also his active engagement with Afrobolivian collective organizing that, despite occasional questioning, determines his status as legitimately Afrobolivian in the eyes of others, as well as his individual positioning. In fact, what most clearly distinguishes Roberto's situation from that of the people he referred to as *Mamanis negros* and *Angolas indígenas* – beyond individual *sentimiento* and *corazón* – is the fact that he actively engages in the affairs of the Afrobolivian community of Cala Cala. As one of the most active community members in terms of political activism and cultural entrepreneurship, for Roberto, being Afrobolivian is rooted in practice, rather than in a merely discursive positioning. Therefore, although his authenticity and authority are occasionally questioned on the grounds that he is *mezcla*, his legitimate belonging and leadership role in the community are generally accepted.

Beyond this particular example, there is of course no reason to suggest that we can establish a clear, unitary way in terms of how racial mixture relates to the question of how any individual positions him- or herself towards Afrobolivianity. On the one hand, parallel to Roberto describing himself as *"mezcla"* and yet clearly identifying with Afrobolivian culture, political organization and communal values, there are numerous cases in which individuals with mixed racial ancestry express and practice strong ties to Afrobolivian identities and ethnoracial networks in urban as well as rural contexts. On the other hand, there are people unanimously classified as *negros carbones* who do not engage with Afrobolivian organizations, sometimes even preferring to claim foreign origins in urban settings, show no interest in *saya* and consider Afrobolivian culture something only remotely – if at all – important in their lives. As the following cases illustrate, however, there are certain tendencies regarding how the relationship between physical appearance, ancestry and legitimate belonging are interpreted, especially in urban settings where people do not know all potential members of the 'Afrobolivian community' personally, as is the case in the fairly small *comunidades* in the Yungas.

"Can just any white person dance here?" – An urban perspective on phenotype, ancestry and legitimate belonging

The following account is a transcription of a discussion within the La Paz-based organization *Movimiento Cultural Saya Afroboliviana (MOCUSABOL)* and a subsequent conversation I had with one of the members that participated in the discussion. It is an interesting example of the ways phenotypical appearance, cultural authenticity and identity are commented on and negotiated within urban Afrobolivian organizations.

At a MOCUSABOL meeting I attended in La Paz, great controversy was sparked by the comments of Marco, a long-time member of the organization. Marco 'originally' comes from Coripata, which means that his family is from that municipality/region in the Yungas, even though he migrated to La Paz at a very young age. The present group members were just discussing an upcoming performance and compiled a list of the members that were to participate when Marco addressed the *mesa directiva* (board of directors) with a question. He wondered, he said, since when it had been allowed for "any white person" *("cada blanco")* to dance *saya* with the group. At a past performance, he recalled, he had seen two "white girls" *("chicas blancas")* dancing with the group; "white girls" he had never seen before and did not know personally. He expressed serious worries with regard to the image the participation of "whites" would create for the audience and the general public. He went on to complain that the two girls in question had not even formally introduced themselves before starting the performance, something he interpreted as a lack of respect for himself, the group and Afrobolivian culture in general. His interpretation of the situation was that people from outside of the community were trying to appropriate Afrobolivian culture for themselves, contributing to an image of MOCUSABOL that he did not consider adequate. For him, *saya* was and should continue to be an Afrobolivian affair without the participation of outsiders. Many of the present members commented approvingly on his intervention.[16] The unfolding discussion among the members of MOCUSABOL centered on the relationship between phenotypical appearance and legitimate group membership. The main quarrel was about the fact that the two girls where considered "white" by some members of the organization. After some heated debate, another member pointed to the fact that the girls in question are the nieces of a man who was a well-known member of MOCUSABOL and whose Afrobolivianity was clearly beyond question. That piece of information calmed the mood significantly, yet questions of how to deal with 'white-looking' people continued to loom in the background. At some

16 It is important to know that participation in public performances is a much debated and highly contested topic within Afrobolivian organizations, mainly because of the economic gain participants can obtain through participation.

point, a member of the *mesa directiva* took the initiative and reminded the present members of the MOCUSABOL statutes that clearly established that the only prerequisite for becoming a member of the organization was "African ancestry" (*"descendencia Africana"*) and not black phenotypical features (*"no tiene que ser negro"*). Since this was clearly and without any doubt established in case of the two girls, the matter need not be discussed any further. Subsequently, he reminded the assembled members of the contents of different workshops that MOCUSABOL had been organizing with regard to Afrobolivian identity and the importance of self-identification (*"autodeterminación"*). He cautioned the participants against judging too quickly based on a person's skin color and jumping to conclusions regarding their claim to legitimate membership. With that said, the meeting resumed its course and the problem was not discussed further.

Some days later, I had lunch with Paola in a crowded restaurant in La Paz' busy Uyustus market district. She is a stable member of MOCUSABOL who had also witnessed the debate. We discussed the events of the meeting and Paola expressed her support for the official position on the subject of requirements for membership (focusing on ancestry and limiting membership on these grounds), and also showed great understanding of the critical inquiries Marco had made concerning the circumstances of the two "white" girls' participation. When I somewhat provocatively asked her how far back in a person's family tree the "black" person could be located and what other criteria might be considered valid if the genealogy background check did not render clear results, she explained the matter to me by referring to her own situation, her family background and her biography. She started by saying: "I am *mestiza*, but I feel Afro." (*"Soy mestiza, pero me siento Afro,"* note the parallels to the case discussed at the beginning of the chapter). She explained that she considered herself to be *mestiza* because her Afrobolivian grandfather had children with an indigenous woman, one of them being Paola's mother. From that point onwards, her family became mixed. As a child, she recalled continually being confronted with the Afrobolivian ancestry in her family. In her words, this was due to the fact that she was "the blackest among the siblings" (*"la más negra de todos mis hermanos"*), i.e. she was given the impression by others that her physical appearance showed clear markers of Afrobolivian ancestry. Her siblings, on the other hand, did not look as "black" as she does, their physical appearance thus generating less comment referring to Afrobolivianity. To this situation she attributes the fact that she does "feel Afro," self-identifies as Afrobolivian and actively participates in the *saya*, whereas none of her siblings do. They rather feel inclined toward the indigenous/mixed aspect of their ancestry. But since she was always "the black of the family" (*"la negra de la familia"*) she actively embraced that part of her ancestry. In her case, the visibility of black physical features sparked discussion on her racial ancestry. This in turn led to her self-identification as Afrobolivian.

From all I know about how Bolivians usually identify a 'black person' *(negro/a)*, Paola would have easily passed as 'non-black' if she hadn't chosen to emphasize her Afrobolivian ancestry. The same is true for Marco – the man who initially started the conversation. In fact, people from Cala Cala that know him personally even commonly referred to him as *"blancón"* (lit.: "white-ish"). Judging only from their phenotypical appearance, Paola and Marco could easily have been subject to the same doubts that Marco expressed with regard to the "white girls" – namely that they were not 'black' (enough) and thus not entitled to participate in the *saya*. Yet Paola expressed little consideration for the "white girls" whose legitimacy as Afrobolivians had been questioned. She considered it indispensable for the organization to inquire into the background of its stable members. For her, the "black blood" *("sangre negra")* that runs in her veins legitimizes her claim to membership and also determines the degree of her authenticity as *"Afro."* In her view, it is a matter of biographical circumstance and individual choice how a person deals with his or her ancestry, yet "black blood" is indispensable for claiming membership of the Afrobolivian community and also a prerequisite for performing *saya* authentically. "*Saya* is in our blood" *("La saya, la llevamos en la sangre")*, she added towards the end of our conversation, hinting at the widespread belief that a non-black person, cannot 'feel' *saya* as a black person can and is also not able to perform it with the degree of authenticity needed to be a member of MOCUSABOL and thus a representative of Afrobolivian culture.

'Social blackening' and the appeal of *"lo Afro"*

The fairly essentialist views on Afrobolivianity shining through Marco's and Paola's statements and MOCUSABOL's statutes notwithstanding, there is a great deal of flexibility with regard to identifying as *Afro* in Bolivia. This is true in many ways. As much as Marco and Paola could have 'whitened' their biography and appearance – something many mixed race people do in Bolivia and elsewhere for a variety of reasons – it is also possible to undergo such processes in the opposite direction. One fairly extraordinary but very telling case is that of Valeria, a young Afrobolivian woman from Santa Cruz. She was born to an urban-based, *"mestiza"* mother (neither self-identified indigenous, nor Afrobolivian) and hardly knows her father. As far as she told me, her father is neither visibly 'black' nor has he self-identified as Afrobolivian at any time. Her mother – she told me – has never mentioned anything that would have led her to believe that she was Afrobolivian or had Afrobolivian ancestry. She did not consider herself to be *"negra"* and even told me that she considered her skin color to be lighter, rather than darker, than what she called the "Bolivian average" *("los Bolivianos en general")*. Yet she told me that because of her curly hair, in high school she was continually approached by a handful of Afrobolivian students who wondered whether she did in fact have Afrobolivian ancestry. They eventually became friends and by being associated with the *"negros,"* she underwent a process that might best be described as 'social blackening.' On the one hand, she started dancing *saya*, which is certainly an important aspect of her becoming Afrobolivian. On the other hand, she emphasized that in day-to-day contexts, she expresses her Afrobolivian identity mostly by wearing her curly hair more openly, not trying to suppress the *"Afro"* look of it. Additionally, she started wearing clothes with 'African' patterns *("estilo dashiki")* that are increasingly associated with the 'Afro' look in Bolivia and that clearly reference a diasporic perspective on Afrobolivianity. She eventually met an Afrobolivian *(negro)* man through her Afrobolivian friends, whom she ultimately married and had a child with. Nowadays she firmly identifies as Afrobolivian and is one of the most visible figures in Santa Cruz' Afrobolivian scene, as she works for the *Instituto de Lengua y Cultura Afro (ILC-AFRO)*, the Afrobolivian branch of the government-sponsored *Instituto Plurinacional de Estudio de Lenguas y Culturas (IPELC)*, an entity whose main objective is to assist the *pueblos* recognized by the Constitution to preserve and/or revitalize their languages and cultures. As far as she told me, her claim to Afrobolivian identity was never questioned; not when she started to dance *saya* and entered the more formalized group in Santa Cruz, nor when she applied for the job at ILC-AFRO. This is quite surprising, given the fact that she managed to secure a position as a government employee through the *Afro* slot, something many activists aspire to. These positions are therefore usually very jealously guarded. Thinking along the lines of Marco – and he is far from an isolated example – the legitimacy of Valeria's claim to Afrobolivian identity could have been questioned on a variety of grounds. She is not *"negra,"* claims no ties to any specific Afrobolivian ancestor and has no connection to a community in the Yungas. Her engagement of Afrobolivianity, albeit sparked by an isolated feature of her phenotypical appearance, is mainly rooted in her firm self-positioning as Afrobolivian and her embracing of an increasingly diasporic perspective on Afrobolivianity.

Conclusion: Race, identity politics and the invisibility of *"Afro-Aymara"*

In this chapter, I have identified the main discursive threads relevant in the articulation of Afrobolivianity. Representing Afrobolivians as 'the people of the Yungas,' characterized by distinctive cultural features, this process of articulation involves engaging a language of indigeneity, mainly through references to culture and place. At the same time, a transnational, diasporic perspective on Afrobolivianity is emerging. Finally, I have shown that despite the growing importance of those discourses, Afrobolivianity is also importantly a matter of racialized difference. As the three ethnographic vignettes have shown, the way these threads interact varies according to context.

On (the invisibility of) *Afro-Aymaras*

At the beginning of the chapter, I raised the question of how indigeneity and blackness might relate to each other in Bolivia and – following Mark Anderson's remarks – whether there is "the possibility that the terms [Afro and indigenous] modify each other so that we might speak of 'indigenous blackness' or 'Afroindigeneity'" (Anderson 2007:407). Anderson also reminds us, however, that "we should critically analyze the way that hyphen marks similarities and differences, disjunctions and articulations" and in what remains of this chapter, I want to briefly address the question of how and under what circumstances the invocation of similarities allows for articulation, and when and why disjunction and an emphasis on difference prevail. As I have shown, discursive articulations of Afrobolivianity draw on the language of indigeneity, and in political and legal realms Afrobolivians also position themselves and are regarded in many instances "like indigenous people" (cf. Anderson 2007). What is more, as my discussion of Cala Cala, as well as other authors' depictions of different communities in the Yungas show, *Yungueño* culture, oral tradition, political and economic institutions and festive culture could be interpreted as Afro-indigenous, since they were forged over the years by Afrobolivian and indigenous *peones* and *comunarios* living together in a common geographic, economic and social space (Busdiecker 2007; Léons 1966; Léons 1972; Spedding 2009; Sturtevant 2013).

Yet not one discussion of the Yungas that I am familiar with applies this terminology ("Afro-indigenous"). Moreover, for most Afrobolivians I have met over the years, Afro-indigeneity or indigenous blackness are not viable concepts for describing their social reality or options for conscious and explicit self-identification. This is true in everyday processes of social differentiation, as well as in more politicized contexts where structural and discursive similarities do exist, yet any conceptual association with *"los indígenas"* is downplayed by Afrobolivians. I have come across countless statements explicitly denying any allegations that Afrobolivians are in any way *'indígenas'* or even 'like *indígenas*' and also heard numerous complaints by Afrobolivian activists that "they always have to move alongside the *indígenas*."[17] For example, at some point during my fieldwork, Afrobolivians discussed a documentary on Afrobolivians in the Yungas aired on Argentinian television and entitled: *"Los negritos de Bolivia: descendientes de africanos con vidas aymaras"*; "The little blacks of Bolivia: descendants of Africans with Aymara lives." Although the short film does not depict Afrobolivian lifestyles in any different way to the countless clips many people proudly showed me as representing part of their 'culture,' what caused outrage among most Afrobolivians was the allegation that they were leading "Aymara lives" and thus were culturally indistinguishable from Aymara. Attempts to

17 *"Siempre tenemos que ir con los indígenas."*

emphasize the many similarities they share with other Bolivians, rather than the things that set them apart, are often met with open rejection. Although Afrobolivianity is articulated very much like indigeneity in Bolivia, and this articulation has been sanctioned by legal recognition, for most of my interlocutors, *Afro* and *indígena* remain two separate spheres of belonging, culture and sociality.

Even the few references I have encountered that employ a certain terminological approximation – "*doble Afro-indígena*," "*Angolas indígenas*," "*Mamanis negros*," "*zambo*," "*mezcla*" – are first of all fairly rare and second of all, I argue, point in a direction that makes me think rather of "disjunctions" than of "articulations," to use Anderson's (2007:409) terms. The woman quoted at the outset of this chapter lamented the fact that she could not contribute any details to the discussion of Afrobolivian language or culture and apologetically explained that by pointing to her lifelong close associations with indigenous people. She has by way of being "*doble Afro-indígena*," become less "*Afro*." The same is true for Roberto's representations of "*Angolas indígenas*" and "*Mamanis negros*," whose alleged lack of commitment to Afrobolivianity he sees as a threat to Afrobolivian groupness. The occasional questioning of his leadership role in Cala Cala on the grounds that he is *zambo* points in a similar direction. The approximation of "*Afro*" and indigenous, their blending and interaction, no matter whether this process is imagined as a matter of race, culture or both at the same time, is not interpreted as something productive. Only once have I heard an individual identifying as "*Afro-Aymara*." The young man spoke up in the plenary of the same CONAFRO congress in 2014 and demanded that CONAFRO make the question of how to deal with mixed people (*hermanos mezclados*, lit.: mixed brothers) a central concern of the organization, since people like him – "Afro-Aymara" – were often discriminated against by "their own people" ("*nuestra propia gente*") for not being purely Afrobolivian. I met this individual several times during my fieldwork and in subsequent conversations had the impression that he indeed thought of his identity in ways that would make it possible to speak of articulation, rather than disjunction. Although firmly rooted within Afrobolivian identity and cultural discourse, politically very active and in close contact with CONAFRO and other organizations, he spoke a lot about the great influence his mother – an Aymara woman – had on his life, his values, his ways of seeing the world and how he could not consider himself "only Afrobolivian" ("*solamente Afro*"). However, his was an isolated case and the CONAFRO plenary that day did not respond to any of the issues he raised in his intervention.

I interpret this silence on "Afro-Aymaras," as well as the various comments that aim at explicitly separating *Afro* from indigenous as pointing very clearly into one direction: the disjunction of Afrobolivianity from indigeneity and mixture rather than its close association with it. By stating "*soy doble Afro-indígena*," "*Ya soy mezcla, pero me siento Afro*," "*soy mestiza, pero Afroboliviana*," or "*soy zambo, mezcla, pero me identifico como Afrodescendiente*," people acknowledge that racial mixture and cultural similarities are a social reality, yet they try to disentangle Afrobolivianity and indigeneity. In my view, this situation is rooted in two interrelated dimensions. On the one hand, the still widespread tendency to conceptualize Afrobolivianity as essentialized racialized difference and on the other, the pervasive influence of equally essentialist identity politics that shape the articulation of Afrobolivianity as a matter of 'cultural difference.'

Afroboliviano as *negro*

Racialized notions of Afrobolivianity are highly essentialist. Markers of Afrobolivianity – even though they are represented as 'cultural' as in the case of *saya* – are very often seen as essential, heritable qualities that 'run in the blood' and are thus naturalized to a great extent and tied to ancestry (cf. for example Wade's [1993:249f] remarks on *"sangre caliente"* as a heritable quality of Afrocolombians). Although an individual's phenotype by no means determines self-identification and does not tell us anything reliable about someone's 'culture,' racialized physical traits are still by far the most commonly given explanation in accounting for what being Afrobolivian is about. This is exemplified by the tendency that *"los más negros"* ("the blackest") are in most cases exempt from further inquiries into their ancestry, kinship ties and/or geographical roots or cultural skills in order to legitimize their Afrobolivianity. This is not to say that those topics do not play a role for those *'negro'* individuals. Even *"los más negros"* comment on their geographical origins and genealogical ancestry; they just do not need to further legitimize their Afrobolivianity with it. It is taken for granted that a *negro* individual is legitimately *Afroboliviano* – no matter how bad a *saya* dancer one might be, how little contact with the Yungas a person might have or how the individual in question relates to his or her Afrobolivian kin in practice. Given that racial mixture is making phenotypical blackness less clearly distinctive in many cases, equally essentialist references to ancestry are emerging as an increasingly important factor in marking the boundary of Afrobolivianity. Although categorizations like *zambo, mezcla* and *mestizo* denote mixture, they still tacitly posit the existence of pure categories as the foundation for mixture (Wade 2005). Consequently, when 'white-,' 'mixed-' or 'indigenous-looking' individuals are questioned with regard to the legitimacy of their claims to belonging, they resort first and foremost to referencing a *negro* or *negra* ancestor.

Afrobolivianity is thus to a large extent a matter of race – either defined through phenotype or through biological ancestry – even though many individuals tirelessly argue that what makes somebody Afrobolivian is first and foremost culture and self-identification. As Roberto's remarks on the *Angolas indígenas* suggest, racial admixture – a very widespread phenomenon in Bolivia both historically and in the present – is considered a possible liability and an obstacle to embracing *(asumir)* Afrobolivian (collective) identity and representing Afrobolivian culture. His own story and the awareness of his mixedness notwithstanding, he suspects that mixed individuals and their lack of commitment to the Afrobolivian cause put the continuity of the collective in danger. Both the lack of visibly black features (as exemplified by the *Angola indígena*) and the cultural influence of 'others' (as exemplified by the *Mamani negro*) are seen as contributing to the weakening of Afrobolivian collectivity. It repeatedly struck me as quite remarkable that it is often the less visibly black individuals who deployed this type of argument, when their own life stories would suggest that racial mixing might not have the results they generally fear.

Afroboliviano beyond *negro*

The articulation of Afrobolivianity beyond racialized difference is, in practice, not less essentialist. It builds on the logics of multicultural and plurinational identity politics that presuppose and propagate clear-cut distinctions between groups, either-or-logics of categorization and identification, and difference rather than similarity as a basis for inclusion and empowerment. As I will detail in chapters 8 and 9, the notion of political Afrobolivianity beyond *negro* is so deeply rooted in the political and legal context of multiculturalism and plurinationality – the term *Afroboliviano* only emerging in the late 1980s – that it cannot be grasped without always keeping in mind what conceptual baggage this entails. And the plurinational regime of recognition is equally essentialist as racialized notions of difference. As the population census in 2012 vividly exemplifies, individuals can only be counted as Afrobolivians – in the strict sense of the word – not as *zambos, mezclas* or *Afro-Aymaras*. The avenues to representation, political empowerment and economic benefits are also to a large degree dependent on exclusive, clearly circumscribed and legally sanctioned identities. Although individual positioning practices and the way people frame their identities and aspirations are often less essentialist and much more dynamic than the rhetoric of Bolivian ID-ology or racialized essentialism suggest, there are few contexts where these alternative visions can be brought to bear. The essentialist perspectives expressed in the notion of Afrobolivianity as racialized difference, as well as in the notion of a culturally defined multicultural/plurinational Afrobolivianity, thus preclude a thorough and productive engagement with entangled concepts like black indigeneity or indigenous blackness.

In the next chapter, I will elaborate on this topic by examining the making of 'Afrobolivian culture,' a process that is based fundamentally on defining, cataloging and structuring Afrobolivian 'cultural elements,' conceptually separating them from regional and/or indigenous culture in order to make them legible and politically meaningful.

Chapter 7: "We are Culture, not Color"
Musicians, Technocrats and the (Re-)Making of 'Afrobolivian Culture'

As I have shown in the preceding chapter, references to phenotypical appearance and genealogical ancestry have been enhanced by references to 'Afrobolivian culture' as a defining feature of Afrobolivian identity and groupness. Moreover, 'distinct culture' is an important conceptual basis for political mobilization and ensuing legal recognition in multicultural and plurinational times. Just as the shirt of the young man in the photograph below indicates (see fig. 16), the articulation of Afrobolivianity, as well as political mobilization and demands for recognition, heavily focus on discourses that foreground *"cultura"* as the defining aspect of being Afrobolivian.

Figure 16: Afrobolivian saya musician with a shirt stating: "Soy cultura, no color" – "I am culture, not color." (photograph by the author).

In this chapter, I will approach the subject of 'Afrobolivian culture' in two contexts. First, I will discuss the Afrobolivian dance *saya*, analyzing the changing contexts, meanings and discursive roles of the dance as a "cultural performance" (Cohen 1993; Guss 2000; Parkin, Caplan, and Fisher 1996), as a strategic asset of mobilization, and as an important symbol of Afrobolivianity more generally. Second, I will discuss processes of compiling, organizing and codifying 'Afrobolivian culture' during the implementation of state-sponsored programs that aim at establishing an objective definition of 'Afrobolivian culture.'

Saya as cultural performance

In September 2014 I attended the *III. Festival de la Saya Afroboliviana* taking place at the Plaza San Francisco, the main square in the city of La Paz. The event was organized by CADIC and Jorge Medina and was held on a stage with amplification and professional lighting similar to a pop concert. Its program consisted of performances by *saya* groups from different places in the Yungas and from the city of La Paz. Parallel to the festival, CONAFRO was hosting its biannual congress that also counted on the participation of various community leaders from the Yungas, as well as leaders of the various urban groups from Santa Cruz, Cochabamba and La Paz. I arrived at the festival shortly before its official opening and was accompanied by Francisco and other representatives from the *comunidad* of Yábalo-Thaco (Sud Yungas), including his wife. As we waited for the show to start, we discussed the events of the CONAFRO congress we had just attended. More and more people flocked onto the plaza, among them other delegates of the congress, but also the general public passing by the central plaza. Francisco calmly observed the preparations and was pleased by the great interest of the public in the *saya* performances. Finally, Jorge Medina took the stage and gave his opening speech. He emphasized the great importance *saya* has for the Afrobolivian people and gave a short introduction to its history. Brought to Bolivia from Africa by slaves in colonial times, he summarized, *saya* had been practiced by Afrobolivians in the Yungas for generations and, as of now, represented the most important 'cultural tradition' of Afrodescendants in the country. He went on to inform the public that as a result of his interventions in parliament *(Asamblea Plurinacional)*, *saya* had been recognized by law as being part of the 'cultural patrimony of the nation,' as "belonging to the Afrobolivian people" and, furthermore, that it was the state's obligation to foster and promote its performance as part of the national cultural heritage.[1] He ended his introductory speech with a summary of his legislative efforts on behalf of the

1 *Ley 138: Declarase Patrimonio Histórico Cultural e Inmaterial del Estado Plurinacional de Bolivia a la expresión artística cultural viva "Saya Afroboliviana" perteneciente al Pueblo Afroboliviano.*

Afrobolivian people and then introduced the hosts for the night's entertainment, two radio journalists who were to be in charge of announcing the different acts and enlivening the crowd. Besides the *saya* groups, they announced, the spectators were to be entertained by a performance of capoiera, another "traditionally African expression," and by different musical groups, including *Alaj Pacha*, a fairly well-known folklore band of *mestizo* origin. A significant crowd had assembled by that time and the performances began.

What followed was in some sense a contest between different *sayas*, displaying their mastery of the dance, spicing up their performances with various gimmicks – even though there were no judges or prizes and no explicit mention of a competition was made by any of the participants. One group exhibited a great variety of different dance steps and choreographed sequences, whereas in the performance of another group, a particularly talented singer took center stage, singing some of the *coplas* as solos. Yet another group prominently placed young children at the front of the performance, exhibiting the skills of the youngest members of their group. They were complimented with a lot of applause by many of the spectators and the atmosphere was in its majority cheerful and festive. The people in the audience seemed to enjoy themselves greatly and some people even approached the stage and danced along with the performers. It struck me as remarkable that among the most enthusiastic individuals in the audience there were very few Afrobolivians. Francisco also stood in the back rows of the crowd and observed the spectacle with little outward signs of emotion, looking – if anything – puzzled. Given the fact that in between the performances the hosts – as a means of complimenting the performers for their skillful presentations – repeatedly shouted that "here, we are seeing the 'joyfulness of a people'" (*"la alegría de un pueblo"*) and "the essence of Afrobolivian people and culture" (*"la esencia de la cultura y del pueblo Afroboliviano"*), it was an odd situation to observe the self-identified members of this *pueblo* occupying the role of puzzled bystanders at the sight of 'their culture' being performed publicly to a zealous crowd. Since the loud music made it impossible to talk, I could do little to inquire into Francisco's impressions of the whole thing and we stood side by side watching the show. Only after some time, during a short break, did he turn and address his wife and me, saying: "They are stylizing it too much. It is going to be lost" (*"Mucho lo están estilizando, se va a perder"*). His wife nodded in agreement and they both turned again to keep watching the unfolding event. After the *saya* performances, it was the turn of the capoeira group to take the stage. They performed a short series of 'games' in an improvised *roda* (see Downey 2005) and shortly afterwards took their leave.[2]

2 Initially, the organizers had also announced the participation of a musical group from Africa, allegedly from Kenya, via some local newspapers. Although this performance did not

The show was then interrupted for the preparations for performances by different musical groups and I asked Francisco what he had meant with his previous comment. He started by telling me that he was very happy to see young people dance *saya* and that he was very pleased at how the crowd had received the dancers and that so many people had come in the first place. Yet the way he saw *saya* being performed that day made him worry. The *saya* he knew, the *saya* from his community, was different, he told me. It was slower *("más pausada")*, he explained, less spectacular *("más sencilla")* and not as conventionalized as the performances he had seen. And it was not only the *saya* performances that had made him uneasy. The capoeira group and their performance did not make sense for him in this context. "That has nothing to do with Afrobolivians" *("No tiene nada que ver con el pueblo Afroboliviano")* he noted. Being a man of very few words, Francisco did not further elaborate on his statement and told me he had to leave in order to find the hostel that had been provided to him by CONAFRO for attending the conference. What I took from his comment and his brief explanations was a general inquietude towards the matter of *saya* performances such as those we just witnessed. It would seem exaggerated to speak of disapproval – recall his happiness about the fact that young people were performing *saya* – and I prefer to interpret his statements as a fundamental puzzlement in light of the changes he perceives are happening in regard to *saya*. He did not express dissatisfaction explicitly; it seemed rather like a slightly nostalgic disbelief in what he saw, paired with a silently expressed acknowledgement that these changes, however puzzling they appeared to him, also had a positive side and would continue to shape what is perceived as 'Afrobolivian culture' in Bolivia today.

This short episode exemplifies the central importance of *saya* for any discussions of 'Afrobolivian culture.' First and very importantly, *saya* is still by far the most visible part of Afrobolivian presence in the public sphere. Only through *saya* do Afrobolivians gain such wide visibility as afforded by a show in La Paz's most important plaza. While the more politically oriented CONAFRO congress we were coming from was held behind closed doors inside an auditorium with little to no outside participation or media interest, the *saya* festival was held at Plaza San Francisco, one of the most important public spaces in La Paz. Yet the context of the festival also alerts us to the fact that in its moments of greatest visibility and coverage, Afrobolivian culture appears mostly in a framework of folkloric performance. The festival's program gave a fairly palpable impression of the location of *saya* and Afrobolivian culture within the conceptual space of Bolivia as a nation, showcasing the Afrobolivian dance alongside popularized Andean music referencing Bolivia's indigenous musical tradition (cf. Bigenho 2002). The capoeira per-

materialize that day, it is not unusual for *saya* to be performed alongside 'African' music or dance.

formance, in turn, points to the fact that *saya* is nowadays also associated, in the broadest of senses, with cultural expressions of the African Diaspora. Albeit briefly and only in passing, Jorge Medina also commented on his legislative efforts with regard to *saya*, most notably the passing of Law 138, hinting at the fact that *saya* (and Afrobolivian culture more generally) is now the object of legal regulation. Finally, through Francisco's statements, we also get a glimpse of the contested nature of Afrobolivian culture. His comments invite us to think about the relationship between performers and spectators, between Afrobolivians from different regional backgrounds, as well as between different generations, paying special attention to competing political orientations, aesthetic preferences and perceptions of cultural change.

Cultural performances are – as David Guss (2000) has argued following Abner Cohen (Cohen 1993) – best understood as "important dramatizations that enable participants to understand, criticize, and even change the worlds in which they live" (Guss 2000:9). Cultural performances are dialogical and even polyphonic sites of discursive reflection, but also sites of "cultural production" (Guss 2000:12). Analyzing *saya* as cultural performance is thus a fruitful vantage point from which to analyze the changing meanings and roles of 'Afrobolivian culture' and the discourses surrounding it. Compared to other aspects of Afrobolivianity, the literature on *saya* is quite substantial. The (mostly unknown) history and origins of *saya*, its material characteristics, rhythmic and musical aspects, as well as the fundamental role it plays in Afrobolivian cultural revival and mobilization have been widely covered (see, among others, Ballivián 2014; Busdiecker 2007: chapter 5; Centro Pedagógico y Cultural "Simón I. Patiño" 1998a; Quispe 1994; Revilla Orías 2013b; Rey 1998; Rocha Torrez 2007; Rossbach de Olmos 2007; Sánchez Canedo 2010; Sánchez Canedo 2011; Templeman 1995; Templeman 1998). Those works have also documented and analyzed *saya* as a cultural performance through which people "are able to talk about local life and tradition, about change over time in the community, about local needs, individual relationships, and about being black" (Busdiecker 2007:205). In her ethnography of blackness in Bolivia, Sara Busdiecker writes:

> "Saya is not simply what is 'most important' to Afro-Bolivians nor is it merely what Afro-Bolivians are 'best known for'; rather, saya is powerfully implicated in not only notions of color and race, but also notions of ethnicity, culture, and peoplehood as they relate to blackness in Bolivia. In other words, the very construction of the present-day experience and meaning of blackness by Afro-Bolivians and non-Afro-Bolivians alike is inextricably tied to saya." (Busdiecker 2007:165–166)

Indeed, it is hardly possible to discuss any topic with Afrobolivians from any background without at least touching the subject of *saya* and, more often than not, *saya* or discussion of the dance takes center stage.

In what follows, I will highlight some aspects of *saya* that I consider especially important. On the one hand, through *saya*, Afrobolivians express and negotiate notions of history, authenticity and cultural change. In this sense, *saya* is a crucial discursive device in the process of articulating Afrobolivianity. *Saya* is also often identified by Afrobolivians themselves as their most important strategic asset for gaining visibility and recognition. Moreover, as the fundamental cultural emblem of Afrobolivianity, *saya* supplements "more local village or kin-based affiliations" (Clifford 2013:222) in processes of articulating Afrobolivianity – parallel to what Clifford has discussed with regard to indigenous identifications.

Debating history, authenticity and cultural change: *saya de antes* and *saya de ahora*

The origins and early history of *saya* are unknown. Afrobolivians nowadays refer to "the time of the *hacienda*" (*"el tiempo de hacienda"*) in order to account for its temporal origins and most regularly only mention *los Yungas* as the region where *saya* originated. By Afrobolivians themselves, *saya* is thus represented as genuinely Afrobolivian, rather than as an 'African tradition' as some journalistic accounts of the dance sometimes state. Afrobolivians also agree on the fact that traditionally *saya* used to be played and danced mainly at patron saint fiestas and wedding festivities in Afrobolivian communities and this practice is reported to have remained intact until the Agrarian Reform in 1953. After the Agrarian Reform, *saya's* importance steadily declined and this period is remembered by many of my Afrobolivian interlocutors as the time when *saya* "was lost" (*"se perdió"*). The dance was then re-vitalized, recuperated and salvaged in the 1980s and 1990s by young migrants in urban settings. What is important to note is that as a part of revitalization, the dance has been increasingly shaped towards being a performance for an audience of outsiders, i.e. people that are not part of the group of people that actually performs. Whereas in the years before the Agrarian Reform, *saya* was performed on occasions that were important for social relations within the rural community, the revitalized *saya* was not grounded in rural community life, but in urban settings and the experiences of young migrants in Bolivian cities. Most importantly, it was directed at the outside world as much as it addressed Afrobolivians. As Julia Pinedo, one of the principal actors of early revitalization and one of the founders of MOCUSABOL told me, the process of "revitalizing" on the one hand entailed consulting elders from the Yungas on their memories of *saya*, but on the other hand also required a lot of creativity from the founders of the group. They adjusted the lyrics to their experiences in urban contexts, displacing topics such as love and community life with matters of Afrobolivian identity, migration and political mobilization. They also adjusted the performance of *saya* to the prevailing models of both Bolivian *entradas* (folklore street parades) and the requirements of the organizers of dance performances. For example, Julia recalled how she and other women invented choreography for *saya* that was compatible with performing it on a stage in a theatre, as well as in an *entrada* in the streets. Subsequently, different *saya* ensembles had to adjust their performance to varying needs, including trips to international folklore festivals, as well as the recording of CDs, the shooting of videos, performances on TV, at night clubs and in restaurants.

In general, people distinguish between *la saya de antes* (the *saya* from before the Agrarian Reform) and *la saya de ahora*, the *saya* that is danced now and that arose from the revitalization in the 1980s. Although the differences cited by my interlocutors show slight variations, the biggest differences are said to be found in terms of the lyrics, the composition of the ensemble of dancers, their clothing and the context of the performance of *saya*. Whereas in *la saya de antes* topics such as love, romantic courtship, community life and hardships of the peasantry dominated, *la saya de ahora* is much more concerned with topics of Afrobolivian identity and political messages. In terms of instrumentation and ensemble, *la saya de antes* required three sizes of drums (*Tambor Mayor, Tambor Menor, Ganyingo*), the *Cuancha* and metal bells *(cascabeles)*, that the *Caporal* or *Capitán de Baile* – the leader of the dance – would wear around his legs in order to set the pace of the dancers. Besides the *Caporal*, there were other symbolic roles important to *saya* performances, such as the *alcalde* (lit. mayor). Thus, *la saya de antes* could also be read as a display of hierarchies within the community. Nowadays, performances include far fewer of the above-mentioned instruments, focusing on *Tambor Mayor, Tambor Menor* and *Cuancha*. The specific roles are also only rarely included, since the focus is much rather put on the lyrics communicating specific messages and on the choreography that has been adjusted to fit the dynamics of street parades *(entradas)* and stage performances respectively. Another key distinction is made in terms of the clothes used for dancing *saya*. Most of my interlocutors agree that before, *saya* was danced in very simple white cotton shirts (men) and *polleras* (women). The dancers are said to have worn *abarcas* (sandals made of tire rubber, very common in the Bolivian countryside) or even to have danced barefoot. While *abarcas* are still the most common footwear used in *saya* groups, the hitherto simple outfits have evolved into colorfully embroidered *trajes*. In general terms, and certain exceptions notwithstanding, *la saya de ahora* is at once simpler in its instrumentation and the distribution of roles, and more complex in its lyrics conveying political messages. The style of the performance (i.e. having choreography) is much more suitable for performing it on stage or in the context of an *entrada*. The clothes people wear show the influence of the colorful outfits common in many folkloric dances of Bolivia. Most importantly for my analysis, the contexts and the audiences that are addressed with *saya* are different. Whereas for the *saya de antes* the main frame of reference was the Afrobolivian rural community, *la saya de ahora* is directed mostly at an audience of outsiders.

Naturally, the distinctions made here are not as clear as they may seem at first. There is a certain amount of debate, both in terms of the content and style of *saya de antes* vs. *saya de ahora* and in terms of the clear before-after timeframe of the Agrarian Reform. For example, in many narratives people recall an event in 1977, a coffee festival organized in Coroico, as the first glimpse of a revitalized *saya* before the events of the early 1980s that sparked more profound and durable efforts at reorganizing the *saya* groups. Yet I have also spoken to various individuals that recall 1977 not as the beginning of revitalization, but as the last time *la saya de antes* was performed before disappearing into oblivion. What is more, this debate only encompasses the Nor Yungas region, and circles explicitly around the *saya* of Tocaña, leaving the Sud Yungas Province and Chicaloma, *"el pueblo de los negros,"* out of the picture.

Even though the most commonly cited distinction pits the pre-reform *saya* against the new *saya* of the 1980s, *saya's* transformation is not limited to the early years of revitalization, but is still ongoing. The performances I have witnessed during recent years have all emphasized different aspects, varied significantly in style, size and sophistication and have occasionally introduced completely new elements. A vivid example is provided by the so-called *"Mama África"* characters introduced by a Cochabamba-based *saya* group in 2017 (see fig. 17), which also mirror the growing importance of references to Africa by Afrobolivians.

Figure 17: "Mama África" characters as part of a saya performance during a Carnaval parade 2017, Cochabamba (photograph by the author).

On the other hand, there are also initiatives that point in the opposite direction of recreating the pre-reform *saya*. The supporters of such initiatives are generally critical of introducing new elements to *saya* and rather aim at re-introducing elements that have now been abandoned. One such initiative, for example, purported to reintroduce the *Ganyingo*, a small drum that was an integral part of the instrumentation of the dance in earlier days, but is hardly used at present.

Saya's history and the transformations it underwent – as well as the way Afrobolivians position themselves towards those issues – thus reflect the socio-cultural transformations affecting Afrobolivians in recent decades. *Saya's* transformation reflects Afrobolivian migration and the experience of discrimination, as well as engagement with Bolivian folklore as an important context for gaining visibility and recognition. Moreover, through *saya*, Afrobolivians refer to the Yungas as ancestral territory, but increasingly also incorporate diasporic references as an important element of what they consider Afrobolivian culture.

Saya as a strategy of visibilization

Saya is not only important as a performative and discursive device through which Afrobolivians engage with their history, tradition and perceived cultural change. Many of my interlocutors, and particularly the ones engaged in some kind of organized political effort, also explicitly highlighted the role of *saya* as an emblem of Afrobolivian culture and as a strategic communicational device directed at an audience beyond Afrobolivians. This discourse has been made prominent by the contributions of Mónica Rey, a leading figure in the Afrobolivian movement. Rey studied *Comunicación Social* at the Universidad Mayor de San Andrés (UMSA) in La Paz in the 1990s and wrote her thesis on *saya's* role as a communicational device. To this day, she remains one of the leading figures of the urban Afrobolivian movement and enjoys particular visibility and respect among Afrobolivian activists. Therefore, her stance on *saya* is widely known among Afrobolivians and shapes the way many people think and talk about *saya*.[3] Rey (1998) argues that *saya* serves two communicational purposes for the Afrobolivian movement. On the one hand, it is a means to unite the Afrobolivian community and make them embrace their identity (see also Templeman 1998). *Saya's* second communicational purpose is, according to Rey, to propagate the messages of the movement to the wider public. *Saya* very literally 'gives Afrobolivians a voice' and through *saya* the Afrobolivian movement was able to express its discontent with the situation of the Afrobolivian population, and raise awareness for issues such as racism, poverty, discrimination and 'invisibility.' At the same time, through *saya* the movement articulated its demands and overcame the limitations with regard to effective political participation that Afrobolivians encountered at the beginning of their mobilization.

3 In 2014, she has been elected *Asambleista Supranacional* for the ruling MAS party and also occupies a very prominent position in CONAFRO.

Ethnomusicologist Robert Templeman – who carried out fieldwork among *saya* groups in the 1980s and 1990s, subscribes to a similar view. He analyzes the roles *saya* has played in the mobilization of the Afrobolivian people and highlights how through *saya*, the movement's messages are communicated to the public. For Templeman, the communicational strategy is twofold: On the one hand, Afrobolivians, through *saya*, challenge their 'invisibility' by presenting emic perspectives on Afrobolivian livelihood and making them known to the public. On the other hand, the lyrics convey a positive image of blackness as something beautiful that Afrobolivians do not have to be ashamed of. Building on the interpretation of *saya* as a communicational device, the dance is also occasionally framed even more explicitly as a political strategy. Many Afrobolivian activists refer to *saya* as a tool of political strategy functionally equal to road blockades, marches and strikes, forms of collective action very common in Bolivia, especially in the context of indigenous mobilization and other popular sectors' efforts to reach their goals. For Afrobolivians, *saya* serves the same purpose and is employed strategically when deemed appropriate. In various conversations on the subject, Juan Carlos Ballivián – former CONAFRO secretary general – attributed the strategic advantage of *saya* to a variety of factors: besides the already mentioned aspect of communication, *saya's* playful character is in his view less inviting of direct repression by the state. In contrast to roadblocks, marches or strikes, a *saya* performance is much less likely to be disbanded violently by the police. Finally, since it is not always and immediately identifiable as 'politics,' it can be employed in spaces not accessible to political activism as such. What is more, and even though most Afrobolivians often comment very critically on the association of *saya* with Bolivian folklore and reject any attempt to reduce the expression to this category, many organizations and individuals very actively seek out spaces of folkloric performance in order to publicize *saya* and Afrobolivian culture more generally. Since 2011, *saya* has been recognized as part of the cultural and historic patrimony of the nation, alongside other dances that clearly pertain to the realm of folklore. As folklore, *saya* has become a marketable commodity and, as such, is an important economic factor for Afrobolivian organizations, as well as for individuals. Performing *saya* for money enables many individual members to earn some extra cash that would otherwise not be available to them and serves as a key funding mechanism for many Afrobolivian organizations. Beyond the economic aspect, as patrimony, *saya* also offers a way for Afrobolivians to relate to discourses of Bolivian cultural and national identity. In fact, being recognized as part of the folkloric panorama and lately as historical and cultural patrimony of the nation, is a key area of Afrobolivian visibility and a significant source of pride for many Afrobolivians (for a recent contextualization of Afrobolivian *saya* as part of Bolivian national folkore see Sigl and Mendoza Salazar 2012, chapter 6.1).

The centrality of *saya* in representations of Afrobolivian identity and culture can be explained by a combination of factors. Most importantly, *saya* was fairly easily translatable into the logics of the nascent multicultural Bolivia. In the late 1980s and early 1990s, in the context of multicultural reforms, the folklore industry (especially music and dance) emerged as an important realm within which Bolivia's diversity was not perceived as threatening, but could be accommodated as 'harmless difference.' *Saya* was perceived as a non-confrontational expression of Afrobolivian otherness that fit the discourses of Bolivia as diverse in cultural and ethnic terms, while at the same time not threatening political unity or tackling widespread political, social and economic inequality too directly. Thus Afrobolivianity was accommodated in multicultural Bolivia through *saya*, whereas the pervasive racism and discrimination that Afrobolivians faced were effectively muted. Yet *saya* cannot be entirely reduced to folklore; its inchoate character as floating between folklore and politics has become its major strategic advantage and through *saya* Afrobolivians have been able to some extent to voice political demands and create a collective space of political articulation.

Saya as the emblem of 'lite' Afrobolivianity

The centrality of *saya* in the realms of folklore, politics and discourse, however, must not divert our attention from the fact that *saya* ceased to be an important part of everyday practice in the Yungas in the years after the abolition of the *hacienda* system. In Cala Cala, although there have been efforts at revitalization and people told me that *saya* is performed occasionally, the dance is not part of everyday life and is also secondary to articulating a sense of Afrobolivianity. In Cala Cala, as elsewhere in the Yungas, social institutions that are not specific to Afrobolivians – mainly the *sindicato campesino*, the peasant union – are central for mediating community relations and framing belonging.

In its current form, *saya* is a re-instatement developed out of the experiences of Afrobolivians in urban settings and their engagement with folklore, emerging multicultural and plurinational regimes of recognition and diasporic identity politics. The central symbolic importance of *saya* for the articulation of Afrobolivianity also stems from urban contexts. When expressed through *saya*, Afrobolivianity has thus become a modality of identification that "coalesces around key symbols [...] but is not generally rooted in daily practice" (Canessa 2018:30). Andrew Canessa has observed a similar tendency with regard to indigeneity in Bolivia. On the one hand, there is the modality of indigeneity he observed in a small Andean village where "indigeneity is rooted in a community life with reciprocal labor practices and a set of rituals that bind the community and ancestors together" (Canessa 2018:31). On the other hand, he argues, there is the indigenous discourse developed by Evo Morales and his government in Bolivia. This discourse relies heavily on "symbols of national indigeneity" like the Indigenous New Year celebration and the coca leaf as a symbol of indigenous customs, identity and worldview that are "rooted in the national rather than the local community" (Canessa 2018:31). Following Thomas Grisaffi, who has studied indigenous identifications among coca growers in Cochabamba, Canessa argues that Evo Morales' government propagates a specific articulation of indigeneity, "a more flexible indigenous *lite* version of identity" that enables many people in Bolivia to "support an [indigenous] ethno-nationalist project without actually having to be all that indigenous themselves" (Grisaffi 2010:433) (i.e. without living in indigenous rural communities or speaking an indigenous language). In a similar vein, *saya* functions as the key symbol of a "lite" Afrobolivianity. This "lite" Afrobolivianity is rooted in the discourses of nationally dispersed urban Afrobolivian communities and not in daily economic and social life in local communities. Through *saya*, urban Afrobolivians thus have a way of engaging with Afrobolivianity, although they do not engage in any other particular social, economic and/or ritual practices that would distinguish them from the rest of society.

I think that this also explains why in urban settings people make so much of the affective capacity of *saya* and constantly emphasize its emotional value, whereas in the Yungas, discussions of *saya* are much less frequent and rather sober in tone. Many urban Afrobolivians emphasized that by performing *saya* they "embraced," "realized" or "learned about" their "true identity" as Afrobolivians. They also stress that it is through the bodily practice of performing *saya* (drumming, singing and dancing) that they most strongly "feel" their Afrobolivianity. Therefore it is crucial to acknowledge that *saya* – beyond its strategic value and its discursive role – is also very importantly a bodily practice of drumming, singing and dancing that has a heightened affective capacity. In various conversations I had with Afrobolivians throughout the years, at some point people would offer an account on how actively performing *saya* – for them – made their "identity as Afrobolivians" *("la identidad como Afroboliviano/a")* emotionally and affectively accessible.[4] Interestingly, the second most important context urban Afrobolivians mention with regard to engaging Afrobolivianity are workshops *(talleres)*. It is quite remarkable that, on the one hand, Afrobolivianity is engaged in highly formalized contexts and, on the other hand, through *saya*. In a way, *saya* can be regarded as the experiential counterpart to the formalized identity politics of workshops. I have thus come to think of both contexts – *saya* and *talleres* – as temporally and structurally marked dramatizations and culminations of Afrobolivianity. *Saya* is the experiential, emotional and bodily counterpart to workshops and political rallies in the sense that both contexts "activate" Afrobolivianity as a meaningful frame for people's self-identification (see Eidson et al. 2017).

4 I cannot systematically explore this aspect here, since my material from Cala Cala simply does not offer any fundamental insights with regard to the affective capacity and the bodily practice of *saya*. In Cala Cala, *saya* is not generally practiced and discussions of *saya* – limited as they are to begin with – focus on historical dimensions.

Saya is, however, not the only context in which notions of 'Afrobolivian culture' are negotiated and framed as meaningful. In what remains of this chapter, I will discuss processes of debating, cataloging and structuring 'Afrobolivian culture' in the context of government-sponsored programs. My discussion of Afrobolivian culture will thus move beyond *saya* by introducing additional elements that are considered important for Afrobolivian culture and by highlighting the fact that beyond the realm of cultural performance, contexts mediated by state institutions and certain legal regulations are emerging as key sites of often fairly strategic and guided efforts to catalog elements of Afrobolivian culture and make them a meaningful resource for articulating Afrobolivian identity in Bolivia.

Cataloging 'culture,' and sketching the contours of a *pueblo*

Similar to many other Afro-Latin American groups (see Minority Rights Group 1995), Afrobolivians have – for the most part with good reason – argued that they have been "invisible," "forgotten," "ignored" and "excluded" (cf. Busdiecker 2007:230) in their country. Beyond the realms of politics, rights and the economy, many Afrobolivians assert that this also holds true for the history and notions of national culture in Bolivia, where Afrobolivian contributions are generally obscured, neglected and minimized to the point of invisibility. Moreover, the few sources on Afrobolivian culture that are available have been produced by non-Afrobolivians and in ways that Afrobolivians do not agree with.[5] In recent years, however, there has been a significant increase in efforts at compiling elements and publishing findings on the subject of Afrobolivian culture and, some minor debate aside, a fairly stable list has been produced of musical expressions *(expresiones músico-danzisticas)*, cultural elements *(elementos culturales)*, historical and cultural contributions *(aportes y contribuciones históricas y culturales)*. More recently, and sparked by linguistic research (Lipski 2007; Lipski 2008; Pérez Inofuentes 2015; Sessarego 2011a; Sessarego 2014), Afrobolivian organizations have included references to Afrobolivian language *(la lengua Afro)* to their repertoire of elements. In local contexts, however, *la lengua Afro* hardly plays a role. People occasionally comment that they speak bad Spanish *("español mal hablado")*, but a proper Afrobolivian language does not play any part in their sense of being Afrobolivian.

Efforts at cataloging Afrobolivian culture must be seen as an integral part of the plurinational impetus of state institutions in their quest to implement the *"proceso de cambio"* – the envisioned political and cultural revolution in Bolivia. The

5 This mirrors the tension between self-presentation and representation (by someone else) that has been identified as a decisive feature of debates on Afrobolivian culture in the realm of folklore (Rossbach de Olmos 2007).

very practice of compiling allegedly stable 'elements' that constitute a generalizable 'Afrobolivian culture' mirrors important basic assumptions of plurinational discourse and the idea of discrete *pueblos*. It is based on the premise that each *pueblo* possesses a 'culture' that can be adequately described by listing specific elements. This 'culture' not only defines the *pueblo* in question, but also distinguishes it neatly from other *pueblos*. The essentialist and homogenizing outlook of the plurinational ID-ology machinery bluntly glosses over local variation in Afrobolivian lifestyles, as well as the contested nature of some expressions, let alone the fact that there are many more things Afrobolivians share with fellow Bolivians compared to the few 'elements' that are fashioned into the basis for their distinctions. Moreover, since the task of compiling and subsequently representing those elements in codified form has been attributed to specific institutions under the tutelage of the *Consejo Nacional Afroboliviano (CONAFRO)*, Afrobolivian culture is subject to political manipulation as well as to a certain bias in terms of which communities are taken into account in the process of compilation.

Before I address a set of concrete contexts in which the compilation of Afrobolivian culture takes place, it is useful to take a look at the 'elements' that have been established and are most widely accepted as constituting 'Afrobolivian culture':

- Dances: *saya, semba, matrimonio negro* (also occasionally referred to as *huayño negro, baile de tierra* or *cueca negra*)[6]
- *"El Rey Afroboliviano"*: the symbolic Afrobolivian monarchy
- Funeral rites: *mauchi* and *la chiguanita*
- Material Culture: *saya* instruments, *saya* clothes
- Language: *lengua Afro*

The fact that the prevailing idea of 'Afrobolivian culture' can be transcribed as a mere list of elements is significant in itself. The document pertaining to the Afrobolivian school curriculum treated below, for example, amounts to almost 300 pages. However, the document consists of tables and lists almost in its entirety.[7] The parts of the documentation that are not presented in tables or lists are summaries of the

6 There seems to be a lot of variation and even confusion regarding the exact terminology and the distinctions between *matrimonio negro, baile de tierra, cueca negra* and *huayño negro* (cf. Busdiecker 2007:156). In Tocaña, *baile de tierra* is the most commonly used name for a dance mostly danced at Afrobolivian weddings *(matrimonios)* in the past (thus the relation to *matrimonio negro*). That same dance is occasionally referred to as *cueca negra*. In Cala Cala, people spoke of *huayño negro* being performed alongside saya at Afrobolivian weddings and were not familiar with the designation *baile de tierra*.

7 For example, over 200 pages of tables indicate which elements can be subsumed under which official category. Furthermore, these tables indicate at what age and through which didactic methodology the elements ought to be taught to students.

legal and epistemological foundations of the educational reform that can be found in a strikingly similar fashion in all of the *currículos regionalizados* that have been made available to the public.[8] The document contains hardly any contextualized information on the meanings and practices associated with the listed elements. An interesting case in point is the symbolic Afrobolivian monarchy known as *"el Rey Afroboliviano"* (formerly also referred to as *"Rey Negro"*). The curriculum mentions *"el Rey Afroboliviano"* at the outset in the preamble, stating that:

> "It would be difficult to think of the *Pueblo Afroboliviano* without making reference to the meaning of the lineage of Rey Bonifacio Pinedo and his current heir, Julio Pinedo I., *Rey del Pueblo Afroboliviano*, principal political authority and in whom all the pillars of this *pueblo* are based"[9]

Yet, similar to other elements, *"el Rey Afroboliviano"* is merely listed and the institution is not further explained. An exploration and contextualization of this tradition, however, renders interesting results and is in many ways instructive of how *elementos culturales* are shaped in discourse and practice (for a recent discussion see Busdiecker 2019a).

The *Rey Afroboliviano* in context

The current Afrobolivian King (*Rey Afroboliviano*) is the grandson of *Rey Bonifacio Pinedo*, who died in the 1960s. According to the first and very prominent version of the story, the institution of the *Rey Afroboliviano* dates back to an unspecified moment in the colonial period when a slave of unknown African origin (some refer to the Congo, others to Senegal), was brought to work on the *hacienda Mururata* in the Nor Yungas province. The slaves of the *hacienda* are said to have discovered that this slave was of royal birth and referred to him as *Príncipe Uchicho*. They petitioned the owner of the *hacienda* to exempt him from his responsibilities and offered to do more work themselves in exchange for *Uchicho* to be left alone. This version has been recorded by Pizzarroso Cuenca in his publication *"La cultura negra in Bolivia"* without mentioning precise sources, attributing the information merely to *"tradición oral"* (Pizarroso Cuenca 1977). Bonifacio Pinedo, the last king whose existence can be accounted for in oral tradition today and who died in the 1960s, as well as Julio Pinedo, the current king, are regarded as direct descendants of *Príncipe Uchicho*. It

8 As of July 2018, nine *currículos regionalizados* have been published by the *Ministerio de Educación* (http://www.minedu.gob.bo/curriculos-regionalizados.html [28/07/18]).

9 *"Sería difícil pensar en el Pueblo Afroboliviano sin hacer referencia en lo que significa todo el linaje del Rey Bonifacio Pinedo y su actual heredero Julio Pinedo I" Rey del Pueblo Afroboliviano, máxima autoridad Política y en quien se cimientan todos los pilares de este Pueblo."*

is, however, unclear how the line of Afrobolivian kings was carried on from colonial times into the 20th century (Revilla Orías 2014b).

There is, however, a competing narrative accounting for the *Rey Afrobolivano* tradition. It appears in the testimony of an elderly inhabitant of Tocaña (the *comunidad* directly neighboring Mururata) that was recorded in the 1990s and published as a part of the *Tambor Mayor* project (Centro Pedagógico y Cultural "Simón I. Patiño" 1998b). This testimony neither makes any reference to the tradition dating back to colonial times, nor mentions an African prince as the origin of the tradition. According to this testimony, Bonifacio Pinedo was a very astute and clever *peón* of the *hacienda Mururata*. He was the *capataz* of Mururata (a sort of foreman coordinating the workforce under the supervision of the *hacienda* administrator) and also occupied a special position in the religious hierarchy of the community, assisting the Catholic priest in the celebration of the Holy Mass. According to the testimony, he used those positions to accumulate a significant amount of material wealth, despite the fact that he had to serve the *hacienda* owner as a *peón* just like any other resident of Mururata. He eventually became so rich that he could not only afford to build a house with a corrugated iron roof for himself located on the margins of the *hacienda* property, but also to pay fellow *peones* to take over his labor responsibilities towards the owner of the *hacienda*. In order to underline his special position among the *peones*, the testimony asserts, he travelled to La Paz and had a crown, scepter and coat fashioned by an urban artisan. Then he declared himself king, "King of money, King of gold, King of all the blacks" (*"Yo soy Rey de plata, Rey de oro, Rey de todos los negros"* [Centro Pedagógico y Cultural "Simón I. Patiño" 1998b:114]). He enjoyed an elevated status among the *peones* of Mururata and was frequently sought out for counsel and to settle disputes among the inhabitants. When he died without leaving a male heir in the 1960s, no successor was crowned and the institution of the *"Rey Afroboliviano,"* alongside other Afrobolivian cultural particularities, transformed from a practice to an account of local oral history.[10]

Only in the 1990s, following the first wave of revitalization of Afrobolivian culture, did the tradition of the "black king" again receive attention. In 1992, a wealthy hotel owner from Coroico approached Bonifacio's only known relative, his grandson and current king Julio Pinedo, and convinced him to be crowned as *Rey Afroboliviano* as part of a cultural festival held in Coroico to promote tourism in the Yungas (Rossbach de Olmos 2011:34). Since then, the *Rey Afroboliviano* has mainly appeared in journalistic accounts depicting Julio Pinedo as "the only African king in South America" (The Guardian 2007), "The last king of the Americas" (El País 2016), or the monarch of the "hidden kingdom of the Afro-Bolivians" (BBC News 2009), to name

10 *Cala Caleños* repeatedly asserted that no account of the *Rey Afroboliviano* circulated in Cala Cala until well into the 21st century. As far as the available sources go, the *Rey Afroboliviano* was only ever known in Mururata, and the neighboring *comunidades* of Chijchipa and Tocaña.

just a few of the exoticized images these articles tend to conjure up. Almost a decade after the coronation ceremony of 1992, in the early 2000s the urban Afrobolivian movement discovered the *Rey Afroboliviano* as a tradition potentially translatable to political strategy. Activists began positioning Afrobolivians as an ethnic group (*"etnía"* and later *"pueblo"*) analogous to indigenous people in Bolivia. In this context, a "traditional" institution and figure of authority became an important discursive asset. This process of political appropriation reached its peak in 2007, when another crowning ceremony for Julio Pinedo was organized in the *Prefectura* (regional government) of La Paz. During this ceremony, the governor of La Paz recognized the symbolic authority of the *Rey Afroboliviano*, declaring him the highest representative of the *pueblo Afroboliviano*. The well-known Afrobolivian activist Jorge Medina, who coordinated this event, has repeatedly explained the message he intended to send: if indigenous Bolivians now had 'their president' Evo Morales, Afrobolivians had their king. In political practice, however, the role of the king is minimal. He is occasionally invited to public events representing Afrobolivians in a purely ornamental fashion and his role as a symbolic authority is not even salient in his native Mururata, where the tradition originated (Busdiecker 2007).[11]

The institution of the *"Rey Afroboliviano"* thus has multiple roles: it has been transformed from a purely local symbolic figure with contested origins, surviving only in isolated accounts of oral history, to a performance orchestrated by non-Afrobolivians for journalistic and touristic ends beginning in the 1990s. In the 2000s the Afrobolivian monarchy became a contested symbol for political strategy, manipulated by urban Afrobolivian activists. Most recently, *el Rey Afroboliviano* has been included as another *elemento cultural* in the growing list of markers constituting the culture of *el pueblo Afroboliviano*. In this last role however, *el Rey Afroboliviano* is reduced to a mere 'element' on a list and hardly any details on the history or the current role of the king appear in the document.

---

11 Most recently, events took an even more unexpected turn that even surprised many Afrobolivian activists. Apparently, several years ago, Julio Pinedo was approached by a Spanish citizen who runs an online blog concerned with genealogical research, especially of families related to Spanish nobility (http://www.docelinajes.org/blog [24/06/18]). One of the few individuals in Bolivia who told me that he had met him in person referred to him vaguely as "a man from Spain with a lot of money doing something with lineages." Most likely his interest in Rey Julio Pinedo was sparked by one of the many journalistic accounts that have appeared in newspapers around the globe. I have not been able to document the relationship that developed out of this encounter. One of the results, however, is the official webpage of the *"Casa Real Afroboliviana"* that documents not only the King's activities, but also contains information on the history of the Afrobolivian monarchy.

Arbitrariness, political manipulation and the Tocaña bias

As I have come to understand through conversations with people in Cala Cala, the above-cited list claiming to represent universal 'Afrobolivian culture' is highly arbitrary and it was often met with open rejection or at least confusion by many of my interlocutors. Their criticism was twofold: on the one hand they argued that important 'elements' from Cala Cala were missing in the compilation, mainly aspects of local history and specific aspects of Cala Cala's *saya*. On the other hand, they were displeased that certain 'elements' not found in Cala Cala were represented as being important to all Afrobolivians nationwide – not least the *Rey Afroboliviano* that I have just discussed. People in Cala Cala often explained the differences between what they considered 'their culture' and what many publications represent as Afrobolivian by identifying the latter as rooted in a lack of knowledge and commitment to thorough research on the part of the compilers. Yet I have also come across various cases of quite straightforward manipulation for political ends. What is more, most representations of Afrobolivian culture rely on the context of one particular community and are thus imprecise when applied to all Afrobolivians in the country. In what follows, I will first introduce two short examples of political manipulation. Then I will discuss the Tocaña bias, i.e. the tendency for a particular Afrobolivian community (Tocaña) to be established as an index for Afrobolivian culture.

A vivid example of the processes associated with the compilation and the intentional manipulation of what is listed and represented as 'Afrobolivian culture' is an anecdote surrounding the elaboration of a monograph on Afrobolivian history, culture and economy developed jointly between CONAFRO and the Cochabamba-based research institution FUNPROIEB-Andes *(Fundación para la Educación en Contextos de Multiligüismo y Pluriculturalidad)*.[12] As one of the members of the research team recalled, people in the Yungas were asked to name "typical Afrobolivian dishes" to be included in the book. Responding truthfully, most people said that "*arroz con huevo*" ("rice with eggs") was the most common dish eaten by Afrobolivians every day. Juan Carlos Ballivián, then secretary general of CONAFRO and head of the research team, pushed for this information to be left out of the publication, since he considered "*arroz con huevo*" to be too trivial a dish to represent 500 years of Afrobolivian presence in the country. He even went as far as to consider this a disgrace, showing Afrobolivians as living in poverty and misery. As far as we can judge from the publication, his intervention was successful: alongside typical regional *Yungueño* dishes that are not specific to Afrobolivians, the book eventually listed references to "Mondongo, Anticuchos, Chicharón [sic!] and Patasca" as being dishes that Afrobolivians "might have exported to other regions of the country"

12 Foundation for Education in Contexts of Multilingualism and Pluriculturality.

(*"comidas que el Pueblo Afroboliviano habría exportado a otras regiones del país"*). The description continues:

> "Even though we do not have proof that the aforementioned dishes were an African contribution, among Afrobolivians it is known that those dishes originated in Afrodescendant communities [...]. According to activists, a proof of this is that in Afrodescendant communities in neighboring countries, those are typical dishes of their people. Thus, every Bolivian local population has probably added its own particularities, but the African essence and heritage have not been lost." (Zambrana B. 2014:205, my translation)

This short paragraph is instructive in a variety of ways: First of all, the information collected in Afrobolivian communities was overruled by a small group of specialists that had decided what kind of information was suitable for their project, even though they claim that "Afrobolivians" are the source of their information. Secondly, we learn from the quotation that "activists" have discovered parallels with Afrodescendant groups in neighboring countries, which serves as proof that those dishes are Afrobolivian. Simple analogies like this, establishing an unquestioned link between Africa, Afrodescendants in the Americas and Afrobolivians are often cited by Afrobolivian organizations and individuals in order to account for Afrobolivian cultural particularities. It is important to note that the logics shining through this example are neither limited to the topic of food, nor to this specific publication, but permeate most discussions, compilations, representations and negotiations of Afrobolivian culture. Sometimes they are framed as recuperations and revalorizations of purportedly 'lost cultural elements' and sometimes they are represented as the mere compilation thereof. Occasionally, as is the case for example with the growing trend of dressing in "African clothing," Afrobolivians explicitly address such practices as being part of *"etnogénesis"* (see for example Zambrana B. 2014:211).

Another very telling and visually accessible case is the cover design of a compendium of Afrobolivian culture sponsored by the *Minsterio de Educacíon*. The Afrobolivian researcher Juan Angola Maconde was assigned to coordinate the compilation and pen the publication. He also designed a cover image (see fig. 18), yet this image was replaced with the image of a *saya* dancer on the final publication.

Juxtaposing the two images, Juan Angola made the following comment in a Facebook group on Afrobolivians that he manages:

> "For the cover of the book I created a historical thread. Therefore I divided the drawing into two parts. The upper part reminds us of the African presence in the Villa Imperial de Carlos V. [Potosí] [...]. The lower part of the illustration makes reference to the Yungas [...]. In this region [the Africans] learned how to cultivate coca from the natives, the product that is the backbone of the Yungas economy until the present. Thus the region has become lived history of the African presence

Figure 18: Original cover design by Juan Angola Maconde (left) and the cover of the final publication (right) (images courtesy of Juan Angola Maconde/ Ministerio de Educación).

> in the Department of La Paz of what is today the Plurinational State of Bolivia. But the cover and back cover, I do not know for what motives, reasons and on what grounds, were changed to *saya*, making it look as if the contributions can be reduced to dance. Who provided the photographs for the cover? Where are the ethics?"[13]

He suspected CONAFRO and the *Minsterio de Educación* to be behind it, albeit that this was never confirmed and I have no knowledge of how the matter was settled. The case is telling in a variety of aspects. It shows the possibility of political manipulation by both Afrobolivian organizations and state institutions. It reminds us again of the centrality of *saya* and how it tends to overshadow other elements of 'Afrobolivian culture.' And, most importantly, it alerts us to the fact that what is

13 *"Para la tapa del libro creé un hilo histórico, para ello, hice el dibujo dividido en dos partes. La parte superior, hace memoria de la presencia africana en la Villa Imperial de Carlos V. [...] La parte baja de la ilustración, hace referencia a los Yungas [...]. En esta región [los Africanos] aprendieron a cultivar la coca de los nativos, producto que forma parte de la columna vertebral de economía yungueña hasta el presente. Convirtiéndose la región en historia viva de la presencia africana en el departamento de la Paz y de lo que hoy en día es Estado Plurinacional de Bolivia. Pero, la tapa y retapa, no sé por qué motivos, razones y fundamentos fue cambiado por la saya. Haciendo ver que, los aportes, se reducen al baile. ¿Quién proporcionó las fotos para la cubierta de la tapa? ¿Dónde queda la ética?"*

represented as 'Afrobolivian culture' very often tends to focus on simplified, folklorized images of harmless difference and does not take historical entanglements and lived reality into consideration. What is more, focusing on *saya* means granting Afrobolivian difference center stage, whereas similarities with other groups – expressed by Juan Angola by mentioning the importance of Afro-indigenous interaction in the coca economy – remain underrepresented.

The Tocaña bias

Beyond a rather narrow focus on *saya* and open political manipulation, another common tendency is to conceptualize 'Afrobolivian culture' with reference to one single community: the *comunidad* of Tocaña in Nor Yungas province (for a detailed ethnography of the community see Busdiecker [2007]). The force of that referencing has led to what I have come to think of as the *Tocaña bias* whenever Afrobolivians discuss matters of 'culture,' as well as when measuring degrees of authenticity. On the one hand, the Tocaña bias establishes a set of normative expectations with regard to what constitutes meaningful Afrobolivian 'cultural elements.' On the other hand, the expectations also refer to how certain 'cultural elements' are actually practiced: this encompasses *saya* performances, as well as the use of Afrobolivian Spanish, certain religious rites and other 'customs' like the making of *saya* drums and clothing. The bias has collective and organizational as well as individual dimensions and has recently been firmly and officially established by the state through its new law of education (see below).

Besides *saya*, which is known and has been practiced in all Afrobolivian communities that I am familiar with, the dances of *semba* and *baile de tierra* are also considered to be uniquely Afrobolivian dances, despite the fact that many communities – Cala Cala for instance – do not have any memory of these dances, let alone actively perform them in the present or the recent past. Additionally, the funeral rite *mauchi*, as well as the Afrobolivian monarchy *(el Rey Afroboliviano)*, count as important features of 'Afrobolivian culture' – even though not a single community other than Tocaña and the surrounding hamlets have any recollection of these elements (for details on the contested nature of the "*Rey Afroboliviano*" tradition see: Busdiecker 2007; Revilla Orías 2014b; Templeman 1998). A very common explanation for this situation, which is largely accepted in many other Afrobolivian communities, is that Tocaña has simply retained more 'African' elements than the other communities and is both the cradle and the "last bastion" of 'Afrobolivian culture' (cf. Busdiecker 2007).[14] Yet by taking a closer look, it becomes clear that Tocaña

14 Other explanations that cite much more recent and less 'African' roots for certain practices do exist, but have not gained such prominence within and beyond the Afrobolivian community.

has been made the reference for how 'Afrobolivian culture' and community ought to look through a long process rather than by virtue of 'objective' criteria.

The Tocaña bias as an assemblage of expectations – and lately as quasi-official reference for indexing 'Afrobolivian culture' – has its roots in a variety of sources. Firstly, Tocaña and its inhabitants and/or representatives have been very successful at almost monopolizing attention from scholars, the media, the Bolivian national government, tourism and international cooperation. This particular attention is in part rooted in Tocaña's seminal role in the early efforts at revitalization of Afrobolivian culture, making it a particularly visible community for quite some time. As will be detailed in chapter 8, individuals from the village and migrants somehow related to Tocaña or neighboring communities have been crucial actors in the establishment of the first urban *saya* groups and Afrobolivian organizations. As a consequence of this, the most prominent Afrobolivian political leaders are from Tocaña or are the offspring of migrants from the region, thus ensuring the prominent position of the community in most Afrobolivian organizations. Through its privileged position with regard to the attentions of activists, scholars and state agents, Tocaña's fairly particular demography, as well as the overall make-up of the *comunidad* and the equally particular panorama of cultural practices has been established as 'representative' of Afrobolivian communities and culture. The process by which Tocaña alone has been established as 'representative,' was also aided by the fact that Tocaña, more than most other Afrobolivian communities, fits the basic assumptions of what constitutes a "legible" (Scott 1998) community in multicultural, post-multicultural and plurinational Bolivia: cultural difference, ethnoracial homogeneity, and clear boundaries. Being the most homogenous Afrobolivian community to be found in the Yungas, with only a handful of Aymara inhabitants and hardly any interethnic marriages, Tocaña best fits the plurinational fantasy of discrete ethnoracial groups with clear cultural and geographic boundaries. The *comunidad's sindicato* is predominantly made up of Afrobolivian members, resulting in an almost complete overlap between ethnoracial affiliation and the social institution most consequential for daily life. In Tocaña, unlike in any other *comunidad* with Afrobolivian presence that I am aware of, residence patterns, *sindicato* organization, kinship and most of the political, economic and social networks do coincide with ethnoracial identity.

Its exceptionality notwithstanding, Tocaña has been established as being the most 'typical' and most 'authentic' Afrobolivian community and this has far-reaching consequences: Tocaña's 'culture' is taken to be the index of Afrobolivian culture in terms of the content (i.e. *elementos culturales*) and all other communities and people are assessed against the backdrop of Tocaña and its cultural expressions. Similar to the Colombian case, where the *comunidades negras* of the Pacific coast have "[provided] blackness with a stable, if narrow referent" (Wade 2009c:176), Tocaña has become that referent for Afrobolivian culture. Afrobolivian communities and individuals must refer to this index in one way or another. For many community representatives aiming to position their community as Afrobolivian in any politically meaningful sense, this means aspiring to compile as many sanctioned cultural elements as possible. In many cases this has led to a tendency to objectify culture to a great extent, making difference and 'authenticity' (and with that deservingness) a matter of quantifiable *elementos culturales* and *Afroboliviano* a category that is measured against the backdrop of Tocaña. In a more subtle way, the Tocaña bias also functions as a blueprint when questions of interethnic relations and the position of Afrobolivians in regional and national society are negotiated. Tocaña's historical, demographic, social and political circumstances are generalized and presented as the pattern for the kind of social relationships Afrobolivians have with other *pueblos* in Bolivia. Negating specific local situations and differences in time and space, Tocaña's very particular situation is established as the conceptual starting point for thinking and talking about Afrobolivian communities and their relationships in general. The logics entailed in the Tocaña bias require Afrobolivians everywhere not only to resort to an almost stereotyped list of cultural markers authorized by certain forces as valid for cultural distinction, but also to conceive of their situation and their relationships in a way that might not reflect their everyday experiences. This is true for rural Afrobolivians from other communities that are historically or demographically different from Tocaña, as well as for urban Afrobolivians who are trying to make sense of what distinguishes them culturally from other members of Bolivian society. What is lost along the way are the much more subtle distinctions that nevertheless have much greater significance in day-to-day interactions and in the construction of an Afrobolivian consciousness in various different settings of the Afrobolivian reality, urban and rural.

The few competing narratives decentering the Tocaña bias in political rhetoric and discursive articulations of Afrobolivianity have for the most part lost traction or have been superseded by the dominant position of political leaders from Tocaña. In the past, the Sud Yungas village of Chicaloma was known throughout Bolivia as "the village of the blacks" *("el pueblo de los negros")* (Léons 1972; Sturtevant 2013). *Chicalomeños* also claim the title "cradle of the traditional *saya*" *("cuna de la saya tradicional")* for their village. In the 21st century, references to Chicaloma have become rather scarce, though. I attribute this declining discursive importance of alternative local referents for Afrobolivianity to wider trends towards the homogenization of Afrobolivianity. Through their political influence in CONAFRO, people from Tocaña can exert great influence with regard to defining who or what represents 'Afrobolivian culture' on a national scale. For example, Juan Angola Maconde, a well-known activist and researcher from the *comunidad* Dorado Chico, was forced to publicly clarify the range and scope of one of his publications. He had to publicly declare – and did this among other ways through his Facebook page – that his glossary of

Afrobolivian Spanish entitled "The *afroyungueño* vernacular" should more precisely be entitled "The *afroyungueño vernacular of the sector Nor Yungas Coripata*," the region from which he collected most of his data (Angola Maconde 2012).[15] Prior to his public retraction, he was approached by CONAFRO officials and reprimanded for showcasing a supposed language of all Afrobolivians, when in reality he only presented data from one particular locality. So while the Tocaña faction is far from hesitant to hold Tocaña's *elementos culturales* to be valid for all Afrobolivians, and has the political power and institutional backing to actively enforce this point of view, they very jealously defend this privileged position and police the boundaries of what is considered 'Afrobolivian culture.' This of course has to do with access to resources, political and otherwise. The discursive power of the Tocaña bias, paired with the leading role of the Tocaña-dominated CONAFRO in political terms, has not only led to the hegemony of Tocaña with regard to defining what Afrobolivian culture is, but has also benefitted the community in economic (through tourism projects), and political terms (the majority of Afrobolivian elected representatives and technicians are from Tocaña and its surroundings).[16] What is more, and I will turn to the implications of this in the next section, Tocaña's culture and the list of cultural elements compiled from Tocaña has even become 'official' Afrobolivian culture in codified form in the Afrobolivian school curriculum. This was made possible through CONAFRO's and CEPA's close ties to the *Minsterio de Educación* and the crucial role individuals from Tocaña and the surrounding hamlets played in the elaboration of the curriculum.[17]

Currículo regionalizado del pueblo Afroboliviano: cataloging the essence of a people

The compilation and interpretation of 'cultural elements' "pertaining to Afrobolivians" (*"perteneciente al pueblo Afroboliviano"*) is not merely an academic endeavor and is not limited to book publications or debates among activists. The plurinational machinery set in motion by the legal recognition of Afrobolivians has catapulted the question of what constitutes 'Afrobolivian culture' to center stage, most notably in the combined efforts of CONAFRO and the Ministry of Education in developing

15 Original title: *"El habla afroyungueña" vs. "El habla afroyungueña del sector Nor Yungas Coripata"*.

16 Of course there are also people in Tocaña critical of CONAFRO (on these and other grounds) and people from other regions actively contributing to the proliferation of the Tocaña bias for a variety of reasons.

17 In fact, CONAFRO's secretary general *(Secretario General)*, its secretary of education *(Secretario de Educación)* – who at the same time presides over CEPA – and the key *técnico* at the *Ministerio de Educación* were all from Tocaña or neighboring villages at the time of the elaboration of the curriculum's contents.

the so-called regionalized curricula for Bolivian public schools. The idea behind the *"currículos regionalizados"* is detailed in Law 070 (*"Ley 070 de la Educación "Avelino Siñani - Elizardo Pérez"*), the backbone of the educational reform the MAS government introduced in 2010. Law 070 establishes that education in plurinational Bolivia – among other things – ought to be

> "decolonizing, liberating, revolutionary, anti-imperialist, de-patriarchal and transforming the economic and social structures; oriented towards the cultural reaffirmation of the *naciones and pueblos indígena originiario campesinos*, the *comunidades interculturales* and *afrobolivianas* in the construction of the Plurinational State and the *Vivir Bien*." (Law 070, Art. 3)[18]

In addition to the so-called *currículo base* (the basic curriculum applied in schools all over the country), it is the specific goal of the new educational system to implement so-called *currículos regionalizados* to establish certain educational content according to the socio-cultural and linguistic context of specific regions (*"contexto sociocultural y lingüístico"* [Ley 070, Art. 70]). In practice, this meant that the *Consejo Educativo del Pueblo Afroboliviano (CEPA)* had to compile information and, in collaboration with the *Ministerio de Educación*, develop an Afrobolivian *currículo regionalizado* that does justice to Afrobolivian particularities.

The first time I came into direct contact with the processes associated with the elaboration of the *currículo regionalizado* was in August 2012 in the Sud Yungas village of Irupana, where I participated in a workshop *(taller)* organized jointly by the *Consejo Nacional Afroboliviano (CONAFRO)*, the *Ministerio de Educación* and the *Consejo Educativo del Pueblo Afroboliviano (CEPA)*. The workshop was designed to be the platform for Afrobolivian communities to support the Ministry of Education technocrats *(técnicos)* with 'traditional' content for the new Afrobolivian curriculum. The workshop was held with the inhabitants of different communities of the Sud Yungas province, in which various *comunidades* with Afrobolivian populations are located. I had been informed by my contacts from La Paz that this workshop was complementary to a similar workshop that had been held in Tocaña with the participation of Afrobolivians from the Nor Yungas province. Highlighting the Tocaña bias once more, however, the organizers of the workshop brought people from Tocaña in a bus (sponsored by the *Ministerio de Educación*) in order to participate in the workshop in Sud Yungas as well. The goal of the workshop was to compile the Sud Yungas perspective from Irupana and the neighboring *comunidades*. Yet the organizers thought it important to bring in people with experience *(experiencia)* in

18 *"[...] descolonizadora, liberadora, revolucionaria, anti-imperialista, despatriarcalizadora y transformadora de las estructuras económicas y sociales; orientada a la reafirmación cultural de las naciones y pueblos indígena originario campesinos, las comunidades interculturales y afrobolivianas en la construcción del Estado Plurinacional y el Vivir Bien"* (Law 070, Art. 3).

order to orient *(orientar)* the participants from the surrounding *comunidades* in the process of compiling 'cultural elements.' The organizers framed the whole workshop in a way that clearly gave Tocaña a privileged position. The people from Sud Yungas were to merely complement the contents that had already been compiled in Tocaña, leaving no room for contradictory voices and serious debate.

At first, representatives from CONAFRO introduced the organization, its goals and recent milestones of mobilization, as well as the relation between CONAFRO, CEPA and the *Ministerio de Educación* (see chapter 9). After that, CEPA representatives and the *técnico* from the ministry explained the 'theory' behind the new Law of Education, emphasizing its de-colonial impetus, the respect for cultural diversity it purports to foster, as well as the goal of revalorizing indigenous and Afrobolivian knowledge *(saberes y conocimientos del pueblo Afroboliviano)*. Interestingly, the Ministry of Education had invited representatives of two indigenous groups – an Aymara and an Uru Chipaya – who had participated in the elaboration of their respective *currículos regionalizados*. They shared their experiences concerning the technicalities, as well as the contents the Aymara and Uru Chipaya had discussed in the context of the elaboration of their curricula. Even though it was never stated explicitly, the participation of these two indigenous representatives confronted the participants with a certain logic concerning the information the organizers were trying to compile. Tacitly, the Afrobolivian collectivity was equated with an indigenous *pueblo*, establishing a set of markers and certain expectations tied to the logic of being a *pueblo*. Thus, beyond the legal sphere and mere formalities, the workshop contained a moment in which the equation between indigenous and Afrobolivian *pueblo* status was instantiated in practice.

Experts, categories and 'culture'

For the actual process of compiling, the organizers separated the participants into different groups and assigned different tasks to them. There were groups for gathering relevant data on Afrobolivian history, medicine and 'traditional' healing practices, 'traditions' and values, dance and music, their relation to the environment (*"la Madre Tierra,"* lit.: "Mother Earth") and sustainable use of natural resources, as well 'traditional' modes of subsistence. Even though the format seemingly left it to the people to choose what they thought would be relevant content, categories and items, the introductory lecture on the 'theory' of the law established the categories that people should try to accommodate their 'experiences,' and 'knowledge' to. What is more, each group was accompanied by one or two of the 'experts' who guided their brainstorming and directed the process of compiling relevant elements. The influence of predetermining relevant categories of knowledge became obvious when the posters prepared by the participants were discussed in the plenary and contained almost exactly the same categories and technical language the experts had used during their introduction. One case in point is the listing of the category of "bio-indicators" *("bio-indicadores")*. This category stems from the idea that 'indigenous groups' have a profound knowledge of "bio-indicators" that enhance their ability to interpret specific natural phenomena and that go beyond the content of regular educational curricula inspired more by a belief in 'Western' natural sciences. Such technical language is all but absent from the everyday vocabulary of Afrobolivians and was probably coined at some meeting of educational professionals debating the theory of indigenous curricula. This is not to say that Afrobolivians (or other groups for that matter) do not possess this kind of knowledge. The point I am stressing is that this knowledge is neither specific to Afrobolivians in the Yungas, nor subsumed commonly under the rubric of "bio-indicators." Rather, it is part of common Yungas knowledge that has now been designated as something inherently Afrobolivian and codified in a specific way. The workshops thus not only shaped the categories used by people and classified their knowledge, but instructed them to claim it as exclusively Afrobolivian knowledge.

The *Currículo Regionalizado del Pueblo Afroboliviano* as it appears on the homepage of the *Minsterio de Educación* and will eventually be implemented in schools all over Bolivia reflects these conceptual bases and the practices of compilation of the *talleres* in question. The workshop's basic approach and its different dimensions are reflected in large parts of the document. First and foremost, the *currículo regionalizado* conceptualizes Afrobolivian culture as a set of discrete elements that can be listed and categorized in order to be operationalized in programs of education. It furthermore abets the idea that this set of markers applies to all Afrobolivians, thus essentializing and homogenizing a heterogeneous collective. Finally, it posits certain elements, *saberes y conocimientos* as specifically Afrobolivian, downplaying the essentially transcultural and overarching character (in the sense that they are shared by *Yungeños* regardless of their ethnic or cultural affiliations) of many of the items listed as Afrobolivian.

Traditional knowledge, coevalness and plurinational anxiety

What is more, during the workshop, participants were urged to think about how things were done "back in the day" *("como se hacía antes")*. When prompted in this way, some of the older participants were able to recall certain plants and their uses as household medicines, old forms of measuring distances, surfaces and weights or quantities of coca leaf (none of which were specifically Afrobolivian as far as the participants were concerned). Remembering knowledge is of course not a bad thing *per se*, neither is teaching it to children in school. The crux, however, is that their way of life is essentialized and exoticized. That is, Afrobolivians of the past are exoticized as 'others' in the sense of not being coeval (Fabian 2002), not pertaining to 'modernity.' The experts – relying on the new law and its politics of representation – were not interested in how these people actually lived, and those aspects that did not fit their predetermined ideas of the life of an 'indigenous group' were often ignored. For example, everybody was thrilled about the fact that some people remembered a certain plant that was used to wash clothes in the past (probably *Sapindus saponaria*) and eagerly included this piece of information in their database, ignoring the explicit statements by various people that "of course, nowadays, we use *Ace* [a brand of industrially produced detergent available all over the country]." In a similar fashion and during the course of the entire workshop, 'non-traditional' knowledge, the use of 'modern technology,' the dispersal of many Afrobolivian communities due to ongoing massive migration to regional and national urban centers, the growing use of agrochemical products in the coca economy and the influence of mass media were downplayed or even openly ignored. As a result, the information that had been compiled during the course of the workshops presented a *pueblo Afroboliviano* living as it did fifty years ago. The preamble of the *currículo* even states that the document "recovers the values and historical and cultural principles of the *pueblo Afroboliviano* that have remained latently present as a living culture for more than half a century," making the assumptions underlying the *currículo* with regard to different temporal horizons and their significance for the present explicit. The set of cultural traits that should be considered for the purpose of education are located in the past ("half a century ago"), in the time of the *hacienda* and not in the present.[19]

The *currículo* is not the only example pointing in this direction. Very vivid and instructive in this regard is a short documentary movie produced by the *Ministerio de Culturas* in Cala Cala in 2012. This documentary is part of a series of short films aimed at recuperating the oral history and "traditional values" of the thirty-six recognized groups in their respective languages.[20] The Afrobolivian contribution consisted of the re-telling of a legend associated with the coca plant *(la coca era di sacudí)*.[21] The six-minute film presents three temporal horizons: the present, the time of the *hacienda* and an undefined mythical past . It begins with a woman from Cala Cala remembering – in the present – how her grandfather told her the tale of why it is so hard and physically exhausting to harvest coca leaves. Community members dressed as they would have in the times of the *hacienda* perform scenes that show how the story was told in those times. Additionally – introducing a third temporal horizon – the myth located in a moment even further back in time is performed by community members. The relationship between the three temporal

19 *"Se recogen los valores y principios históricos y culturales del Pueblo Afroboliviano que se mantuvo latente como cultura viva por más de medio siglo."*

20 *"Rescate de la historia oral en 36 lenguas y valores humanos a través de cuentos tradicionales."*

21 *"La Coca era de sacudí"* (available at https://www.youtube.com/watch?v=GVXFbeyX-bY [17/01/18]).

horizons is quite interesting. Besides the quasi-mythical times of the forefathers (which in the case of Afrobolivians can be estimated to lie in the 17th century) when the events that were later converted into the legend took place, there is the time of the *hacienda* (when these stories were told to children by their grandparents) and the present plurinational moment of recuperation. Thus knowledge considered 'traditional' and worthy of recuperation and conservation is localized in the times of the *hacienda* from whence it must be retrieved. These tendencies were not at all taken as something negative or even strange by the participants of the workshop or the documentary. The almost generalized feeling of many people that 'traditions' are eroding, lifestyles are rapidly changing and that this leaves them with little of their 'identity' led most of my interlocutors to enthusiastically embrace this kind of approach. Whereas people tend to express pride in 'authentic Afrobolivian culture' that has survived despite a century-long "*invisibilización*" in formal interviews, I gained other impressions from numerous informal conversations with Afrobolivians from all over the country. What many people conveyed to me in these conversations was a certain type of anxiety, as if they felt that the 'culture' they possess and are able to exhibit in everyday contexts somehow falls short of the expectations put forth by the New Plurinational Constitution, its related programs and the ubiquitous experts and agents of plurinationality that stress concepts of cultural difference based on ahistorical, unchanging pureness and homogeneity.

Making the group, freezing the differences

Besides the tendency to exoticize Afrobolivians as a group and localize them and their lifestyle in the past, 'unspoiled by modernity,' the workshops' design, content and logics had another effect. Unquestioned by most of the participants, the mere invitation of Afrobolivians to the workshops postulated the importance and social relevance of this category of identity. For the experts, it goes without saying that "being Afrobolivian" is the most important and socially consequential facet of identity and thus the only logical basis for compiling data on their way of life. Given my experiences in Cala Cala and other regions of the Yungas, and also with regard to migration and the circumstances under which Afrobolivians live in the country's urban centers, this unquestioned salience is less clear than it may at first seem. Yet the educational law, by way of the categories it proposes, establishes and privileges, and through the practices and performances that are part of these workshops, changes the way people think and talk about themselves, others and difference. By gathering people according to their identity as Afrobolivians, such workshops motivate them to think about their way of life "as Afrobolivians," highlighting what distinguishes them from others. The complex machinery comprising activists, NGO workers and government officials, equipped with laws, projects, programs and workshops summons the collective that they are purporting to represent, include and educate. Workshops are sites where Afrobolivian groupness is called into being and their logics not only mark Afrobolivians as different, they also establish the permitted parameters of this difference by culturalizing Afrobolivianity. They localize Afrobolivians and 'their culture' in the Yungas by linking cultural difference to territoriality (most clearly expressed through the notion of regionalized *currículo*) and by indexing Afrobolivian culture as something rural, premodern and 'other.' They largely ignore the similarities Afrobolivians share with other groups in the Yungas, and fail to contextualize the region with its economic and political connections and migratory flows to different regions of the country. Though there is constant talk of interculturality and the coexistence of different *pueblos* within the region, the logics of the educational law stick to the rather rigid ideas of discrete cultural entities and ignore instances of transculturation and adaptation that mark the history of Afrobolivians and other groups in the Yungas that would, of course, complicate the elaboration of discrete curricula for supposedly discrete cultural groups located in discrete territories.

Conclusion

My aim in this chapter was to elaborate on my assertion that references to 'Afrobolivian culture' are increasingly important in articulating Afrobolivianity. Although racialized images of Afrobolivians are still widespread and Afrobolivians themselves continuously debate racial mixture, 'culture' plays an increasingly important role, especially in the realms of political mobilization, the elaboration of legal documents and in public performances of Afrobolivianity.

Analyzing notions of Afrobolivian culture inevitably means engaging with *saya*. Revitalizing *saya* has been the starting point of establishing notions of an Afrobolivian collective identity in cultural terms and *saya* is often portrayed as synonymous with Afrobolivian culture. By approaching *saya* as a reflexive, contingent and often ambiguous cultural performance, an "important dramatization [...] that enable[s] participants to understand, criticize, and even change the worlds in which they live" (Guss 2000:9), I have fleshed out how the dance "may be used to articulate a number of different ideas" and thus "produce new meanings and relations" (Guss 2000:10–11). In the context of *saya* performances, a wide range of aspects important in the articulation of Afrobolivianity are negotiated. Folklorized images of Afrobolivian cultural difference, racialized notions of authenticity (recall the episode from chapter 6 and the question of whether 'white' people should be allowed to dance) and the strategic political positioning of Afrobolivianity all come together in *saya* performances. Moreover, in the context of *saya* performances, competing perspectives on the "roots" and "routes" (Greene 2007a) of Afrobolivian identity and culture are expressed and negotiated by interchangeably or simultaneously referencing the Yungas and 'Africa' through instruments, lyrics and dress.

Saya also vividly exemplifies the transforming social contexts of Afrobolivianity. It reflects Afrobolivian migratory trajectories, the overlaps and contradictions between rural and urban Afrobolivians and the transformations the concept of Afrobolivianity has undergone during the process of being articulated as a matter of cultural difference in multicultural and plurinational times. As a part of this process, *saya* has transcended the local context of Afrobolivian communities and has become a national emblem of an Afrobolivianity that is no longer exclusively located in rural village contexts. The modifications of *saya* this entails are sometimes interpreted as leading to *saya's* meanings being diluted and its essence being lost – recall Francisco's fear that *saya* "will be lost" *("se va a perder")*. I argue, however that rather than being "lost" or stripped of its meaning, *saya* has been creatively adjusted to new contexts: urban Afrobolivian lifeworlds, folkloric spaces of performance, as well as multicultural and plurinational opportunities at representation. What is more, *saya* has a profound emotional value for many Afrobolivians and thus, beyond being the object of strategic political maneuvering, I have argued that *saya* must be seen as the affective counterpart to formalized contexts of identity politics.

Moving beyond *saya*, I have described efforts at cataloging Afrobolivian culture for various ends: academic publications, political lobbying and the elaboration of documents that purport to represent the 'culture' and lifestyles of recognized *pueblos*. The efforts at cataloging Afrobolivian culture and representing it in codified form are important in many regards. First of all, they are a sign of the growing importance of direct state intervention in matters of culture. They also reflect the particular perspective of the plurinational state vis-à-vis the question of how Bolivia's *proceso de cambio* is to be effectuated. As can be identified in the new Law of Education the 'cultural reaffirmation' of the *naciones y pueblos indígena originiario campesinos* is represented as the decisive step in 'transforming the economic and social structures' of the country. Privileging indigenous groups and *el pueblo Afroboliviano* as collective actors whose cultural reaffirmation, empowerment and representation lies at the core of the current political conjuncture makes it increasingly necessary to obtain clear-cut definitions of what a *pueblo* is and what 'culture' can and should be "reaffirmed." During this process, Afrobolivian culture is conceptualized as a list of discrete elements that clearly mark the boundary of *el pueblo Afroboliviano*. This approach not only overshadows variation between different parts of the Afrobolivian population, but also ignores the fact that many elements that are posited as specifically Afrobolivian are, in fact, fundamentally transcultural and of overarching importance in the Yungas. What is more, the efforts to compile and codify culture propagate a static view on culture, downplaying the processual nature of Afrobolivian cultural practice.

In this chapter, I have argued in favor of considering 'culture' an increasingly important aspect of Afrobolivianity. I have based my argument on the central role of *saya* for representing Afrobolivianity and have also highlighted how the plurinational state actively engages with Afrobolivians as a collective subject essentially defined by its cultural characteristics. This perspective is shared by many Afrobolivian individuals – the shirt stating *"soy cultura, no color"* (fig. 16) being just one visual and very clear articulation of a broader narrative. However, as we have seen in chapter 6 and also throughout my discussion of what it means to be *"Afro"* in Cala Cala, this perspective is neither uncontested, nor can it explain Afrobolivianity exhaustively. In fact – and many approaches to Afrobolivianity tend to overlook this important aspect – it is a rather new perspective. It emerged in the 1980s and gained widespread acceptance mainly through the activities of what is often referred to as *"el Movimiento Afro"* – the Afrobolivian movement. Thus the articulation of Afrobolivianity as a matter of 'cultural difference' cannot be understood without reference to this heterogeneous movement. In the next chapter, I will therefore trace the historical roots of this movement in order to show that specific perspectives and conceptualizations that are often taken for granted nowadays only emerged through a contested process of political struggle.

Chapter 8: *"El Movimiento Afroboliviano"*
Cultural Revitalization, Citizenship and Development

What is often simply referred to as *"el Movimiento Afro(boliviano)"* is in fact a heterogeneous conglomerate of organizations representing a wide range of activities and engaging with different political discourses. In this chapter, I will trace the emergence of the *Movimiento Afro* from efforts by a group of high school students to rescue the Afrobolivian dance *saya* in the Yungas town of Coroico up to the formation of various organizations that continue to shape Afrobolivian politics today. *El Movimiento Afro* emerged in a context that was marked by the logics of a Bolivian state that increasingly embraced multicultural politics and topics like cultural diversity and differentiated citizenship. At the same time, Afrobolivian activists also embraced discourses and ideas associated with the wider African Diaspora in the Americas, combining elements of indigenism (Niezen 2003) and multiculturalism with ideas of "diasporic ancestrality" (Walsh and León 2006) and the global struggle against racism. I will show how the struggle for the survival and passing on of certain Afrobolivian cultural practices took on more political dimensions and ultimately crystallized into what has been called *"el Movimiento Afro"* in Bolivia.

In order to get a first glimpse at the evolution of the *Movimiento's* discursive and ideological foundations, it is instructive to analyze the logos of three Afrobolivian organizations that were founded in different periods of history (see fig. 19). The logo on the left belongs to MOCUSABOL, the *Movimiento Cultural Saya Afroboliviana*. MOCUSABOL is regarded as the first Afrobolivian organization in the country and was officially and legally established in 1998, although its roots date back to the late 1980s.[1] Its name vividly exemplifies the thrust of mobilizations in the late 1990s, highlighting culture and especially *saya*. It also uses the denomination *Afroboliviano*, hinting at the efforts to establish this term as an alternative to *negro/a*.

1 It is often difficult to establish an exact date of foundation for many of the organizations. Very often, the process of legally establishing an organization *(obtener personería jurídica)* takes several years. If not otherwise noted, with "foundation" I refer to the moment when the members of an organization consider that it was established, not the date of official registration.

The logo furthermore features the silhouette of Bolivia's national borders combined with two black faces. When I asked the founding members how this logo came into existence, they told me that the graphic was designed in a time when the members of the organization referred to it as *"Movimiento Negro"* and that it was supposed to represent the fact that "there are blacks in Bolivia" (*"También hay negros en Bolivia"*). Later, the organization was officially established as *Movimiento Cultural Saya Afroboliviana* and became nationally known as *"Movimiento Afro,"* though the initial logo was kept. MOCUSABOL's logo and name thus exemplify a first shift and its underlying contradictions: the terminological shift from *negros* to *Afrobolivianos*. They also hint at the importance of *saya*, as well as the central importance of positioning *Afrobolivianos* as part of the Bolivian nation.

Figure 19: Logos of Afrobolivian organizations (courtesy of MOCUSABOL, Mauchi, Afrocruz).

The second logo belongs to *Mauchi*, an Afrobolivian organization founded in the city of Cochabamba around 2010. *Mauchi's* name refers to an Afrobolivian funeral rite considered to be the 'most African' of all Afrobolivian traditions and its logo uses what members describe as "African iconography" (*"iconografía Africana"*). Furthermore, it makes direct reference to the concept of *Afrodescendientes. Mauchi* represents another set of developments shaping Afrobolivian organization. There is no reference to *saya*, but to another 'cultural element' associated with Afrobolivians. It thus represents a move away from the focus on *saya* to include further aspects of Afrobolivian culture. It also replaces the denomination *Afroboliviano* with *Afrodescendiente*, hinting at the growing importance of transnational discourses on *Afrodescendencia*. Furthermore, it visually expresses a link to Africa and what Afrobolivians regard as representative of 'African culture.' It is important to note that *Mauchi* was founded in Cochabamba, whereas the first Afrobolivian organizations were based in La Paz. Throughout the years however, more and more Afrobolivians migrated beyond La Paz (the city closest to the Yungas geographically) and organizations were established in Cochabamba, Santa Cruz and Sucre.

The third logo belongs to an organization founded in Santa Cruz in 2015. It carries a reference to Santa Cruz in its name *"AfroCruz"* and its logo, in addition to the Bolivian flag, also displays the white and green flag of Santa Cruz. It references relations to *"lo Afro"* through a depiction of Afro hairstyle and the red star that the designer of the logo explained to me as being a reference to "African internationalism" *("internacionalismo Afro")*. It furthermore includes references to *saya*, depicting a drum *(caja)* and *cuancha*, the basic instruments of *saya*. Also very interesting is that it includes the image of a whip. In earlier performances of *saya*, the leader of the men would carry a whip, underscoring his authority over the dance troupe, an element of *saya* rarely found in performances nowadays.

Conspicuously, none of the organizations I have introduced so far was founded in the Yungas, the region of Bolivia most strongly associated with Afrobolivians. In fact, the largest part of my discussion of the *Movimiento Afro* is centered in urban contexts. This is due to the fact that beyond the foundational moment in Coroico and the surrounding *comunidades*, Afrobolivian organizations are mostly an urban phenomenon. With the notable exception of Tocaña (see chapter 7), even today there is no explicitly Afrobolivian organization in the Yungas. However, the organizational logics of urban Afrobolivians have been gaining ground in the Yungas, even though strong peasant unions *(sindicatos)* remain the principal institutions of political belonging and mobilization. What is more, and as I will show in this chapter, the emergence of the *Movimiento Afro* is inextricably linked to migration and thus concerns urban and rural Afrobolivians alike. In Cala Cala, the debates described in this chapter have also played only a limited role. *Cala Caleños* did frequently recall and mention two concrete events that I will address in this chapter: the gathering of Afrobolivians at the Governmental Palace in La Paz at the invitation of Vice President Victor Hugo Cárdenas in 1994 and the recording of *saya* by the *Tambor Mayor* project in 1998. They also mentioned that they sporadically participated in workshops and that they were familiar with Jorge Medina because of his radio show. All those things remain isolated phenomena from their perspective, however. *Cala Caleños* have not been thouroughly mobilized according to the logics of the *Movimiento Afro* and their participation remains momentary and relatively volatile. This is also why, in Cala Cala, a localized notion of what it means to be *Afro* largely prevails (see chapter 3) and the activities of the nationally active organizations are often perceived as only marginally important in the local context. As my discussion of a particular project in chapter 10 suggests, however, Cala Cala is increasingly drawn into the discursive spaces that the *Movimiento Afro* has created and confronted with images of Afrobolivianity established by decades of mobilization and debate.

Rediscovering *saya*: Coroico, 1982

When asking an Afrobolivian person to explain how the "*Movimiento Afroboliviano*" was founded and what it was all about, one is normally first told the story of the rediscovery of *saya*. Minor variations notwithstanding, there is a fairly standardized narrative of the rediscovery of *saya*. The following paragraph is a condensed account of the many almost identical narratives that I have heard from countless Afrobolivians:

"On 20 October 1982, for the first time in many years, the village of Coroico in Nor Yungas Province witnessed a public performance of *saya*, a uniquely Afrobolivian dance. The performance was part of the *fiesta patronal* in honor of *La Virgen de la Candelaria*. It was staged by high school students, young people of around seventeen years of age. As the *saya* dancers entered the village plaza, spectators admired the skills of the drummers, singers and dancers and marveled at the 'exotic' and uncommon appeal of the Afrobolivian rhythms and songs. They cheered the young musicians, encouraging them to keep playing. The whole village was thrilled by the sight of this 'black tradition' *(tradición negra)* in the space of public festive performance, since there had not been a similar performance in many years, leading to the assumption that *saya* – and with it the 'culture' of black people in Bolivia – had disappeared and was beyond recovery. The dance had not been performed by Afrobolivians for decades and only persisted in the memories of people in the Yungas. Many older members of the Afrobolivian community reluctantly watched the performance from afar, afraid of mockery and distasteful comments by the non-black audience. Indeed, it was because of mockery and discrimination that they had stopped performing *saya* and valuing their culture in the first place. Only after a while and after witnessing the positive reactions the youngsters' performance sparked among the spectators did they feel confident enough to approach the performance and express their joyfulness. At some point in the *fiesta*, some of the Afrobolivian villagers even joined in the singing, drumming and dancing, and the *saya* performance in Coroico on 20 October marks the moment *saya* was rediscovered and the beginning of its revitalization."

This narrative contains a lot of condensed information and also a number of key components that play an important role in shaping the narratives on culture, history and political mobilization that circulate among Afrobolivians. First of all, it foregrounds the claim that *saya* had almost been lost in the years prior to the performance and that the 'loss' of *saya* corresponds to Afrobolivian culture more generally. This process is attributed to widespread discrimination against Afrobolivians and their culture, which led an entire generation to seek integration by assimilating to the cultural mainstream in the Yungas and Bolivia more generally. Second, it emphasizes the pivotal role the younger generation played in the rediscovery of *saya*; against the will of the older generations, or at least despite their reservations against dancing *saya*, the students managed to stage a performance. Last, by framing the rediscovery of *saya* as the moment of inception of the *"Movimiento Afro"* more generally, this narrative posits the centrality of 'culture' for the Movement and Afrobolivian identity and establishes *saya's* paramount importance for everything that follows. Whether the 20 October performance was indeed the first public *saya* performance in years is not entirely unquestioned. It is also unclear – and this is an issue hotly debated among Afrobolivians – whether *saya* was indeed at the brink of disappearance or just not very frequently performed in public anymore. There are some sparse pieces of information that suggest that there had been other occasions, but none had the profound consequences the Coroico performance was able to generate (see below). This is why the 20 October performance has entered the Afrobolivian collective memory as the moment when the revitalization of their 'culture' began.

After the success of the 1982 *saya* performance, the group repeated the performance for the same occasion in 1983. This time – as participant Julia Pinedo recalled in an interview – the performance had an even greater impact:

> "[In 1983] there was the 'boom' in town [in Coroico]. It was the sensation in town, *la saya*. And the very people from the *comunidades*, for example Tocaña [...] who didn't want to know about dancing *saya* before. They danced indigenous dances in their *fiesta patronal*, they were dancing to other types of music of the indigenous people, but not their own. They heard the *saya* and they said: 'Wow, who is playing *saya*? It can't be the kids from school.' And then they threw themselves in. [...] And the next day, even more. All of them had come to see, they took the drums away from us [...] and they ended up playing."[2]

---

2 *"[1983] ya ha sido pues el Boom. En el pueblo. Ha sido la sensación en el pueblo, la saya. Ya la misma gente de las comunidades, por ejemplo Tocaña [...] que ya no querían saber de bailar saya, ellos bailaban en su fiesta patronal [...] bailes indígenas, estaban bailando otros tipos de música de los indígenas menos lo de ellos. [...] Ellos escucharon la saya y decían:'¿Pucha quiénes son los que están golpeando saya? No creo que sean los chicos de colegio.' Y se lanzan. [...] Al día siguiente ni hablar. Todos se habían venido a ver, nos han quitado los tambores [...] ellos terminaban tocando [...]."*

People in the villages had been aware that a performance was planned even before the official *entrada* on 20 October and on the day of the *fiesta*, many had come to witness the performance and even join the group of dancers. As Julia put it, in 1983 they witnessed a "boom" caused by *saya*, led by the high school class that she was part of, but already spreading to the rest of the Afrobolivian population in the *comunidad* of Tocaña; a population that had been abandoning customs considered Afrobolivian, as her statement about the residents of Tocaña dancing 'indigenous dances' suggests.

After that, many members of the high school class involved in the first performance migrated to the city of La Paz, as many young Afrobolivians do, in order to study at the university. In La Paz, they met only sporadically, keeping in touch mostly through their persistent link with their community of origin and less through formal gatherings in the urban environment. As many of the people stated, in spite of the success and the positive feedback of the *saya* performances, there were initially no efforts to dance *saya* in La Paz and it was only due to an outside interest that some of the 1982 dancers reunited around *saya* once more. Some years after their first performance, the dancers were approached with the idea of forming an Afrobolivian folklore ballet by a foreign dance instructor. Reluctant at first, they nevertheless decided to seize the opportunity and agreed to practice for *saya* performances. Initially, the plan was to stage an international tour that would take them to Spain – a plan that in the end did not materialize. As Fortunata Medina, an important figure in the early days of revitalization, recalls, they started with a very small group and were recruiting members one by one:

> "But what did we do? We went to Avenida Pérez Velasco [one of the most crowded streets traversing the center of La Paz] and looked for black people [*gente negra*] who wanted to join the group. Because it was only me, Julia and my brothers, nobody else. So we went, and given the shyness of our people, they didn't want to. The majority didn't want to know about dancing *saya*. Every Sunday, we would stand there, at 4pm, and every black [*negro*] that passed by, we would talk to them about *saya*. And that's how we built it [the group]."[3]

Finding new members for the nascent organization proved difficult due to the reluctance of many Afrobolivians to join a *saya* troupe. Besides finding more people to participate in the city of La Paz, the group also had to get in touch with people from the rural villages – mainly Tocaña – in order to be taught how to build the

3 *"¿Pero cuál era nuestro trabajo? Salir a la Pérez Velasco y buscar a gente negra que quiera incluirse al grupo. Porque era Julia y mis hermanos, nadie más. Salíamos y con la timidez que tenía nuestra gente, no quería. La mayoría no querían saber de bailar saya. Todos los domingos estábamos parados a las 4 de la tarde en la Pérez Velasco, todo negro que pasaba le hablábamos de la Saya y así fuimos formando."*

instruments *(cajas)*, learn more lyrics, and master the drumming and dance moves. They raised money from the ranks of the few members to bring skilled individuals from Tocaña to La Paz and kept the rehearsals going for almost a year, waiting for the chance to perform in public. As they realized that the international tour they were promised was most likely not going to happen anytime soon, they decided to take matters in their own hands. Together with Vicente Gemio, a well-known *saya* composer from Tocaña and one of the specialists teaching the students in La Paz, they set out to perform yet again at the fiesta in Coroico on 20 October 1988. This date is today also represented as the date that the *Movimiento Cultural Saya Afroboliviana (MOCUSABOL)* was founded. The performance group in 1988 was composed of about fifteen residents of La Paz (the folkloric ballet) and some individuals from Tocaña who joined the *saya* on that occasion.

A decisive encounter happened the following year. In 1989, the La Paz residents and the performers from Tocaña again danced together on 20 October and caught the attention of Fernando Cajías de la Vega, a renowned colonial historian and at that time newly appointed Prefect of the *Departamento La Paz*. Cajías was known to be a promoter of 'Bolivian cultural traditions' and offered the *saya* not only material support, but also gave them the opportunity to participate in a *Prefectura*-sponsored tour of the country. *Saya* was to be included as a *'tradición paceña'* and presented alongside other dances and musical genres in different Bolivian cities including La Paz, Cochabamba, Sucre and Potosí. Fortunata very vividly described this time as a decisive shift:

> "And that is how it grows, the cultural movement, the *saya Afroboliviana* keeps growing, many people are losing fear, losing shyness, losing embarrassment. Because many were embarrassed. If they dance they are going to hit them, if they dance, what will they say? So this fear was going away."[4]

For her, the most important step was to get people to forget their doubts and reservations about dancing *saya* – the doubts that made the older generations frown upon the first performance in 1982 and also became an obstacle to recruiting members for the first dance group. The official support, a first wave of media coverage and national and international interest sparked a process that eventually led to the formation of a more formally organized group. In the early years, there was a loosely connected group of *saya* performers composed of La Paz residents (among them the members of the original *ballet folklórico*) and individuals from Tocaña that would get together on special occasions but then dissolve quickly into their component parts. Most members describe the early stages of the group's development

4 *"Y así es como crece, el movimiento cultural, la saya Afroboliviana va creciendo, mucha gente va perdiendo el miedo, va perdiendo la timidez, va perdiendo la vergüenza, porque muchos tenían vergüenza de que si bailan nos pegan, si bailan, ¿qué nos dirán? Entonces ese miedo se ha ido perdiendo [...]."*

less as a type of formal organization than as a way of getting together with people that inhabited the same situation as fairly recent migrants from the Yungas to La Paz and could provide support and a certain degree of assistance in times of economic hardship. Besides this function as a vehicle for group cohesion and an informal network for Afrobolivian migrants, *saya* soon became a vehicle for two related goals.

Visibilizing the community *("Visibilizar la comunidad")*

According to the founding members, there were two main goals in the early days of the organization besides efforts to unite Afrobolivians and 'make them identify with their culture' by promoting positive images of blackness (cf. Templeman 1998). First, what they refer to as "visibilization," i.e. the creation of a consciousness among Bolivians that there are Afrobolivians in the country and second to (re-)claim ownership of the term *saya* and the music and dance associated with it (see next sub-chapter).

Most people explain the 'invisibility' of Afrobolivians with reference to situations where it is clearly their visibly different physical appearance that sparks the curiosity of their counterparts. As individuals, Afrobolivians are highly 'visible'; many of them are repeatedly confronted with situations where other Bolivians question their country of origin, expressing the opinion that "in Bolivia there are no black people" and that they must be from Brazil, the Caribbean Islands or from Colombia. The 'invisibility' that they refer to is that of a recognizable Afrobolivian collective that they could be considered as part of. When they state that they are "(made) invisible *(invisibilizado)*" what they mean is that most Bolivians have no knowledge concerning the historical or contemporary presence of Afrobolivians in the country and thus do not consider them part of the country. Occasionally – most commonly in the context of the late 1980s/early 1990s *saya* performances – they also collectively experienced the ignorance of many Bolivians when it came to Afrobolivians. As Julia remembered, during one of their performances, people approached the dancers in order to verify that their faces where not painted and that they were in fact "real black people":

> "Because when we arrived for example in Sucre, many did not believe that we were Bolivians. They said we were from Brazil, that we were from Peru, but not Bolivians. [People said things] like 'But where? In what book are you? You cannot be found in any book. Where are you? How come you are so abandoned? I don't believe that you are Bolivians!' They didn't want to believe us. A child, for example, in Sucre [...] said: 'Mami, Mami' he says, 'Mami, they are not painted after all, they are for real!' Imagine this! And we started laughing, right? We found it a little funny,

but afterwards I started thinking how [widespread] the ignorance is, our own people didn't know that we existed here in Bolivia."[5]

As a reaction to situations like these, the members of the first *saya* ensembles felt the urge to make the presence of Afrobolivians known across the different regions of the country. The strategy to achieve this would be *saya*. Through performances in different cities and locales (festivals, bars, nightclubs) and media coverage, Afrobolivians spread their messages throughout the country. In the early 1990s, the group also recorded its first CD of *sayas* and established a more stable media presence, especially in La Paz. In 1994, Afrobolivians performed *saya* at the Governmental Palace in La Paz at the invitation of Vice President Victor Hugo Cárdenas, an event that was publicized nationally and put Afrobolivian *saya* on the map throughout the country. One particular *saya* was performed that day and its lyrics made specific reference to the special occasion:

"Mister vice president
We appear before you
The blacks *[los negros]* of Bolivia
Asking for recognition"[6]

The group, made up of people from different communities in the Yungas, as well as Afrobolivian migrants living in the city of La Paz, performed several *sayas*. According to Roberto from the community of Cala Cala, this was one of the first times he had personally met many of his fellow Afrobolivians from other communities. He recounted that moment very vividly, emphasizing the importance for the creation of a feeling of belonging to an Afrobolivian community extending across the whole country and not limited to his small rural community in the Yungas and the immediate neighboring communities. For him, performing *saya* that day meant experiencing "unity" and a shared sense of identity. *Saya* played a pivotal role in all this. As he put it: *"Todo era uno."* The word *"todo,"* as he explained to me, hides a variety of differences between the participants he encountered that day. Among those are stylistic differences concerning the drum patterns, the clothing and the lyrics associated with the dance, but also the participants' different regional backgrounds and the different realities of rural and urban Afrobolivians. However, none of this

5 *"Porque cuando llegamos por ejemplo a Sucre muchos no lo creían que éramos Bolivianos. Decían éramos del Brasil, que éramos del Perú pero menos Bolivianos. O sea '¿Pero dónde? ¿En qué libro están? No se los ve en ningún libro! ¿Dónde están? ¿Cómo es que los tienen tan abandonados? No creo que sean Bolivianos.' No nos querían creer. Una, un niño por ejemplo en Sucre, [...] dice 'Mami, mami' le dice [...] 'Mami, no han sido pintados, habían sido de verdad.' Imagínate, ¿no? [...] Y nos hemos puesto a reír, ¿no? Un poco nos causó gracia pero después yo me puesto a pensar cómo es la ignorancia, nuestra misma gente no sabían que nosotros existimos acá en Bolivia."*

6 *"Señor Vicepresidente/ Nos hacemos presentes/ Los negros de Bolivia/ Pidiendo el reconocimiento."*

was important in that specific moment, he said. Roberto was not the only interlocutor stressing the importance of that day in 1994, even though other memories of that moment highlight different dimensions of the invitation to the *Palacio de Gobierno*. Unlike Roberto, who emphasized the personal importance of the event for his interpretation of belonging to a broader community, Julia Pinedo and Mónica Rey, two longstanding members of MOCUSABOL and the latter now a member of the MAS administration, cited the events as a milestone in political terms, more specifically in terms of political visibility and official recognition. The symbolic value of having been received by the second most important man in the state – and the 'visibility' gained through this – was of great significance. What is more, the lyrics of the *saya* performed that day foreshadowed the importance that discourses on 'recognition' would have for later activism.

In a certain sense, the 1994 performance of *saya* for the vice president was a turning point for Afrobolivian activism. The invitation to perform for a national audience in a symbolic space such as the Governmental Palace is interpreted as an important step in terms of the above-mentioned goal of gaining greater visibility. From that follows the related goal of not only being visible, but being recognized as a culturally distinctive collective. The official invitation by a high representative of the government foreshadowed the political opportunities that would arise as a consequence of a rapidly changing political climate in Bolivia. Similar to the continent's other countries, Bolivia embarked on a path to multicultural reforms, shaping state politics regarding 'cultural minorities' and social movements' efforts until today. This shift also fundamentally influenced the political positions of Afrobolivian activists in the years to come and in this sense, the period around the events of 1994 can be seen as both a time of the first important achievements of Afrobolivian activism as well as the starting point for Afrobolivian identity politics under regimes of neoliberal multiculturalism.

Yet it is important to stress the singularity of this event in two different respects. First, the reception by a representative of the state as important as the vice president was a unique occasion not to repeat itself for many years to come; second, the 'Afrobolivian community' appearing before the second most prominent man of the state was not a community in the sense of a group of people with strong and ongoing ties. The staging of the *saya* performance that day was an exceptional effort coordinated by urban activists, uniting representatives from communities from all over the Yungas, something rarely – if ever – naturally occurring in a comparable fashion. Both the state's attentiveness and the make-up of the 'Afrobolivian community' presenting itself in the eyes of the state and society were singularities. The focus on rather spectacular events such as those described above in the foundational narrative and activist discourse overshadows constant tensions between different Afrobolivian communities concerning questions of legitimate representation and the overall effectiveness of the urban organizations' actions.

With and through *saya*, Afrobolivians presented themselves before the eyes of the nation, or as Sara Busdiecker (2007:165) has put it, they "perform[ed] blackness into the nation." *Saya* was not only the main vehicle for making the community visible, it was at the same time the most effective tool for spreading more elaborate movement messages that went well beyond the basic "we are here too" motive. The topics included propagating a more positive image of blackness to black and non-black people alike, encouraging the positive identification of black people with the identity *"Afroboliviano,"* de-racializing notions of blackness and emphasizing black cultural expression in Bolivia, and presenting certain traits of Afrobolivian lifestyles to the audience (see also: Rey 1998; Templeman 1998).

Intimately linked to both the efforts to re-create *saya* as a cultural practice and the mission to make Afrobolivian culture visible to a broader audience was the reclaiming of cultural ownership of Afrobolivians in relation to *saya*. Before turning to the implications of multicultural state politics for Afrobolivian identity politics and collective organizing, I want to briefly sketch this dimension of the early struggles, since it plays a vital role in how the whole political discourse of that time was shaped.

Reclaiming *saya*: authenticity, ownership, appropriation

The struggle to 'reclaim' *saya* as an Afrobolivian tradition has been dealt with extensively: several papers address this issue and stress the paramount importance of questions of ownership and representation (of self and other) in the wider context of Bolivian musical tradition and festive culture (Céspedes 1993; Pérez Inofuentes 2010; Revilla Orías 2013b; Rocha Torrez 2007; Rossbach de Olmos 2007; see also chapter 6 in Busdiecker 2007).

At the heart of the debate on authenticity and ownership of *saya* lies the appropriation of the term *saya* by mainstream Bolivian folklore, mainly by the well-known and internationally recognized group *Los Kjarkas*. Starting in the late 1980s, the Cochabamba-based group – already established as one of the most important representatives of Bolivian folk music – released a number of songs denominated as '*sayas*.' The '*sayas*' of *Los Kjarkas* and other groups are related to a dance genre called *Caporales*. The *caporal* is a figure in Afrobolivian *saya* representing the slave overseer and is commonly impersonated by an experienced member of the group guiding the other dancers with a whip and bells around his feet that mark the pace of the performance. Based on this figure from the *saya*, as well as inspired by the dances *"Tundiqui"* and *"Los Negritos,"* urban folklorists in La Paz created a dance called *Caporales* that soon became popular with the urban middle and upper classes and has become an integral part of the 'traditional Bolivian dances' roster ever since. Not only did the creators and performers of *Caporales* appropriate parts of the *saya*, and a certain terminology, they also – through their lyrics – created the impression that this musical genre was 'traditional' black music from Bolivia, the 'rhythm of the *morenos*' from the Yungas of La Paz. Being of indigenous and *mestizo* background, *Los Kjarkas* claimed to represent Bolivia's Afrobolivian musical tradition. The lyrics of the song *"El ritmo negro,"* for example, read:

> The black rhythm of the heart, the black rhythm
> *Saya*, Bolivian *Saya*, *Saya* of the Yungas
> *Moreno* Flavor
> How the hips are moving to the black rhythm. You can feel fire in the blood, the fire of the *morenos*
> From the Yungas of Bolivia, comes the *saya*, Afrobolivian Music
> *Moreno* Flavor
> Let's dance *saya*, the black rhythm, may the party of the *morenos* never end
> Let's dance Bolivian *saya*.[7]

Most Afrobolivians argued that the music of *Los Kjarkas* did not represent Afrobolivian musical tradition and they strongly opposed the fact that the group spoke of *saya* when performing these songs. Afrobolivians felt that not only were they marginalized in official historiography, ignored in school textbooks and official representations of the nation's population, and were thus largely 'invisible' to the rest of the population; now their 'culture' was being taken away by others, their music manipulated by non-Afrobolivians and presented as authentic. It is indeed ironic that the debate around ownership, authenticity and the appropriation of Afrobolivian culture by outsiders circles around a dance that is based on the figure of the slave overseer. As an intermediary between slaves and masters, often himself a black man and former slave, the *caporal* is often seen as the most despicable representative of the oppressive system. And now this figure was at the core of yet another scheme stripping Afrobolivians of their 'rights' to culture and their opportunities for self-representation. Afrobolivians opposed these tendencies with a *saya* of their own (composed in 1995, see Templeman 1998), stating:

> After 500 years
> You will not exchange
> The beautiful rhythm of *saya*
> With the rhythm of the *Caporal*

7 *"El ritmo negro del corazón, el ritmo negro./ Saya boliviana Saya, Saya de los Yungas./ Sabor moreno./ Como mueven las caderas, al ritmo negro. Se siente fuego en la sangre, fuego en los morenos./ De los Yungas de Bolivia, viene la Saya, música Afroboliviana, Afroboliviana./ Sabor moreno./ Vamos a bailar la Saya, el ritmo negro, que no se acabe la fiesta de los morenos./ Vamos a bailar la Saya Boliviana!"*

> The Kjarkas are confusing
> *Saya* and *Caporal*
> What you are hearing now
> is original *saya*[8]

Through their music and its lyrics, Afrobolivians made claims to authorship and ownership of *saya*, denying the indigenous/*mestizo* folklore industry access to their 'culture.' At the same time, Afrobolivians also demanded that their views and opinions be taken into consideration when it came to the representation of slavery and Afrobolivianity in Bolivian folklore and popular culture more generally. Images of Afrobolivianity and representations of slaves circulate in the dance *Tundiqui/Negritos*, as well as in the well-known *Morenada* and the already mentioned *Caporales*. What all these dances have in common is the fact that they express the views of 'others' (indigenous, *mestizo*) on Afrobolivians and their history. With the revitalization of *saya* and the public performance of the dance, Afrobolivians aspired to present themselves and their view on blackness, as opposed to being (mis)represented by others or obviated completely (cf. Rossbach de Olmos 2007).

Recently, Afrobolivian organizations have focused their critique primarily on the dance *Tundiqui* (occasionally also referred to as *"Los Negritos"*). This dance is performed by non-Afrobolivians in blackface – painting their faces with black shoe polish – and depicts enchained slaves being whipped by their masters (Sigl and Mendoza Salazar 2012:190). Afrobolivians consider the stereotyped depiction of slaves in the dance highly racist and have filed an official complaint with the *Comité Nacional contra el Racismo y toda forma de Discriminación*, an institution established by Law 045 (*"Ley 045 Contra el Racismo y Toda forma de Discriminación"*). Although in 2014 the *Comité* issued a resolution condemning the racist content of the dance, various fraternities still publicly perform *Tundiqui* in La Paz, El Alto and also in the famous Oruro Carnival. The *Tundiqui* case not only serves as a vivid example of the continuing presence of racialized stereotypes that circulate in Bolivian folklore with regard to Afrobolivians, but also clearly demonstrates the limited capacity of the anti-discrimination law. Year after year, Afrobolivian organizations decry the racist depictions of what they consider their ancestors, referring to the anti-discrimination law in general and to the resolution on *Tundiqui* in particular. Yet the public performances of the dance continue and as far as I am aware, there have been no further attempts to settle the matter legally.

---

8 *"Después de 500 años/ No me vayas a cambiar/ El bello ritmo de Saya/ Con ritmo de Caporal./ Los Kjarkas están confundiendo/ La Saya y el caporal./ Lo que ahora están escuchando/ Es Saya original."*

Migration, discrimination and the struggle to consolidate the *movimiento*

As many of the early members repeatedly stated, keeping the group afloat and preventing it from dissolving was a constant struggle. Not only did they lack the economic resources to finance the group's basic needs, they also lacked a stable meeting place and access to communication that would have been necessary to coordinate the members that were dispersed all over the city of La Paz. What is more, many male members of the group did not immediately manage to find stable jobs in the city. This was mostly due to their lack of formal education, paired with a racist urban work environment and the severe economic crisis that Bolivia had to endure throughout the 1980s and early 1990s. This meant that they repeatedly had to return to their communities in the Yungas, especially during harvest seasons, to provide for their families' survival and they were often absent from La Paz for long periods of time. The women, on the other hand, fared better in the urban work environment. Many found jobs as domestic workers, secretaries or shop clerks, thus becoming the economic pillar of their urban households and more strongly integrated into the urban environment. This economic situation in part explains the prevalence of female leadership in the early years of the group's existence, but also its ever volatile status, teetering on the rim of dissolution. Nevertheless, the group made great efforts to become more formally organized:

> "We started to work on our statutes, legal credentials [...] and we went on to do more work, right? Working in a more orderly fashion, so that people know, understand. And through *saya* we have achieved many things, we have achieved visibility for the Afrobolivian people. Because we were very lost, very hidden, without history, without news [coverage], so we started to define what we had to do, right? In terms of respect and everything. They started in the [government] offices, to open doors, to recognize us as Bolivians."[9]

The members set out to define more specific goals, developed formal statutes and started interacting with NGOs and certain state institutions, referred to as "offices" in the statement above. As I mentioned earlier, starting in the late 1980s and intensifying in the 1990s, Bolivia went through a process of economic restructuring and multicultural reforms (including decentralization), a conjuncture for which Charles Hale has coined the term "neoliberal multiculturalism" (Hale 2005). For

9 *"Empezamos ya a trabajar en nuestro estatuto, personería jurídica [...] y fuimos haciendo ya trabajos, ¿no? Un trabajo más ordenado donde la gente sepa, entienda y mediante la Saya hemos conseguido muchas cosas, hemos conseguido, la visibilidad del pueblo Afroboliviano en Bolivia. Porque estábamos muy perdidos, muy escondidos, sin historia, sin noticias, entonces empezamos a marcar lo que tiene que ser, ¿no? Lo que debe ser el respeto y todo. Ya empezaron en las oficinas, abrieron las puertas, a reconocernos como Bolivianos."*

Afrobolivians this meant that they were presented with a number of opportunities to interact with state institutions and transnational NGOs that set out to foster the participation of ethnic and cultural minorities in the newly proclaimed multiethnic society (Bolivian Constitution of 1994). This political climate helped to stabilize the *Movimiento* and opened up new horizons for its organizational development. Very importantly, in 1998 the Cochabamba-based *Centro Pedagógico Simón I. Patiño* organized and funded the work of a team of researchers, as well as a series of meetings and events with the Afrobolivian population. As a result, the center published *"El Tambor Mayor,"* a book with an audio CD including the documentation of Afrobolivian musical traditions and a summary of available information on the history of the communities and the recuperation of *saya*. The book also included first hand testimonies of Afrobolivian villagers on culture and history and up to this day serves as an important reference in academic publications and activist discourse alike. But *"El Tambor Mayor"* was important beyond its quality as a documentary source and academic reference. The efforts to compile the information that the book is based on led a team of researchers (including movement member Mónica Rey) to various communities and many people I spoke to affirmed that it was in the context of those efforts that they became more deeply involved with the organized movement and the revitalization of Afrobolivian culture more generally. Additionally, various Afrobolivian communities from the Yungas participated in a meeting and music festival sponsored by *Fundación Patiño* and the Catholic Church in Coripata (*Festival Luz Mila Patino* and the *I. Encuentro de comunidades negras*), strengthening the ties between dispersed parts of the population and spreading the idea of cultural revival beyond La Paz and Coroico/Tocaña.

Also in 1998, the urban-based movement managed to become a legally established organization by obtaining *Personería Jurídica* under the name of *"Movimiento Cultural Saya Afroboliviana" (MOCUSABOL)*. It is interesting to note that the group had started out as *"Movimiento Cultural Grupo Afro-Boliviano"* in the late 1980s, but changed its name to *"Movimiento Negro"* in 1995 (Templeman 1998:435). However, in 1998, the name that was officially registered – and is still in use today – was MOCUSABOL, abstaining from the term *negro* and emphasizing *"lo cultural"* and the ever-present *saya*. The following years would become decisive in shaping the orientation of the movement and formalizing the political mobilization of Afrobolivians beyond the realm of *saya*. Before I turn to shifts in political orientations, however, there are some aspects concerning the foundational narrative that deserve further attention.

Contextualizing and decentering the foundational narrative

The basic narrative reproduced above has been advanced especially by members of the Coroico/Tocaña faction within the Afrobolivian community and has been propagated through a variety of means. Most prominently, Mónica Rey and Fortunata Medina, members of the high school class that performed *saya* in 1982, have become important spokespersons and representatives for Afrobolivians in general and for the propagation of this particular narrative more specifically. Both from Tocaña, their views contrast significantly with those from other *comunidades* in the rest of the Yungas, but nevertheless have become the main reference for everyone interested in the Afrobolivian community (scholars, activists, politicians and national/international media). Rey wrote her undergraduate thesis (1998) about the meanings and uses of *saya* in the Afrobolivian community and has been interviewed extensively by the media on questions of the history of the movement. As one of the first written sources on the emerging Afrobolivian mobilization, it has also been widely cited in a variety of later sources. She was also part of the *Centro Pedagógico Simon I. Patiño* team that produced the first recordings of *sayas* and published *"El Tambor Mayor"* in 1998. The *sayas* recorded there are almost exclusively from the community of Tocaña, the small village near Coroico that has become the emblematic community of Afrobolivians in Bolivia. Furthermore, Mónica Rey counted on the support of Fernando Cajías, who organized and sponsored most of the early *saya* performances. She served as President of MOCUSABOL and was one of the founders of CONAFRO, the first Afrobolivian organization with explicitly national aspirations. In 2015, she was elected *Diputada Supranacional* for the ruling *Movimiento al Socialismo* and remains one of the most visible and prominent representatives of the Afrobolivian community. Fortunata Medina, for her part, besides actively contributing to the foundation of MOCUSABOL, also spoke internationally about her experiences with the movement and appeared, for example, in a 1998 conference on blackness in America and the Caribbean that lead to the publication of the seminal edited volume by Whitten and Torres (1998). She moved away from La Paz and is as of 2017 one of the leading figures of the Afrobolivian community in Santa Cruz and also closely related to CONAFRO. Both Medina and Rey are without any doubt key figures in the Afrobolivian community and widely respected for their years-long dedication to the cause of the Afrobolivian people. To me, their dedication and ongoing efforts are beyond question. Yet their prominent positions and privileged access to disseminate their version of the story lead to a simplification of the various nuances that can be found and whose importance is put forth by other scholars and activists that do not enjoy such extensive and long-lasting coverage.

In most of the testimonies I collected from activists in La Paz, Cochabamba and Santa Cruz, the basic pillars of the foundational narrative remain relatively stable across the different testimonies. Yet there are certain variations that deserve further attention in order to contextualize what has become 'common sense' among many Afrobolivians when it comes to imagining their political history and the 'revival' or 'salvation' of their culture more generally. First of all, there are various voices that stress the importance of not overlooking specific earlier performances of *saya* in 'public spaces' and more generally the many clues – both in written sources and oral histories – of the continuous importance of *saya* within the different Afrobolivian communities. Martín Ballivián (2014) not only cites evidence of a public *saya* performance in La Paz in the 1950s but also forcefully argues for a reconsideration of the narrative of loss and oblivion so common among Afrobolivians. He states that *saya* has played a major role in festive contexts, as a carrier of Afrobolivian oral history and in community organizing since at least the early 20th century and denies tales of its imminent disappearance in the 1960s and 1970s that have become crucial for the construction of the activist discourse. He goes on to mention the testimony of a well-known composer of Afrobolivian *sayas*, stating that he had composed a new *saya* specifically for a festival held in Coroico in 1977, five years before the alleged salvation of *saya* from oblivion. The same information is mentioned in Robert Templeman's (1998) account of *saya*'s 'revival' in the 1980s.

Ballivián's (2014) description partly resonates with some testimonies I collected in Cala Cala where people have active memory of *saya* performances and do stress the continuous importance of *saya* while at the same time acknowledging the effect the activities of the urban organizations had on their practice and understanding of *saya* in the 1980s. Roberto told me that as far as he remembered from his childhood in the 1970s and early 1980s and from what he learned from his relatives, the people of Cala Cala performed *saya* on special occasions such as the annual *fiesta* in Cala Cala or neighboring Dorado Chico, or at weddings among the Afrobolivian population. Cala Cala always had its own drums *(cajas)* that were kept and taken care of by the community. He went on to describe how in the mid-1990s a group of Afrobolivians from Coroico/La Paz, alongside historians and musicologists and funded by *Fundación Patiño* arrived in the village to record *sayas* from Cala Cala. Indeed, this led to an increasing interest in *saya* in Cala Cala, but it seems exaggerated to suggest that *saya* was on the brink of disappearance within the community. I have been told similar stories in other villages, especially the Sud Yungas village of Chicaloma, another well-known Afrobolivian community (on Chicaloma see: Kent 2001; Léons 1972; Sturtevant 2013).

Besides critically examining the assertions of *saya's* imminent disappearance, it is also important to note that the above-mentioned narrative apparently understates the active participation of people who are not from Tocaña but who also played a major role in the foundation of MOCUSABOL. Again, it is especially Chicaloma – a village in Sud Yungas and the self-proclaimed "cradle of traditional *saya*" *("cuna de la saya tradicional")* – that seems to have played a much bigger role than the Coroico-centered narrative admits. Chicaloma also plays an important role in the ongoing discussions about the specificities of *saya* performances and certain aesthetic features related to the dance.

The pitfalls of folklorization and the shift "from performance to politics"

The focus on *saya* in early mobilizations also had its pitfalls. Afrobolivians were quickly reduced to *saya* and their skillful dancing, and the movement's early focus on *saya* ended up overshadowing other aspects of the Afrobolivian experience. As a consequence of focusing on *saya* and participating mainly in events that relied on this cultural expression, Afrobolivian identity and culture became folklorized and were often reduced to *saya* alone. This led to a tendency that Lioba Rossbach de Olmos (2011) has called *"patrimomialización."* With that term she refers to tendencies to recognize Afrobolivian cultural expressions alongside other folklorized traditions as 'cultural patrimony' without granting Afrobolivians further territorial, political or economic rights. She juxtaposes the Bolivian case with the situations in Colombia (where an ethnicization of blackness prevails) and Cuba (where she speaks of racialization). Formally, this juxtaposition is not tenable as of 2009 when the Bolivian Constitution granted Afrobolivians the same rights (including the right to territory) as indigenous peoples, wherever appropriate *("en todo lo que corresponda")*. Furthermore, and with my remarks on race in Bolivia in mind, it is problematic to analyze the Bolivian case without reference to racialization. In many regards, however, Rossbach de Olmos' description is still quite accurate even today. Reviewing the national laws and decrees (as well as departmental and municipal decrees) concerning Afrobolivians that have been passed in the last decade, it becomes obvious that most of these bills have to do with *saya* and the recognition of Afrobolivian 'patrimony' more generally. Most prominently, Laws 138 and 200 recognize *saya* as "Historical-Cultural and Immaterial Patrimony of the state" and declare 23 September the *"Día Nacional del Pueblo y la Cultura Afroboliviana"*.[10] Even though many Afrobolivian organizations struggled for the passing of these laws and most people I spoke to regard them as important milestones for the Afrobolivian population, most of my interlocutors were keenly aware of the limitations this kind of recognition entails. Harsh critiques of folklorization abound among Afrobolivians and the tendency to see them (and their culture) as merely national patrimony, were voiced in numerous instances. A fairly explicit hint at the overall problem can be found in a statement by an Afrobolivian activist cited in a newspaper article on a CONAFRO congress in 2012. Giving his opinion on matters of justice and discrimination, Edgar Vázquez, a CONAFRO member and Afrobolivian

10 www.gacetaoficialdebolivia.gob.bo [24/09/2018].

activist, called attention to the fact that Afrobolivian women are stereotyped in a variety of ways: they are racialized, sexualized and treated as objects, but also reduced to their potential ability in *saya* dancing:

> "I manifest that Afrobolivian women are seen as objects for being physically well endowed. Furthermore, I comment that many associate them with Afrobolivian dance because they are from the Yungas. 'She must know how to dance *saya*,' they say."[11]

Besides providing a gendered perspective on discrimination, he clearly also sees the firm association of Afrobolivians with *saya* as a problem. The article continues:

> "They do not see the Afrobolivian woman because of her capacity and her knowledge, but from a folkloric point of view. That is also a discriminatory act. It is fine, we have our culture, we respect it very much, but what we want is for people not only to see us as a culture, but as persons."[12]

Besides decrying the objectification of black women – a discriminatory practice most Afrobolivians I spoke to explain in terms of a deeply rooted racism in Bolivian society – Vázquez points out the folklorization of Afrobolivians and the fact that they are not seen as individuals or valued for their capacities and knowledge (*"capacidades y conocimientos"*).

To counteract the tendencies of folklorization, Afrobolivian organizations searched for opportunities to widen the scope of their activities and discourses. In the late 1990s, according to many of my interlocutors, the activities of MOCUSABOL started to become 'political.' The first generation of leaders – the *saya* generation – had been gradually stepping away from the organization. For example, Fortunata Medina moved to Santa Cruz where she would become a key figure in the mobilization of the ever-growing Afrobolivian population in Bolivia's lowland boomtown and Julia Pinedo left the organization to focus on her professional career. Despite these developments, MOCUSABOL remained the center of Afrobolivian cultural and political activism and by far the biggest and most important group. Its leadership was taken on by Jorge Medina, who pressured the group to become more 'politically' active and transcend the focus on dancing *saya*. Many of the people I interviewed associate two things with Medina: *"talleres"* and *"política."*

As Julia remembers:

---

11 *"Manifestó que las mujeres afro son vistas como objetos por ser bien dotadas corporalmente. Asimismo, comentó que muchos las asocian con la danza afroboliviana por proceder de los Yungas. 'Debe saber bailar saya,' dicen."* (El Cambio 2012)

12 *"No ven a la mujer afro por su capacidad y sus conocimientos, sino desde el punto de vista folklórico. Este hecho también es un acto discriminatorio. Está bien, tenemos nuestra cultura, la respetamos muchísimo, pero lo que queremos es que no sólo nos vean como cultura, sino como personas."* (El Cambio 2012)

> "So he [Jorge Medina] takes it up and rebuilds it. But he starts working very little in culture. He starts working more in the identification of the *pueblo afro* but it was not easy to convince the people that we needed to go further, that we couldn't just keep on dancing. So Jorge decides to give workshops, mixing always culture with our history. He starts rescuing and he starts giving workshops to tell us a little bit about our history because we also didn't know what our history was. He tells them and just then, gender equality and all that is en vogue. So he starts working with that and he starts entering institutions and he doesn't do it so much focused on culture, but he does it politically. He entered through culture and afterwards identity, history and all that and he ends up doing what he is now, he is a member of parliament thanks to what the *saya* began to work on, right?"[13]

The workshops he organized were mainly concerned with two related topics: history and identity/identification. Medina's line of argument and subsequent strategy parted from the experience he and other leaders had had in the early years of mobilization: many Afrobolivians did not identify as such and this lack of identification made mobilizing an Afrobolivian constituency very difficult. Secondly, Medina and others adopted a critical stance towards the achievements of the cultural movement based on performing *saya*. They argued that performing *saya* had made Afrobolivians visible as part of the country and had proven to be an effective means of conveying the messages concerning ownership of *saya* to the public. At the same time, however, the focus on dancing and performance had contributed to the stereotyping of Afrobolivians as mere dancers and entertainers, reducing their organization to the status of a dance troupe.

> "Oh no! The little blacks, the dancers, the ones of the *saya*. We were the *saya* dancers. That's how people knew us, as the *saya* dancers. They saw a black person and said: 'Ah, the *saya* dancers, the musicians, the dancers!' So we didn't want that. So in MOCUSABOL I told them: 'People, we have to start thinking politically.' But there was no interest. People were too involved in the cultural part."[14]

---

13 *"Entonces el lo retoma eso y lo vuelve a armar. Pero él empieza trabajar muy poco tiempo en lo que es lo cultural. Él empieza más a trabajar en lo que era identificación del pueblo afro pero no era fácil convencerlos a mi gente que deberíamos ir más allá, que no podáamos quedar solamente bailando. Entonces Jorge decide dar talleres, mezclando siempre lo cultural con lo que era nuestra historia. Empieza rescatar y empieza a dar talleres para contarnos un poco que es nuestra historia porque tampoco sabíamos lo que era nuestra historia. Les cuenta y también justo se pone de moda la equidad de género, todo esto. Él empieza trabajar con todo esto y empieza meterse a instituciones y ya no lo hace esto tan cultural, sino ya lo hace algo político. Él ha entrado por lo cultural y después ya identidad, historia y todo eso y termina haciendo lo que es el ahora, que es diputado gracias a lo que la Saya empieza a trabajar, ¿no?"*

14 *"Ah no! Los negritos, los bailarines, los de Saya, éramos los bailadores de Saya. Así nos conocía la gente, como los bailadores de Saya. Veían a un negro y decían: Ah, los bailadores de Saya, los músicos, los bailadores. Entonces no queríamos eso. Entonces en el MOCUSABOL les digo: Chicos, tenemos que*

In Medina's view, it was a result of that situation that MOCUSABOL had not been able to achieve any significant improvements for the Afrobolivian population. He thus proposed a twofold strategy. Internally, he sought to strengthen the organization by organizing workshops concerned with Afrobolivian identity and history, raising the consciousness of topics such as discrimination, social rights and equality of opportunities among the Afrobolivian population. In addition to that, he approached state institutions in order to obtain funding and lobby for Afrobolivian interests so that they would be on the agendas of ministries and development agencies. His emphasis on 'politics' as opposed to 'culture' eventually led to the creation of *CADIC (Centro Afroboliviano para el Dessarrollo Integral y Comunitario)* in 2006, considered to be the political branch of MOCUSABOL by most Afrobolivians. Through CADIC, Medina sought to institutionalize the divide between culture *(saya)* and politics, reserving the former arena for MOCUSABOL, while working on the latter through CADIC. The organization's objectives no longer make any direct reference to *saya* and instead emphasize other goals such as promoting the formation of new leaders, development projects, and strategic alliances with other organizations, and pushing for public policies such as affirmative action programs.[15] CADIC also puts great emphasis on "strengthening the ethno-cultural identity of Afrobolivians and promoting the integration and development of our communities" *("fortalecer la identidad étnico-cultural de los Afrobolivianos/as promoviendo la integración y el desarrollo de nuestras comunidades")*. This can be read as a first step in the direction of ethnicization, which I will discuss more thoroughly in chapter 9.

From *negros* to *Afrobolivianos/Afrodescendientes*

Very importantly, Medina introduced a major shift in broadening MOCUSABOL's scope in its search for new members, as well as its political discourse. Previously, the group was primarily composed of *negros* – Afrobolivian individuals matching expectations regarding a normative phenotypical blackness – and recruited its members almost exclusively from the ranks of Nor Yungas migrants, mainly from the *comunidades* around Coroico (cf. Templeman 1998:431). Medina sought to include migrants from other regions of the Yungas, as well as the growing population of urban-born Afrobolivians, many of whom were not classified as *negros*, but as one or another intermediate category hinting at racial mixing *(zambo, mulato, mestizo)*. For Medina, as long as they identified with their Afrobolivian heritage, which he sought to strengthen through workshops, and had some Afrobolivian ancestors, their claim to Afrobolivian identity was equally valid. He sought to reach this

---

empezar a pensar políticamente. Pero no había ese interés, la gente estaba metida en la parte cultural."(Jorge Medina quoted in Komadina and Regalsky [2016]).

15 See: www.cadic.org.bo [16/09/2016].

part of the population through the aforementioned workshops, motivating people to learn about Afrobolivian history and embrace their heritage and identity as Afrobolivians. However, not all of the first generation members shared that opinion and according to Bolivian anthropologist Kantuta Cavour (personal communication), who conducted fieldwork among the members of MOCUSABOL in the 1990s, Medina's decision to include individuals with only some degree of Afrobolivian ancestry sparked fierce resistance from certain factions of the group. Those opposing Medina's strategy argued that the movement had been and should continue to be an organization formed of *negros*, defending the interests of *negros*. The tensions engendered by the uneasy relationship between skin color, genealogical ancestry and self-positioning practices in the articulation of Afrobolivianity have not been resolved to this day, as I have shown in chapter 6. On an organizational level, however, Medina's line of argument eventually prevailed. Under his leadership, MOCUSABOL grew steadily and was firmly established as the most visible Afrobolivian organization in Bolivia. Medina also benefitted personally from the success of his mobilization efforts and was long considered the most important Afrobolivian political leader. In 2010, he became the first Afrobolivian member of the *Asamblea Legislativa Plurinacional.*

Beyond broadening the possible membership base of MOCUSABOL, the shift from *negros* to *Afrodescendientes* also meant embracing the transnational politics of blackness gaining momentum in Latin America in the 1990s (Minority Rights Group 1995). Medina's engagement of the term *"Afrodescendiente"* and some of his political projects certainly were inspired by transnationally circulating ideas and discourses. He participated, for example, as a delegate representing Afrobolivians in a series of regional preparatory events for the "World Conference against Racism, Racial Discrimination, Xenophobia and Related Intolerance" held in Durban, South Africa in 2001. One of his first projects as *Asambleísta* (Member of Parliament) was lobbying for an anti-discrimination law. The *Asamblea Legislativa Plurinacional* passed Law 045 (*"Ley 045 Contra el Racismo y Toda forma de Discriminación"*) in 2010. Jorge Medina was heavily involved in its elaboration and many of the articles reflect the language of the Durban Declaration of 2001.[16]

16 The law is occasionally invoked by Afrobolivians when describing everyday racism, but to date, I have not come across a single case where an Afrobolivian individual has filed a legal suit based on the anti-discrimination law. In the debates surrounding the passing of Law 045 in 2010, the topic of racism as a specific form of discrimination was quickly deflected. The debate and media coverage focused instead on the possible curtailing of the freedom of speech, since the law also contemplates sanctions for individuals and media outlets that propagate discriminatory attitudes and opinions. Four years after the passing of Law 045, CONAFRO filed a complaint denouncing the racist attitudes reflected in the dance *Tundiqui* and causing the *Comité Nacional contra el Racismo y toda forma de Discriminación* to issue a resolution condemning the public display of racist stereotypes in *Tundiqui* performances.

From folklore to cultural citizenship

The terminological and conceptual shift described in the preceding section has another important dimension. This is clearly expressed in a MOCUSABOL publication that explains that:

> "The Afrobolivian Movement uses the term Afro instead of *negro*, since *negro is a color, it's not a culture, history, philosophy. In contrast, Afroboliviano is that and much more*, it is the sign of the cradle of humanity and its diaspora in the world [...]" (Emphasis added by the author.)[17]

Some authors interpret statements like this as a clear sign of Afrobolivian organizations approaching politics from an exclusively transnational vantage point. They take the adoption of the language and discourses of transnational organizations on *Afrodescendant* people as indicating a trend of envisioning Afrobolivian politics mostly beyond the national context (Komadina and Regalsky 2016). The very terminology *Afrodescendiente* is taken as an indicator of this, as is the framing of grievances in the language of racial discrimination, references to slavery and the historical injustice it engendered. Debates associated with the term "*Afrodescendiente*" on a transnational level have certainly enhanced the discursive repertoire of the *Movimiento Afro* and many organizations have established ties to organizations spanning the whole continent, participate in events associated with the UN Decade for People of African Descent and clearly express the political importance of belonging to a wider African Diaspora.

I argue, however, that this interpretation fails to acknowledge some important developments with regard to the *Movimiento Afro* and its political discourse. On the one hand, even before Afrobolivians began adopting the term *Afrodescendiente*, they had already replaced the racialized and derogatory terms *negro/a, negrito/a* and *moreno/a* with *Afroboliviano*. The prefix "*Afro*" denotes – as is the case with the widely known Afro-American or African-American – cultural ancestry and ties to the African continent, as I have shown in the quotation from MOCUSABOL's publication above. The second part of the denomination is equally important though: "*-boliviano*" makes clear reference to the claim to national belonging and "recognition as part of the nation" that much of Afrobolivian activism very prominently makes (Busdiecker 2007). "We are Bolivians, too" (*"Nosotros también somos Bolivianos"*), is consequently one of the most important slogans of the movement today.

However, the resolution has not rendered any palpable results and *Tundiqui* performances still occur frequently (for a recent discussion, see Busdiecker 2019b).

17 *"El Movimiento Afroboliviano utiliza el término Afro en vez de 'negro', ya que negro es un color, no es una cultura, historia, filosofía. Mientras que Afroboliviano es eso y mucho más, es el indicativo de la cuna de la humanidad y su diáspora en el mundo [...]."*

This focus on national belonging and the claiming of rights in the name of national citizenship is in part a consequence of the early struggles that emphasized Afrobolivian cultural expression as being part of national cultural diversity. Beyond this cultural dimension, however, it is also the consequence of the widespread tendency in Latin America that indigenous and other marginalized groups must accommodate their claims and voice them within a discourse and language of citizenship (Canessa 2005; Postero 2006; Yashar 2005).

In the context of constitutional reform in Bolivia in 1994, the topic of differentiated citizenship (Kymlicka and Norman 2000) or cultural citizenship (Rosaldo 1994) for indigenous groups was becoming a major buzzword in Bolivian politics and social movement activism (Van Cott 2000). Within this context, Afrobolivian organizations aimed to reposition Afrobolivians in Bolivia's "structures of alterity" (Wade 2010:36) in order to benefit from the multicultural regimes of recognition set in motion by Bolivia's 1994 Constitution. Racialized others *(negros/as)* were repositioned in political contexts as cultural others *(Afrobolivianos/Afrobolivianas)* with a claim to cultural citizenship. Throughout this process of political repositioning, references to *Afrodescendencia*, and by extension to African culture and history, were the basis of claims to a unique and recognizable Afrobolivian culture beyond *saya*. This cultural difference was then employed politically as the foundation for claims to differentiated citizenship equivalent to that of indigenous groups. Very importantly, ties to *Afrodescendientes* and Africa – real and imagined – were used to present claims to the Bolivian state in the language of differentiated citizenship, not as a means to position Afrobolivians as a transnational or diasporic collective in need of a different set of practices of recognition.

The political repositioning of Afrobolivians as "cultural others" has contributed to a variety of developments and processes. Culturalizing blackness politically has enabled Afrobolivians to participate in government- or NGO-sponsored programs addressing issues of cultural diversity and differentiated citizenship in a way that a racialized discourse on blackness would not have offered. The above-mentioned invitation by Vice President Cardenas, the nationwide media presence by way of participating in cultural activities and the funding available through programs latching onto Bolivia's 1994 multicultural constitution would not have been possible otherwise. This shift also laid the groundwork for Afrobolivian mobilization in the context of Bolivia's *proceso de cambio* beginning in 2005, which I will address in chapter 9.

CADIC and the discourse of development

Another of Jorge Medina's political merits was his astute embracement of the discourses of development circulating in Bolivia from the 1980s onward. Besides recognizing the vital importance of the vast mixed-race youth in urban centers for

Afrobolivian mobilization and the opportunities claims to cultural citizenship offered, he engaged with the international development industry in novel ways. Bolivia has been, until very recently, at the top (or close to the top) of any list concerning development funds received or the percentage of foreign aid in relation to GDP. Development, organizations and funds related to it have correspondingly been very important in the country (Carmona 2010). Beyond the organizational and economic dimensions, development discourse has also shaped the country's "complicated modern trajectory" (Goodale 2009:146) in more general terms. Therefore, it is important to discuss the ways development discourse has been used to political ends by Afrobolivian activists, giving relations between the rural and urban realms of Afrobolivian reality a particular twist. What Medina understood was that in order to attract funding for his projects, he had to frame them in the language of development and he designed CADIC accordingly. Given the large scale roll back of the state in Bolivia starting in the mid-1980s and occurring most fiercely in the 1990s, NGOs were on the rise and transnational and development discourse with them. CADIC was founded as "the political branch" of MOCUSABOL and purported to transcend the realms of folklore that MOCUSABOL firmly occupied through *saya* performances. The Afrobolivian leaders involved in CADIC's foundation were sharply aware of the above-mentioned pitfall of folklorization and strategically repositioned the discourses of Afrobolivian activism once more. In its name, CADIC features the buzzword "development," highlighting its "integral" and "communitarian" focus. In a recent statement, CADIC was described as

> "An institution that has the objective of promoting the empowerment of the *pueblo Afroboliviano*, strengthening its ethno-cultural identity through its educational, political and socio-cultural formation, seeking relations with the government, civil society, and international organizations generating actions that contribute to the development of its communities."[18]

Besides the lack of reference to *saya* and cultural performance – which was unheard of for an Afrobolivian organization by the time of CADIC's foundation in 2006 and still stands out as rather unusual – the quote above displays an instructive array of references to key elements of CADIC's work. There is talk of empowerment, ethnocultural identity, education, civil society, international organizations – and how all these factors should ultimately contribute to development in Afrobolivian communities. The 'politics' CADIC has in mind, then, is in the first instance 'development.'

---

18 *"Una institución que tiene el objetivo de promover el empoderamiento del pueblo afroboliviano, fortaleciendo su identidad étnico-cultural a través de su formación educativa, política y sociocultural, buscando el relacionamiento con el gobierno, sociedad civil y organizaciones internacionales generando acciones que contribuyan al desarrollo en sus comunidades."* (http://www.jorgemedina.org/2014/04/cadic-cumple-8-anos-de-vida-en-servicio.html [19/07/2017]).

By development, I mean what Gillian Hart (2001:650) has called "'big D' Development," which she defines as "a post-second world war project of intervention in the 'third world' that emerged in the context of decolonization and the cold war" as opposed to "'little d' development or the development of capitalism as a geographically uneven, profoundly contradictory set of historical processes." One important aspect is the notion of this kind of development as an 'intervention' – the 'first world' intervening in the 'third world' for the sake of development. Mapped onto Bolivia and the Afrobolivian case specifically, this means that CADIC (and with it urban Afrobolivians) intervenes in rural *comunidades* for the sake of development. Obviously, the global dimension of the 'first world' intervening in a 'third world' country such as Bolivia is an important notion in the Afrobolivian case, too. Yet I would argue that for understanding the dynamics of Afrobolivian mobilization and identity politics, the relationship established between the allegedly urban/modern CADIC and 'backward rural communities in need of development' – and the symbolic as well as material and power differences this opposition entails – is of even greater importance. It casts the rural Yungas communities as recipients of development in need of assistance from urban, modern Afrobolivians. Ironically, the more successful CADIC became at channeling development funds, the more dependent the communities became. This relationship of dependence and the discursive construction of urban organizations working on behalf of 'disenfranchised rural communities' has become a pattern that is difficult to overcome both in discourse and in practice (see chapter 9 on CONAFRO). It bars rural Afrobolivian community leaders from participating in decision making and political action in urban settings directly and is one of the main problems CONAFRO faces today in its attempts to position itself as the legitimate leadership of all Afrobolivians, urban and rural.

Talleres (workshops) as spaces of articulation

Jorge Medina's move to engage development discourse had further consequences beyond establishing a specific pattern of relationships between rural and urban Afrobolivians. It also meant that workshops *(talleres)* became the main method of approaching Afrobolivian identity politics. This tendency is not limited to CADIC as an institution. In chapter 5 I described a workshop in Coripata where *Cala Caleños* were prompted "to think about identity" *("tenemos que pensar en la identidad")* and in the previous chapter I showed how cataloging Afrobolivian culture is also achieved at least in part by gathering people in workshops.

Following Eduardo Restrepo (Restrepo 2004:705), who has analyzed the ethnicization of blackness in Colombia, I propose to analyze *talleres* as "techniques that entail the concentration of people in a determined time and space with a specific aim." Beyond the "circulation of a certain kind of speech, of a particular management of the body and of the establishment-reproduction of specific power relationships," these techniques are important in the sense that they aim to "establish relations and assumptions into the matrix of interaction among the attendees at multiple levels" (Restrepo 2004:705). Mark Goodale (Goodale 2009) has also vividly described in his ethnography of human rights discourse in Bolivia that the importance of *talleres* can hardly be overstated. Writing about the program brochure of a workshop he attended during fieldwork, he notes that "the entire range of technocratic knowledge practices are brought together within the four corners of this humble little brochure at the service of, as it turns out, what has become a kind of meta-technocratic knowledge—human rights" (Goodale 2009:132–133). What is more, this is not a new phenomenon only recently introduced and relevant in Bolivia: it is something that has been shaping Bolivian people's sense of themselves, and their view on law, politics and development in decisive ways. As Antonio Rodríguez-Carmona aptly put it:

> "Twenty years is nothing, or it can be a lot. Twenty years of seeing 4x4 vehicles drive by, seeing international cooperation personnel dressed in polar jackets. Twenty years hearing the talk of solutions to poverty, projects, expected results, *twenty years of participating in training workshops [talleres]* [...]" (Rodríguez-Carmona 2009:1, my translation, emphasis added)[19]

What applies to processes of transforming Afrocolombian political subjectivities as described by Restrepo and to human rights in the case of Goodale's study, I argue, also applies to plurinational ID-ology and the propagation of Afrobolivianity as a framework for identification. Each workshop must be seen as one concrete event giving meaning to the category *"Afroboliviano"* as the basis for collective gathering and political action in contexts where this category is often not salient in organizational terms. In rural contexts, identification as *Afroboliviano* competes with *comunario* identity and *sindicato* politics, as I have shown in chapters 3 and 4. In urban settings, Afrobolivians are often dispersed geographically and concrete spaces of communication among Afrobolivians are mostly found in *talleres* or in meetings of Afrobolivian organizations. *Talleres* thus serve to constitute a sense of collective belonging on ethnoracial grounds. In *talleres* people are explicitly addressed as Afrobolivians. They are encouraged to frame their claims as 'Afrobolivian claims' and conceptualize needs and deservingness in collective ethnoracial terms. To cite but one example, in a *taller* organized by CADIC that I attended in Santa Cruz, Medina addressed the audience as follows: "What does the Afrobolivian community of Santa Cruz want?" The people in the audience responded with a long list of desires: a project to create incentives for the formation of Afrobolivian micro-

19 *"Veinte años no es nada o puede ser mucho. Veinte años viendo pasar vagonetas 4x4, cooperantes extranjeros vestidos con chamarras polares. Veinte años oyendo hablar de soluciones a la pobreza, proyectos, resultados esperados, veinte años asistiendo a talleres de capacitación [...]."*

businesses *(micro-empresas)*, a census of Afrobolivian people in Santa Cruz, a direct Afrobolivian representative on the municipal board of the city, an emergency fund for Afrobolivian people that can provide financial aid in cases of sickness or accident, support for an Afrobolivian cultural festival, a school that teaches Afrobolivian *"artes y expresiones culturales"* (artistic and cultural expressions) and health insurance for Afrobolivians *("seguro Afroboliviano")*. As this list shows, matters of economic necessity, political representation, culture and health care were framed as Afrobolivian needs and desires that should be addressed within a framework relying on collective ethnoracial identifications. Even overarching topics such as better access to health care and insurance – doubtless a matter of great interest for many Bolivians – were approached from a perspective foregrounding collective identification as Afrobolivians.

A last point that I only want to briefly introduce here as it will be discussed in more detail in the subsequent chapter is the increasing salience of "rights talk" (Merry 2003) fostered by workshops. Whereas earlier approaches – for example the work of MOCUSABOL and the important efforts of the *Centro Pedagógico Simón I. Patiño* – circled around the revitalization of customs and 'tradition,' as well as the salvaging of 'culture,' the more transnationally inspired approach employed by CADIC advocated for introducing the idiom of rights through concepts such as human rights, women's rights, indigenous rights, minority rights or explicitly *Afrodescendant* rights. Jorge Medina often explicitly adopted a rhetoric inspired by the 2001 Durban Declaration, making the term *Afrodescendiente* an important reference, as well as introducing a more explicit anti-discrimination framework into Afrobolivian politics hitherto framed more commonly in terms of multiculturalism. The legacy of the logics and modes of engagement CADIC first introduced is thus manifold. It shaped Afrobolivian politics to a large extent and with durable consequences by making development a major issue, by firmly establishing the workshop as a context of engagement and interaction, and by broadening the scope of Afrobolivian political discourse to include different facets of "rights talk." The partial shift to a more decidedly diasporic political rhetoric – expressed in the proliferation of the term *Afrodescendiente* – also occurred during CADIC's most active period.

Conclusion

What started in 1982 as the initiative of a few high school students in a small Yungas village had, by the turn of the 21st century, become an increasingly organized network of Afrobolivian organizations. The 'rediscovery' of *saya* and the ensuing propagation of a cultural understanding of what it meant to be Afrobolivian beyond the color of one's skin paved the way for Afrobolivian organizations and individuals to articulate their grievances in national and international contexts. Afrobolivian organizations have ever since been active in the realms of folklore and cultural production, in national politics, international development contexts and transnational fora. Their discourses and strategies mirror all these contexts, as well as the very immediate and local specificities of the Afrobolivian case.

Following the 'rediscovery' of Afrobolivian culture, certain key individuals started organizing primarily black *(negro)* youth in urban centers and embarked on a process of cultural revitalization that they carried into the rural communities from whence they had migrated a few years earlier. Public performances and the spaces offered by the folklore industry were key factors in this regard. Furthermore, the overall political climate and the support of a set of key actors (anthropologists, national NGOs and individual power brokers) favored these efforts and made it possible to consolidate the emergent movement under the banner of MOCUSABOL. The organizational panorama subsequently diversified, and with it the political propositions and discursive framings. The most salient development in this regard is the shift in terminology from *negro* to *Afroboliviano* and all the meanings this shift carries – namely the culturalization of Afrobolivianity and an emphasis on national belonging and citizenship. Additionally, the generally national focus of Afrobolivian politics notwithstanding, diasporic affiliations and ideas circulating within transnational networks of *Afrodescendientes* also had a part to play in Afrobolivian mobilization. Through activists' participation in transnational events – and their subsequent efforts at disseminating the contents of these meetings – Afrobolivians started reflecting on their origins, their relation to the wider African Diaspora and the meanings these links would have for their place in Bolivian society.

In terms of the goals achieved in this formative period of the Afrobolivian movement, visibility stands out as the most important. Through their activities, Afrobolivians "perform[ed] blackness into the nation" (Busdiecker 2007), challenging the widespread silence on Afrobolivianity in public discourse. The relative silence and invisibility of Afrobolivian collectivity and culture was replaced, however, only by partial visibility and recognition as part of the nation's cultural patrimony, leaving little room for representations of more mundane and day-to-day Afrobolivian lifestyles and contributing little to the betterment of living conditions in Afrobolivian communities. This is what I have called the pitfall of folklorization and the perceived limitations of early mobilizations inspired Afrobolivian activists to search for a number of alternative strategies to overcome this situation. Two stand out as most important: first are the discourses associated with development and second is the proliferation of "rights talk." While the former has marked contexts and genres of political engagement and interaction to a large extent, the latter became increasingly salient in the Afrobolivian campaign surrounding the Constituent Assembly convened by the newly elected government of the *Movimiento al Socialismo (MAS)* and its leader, Evo Morales, in 2006. It is to the processes around this event – usually referred to as ground-breaking and epochal – and its aftermath that I now turn.

Chapter 9: Rights, Recognition, and New Forms of Organization

The Judicialization of Afrobolivian Activism and the Rise of CONAFRO

In a recently published account, the *Consejo Nacional Afroboliviano* (CONAFRO) describes the decade starting in 2010 as the time when the Afrobolivian people finally began to step out of the 'invisibility' of the past to become active and visible social and political actors in Bolivia. This is attributed to the foundation of CONAFRO and a process of ethnic and cultural revival, as the introduction of the text explains:

> "The *pueblo Afrosdecendiente* in Bolivia, since the beginning of this decade and after a long process of ethnic and cultural mobilization, has managed to found a proper national political instance through which, in a short time and unlike other indigenous peoples, it *[el pueblo Afrodescendiente]* has had the opportunity to become one of the principal actors in the current sociopolitical conjuncture. We refer specifically to the *Consejo Nacional Afroboliviano*."[1]

The authors go on to state that:

> "the Bolivian state, after a long process of invisibilization and as a response to the insistent demands, could not help but accept the *pueblo Afroboliviano* as a legal subject with the same rights, collective and individual, as the other *pueblos indígenas originarios campesinos* that live within national territory. The *pueblo Afroboliviano*, therefore, is now included in the new laws, and on the basis of that, is fighting for its political project to be taken into consideration in public policy aiming

1 *"El Pueblo Afrodescendiente en Bolivia, desde principios de la actual década y luego de un largo proceso de explicitación étnica y cultural, ha logrado conformar una instancia política nacional y propia [con su respectivo brazo educativo] que, en poco tiempo y a diferencia de otros pueblos indígenas, le ha posibilitado constituirse en uno de los principales actores protagónicos en la actual coyuntura sociopolítica del país; nos referimos, específicamente, al* Consejo Nacional Afroboliviano (CONAFRO) *[y a su secretaría de educación, el* Consejo Educativo del Pueblo Afroboliviano [CEPA]*]."*

at improving its quality of life in economic/productive, social/organizational and cultural/educational terms."[2]

These two excerpts include a significant number of important points and developments that I want to detail, contextualize and analyze in this chapter. As I described in the previous chapter, Afrobolivian activism initially started with efforts of cultural revitalization and public performance, later introducing logics of development, diasporic politics, differentiated citizenship and ethnic rights. These efforts laid the groundwork for Afrobolivians' (informal) participation in the 2006 Constituent Assembly that culminated with the official legal recognition of the collective subject *el pueblo Afroboliviano* in the new Bolivian Constitution ratified and promulgated in 2009. As will become clear, in recent years Afrobolivian activism has evolved in a number of key aspects and three related developments stand out as most relevant: Firstly, 21st century Afrobolivian activism relies heavily on the concept of rights. This entails a legalized language, a certain judicialization of protest and politics more generally and most strikingly an upsurge in "rights talk" (Merry 2003). Secondly, the idea of articulating demands and claiming rights on behalf of a collective subject called *el pueblo Afroboliviano* has gained significant momentum. This also entails emphasizing ethnic identity, culture, territoriality and language as the basis for collective identification rather than pointing out race, skin color and phenotype. Finally, the emphasis on *pueblo* status has sparked new forms of collective organizing that differ greatly from the prevailing modes of mobilization (as *saya* performance ensembles or NGOs in search of development funds) and draws inspiration from indigenous and other popular organizations in Bolivia.

In the first part of the chapter, I argue that a growing proliferation of rights talk and the framing of political demands as rights became fundamental to making Afrobolivian claims compatible with the logics of the Constituent Assembly. In this sense, Afrobolivian activism mirrors emerging trends of judicialization in Latin American politics (Huneeus, Couso, and Sieder 2010:8; de Sousa Santos 2002). Moreover, I argue that the logics of multicultural and plurinational recognition made it vital to frame these demands-cum-rights in collective terms. The concept that made this articulation possible is *el pueblo Afroboliviano*, heavily inspired by transnationally circulating concepts of indigenous peoplehood adjusted to Bolivian circumstances (Niezen 2003; for Bolivia see: Canessa 2012b). In terms of political

2 *"[A]l Estado boliviano, luego de un largo proceso de invisibilización y como respuesta a la insistente demanda, no le quedó más que asumir al Pueblo Afroboliviano como un sujeto jurídico con los mismos derechos, colectivos e individuales, que los otros pueblos indígenas originarios campesinos que habitan en el territorio nacional. El Pueblo Afroboliviano, por eso, ahora está incluido en las nuevas leyes y, sobre ese fundamento, está luchando para que su proyecto político y de vida sean tomados en cuenta en las políticas públicas con el propósito de contribuir al mejoramiento de su calidad de vida en los ámbitos económico productivo, social organizativo y cultural educativo."*

organization and mobilization, the formation of the *Consejo Nacional Afroboliviano (CONAFRO)* marks a decisive shift representing a turn to a different pattern of mobilization from the development NGO organizations and the cultural/dance groups of the 1980s and 1990s. CONAFRO presents itself as the *ente matriz* (lit.: mother institution) of all Afrobolivians in much the same way as the large indigenous federations in the country. Taken together, I argue that the three trends – judicialization, the emphasis on *pueblo* status and the proliferation of new modes of mobilization – have marked Afrobolivian engagement with the state and international institutions to a great extent. In the eyes of CONAFRO, the outcome has been fairly clear and positive: hitherto marginalized Afrobolivians have achieved visibility as a collective subject of rights and are in a position to effectively push for their political project to be taken into consideration by the Bolivian state. Yet there are also critical voices and important contradictions inherent in the processes of mobilization and recognition, as I will show at the end of the chapter.

"500 years give us rights!" Framing political demands as rights to be claimed

My first encounter with an Afrobolivian organization in 2010 was instructive for a variety of reasons. I was in Bolivia in search of a new research project and was conducting preliminary fieldwork. Since I was interested in the Afrobolivian population, I casually paid a visit to the most visible Afrobolivian organization (at that time the *Centro Afroboliviano para el Desarrollo Integral y Comunitario [CADIC]* in La Paz). I was quickly called into the office of its president, Jorge Medina. Medina had just been elected to congress on the *Movimiento al Socialismo (MAS)* ticket of the special indigenous electoral circumscription *(circunscripción especial indígena)* for La Paz and received me openly and in a friendly manner. After explaining the reasons for my visit and offering to help with anything CADIC might need, he gave me the following task: compile and translate the anti-discrimination laws of various countries (he was especially interested in Brazil and South Africa and, given my nationality, asked me to include Germany). I did as he asked and stopped by his office a few days later to present my translations and discuss my findings. He was mostly interested in debating how the foreign laws might be adjusted to the Bolivian situation, since he was himself planning to propose a law against discrimination in parliament. In most of our meetings, we were accompanied by his closest assessor, who was at the same time his lawyer and had the expertise to translate Medina's ideas into legally adequate language as well as foresee possible legal trapdoors in the process. My first months of engaging with Afrobolivian politics were thus marked by laws and bureaucratic technicalities. These circumstances certainly shaped my perspective on the subject. It differs significantly from what other researchers have written about and shared with me in personal communications. During most of the 1980s and 1990s and even into the 21st century, *saya*, culture and 'visibility' were the currencies of Afrobolivian mobilizations (Busdiecker 2007; Komadina and Regalsky 2016; Rossbach de Olmos 2007; Templeman 1995). Accordingly, scholars shaped their arguments in terms of these topics and some have questioned the relevance of legal discourse and the claiming of rights in understanding Afrobolivian reality.[3] I argue, however, that a closer look at these instances of Afrobolivian mobilizations is long overdue. One cannot deny the increasing salience of these topics in current political discourse. Many of my interlocutors also expressed a sense of increased importance of rights, legal reform and judicialization for Afrobolivian politics.

Afrobolivians "on their way to the Constituent Assembly"

Bolivian politics in the early 21st century was marked by various episodes of civil unrest, culminating in the 2002 "water war," *("Guerra del Agua")* the 2003 "gas war" *("Guerra del Gas")* and the subsequent toppling of President Gonzalo Sanchez de Lozada's neoliberal and multicultural government. Beyond matters of basic service privatization (water) and the overall economic project pursued by neoliberal governments since the 1980s (such as the selling of primary resources, e.g. gas), the protests were concerned with social inequalities, neo-colonial power relations and the large-scale disenfranchisement of vast parts of the population (poor, peasant, indigenous, etc.) more generally. In the wake of these mobilizations, Evo Morales and the MAS party won the elections in 2005, took power in 2006 and immediately called for a Constituent Assembly *(Asamblea Constituyente)* in order to rework the country's fundamental legal basis and tackle social inequality and colonial domination (Kohl and Farthing 2006).

In the years and months leading up to the *Asamblea Constituyente*, Afrobolivian mobilization had arrived at a critical juncture. It was faced with the limitations of mobilizing in the realm of folklore, and of Jorge Medina's NGO-style approach to activism. Even though CADIC was reaching different urban and rural communities with small-scale development projects and workshops, and *saya* groups had been established in all major cities, delivering a certain degree of visibility, no significant improvements for the Afrobolivian population were being achieved, according to many of my interlocutors. Through *saya*, Afrobolivians had managed to become a visible part of the folkloric mosaic of the country. They remained, however, disproportionately poor, uneducated, discriminated against and marginalized in political life, the workplace and everyday contexts. There was, in short, a lot to be done from

3 However, see Busdiecker (2009b) for an analysis pointing at the increasing importance of legal discourse.

the perspective of Afrobolivian leaders as well as from the vantage point of urban and rural communities. From the perspective of many Afrobolivians, the problems they were facing as a collective were exemplified by the failed campaign to include *Afroboliviano* as a category of self-identification in Bolivia's population census of 2001. As the first census to be undertaken after the multicultural reforms of the 1990s, the questionnaire included questions concerning proficiency in indigenous languages and cultural identity: "Do you consider yourself to belong to any of the following *pueblos originarios* or *indígenas*?"[4] Possible categories of identification were: *Quechua, Aymara, Guaraní, Chiquitano, Mojeño, otro nativo* (other native), or *ninguno* (none). Afrobolivians considered the omission of the option *Afroboliviano* as a clear sign of their marginalization in official discourse. They were not satisfied with the option to mark "*otro nativo*" and specify "*Afroboliviano,*" which was indeed possible, since they did not consider themselves natives *(originarios)* or indigenous. Marking "none," in turn, would downplay their cultural uniqueness and their status as a collective that can be distinguished from the national mainstream. They felt they had been made 'invisible' as a culturally different collective in need of special attention. As had previously happened, this experience of frustration led to an active campaign – led by MOCUSABOL and CADIC – to push for official recognition. The opportunity to put these claims into practice presented itself in the context of the *Asamblea Constituyente*: from 2006, Bolivia began to debate and elaborate a new constitution that promised to put an end to 'more than 500 years of colonialism.'

In this context, there are a number of examples of the tendency to frame political demands as rights, one of the clearest being MOCUSABOL's campaign in the context of the *Asamblea Constituyente* that stated: "*Más de 500 años nos dan derechos*" ("More than 500 years give us rights"). Here, MOCUSABOL very clearly stated that "we have to achieve recognition as a *pueblo* and demand the right to land and territory."[5]

The focus on rights and recognition that was formalized in MOCUSABOL's claims in light of the Constituent Assembly had its roots in earlier campaigns demanding inclusion in the National Census of 2001 and can be discerned as an emerging topic in *saya* lyrics as early as 1994 (cf. Templeman 1998). Yet it was only in the context of elaborating a new constitution that these demands took center stage and Afrobolivians mobilized to seize the opportunity to be included in the far-reaching reforms that the government promised would be achieved through constitutional reform. This of course also entailed framing and articulating demands in a way that was compatible with the logics of constitutional reform in Bolivia. Fundamentally,

---

4 "*¿Se considera perteneciente a alguno de los siguientes pueblos originarios o indígenas?*"

5 "*Debemos lograr el reconocimiento como pueblo y posteriormente exigir el derecho a tierra y territorio*" (MOCUSABOL BOLETIN 2005-06).

Figure 20: Cover of a MOCUSABOL leaflet summarizing the demands of Afrobolivians in the context of the Constituent Assembly (courtesy of MOCUSABOL).

it meant that demands had to be formulated as rights to be claimed. Sara Busdiecker (2009b), who did extensive fieldwork among Afrobolivians at the turn of the millennium, also described a shift from the "performative to the political" in Afrobolivian mobilization. She remarked that Afrobolivian organizations that were at first mainly concerned with revitalizing and performing *saya* broadened their focus to include political demands and new forms of organization beyond the performance of *saya* to counter political, legal and statistical invisibilities. In light of the Constituent Assembly, the legal dimension was of ever-growing importance.

Afrobolivians in the Constituent Assembly: formal absence, changing alliances and the ever-present *saya*

In the process of participating in the Constituent Assembly, Afrobolivian organizations have come into close contact with legal instruments and discourses as well as with the argumentative repertoire of a variety of other social movements. As Komadina and Regalsky (2016) report, Afrobolivians were not able to secure direct participation through an Afrobolivian representative and were thus forced to look to other avenues to make their claims heard. Many of my interlocutors heavily criticized the fact that before the passing of the New Constitution in 2009, Afrobolivian organizations and demands were, if not systematically rejected, at least not systematically or officially included. This furthermore intensified the impression that only legal recognition could remedy Afrobolivian exclusion.

At first, MOCUSABOL teamed up with a variety of small organizations to form an eclectic alliance of Afrobolivians, gays and lesbians, street children and other small minorities. Soon, however, MOCUSABOL and CADIC formed an alliance with the *Consejo Nacional de Markas y Ayllus del Qollasuyu (CONAMAQ)* – an indigenous organization based in the Aymara communities of the Bolivian highlands – that would serve as their way into certain contexts of decision making. This alliance was upheld even after the New Constitution was passed. Through the alliance with CONAMAQ, Afrobolivians were included in certain sessions of the *Pacto de Unidad*[6] commissions and in commission meetings held by the ruling MAS party, which held the majority of seats in the Assembly and would thus be of great importance. As Schavelzon (2012) details in his ethnography of the Constituent Assembly, Afrobolivian voices intervened especially with regard to the formulations that would become Article 3 of the Constitution, summarizing the notion of the "Bolivian people" *(el pueblo Boliviano)* and determining who would be considered part of the entity in the New Constitution. At the same time and in addition to the strategy of participating in commissions through CONAMAQ, Afrobolivian individuals successfully approached the formal representatives of certain commissions and were given a chance to present their demands (Komadina and Regalsky 2016). There was some resistance, however, to including Afrobolivians explicitly in Article 3. Some *constituyentes* argued that singling out Afrobolivians by naming them explicitly while subsuming the other *pueblos* under the name *pueblos indígenas originarios campesinos* would be unjust and that either all *pueblos* or none at all should be mentioned in the article (Schavelzon 2012:128f). Others argued that naming them in such a prominent place would give the impression that Afrobolivians are "a macro-*pueblo*, when in reality they are only 500 people" *("un macro-pueblo cuando sólo son 500 personas")*

6 See chapter 2, footnote 15.

(Schavelzon 2012:128 quoting an anonymous *constituyente*). In the end, the MAS delegates (who had a vast majority in the *Asamblea*) agreed to include the formulation *"comunidades Afrobolivianas,"* alongside the *"naciones y pueblos indígena originario campesinos"* and the *"comunidades interculturales"* in Article 3 of the New Bolivian Constitution of 2009).[7] It is interesting to note that here the plural formula *"comunidades Afrobolivianas"* prevailed, whereas later the term *"el pueblo Afroboliviano"* emerged. The discrepancy between the articles, in my view, hints at the fact that the notion of *el pueblo Afroboliviano* was not completely stabilized by the time the Constitution was debated and the status of Afrobolivian collectivity was still a matter of debate.

Once Afrobolivians had been included in the foundational definition of what constitutes the "Bolivian people" *(el pueblo Boliviano)* it was possible to pursue the goal of claiming special rights analogous to indigenous groups. This goal was achieved through Article 32, which recognizes that *el pueblo Afroboliviano* possesses the same rights as indigenous groups *(naciones y pueblos indígena originario campesinos)*, "wherever appropriate" *("en todo lo que corresponda")*. In order to ensure that Afrobolivian demands were met and the Article in question could not be erased from the final document (as had happened several times before according to many of my interlocutors from different Afrobolivian organizations), MOCUSABOL and CADIC decided to stage a massive gathering of *saya* dancers and enter the building in Sucre with drums, singing and dance while the Assembly was in session. In recounting their experiences in Sucre, my interlocutors paid this moment the most attention, seemingly confirming the widespread allegations that Afrobolivians have achieved every political milestone through *saya*. This framing nevertheless downplays the importance of barely visible, semi-official negotiations around the Constituent Assembly and overshadows the various adaptations that Afrobolivian demands underwent during this process. The watershed moment of being officially recognized has significantly changed Afrobolivian political opportunities and has enhanced opportunities for participation. At the same time, the legal provisions that come with official recognition established the parameters that Afrobolivian participation must take and identified specific topics as relevant realms of recognition while excluding others. Most importantly, official legal recognition has stabilized the notion of a nationally homogenous *pueblo Afroboliviano*, which was circulating before but has gained currency most significantly since being legally established in 2009.

7 The term *Afroboliviano* was ultimately chosen instead of the wording *Afrodescendiente* since some representatives feared that writing *Afrodescendiente* would grant further rights to *"brasileros"* (Schavelzon 2013:129), i.e. Afrodescendants from other Latin American countries.

The aftermath of recognition: *el pueblo Afroboliviano* as the subject of collective rights

Besides foregrounding the claiming of rights as adequate tools to alter past and present injustices and to improve the situation of their constituency, Afrobolivian activists began shaping their demands by way of appealing to the Bolivian state and international institutions under the logic of what Shane Greene (Greene 2007a) has called the "holy trinity of multicultural peoplehood" (culture, territory and language). The importance of this cannot be overstated. In most cases, it was not individual rights that were the center of attention, but collective ones. This in turn generated the question of how and by what means this collective subject of rights could be defined. Making Afrobolivian claims *legible* (Scott 1998) entailed positioning themselves as a legitimate *pueblo*. The Constitution is fairly specific when it comes to defining what a *pueblo* consists of (adding "historic tradition" and "worldview" to the triad of language, territory and culture). According to Article 30 of the New Bolivian Constitution:

> "A nation and rural native indigenous people consists of every *human collective that shares a cultural identity, language, historic tradition, institutions, territory and world view*, whose existence predates the Spanish colonial invasion." (translation by Constituteproject.org, emphasis added)[8]

Shaping their demands to fit this definition was not completely new for Afrobolivian activism. References to *"el pueblo negro," "el pueblo Afroboliviano,"* or alternatively *"el pueblo Afrodescendiente,"* can be traced back to the early 1990s when the revitalization of *saya* sparked a boom in publications on Afrobolivians and the multicultural reforms in Bolivia had already led the way to articulations of collective identity very similar to those promoted by the 2009 Constitution. Yet in scholarly and press publications, as well as in documents elaborated by Afrobolivian organizations, references to *"el pueblo"* coexisted with references to *"la cultura negra/Afroboliviana," "la comunidad negra," "las comunidades Afrobolivianas," "la etnia Afrodescendiente"* and so on. Reviewing these documents gives the impression that the movement was trying to consolidate itself, both in organizational terms, as I have described in chapter 8, and in terms of the concepts to be used. Each of the denominators just mentioned carries slightly different connotations and emphases. On the one hand, there is the terminological distinction between *"negro," "Afroboliviano"* and *"Afrodescendiente."* In political discourse, *"negro"* (connoting skin color) has fallen out of use and has been replaced by *"Afroboliviano"* (highlighting culture and national citizenship)

8 *"Es nación y pueblo indígena originario campesino toda la colectividad humana que comparta identidad cultural, idioma, tradición histórica, instituciones, territorialidad y cosmovisión, cuya existencia es anterior a la invasión colonial española."*

and *"Afrodescendiente"* (highlighting culture and diasporic affiliations). Equally important, however, is the distinction between *"cultura," "comunidades"* (plural), *"la comunidad"* (singular), *"la etnía"* and *"el pueblo."* Referring to *"cultura"* leaves open the question of whether and in what sense this *"cultura"* relates to individuals, groups or a group. Speaking of *"comunidades"* in the plural implies acknowledging multiplicity and possible heterogeneity. The singular *"la comunidad,"* in contrast, rhetorically implies homogeneity and uniformity. Referring to *"etnía"* and *"pueblo"* additionally implies assuming specific characteristics of a community. The matter of terminology is far from conclusively settled. As I showed in chapter 6, articulations of Afrobolivianity are shaped by entangled references to phenotype, race, culture, region, indigeneity and diaspora. Even the constitutional text is not conclusive on the subject. As I have mentioned, Article 3 refers to *"las comunidades Afrobolivianas,"* whereas Article 32 speaks of *"el pueblo Afroboliviano."* I argue, however, that in the current political discourse, alternative terms and perspectives are increasingly overshadowed by the specific articulation of Afrobolivian collectivity as a *pueblo*, which started gaining currency in the years between 2006 and 2009 (during the Constituent Assembly) and most clearly after 2009 when the New Constitution was being promulgated.

Re-articulations of Afrobolivianity and the dynamics of *pueblo*-ization

Whereas in 2005 and 2006 MOCUSABOL was voicing the demands of *"comunidades Afrodescendientes"* directed at the *Asamblea Constituyente* (see fig. 20 above), in 2014 CONAFRO stated its mission as being to work for a *"pueblo Afroboliviano fuerte y mancomunado"* ("a strong and unified *pueblo Afroboliviano*").

I argue that the transformations this shift expresses go well beyond changing the terminology of leaflets and action plans. The political and legal re-articulation of *"comunidades Afrobolivianas"* as *"el pueblo Afroboliviano"* exhibit clear parallels to the processes that Eduardo Restrepo has described for Afrocolombian mobilization and which he termed "the ethnicization of blackness." According to Restrepo (2004:699),

> "the ethnicization of black political subjects and subjectivities must be understood as an ongoing process of the articulation of blackness in Colombia that has established a specific relationship between territory, identity, cultural tradition, nature and otherness."

In Bolivia as well as in Colombia, this process has – especially on the level of political subjectivities and mobilization strategies – led to the prevalence of "novel modalities of collective action closely tied to the logic of the [...] state" (Pardo and Alvarez 2001 quoted in Restrepo 2004). In the Colombian case it involved the configuration of an ethnic black political subject (the black community as an ethnic group) (Restrepo 2004:706), whereas in Bolivia, it has led to the articulation of Afrobolivian collectivity as *el pueblo Afroboliviano.* The two processes exhibit certain similarities but differ in terms of specific content due to the different discourses pertaining to blackness and indigeneity in the two countries.

According to Restrepo (2004), in Colombia, the question of territory was crucial, since the logics of recognition established by Colombian legislation made the territorial integrity of a given ethnic group an important aspect in determining their legitimacy. In Bolivia, the politics and the language of indigeneity as well as the ensuing regimes of recognition differ from the Colombian case. Bolivian discourses on indigeneity have been in constant flux and include shifting references to language, dress, the colonial encounter, self-identification and marginalization (for a concise overview see Canessa 2007). The discourses of regimes of multicultural recognition that are most relevant to the Afrobolivian case are the Law of Popular Participation and more broadly the multicultural Constitution of 1994, which have been circulating in many communities. As criteria for being considered indigenous, they emphasize pre-colonial origins, history, language and culture, and self-positioning as belonging to the same socio-cultural unit (Canessa 2007:203f.). Another important factor is the very strong association of Afrobolivians with *saya,* stemming from the fact that the revitalization of *saya* was the backbone of the emerging movement and Afrobolivians became visible in Bolivia first and foremost as *saya* dancers. The process of recognition emerging from this combination was what Lioba Rossbach de Olmos (2011) has called *patrimonialización* (i.e. being recognized as cultural patrimony of the nation) and what many of my Afrobolivian interlocutors refer to as *folklorización* – mostly with a negative connotation. In the wake of official recognition, folklorization and patrimonialization have been enhanced in certain ways, adding up to what I term the *pueblo*-ization of Afrobolivian collectivity.

Pueblo-ization moves beyond the association of Afrobolivians with folklore by introducing further elements that contribute to a cultural and historical definition of Afrobolivianity, following the Constitution's definition of a *pueblo* as a collectivity that should possess "cultural identity, language, historic tradition, institutions, territory and world view." In order to plausibly articulate the Afrobolivian collectivity as a *pueblo,* Afrobolivian organizations smoothly latched onto representations of *saya* as authentic Afrobolivian culture, yet made great efforts to emphasize its value as cultural practice beyond folklore. One vivid example is Martín Miguel Ballivián's (Ballivián 2014) claim in the context of his analysis of *saya* as a space of encounter and education in Afrobolivian communities. He asserts that *saya* means "living well with happiness in community, from our worldview" *("resulta ser el Vivir Bien con Alegría en Comunidad, desde nuestra cosmovsión")* (Ballivián 2014:13) positing *saya* as the backbone of an Afrobolivian *cosmovisión*, analogous to the indigenous concept of *Buen Vivir/Vivir Bien* (Acosta 2015). In the same vein, Afrobolivian organizations have been very active in promoting the symbolic monarchy *"el Rey Afroboliviano"* as an example of historical continuity of Afrobolivian leadership and have furthermore positioned the king as a sort of 'traditional' authority figure for the Afrobolivian people (see chapter 7 and also Busdiecker 2007; Revilla Orías 2014b). Similarly, certain other 'cultural elements' like the funeral rite *mauchi* and dances like *zemba, baile de tierra* and *cueca negra,* have been introduced to a wider public. In the context of fostering an image of cultural distinctiveness, references to Africa and African culture have also been on the rise in conceptualizing Afrobolivian culture. Yet references to Africa and African cultural roots are employed to legitimize claims to a unique and recognizable Afrobolivian culture that is put forth politically as a founding claim to the *pueblo* status equivalent to that of indigenous groups, not as a means to position Afrobolivians as a different kind of collective (transnational, diasporic) in need of a different set of practices of recognition.

Another striking example is the campaign to revitalize Afrobolivian Spanish *(la lengua Afroboliviana),* a historically distinct creole variant of Spanish that has fallen out of actual use. Afrobolivian individuals and organizations have been taking up the findings of linguists researching this Afrobolivian Creole language (Lipski 2008; Pérez Inofuentes 2015; Sessarego 2011a; Sessarego 2014) in order to substantiate their claim to the status of a *pueblo*. For example, Juan Angola Maconde (2012) has recently published a dictionary of Afrobolivian Spanish terms and the "long-lost 'black Spanish'" (Lipski 2007:1) has also been introduced as a part of the *Currículo Regionalizado del Pueblo Afroboliviano*.

Similarly, the ubiquitous references to the Yungas as the region most traditionally associated with Afrobolivians and their culture (see for example Busdiecker's [2009a] discussion of the importance of place for concepts of Afrobolivianity) are now discursively pitched to resonate with discourses around indigenous territories *(territorios indígenas)* very common in political and legal discourse in Bolivia. The struggle for land was particularly important in the mobilization of various indigenous groups in the Bolivian lowlands who had not benefitted from the land reform in the 1950s (Lacroix 2012). In 1996, the Bolivian government issued an updated law of land reform *(Ley INRA)*, recognizing collective indigenous ownership of land. This law was heavily influenced by ILO declaration 169, and reflects the declaration's demand that "governments shall respect the special importance for the cultures and spiritual values of the peoples concerned of their relationship with the lands or territories [...] which they occupy [...]" (ILO 169, Art.13). The Bolivian Constitution of 2009 also includes references to indigenous territory and many of the special entitlements granted to the recognized *pueblos* in the Constitution are explicitly or implicitly tied to notions of territoriality.[9] As far as most sources up

9 On the one hand, in Article 30, which defines the concept of *"nación y pueblo indígena originiario,"* territoriality is listed as one of the markers of a *pueblo*. Several of the special rights

until very recently go, references to the Yungas as 'Afrobolivian territory' or the 'region of Afrobolivians' went no further than to say that a significant part of the Afrobolivian population historically lived there and that there are still many *comunidades* where Afrobolivians make up a significant proportion of the population. By no means did it add up to an exclusive claim to that territory by Afrobolivians which would put them in direct competition with other segments of society. As land rights and territory are among the most tangible and economically significant (and thus most highly contested) aspects of the *pueblo* status, Afrobolivian claims in this regard have not been as straightforward as they have been in the realms of culture and language. Afrobolivian activists are very keenly aware that touching on the subject of exclusive land rights in the Yungas might mean losing most of the support that they have enjoyed from indigenous groups. This does not stop them from invoking the concept in their action plans, agendas and programs though, as CONAFRO's most recent agenda shows. CONAFRO instated a *Secretaria de Tierra, Territorio y Medio Ambiente* whose central responsibility is to "push for [the land of] Afrobolivian communities being recognized as our territory."[10] I have described notions of Afrobolivian autochthony in the local context of Cala Cala (see chapter 3) and have also hinted at the importance of the Yungas in articulations of Afrobolivianity more generally (see chapter 6). As a consequence of *pueblo*-ization these discourses have now also entered political rhetoric.

Finding ways to argue for Afrobolivian cultural distinctiveness, historic tradition, language and a relationship to territory similar to that of indigenous peoples was an important step on a discursive level. What Afrobolivian activists very quickly and astutely learned in the months after the promulgation of the New Constitution and the following general elections held in late 2009 was that in order to open up spaces of participation and harvest more concrete benefits of recognition, one further step was necessary: *el pueblo Afroboliviano* needed an *ente matriz* – literally a "mother entity," meaning a single institution that represents a "strong and unified *pueblo Afroboliviano*."

---

listed in Article 31 are also linked to territoriality (self-determination, prior consultation, the right to participate in the benefits of the exploitation of natural resources). What is more, territoriality can also serve as a foundation for claims to political autonomy of an indigenous group within the boundaries of a specific territory.

10 *"Gestión para que las comunidades Afrobolivianas sean declaradas nuestro territorio."*

The *Consejo Nacional Afroboliviano* (CONAFRO): the organizational response to the *pueblo* discourse

The history behind and around CONAFRO's foundation is instructive for a variety of reasons. First of all, it shows the great influence of newly opening spaces and possibilities for Afrobolivian individuals and organizations in the Plurinational State. Economic funding from the Ministry of Education, specific legal provisions, and institutional support from a variety of state institutions were crucial in the founding of CONAFRO. Secondly, CONAFRO as an organization mirrors the changing political articulations of Afrobolivianity in its structures, goals and aspirations in the sense that CONAFRO is the idea of *el pueblo Afroboliviano* turned into an organization. Conceptualized as a nationally active organization that represents dispersed communities and local grassroots organizations with a unified voice and under a centralizing logic, CONAFRO as an organization is the outcome of Afrobolivian interpretations of indigenous social movements *(movimientos sociales)*. *Movimiento social* has become a ubiquitous term in Bolivian politics nowadays, and even members of the current government repeatedly speak of themselves as being "the government of social movements" (see also Torrez and Zegada 2008). For most of my interlocutors, the term describes certain practices and modes of legitimation of power and representation that allegedly counter hegemonic neoliberal forms of governance. For them, a *movimiento social* and its leaders represent the people *(el pueblo)*. Its representatives' authority is legitimized by the base through voting and ongoing participation in debates and the exchange of ideas. Interestingly, many adherents of this view conceptualize their way of doing politics in opposition to the very widespread NGO-like structures of organizations and their technocratic, developmentalist attitudes and actions. Compliance with this model seems to be a prerequisite for obtaining any attention from state institutions. One of the main characteristics of this model is the existence of a national-level organization that represents the group in question vis-à-vis central state organs, while the regional and local levels are the arenas in which most of the debates take place. Only if an organization fits this definition can its members hope to benefit from state-funded programs that are channeled through *movimientos sociales*. One of the main obstacles to Afrobolivian mobilization, activists stated, was the fact that no national organization existed before the foundation of CONAFRO and that they were not able to make any substantial progress due to this situation.

Envisioning CONAFRO and the logic of *movimientos sociales* as a form of governance

The meetings that would eventually lead to the creation of CONAFRO started out as rather informal gatherings in the city of La Paz. According to Juan Angola Maconde, it was mainly Afrobolivian public functionaries – employees of the *Ministerio de Educación*, the *Ministerio de Desarrollo Rural y Tierras* and the *Viceministerio de Comercio Exterior* – as well as Angola himself who conducted the initial meetings at *La Prensa*, a restaurant in the government district of La Paz. They were sometimes accompanied by non-Afrobolivian co-workers from state institutions and occasionally by other urban Afrobolivian activists. During these meetings, they came up with the idea of founding a nationwide Afrobolivian organization, *"un ente matriz"* for the *pueblo Afroboliviano*. Planning the founding of an *ente matriz* was their response to repeated rejections of Afrobolivian demands by national and international institutions due to the fact that there was no nationally active, representative Afrobolivian 'mother institution' through which funding could be channeled or representation organized. For example, there was no formal mechanism or transparent election on behalf of the Afrobolivian constituency to elect Jorge Medina as their candidate to run for the post of *Asambleísta Nacional* in 2009. Medina always claims to have been elected democratically during an *ampliado* (public gathering) of the *pueblo Afroboliviano* held in La Paz. His critics argue that he seized the opportunity and used his contacts established as leader of CADIC to take advantage of a vacuum in the ranks of the MAS party to be elected as the only available candidate. Be this as it may, the Afrobolivian leaders meeting in *La Prensa* in 2010/11 recognized that their project lacked institutional backing and representation in the eyes of the state. This is why they decided that *el pueblo Afroboliviano* needed an institution representing it on a national level.

In this regard, they explicitly pointed to indigenous groups whose nationally active organizations had accomplished nationwide recognition and representativeness in the eyes of state institutions. Since MAS's rise to power in 2005/2006, these indigenous organizations have enjoyed an unprecedented level of direct influence in national politics. As members of the *Pacto de Unidad* (see footnote 15, chapter 2) and coordinated by the *Coordinadora Nacional por el Cambio (CONALCAM)*, the large indigenous *movimientos sociales* have exerted great influence on the national government since 2005. Certain key leaders of these movements have also been integrated into the structures of the state. As Nancy Postero (2017:31) has recently reminded us, the *Movimiento al Socialismo* (MAS) party – also according to repeated statements by Evo Morales himself – is not supposed to be "a traditional party, but the political instrument of the social movements that form its base."[11] By the time Afrobolivian leaders were envisioning CONAFRO, they were keenly aware of these new forms of governance in what has been termed the "New Indigenous State of Bolivia" (Canessa 2012a) or Bolivia's "post-multicultural" moment (Postero 2006).

11 By 2017, the accuracy of these kinds of statements is in doubt as the MAS has concentrated power in state institutions to a great extent, creating open dissent from various social movements (see Postero 2017:17).

With this in mind and their experiences from the Constituent Assembly still vividly present, they developed a strategy to found an Afrobolivian organization that would meet the standards of an *ente matriz*, a legitminate *movimiento social.*

It is crucial to note that the idea to found CONAFRO did not arise from the rural communities that are often represented as the backbone of the organization: it was envisioned within the ranks of a very limited number of formally educated, politically connected and urban-based activists. They realized that the MAS government had shifted its focus from NGOs and the traditional development sector to what government rhetoric called *movimientos sociales*, organizations *representing* a certain constituency, not merely *working on behalf* of somebody. The political shift away from organizations like CADIC – that responded to the developmental ideals of the neoliberal multiculturalist state and never pretended to represent the Afrobolivian people, but rather worked on their behalf – made it necessary to envision a completely new Afrobolivian 'entity': an 'entity' that could legitimately claim to represent the whole of the Afrobolivian population throughout the country and not only certain factions of urban residents, rural communities or political allies. In order to achieve this level of representation, they based their plan on the ideal of forming an organization committed to "organic leadership" *(liderazgos orgánicos)*, a mayor buzzword in Bolivian politics and part and parcel of the MAS government's claim to legitimately govern by the will of the people *(gobernar obedeciendo)*. In order to claim "organic leadership," they decided that it would be necessary to convene a national Afrobolivian meeting in order to discuss their plan, hold elections and spread the word. Consequently, they then set out to find an institution that would fund a National Afrobolivian Congress in order to be able to consult with the constituency and ground the organization in democratic procedures. However, initial attempts to secure funding from the UN High Commissioner on Human Rights failed due to conflicting interests and competing leaders' interventions. The anti-CONAFRO faction mainly comprised of Jorge Medina and his followers associated with CADIC, who branded CONAFRO supporters as opportunistic *"arribistas"* (parvenus), unrightfully seizing the opportunities created through the years-long mobilization of the older generation of leaders. The proponents of CONAFRO in turn denounced the sectarian practices of Medina's followers as hindering Afrobolivian political mobilization in order to secure personal benefits. This dispute has still not been resolved today and is mirrored by the conflicts between competing organizations at the local, regional and national levels.

Eventually, the proponents of CONAFRO seized an opportunity directly linked to new legal provisions and the generalized political opening for Afrobolivians following the passing of the New Constitution in 2009. In the aftermath of the passing of a new educational law (Ley 070) in 2010, the *Ministerio de Educación* approached Afrobolivians and urged them to found a *Consejo Educativo*. The thirty-seven groups officially recognized by the New Constitution (including Afrobolivians) were to play a crucial part in the reform of the educational system that was high on the agenda at that time. Law 070 had ratified the institution of *Consejos Educativos de Pueblos Originarios* originally instated by the last educational reform in the 1990s *("Ley No. 1565 de la Reforma Educativa del 7 de Julio de 1994")* and granted these councils new rights and responsibilities. Each *pueblo* – through its respective *Consejo Educativo* – had to elaborate the fundamental tools for introducing a new kind of education that would accompany, deepen and broaden the country's process of decolonization and change. Since Afrobolivians did not have an educational council (the legal provisions of 1994 only envisaged councils for *"Aymará, Quechua, Guaraní y Amazónico multiétnico y otros")* the Ministry of Education urged them to create one. For that purpose, the Ministry of Education agreed to economically and logistically support a National Afrobolivian Congress and the proponents of CONAFRO took advantage of that opportunity to not only found a *Consejo Educativo* but to simultaneously launch their *ente matriz.*

The *"I. Congreso Nacional Afroboliviano"* was held on 2 and 3 September 2011 at Casa John Wesley in La Paz. According to the organizers, the event hosted representatives from all major cities in the country as well as a great number of communities in the Yungas. The objectives of founding a *Consejo Educativo* as well as electing representatives and ratifying the structures for the newly established CONAFRO were accomplished. Most members of the original group did end up in important positions as official representatives and continue to shape the work of CONAFRO today.

Structural and ideological basics or: what it means to be an *"ente matriz"*

The conceptual basis for CONAFRO's activities is the idea of a collective Afrobolivian entity with similar life conditions, problems, goals and aspirations. Similar to the Constitution, which made *"el pueblo Afroboliviano"* the subject of collective rights without further explanation, the founders of CONAFRO took this collectivity *(el pueblo Afroboliviano)* and its boundaries for granted as self-explanatory. CONAFRO has subsequently tried to position itself as the 'natural' representation of this *pueblo*. The organization's agenda specifically states that a strong and unified *pueblo Afroboliviano ("un Pueblo Afroboliviano fuerte y mancomunado")* lies at the heart of their political efforts. CONAFRO is thus a clear step towards a unifying discourse on a national scale and tries to counter regionalist tendencies and the often cited rural-urban divide. While previously, people regularly addressed issues referring to *"los negros," "los Afrobolivianos," "las comunidades Afrobolivianas"* or *"la cultura Afroboliviana,"* CONAFRO's agenda exclusively works with the term *"el pueblo Afroboliviano":* the political articulation of a variety of different Afrobolivian communities (urban and rural) under a single banner. This very specific rhetorical, political and legal articulation of an Afrobolivian collectivity as *un pueblo* has a variety of consequences. In the field of political organizations it requires the existence and at the same time strengthens the position of a unified representation (i.e. CONAFRO). Rhetorically, it aligns Afrobolivians' political programs with indigenous politics, thus rendering them politically and legally compatible but also creating potential for rivalry in view of limited resources. As I mentioned at the outset, the foundation of CONAFRO must be seen as a response to the overall political climate in Bolivia *(el proceso de cambio)* and specific opportunities and obstacles for Afrobolivian organizations and representatives at certain moments. As we have seen, official recognition and favorable circumstances for a certain type of organization motivated the founders of CONAFRO to a great extent. In this respect, it is also telling to analyze the organizational structure and the political discourses of CONAFRO and its leaders. This analysis will further strengthen my point that CONAFRO is envisaged as a very specific, new type of organization at the same time responding to and envisioning the idea of a *pueblo Afroboliviano*.

Structurally, CONAFRO purports to mirror both peasant union structures and elements of the nationally active indigenous and peasant organizations like CONAMAQ, CIDOB and CSUTCB. It consists of different *secretarias* which work in different thematic areas and thus resembles the *sindicatos* of most Yungas *comunidades*. Interestingly, CONAFRO's statutes have ever since the outset envisioned the possibility of creating regional and local branches of the organization. At least informally, such sub-groups now exist in Cochabamba and Santa Cruz. Yet CONAFRO remains a top-down project to a large extent.[12] Rather than being born though the 'organic' agglomeration of local organizations – as official rhetoric has it – CONAFRO first created a national super-structure that it now tries to fill with local organizational life. This drive to be the all-encompassing organization for all Afrobolivians is what differentiates CONAFRO from its predecessors. Another important difference – especially in contrast to CADIC, its most serious competitor for funds, legitimacy and followers – is that the people occupying positions within CONAFRO are elected representatives rather than employees chosen by appointment. Accordingly, neither the board of directors/executive committee nor the technical commission are the most important groups in deliberation and decision making. This role is – again, at least theoretically – reserved for the National Congress, which purports to unite the whole *pueblo* and reach decisions by consensus. CADIC, on the other hand, is organized much more hierarchically and answers to a completely different organizational logic. It has a self-appointed founder-director (Jorge Medina) who hires employees to work in the different areas the organization tries to cover. The fact that Medina was at the same time the director of this company-

12 In this sense, CONAFRO mirrors the perspective and the practices of government-led development projects that are equally top-down in many instances, as my discussion of a project in Cala Cala in chapter 10 will show.

like NGO and positioned himself as the most legitimate representative of his *pueblo* sparked fierce criticism and lead to a great amount of conflict between Medina and the emerging CONAFRO. In terms of their general political discourse, official mission statement and objectives, CONAFRO differs only marginally from CADIC. The small differences that do exist, however, point in the same direction as the organizational differences already mentioned, namely that CONAFRO first and foremost claims to represent an Afrobolivian constituency and lobby for it politically. The same is true for the activities CONAFRO is mostly responsible for. The organization is much less involved in workshops, projects and training courses, but focuses rather on lobbying, intervening in political discussion and placing CONAFRO members in government institutions and ministries.

An important claim always put forth by CONAFRO activists is that "CONAFRO belongs to the *comunidades*" (*"CONAFRO es de las comunidades"*). Ideally and in discourse, CONAFRO is designed to function as a national confederation of local Afrobolivian community organizations. This discursive move is crucial in the struggle for legitimacy, since only the national representation of a legally recognized collective subject can hope to convince state institutions of its legitimacy. Yet in practice, there are no communal Afrobolivian ethnic organizations, since there are no exclusively Afrobolivian communities. The only organizational CONAFRO member from the Yungas is Tocaña's *Centro de Expresión e Integración Cultural Afroboliviano (CEICA)*, an organizational remnant from the times of *saya* revitalization in the 1990s that organizes *saya* performances in the community. Besides that, there are no formally established Afrobolivian communal organizations that could become part of CONAFRO. The 'representation' of communities that CONAFRO purports to effectuate is based on certain community representatives' participation in the National Afrobolivian Congresses and is thus highly informal, opaque and volatile. Especially beyond the CONAFRO strongholds in the Yungas around the town of Coroico (mainly the *comunidades* of Tocaña and Mururata) and the urban organizations in Cochabamba and Santa Cruz, CONAFRO's legitimacy as the representative of Afrobolivian interests is highly contested. Cala Cala's residents, for example, took considerable pride in having "sent away" CONAFRO representatives that were trying to "take advantage" of the community and its members and did not work for or speak on behalf the "*comunidad* Cala Cala." Even though they later expressed their allegiance to CONAFRO on paper for strategic purposes, individual members kept on insisting that they did not feel represented by or did not actively participate in CONAFRO activities.

Strategies and achievements

According to its official mission statement, CONAFRO is fighting for an Afrobolivian presence in contexts of public decision and policy making in order to advocate for development projects that benefit its constituency. Interestingly, this general mission statement hints at the logics and strategies that marked Afrobolivian politics and mobilization in the past (development) and at the same time directs attention to the newly established spaces of official participation in government-related spheres as the main site of struggle in the present. Indeed, up to today, CONAFRO has mainly tried to place its members in political and administrative positions. This inevitably leads to disagreement and conflict, since the expectations of hired and salaried government employees on the one hand and social movement activists and representatives on the other tend to differ greatly. Whereas government employees (at least ideally) should go about their tasks impartially, activists are expected to take sides, fight for their cause and lobby for the interests of their constituency. CONAFRO leaders who have managed to obtain administrative positions struggle to balance the expectations related to these different roles – mainly with limited success. Given the reduced opportunities to exert concrete political influence from an administrative position that most of the activists-turned-*funcionarios* have to deal with, this is hardly surprising. Of course, the presence of Afrobolivians in spaces of public administration has long been overdue – and in some cases the mere fact that an Afrobolivian person sits behind an official desk is a political message – but for the large bulk of Afrobolivians the situation has hardly changed and the effects of CONAFRO's actions remain largely symbolic. Critics argue that CONAFROs strategy only benefits its leaders (who end up in lucrative government jobs) and does little to improve the situation of their constituency. To the contrary: CONAFRO's strategy even facilitates cooptation and weakens the organization's overall power to fight for a common cause instead serving a select few that pretend to work for their people but claim all the benefits for themselves. From the perspective of CONAFRO's leaders, however, it is only from within the state and government structures that Afrobolivian mobilization can succeed and reach the desired goals. For them, the aspiration to enter government jobs is neither a form of cooptation of the organization, nor a matter of individual activists reaping the benefits of collective mobilization *(buscar los apetitos personales)*. Rather, it is the logical consequence of the legal empowerment and the official inclusion granted by the New Constitution. Where, if not in government offices, could Afrobolivian people request inclusion on the basis of the Constitution? How, if not through the alignment of CONAFRO with the governing MAS party, could this inclusion be accomplished? These are common rhetorical questions CONAFRO leaders direct at their critics, thus making a case for their kind of mobilization. CONAFRO leaders are, obviously, aware of the risks such a strategy entails. In particular, the close alliance with the MAS party is considered a possible future liability and is not unanimously supported by the leadership. What is more, few if any of the CONAFRO leaders I have met struck me as particularly fond of the MAS party on purely ideological grounds. Even though they may swear allegiance to Evo Morales, MAS and the *proceso de cambio,* they mainly do so on strategic grounds. Whether the strategy is beneficial for Afrobolivians in general or rather directed at personal benefit for certain individuals – as some critics argue – is an open question.

The widespread criticism and conflicting claims notwithstanding, CONAFRO has managed to position the organization as the legitimate representation of Afrobolivians, at least in the eyes of most government institutions. The *Ministerio de Educación* is firmly allied to CONAFRO for a variety of reasons. First of all, various CONAFRO members work for the Ministry of Education, blurring the boundaries between government functionaries and social movement activists. Secondly, CONAFRO institutionally integrated the Afrobolivian *Consejo Educativo (CEPA)* as its *Secretaria de Educación,* thus fusing an officially recognized institution with its social movement organizational structures. In practice, this means that all efforts to work with CEPA must necessarily go through CONAFRO since their secretary of education is at the same time the director of the *Consejo Educativo.* This double role is a direct consequence of the parallel founding of CEPA and CONAFRO, and effectively makes CONAFRO the exclusive gatekeeper for educational programs directed at Afrobolivians by the Ministry of Education. What is more, CONAFRO has successfully managed to monopolize access to government-sponsored positions for advisors and functionaries of the newly founded *Instituto Plurinacional de Estudio de Lenguas y Cultura (IPELC)* and its Afrobolivian branch, the *Instituto de Lengua y Cultura Afroboliviana (ILC-AFRO).*

Working with the *Ministerio de Educación* served as a key argument for CONAFRO activists positioning themselves as the legitimate representatives of the *pueblo Afroboliviano* vis-à-vis other government institutions. Having established a precedent through the close alliance with the Ministry of Education, CONAFRO representatives managed to secure important supporters in favor of their claim to legitimacy. Very importantly, CONAFRO managed to successfully negotiate their way onto the governing MAS party's electoral ticket. In the 2014 elections, for example, it was CONAFRO co-founder and Secretary of International Relations Mónica Rey who ran for the position of *Diputada Supranacional* for MAS and was eventually elected for a five-year term starting in 2015. More recently, in the same vein, CONAFRO managed to place their former executive Juan Carlos Ballivián in an important position in the *Defensoría del Pueblo* that is run by an ombudsman closely linked to the MAS party since 2016. Through their close alignment with the ruling MAS party, they also secured support from the MAS-led regional government *(prefectura)* of La Paz and its *Prefecto* Cesar Cocarico (2010-2015), from MAS representatives in different regional and municipal parliaments, as well as government-friendly NGOs and media. Successful mobilization, in turn, allowed CONAFRO to secure funds and deliver programs, projects and workshops to various communities. What is more, the visibility of CONAFRO leaders in the aforementioned positions convinced many Afrobolivians that CONAFRO would be able to effect palpable changes and adhere more strongly to the narrative of representing the Afrobolivian people since CONAFRO leaders had successfully managed to get into those positions.

Beyond placing individuals in strategic positions within the government hierarchy, public administration and the ruling MAS party, CONAFRO has mobilized the media in order to generate support for the organization. What is more, CONAFRO has managed to affiliate most of the urban organizations in all major Bolivian cities (with only a few exceptions remaining loyal to Jorge Medina and rejecting CONAFRO's leadership), thus channeling the regional support base of these organizations. Additionally, CONAFRO has been involved in a series of publications and scholarly projects, most prominently in a collaborative project with FUNPROEIB-Andes increasing its visibility and thus its scope of operation and legitimacy.[13] Yet, as the next section will show, neither the conceptual basics of the New Constitution, nor the organizational perspective represented by CONAFRO are uncontested.

The limits of recognition

First and foremost, it is important to recognize the groundbreaking character of the New Constitution for Afrobolivians. In light of the country's history and the prevailing discourses on national identity and cultural diversity that are in their majority mute on issues concerning Afrobolivians, it can hardly be overstated what this kind of symbolic inclusion means for many Afrobolivians. It is the long-desired visibilization, inclusion and acknowledgement that so many people have fought for in recent decades. It is the official acknowledgement by the state that Afrobolivians are, in fact, "Bolivians, too" (Busdiecker 2007). The extremely high hopes many Afrobolivians invested in the subject of recognition also explain, at least in part, why the palpable effects (or rather the lack thereof) are so meticulously scrutinized.

There are a number of factors I would like to highlight as pointing to the limits of legal recognition and with that also to the limits of mobilizing Afrobolivians as a *pueblo* in the sense of the Constitution. I have addressed the more subtle tensions between Afrobolivian everyday sociality and the logics of the Constitution in chapter 5 and will elaborate on the subject from the perspective of Cala Cala in the next chapter. Here I will focus on the consequences as experienced in the realm of political mobilization and organizational life more broadly. The limitations of the prevailing modalities of recognition my interlocutors most commonly expressed relate to different aspects. On the one hand, there are certain contradictions with regard to the collective subject of recognition: *el pueblo Afroboliviano*. On the other

13 See http://fundacion.proeibandes.org/proyectos/conafro.php [18/07/2017]

hand, the specific rights granted to this collective subject do not escape criticism. Finally, and this is a problem not limited to the realm of legal recognition but concerns Afrobolivian activism more broadly, the question arises whether it is indeed possible to articulate a sufficiently cohesive Afrobolivian collectivity in practice. I will now address these criticisms in more detail.

In the sections above, I have pointed out the seminal importance of the concept of *pueblo*, as it has important consequences for the way an Afrobolivian collectivity is imagined and mobilized. In their mission statements, Afrobolivian organizations were very successful at making their claims compatible with the language of recognition; they furthermore managed to convince the *Asamblea Constituyente* that a distinct Afrobolivian collectivity should be recognized under the premises of the *pueblo* status; and finally, they were quite successful in arguing their case in negotiations with different government agencies. Remember that Afrobolivians have the same rights as indigenous peoples *"en todo lo que corresponda,"* "wherever appropriate," leaving it to the interpretation of the parties involved in a specific project, law, initiative or court case whether and to what degree a certain situation justifies the extension of indigenous rights to Afrobolivians. What is more, as I have described in the section on CONAFRO, the Afrobolivian leadership has managed to establish a legally registered, nationally active and – in the eyes of the state – widely accepted national organization. So it might seem that official recognition was a success story. Yet there is one decisive aspect where the success story is increasingly dubious. Whereas the state (for example, different ministries, parliaments and the *Instituto Nacional de Estadística*), the governing MAS party and international cooperation have embraced CONAFRO as the legitimate representation of *el pueblo Afroboliviano*, CONAFRO's leadership is repeatedly questioned by large parts of the Afrobolivian population. Although framed mostly as a critique of individual leaders, I would argue that behind the criticism directed at CONAFRO and its leadership by many individuals lies discontent with the underlying logics of recognition that CONAFRO can hardly change. This is also something CONAFRO leaders recognize, yet they point to the fact that the regime of recognition they have to operate with does not allow for certain things the population would most urgently demand.

Robert Albro (2010a) has pointed out that the New Bolivian Constitution recognizes only a very specific collective indigenous subject to the exclusion of others. For him and others, the definitions of what constitutes an indigenous *pueblo* in the 2009 document reflect a strongly Aymara-centric view, legally privileging a certain collective indigenous subject while at the same time marginalizing alternative versions of indigeneity – in Albro's case urban indigeneity in provincial towns (cf. Shakow 2014). His critique goes further than the concerns that have been voiced by the self-represented *mestizo* population of the country – namely that the representation of Bolivia as a mostly indigenous country leaves out an alleged *mestizo* majority – to suggest that even though the New Constitution must be seen as a milestone in the struggle for indigenous rights, it nevertheless fails to recognize a large part of the self-identified indigenous population. A similar argument can be made for the Afrobolivian population since Afrobolivian recognition is based on the same limited premises as indigenous recognition. For Afrobolivians in urban contexts, the utility of official recognition is highly doubtful, since the collective subject and the associated rights aim at homogenous, territorially bounded communities and their purported way of life. Thus the rights do not resonate with the grievances of individuals living in highly diverse urban environments, and recognition remains an elusive achievement with no practical consequences for most urban Afrobolivians.

And even in rural settings, the question remains whether it is possible to mobilize people and also to work on their behalf within the logics of the New Constitution. Due to the Constitution's homogenizing impetus and its narrow definition of community, it is hardly able to grasp the reality of the Afrobolivian presence in rural *comunidades*. Being a direct organizational response to the Constitution and its ensuing political logics, CONAFRO suffers from the limitations these conceptualizations have inscribed in its organizational structure. Taking cues from large national indigenous confederations, the basic idea behind CONAFRO is to agglomerate territorially based, ethnically homogenous Afrobolivian communities in its organizational structure. The problem is that such homogeneous Afrobolivian communities do not exist. This situation is not limited to CONAFRO, but has accompanied Afrobolivian activism since the very beginning. When Afrobolivian organizations aimed to spread their logics and demands throughout the rural Yungas and engaged in a process of mobilization that transcended the urban context, they often encountered the same set of problems. The idea of the existence of a unified *"pueblo Afroboliviano"* required rural communities to subscribe to it in order to legitimize the leadership of its proponents. Besides recruiting urban residents with at least some Afrobolivian ancestry to strengthen the urban bases of the movement, leaders sought support from rural Afrobolivian communities and their leaders. The problem they encountered was the generalized absence of a clearly defined Afrobolivian leadership in most rural communities. With the exception of Tocaña, Afrobolivians in the Yungas are a minority in all *comunidades* and since they are integrated into the system of peasant unions across ethnic boundaries, there was no such thing as an Afrobolivian leadership in the Yungas – at least not in a formal, widely accepted sense. This led to complicated issues: If there is no formally agreed upon leader of a given community, who can be addressed as representing community A or B? In most cases, urban organizations turned to specific individuals who showed interest in CONAFRO and who claimed to enjoy an elevated informal status within their respective community. However, this practice was very volatile in gathering support and longstanding alliances. Additionally, the informally chosen representatives did not go unquestioned and in many cases their claims to leadership were strongly challenged. This led to conflicts within and between rural communities and made the mobilization of a constituency defined in ethnic terms highly problematic.

Similar to the case that Restrepo describes for Colombia (2004:706), there are no ethnic organizations of Afrobolivians in the Yungas that could form the basis of an ethnic movement or become the pillars of an organization claiming to represent *un pueblo*. Mónica Rey (1998:91) has argued that, beginning in colonial times, the *saya* groups in *comunidades* with Afrobolivian populations had functioned as a "hidden organization" *("organización oculta")* providing Afrobolivians with the possibility of salvaging their "ancestral tribal organizations" *(organización ancestral de carácter tribal")* in the context of slavery. This view is corroborated by descriptions of complex hierarchies structuring the *saya* until the first half of the 20th century. In an often cited testimony by Manuel Barra – one of the oldest inhabitants of Tocaña – he meticulously describes how certain leadership positions structured *saya* performances (Centro Pedagógico y Cultural "Simón I. Patiño" 1998b). In the same vein, Martín Ballivián (2014) argues that *saya* groups had important social and political meanings in the time before the Agrarian Reform of 1953. As far as the information I collected during my fieldwork goes, there was not much left of these structures by the time the urban residents sought to establish links to rural communities in the 1980s. They relied instead on groups that had been constituted fairly recently and dated back only to the late 1980s and early 1990s. Their foundation was mainly motivated by workshops organized by the urban residents, the nationally publicized hype around *saya* and the economic possibilities associated with *saya* performances for certain audiences. Thus, by organizing dance groups, rural residents recreated a space conceptualized as exclusively Afrobolivian that in some instances could serve as the basis for a proto-ethnic organization. The question is to what extent the *saya* groups can be considered as an organizational space parallel to the peasant unions and whether they can serve as the organizational matrix to articulate an Afrobolivian ethnic movement in the Yungas that would give substance to CONAFRO's claims to leadership. The cases of Cala Cala and other *comunidades* – where no exclusively Afrobolivian political organizations have emerged – suggest that this is rather not the case.

Conclusion

As I have shown in the preceding chapters, there is a great number of parallel processes that shape Afrobolivian mobilization and the articulation of a collective Afrobolivian subject. Rooted in the efforts to revitalize Afrobolivian dance and culture in circumstances marked by migration, discrimination and the appropriation of Afrobolivian traditions by *mestizo* popular culture, the *Movimiento Afro* in Bolivia embarked on different organizational and political routes in order to make its claims heard. Some strategies meant appealing to the logics of multicultural reform and stressing parallels with indigenous groups in terms of suffering and disenfranchisement. Others relied on embracing the opportunities for public visibility provided by folklorized culture or engaging in continental networks of Afrodescendants, foregrounding African roots as a means of claiming cultural uniqueness and differentiated citizenship. The responses to these claims are as varied as the strategies employed. In some instances Afrobolivian demands have been heard and accepted, and certain goals have been achieved. In other cases the struggle for recognition and equality continues.

In this chapter, I have highlighted three more recent developments: the judicialization of Afrobolivian activism, the discursive consolidation of el *pueblo Afroboliviano* and the foundation of a nationally active *ente matriz*. Afrobolivian political activism has undergone a decisive transformation in the sense that political goals have been reformulated as rights to be claimed from the state. This judicialization of politics resonated with trends on a regional scale (Sieder, Schjolden, and Angell 2005b; Couso, Huneeus, and Sieder 2010; Sieder 2010), as well as with the national political context dominated by the Constituent Assembly and the eventual promulgation of the New Constitution between 2005 and 2009 (cf. Schilling-Vacaflor 2010). The framing of political demands in legal language and the strong focus on making an impact within the constitutional reform process in turn fostered the discursive consolidation of the concept of *el pueblo Afroboliviano* and eventually sparked an organizational response through the formation of CONAFRO in 2011. CONAFRO's limitations in terms of making a political impact, as well as the serious doubts many Afrobolivians express with regard to the legitimacy of its leadership, point us towards more general limits of recognition. These limits have to do with the frictions caused by the contrast between the Constitution's definition of community and actual conditions on the ground. Whereas the former relies on the idea of ethnically homogenous and territorially bounded communities *(pueblos)*, the latter are shaped by ethnoracial heterogeneity, deep economic entanglements and historically grounded social integration.

Even though Afrobolivian organizations have been able to benefit from a limited number of government policies that favor officially recognized *pueblos*, the prevailing logic of mobilization as a *pueblo* is highly contested, as is the question of leadership. The mobilization of Afrobolivians based on the propagation of a homogeneous collective subject expressed in the idea of *el pueblo Afroboliviano* is fraught with contradictions and remains an unstable and volatile political project. By subsuming the experiences and particularities of very small and dispersed rural and urban communities, it obscures many decisive facets of what it means to be *Afro* in different contexts in Bolivia. Even the much less homogenizing term 'Afrobolivian communities' (in English and in the plural), that I use as a shorthand to refer to the *comunidades* in the Yungas with varying levels of Afrobolivian population, is not unproblematic. As I showed in chapter 3, what it means to be *Afro* in Cala Cala is so intimately tied to the history of this particular place, and in many cases even to specific individuals, that it cannot be generalized to apply even to the neighboring *comunidades* and even less to a shared sense of Afrobolivianity on a national scale. Speaking of a single, unified, and homogeneous *pueblo Afroboliviano* presupposes a level of Afrobolivian groupness that I have not encountered in Cala Cala or elsewhere.

Thus the "*Movimiento Afro*" remains fragmented despite the efforts at unification pursued by CONAFRO. Quarrels between rural and urban, between Nor and Sud Yungas, between families, political factions and generations are still very common. The unifying efforts of CONAFRO notwithstanding, different leaders rally support independently and Afrobolivian mobilization is hampered by factionalism and strong competition between certain charismatic personalities. Most organizations only rhetorically address a nationwide audience and a single *pueblo*, but in political practice focus their actions on certain cities or *comunidades*. It is in this context that the foundation of CONAFRO and the impact of its mobilizations must be analyzed. Its formation is a top-down project, responding more to the plurinational logics of recognition and the rhetoric of *pueblo* status than to the grassroots initiatives of local organizations.

In the next chapter, I discuss a case from Cala Cala that reflects many of the contradictions that emerge when the concept of *el pueblo Afroboliviano* is engaged in local contexts. Through the analysis of a tourism project based on 'Afrobolivian culture' in Cala Cala, I shed light on the local engagements of nationally circulating ideas of Afrobolivianity. I will draw together the arguments made with respect to the notions of what it means to be *Afro* in Cala Cala and my analysis of broader articulations of Afrobolivianity, fleshing out concrete contexts in which the plurinational perspective on Afrobolivianity is engaged and negotiated by *Cala Caleños* against the backdrop of local understandings of community and belonging.

Chapter 10: Plurinational Afrobolivianity on the Ground and Built Identity Politics

La Casa Cultural Afro Cala Cala and the *Centro de Interpretación de la Cultura Afroboliviana*

The project I will address in the following sections is a community tourism project that people from Cala Cala were developing with assistance from the IDB (Interamerican Development Bank) and the Coripata Municipal Government in the framework of the PNTC (*Programa Nacional de Turismo Comunitario,* National Community Tourism Program). The project initially consisted of funding the construction of a community center and shelter for tourists named *La Casa Cultural Afro Cala Cala*. When I first arrived in Cala Cala in late 2014, the project was in the planning stage and I constantly found myself involved in meetings and discussions on anything from architectural plans or environmental sustainability certificates to statutes for a communitarian tourism association. Moreover, I accompanied people from Cala Cala in various meetings with municipal officials in Coripata or PNTC representatives in La Paz. Talk of the project was ubiquitous and even though the number of individuals seriously involved in the planning and organization was fairly limited, they continually engaged all other members of the community in conversation about the project. The project was the talk of the moment and seemed to occupy an important place in the community's collective consciousness. When I left Cala Cala in mid-2015 after my initial research stay, the necessary documentation had just been handed in to the PNTC and was awaiting evaluation. The project was granted funding in October 2015 and by the time of my return to Cala Cala in early 2017 for a follow-up research stay, the construction was almost finished. People in Cala Cala were awaiting the arrival of PNTC officials and the *Viceministro de Turismo* (vice minister of tourism) to approve their efforts and give the green light for the opening of the *Casa Cultural*. With the opening just around the corner, the tourism project was of course still an important point of discussion, and the subject of meetings and organizational activities. As far as my interlocutors told me, the tourism project was unprecedented in the sense that throughout the construction phase the whole *comunidad* – including Nogalani – had been highly engaged in terms of the money and manpower that every member of the *comunidad* contributed to the construction.

What sets the tourism project apart (at least with regard to Cala Cala) from other projects or workshops, is the significant amount of money the government, as well as people from the *comunidad*, invested and the immediate tangible material benefits it promised to deliver. This explains why the project became the center of attention for many in the community, more than any workshop or rights campaign ever could have. People felt that there was much more to gain from this project than from an ephemeral training workshop or from some abstract political rights in the future. A whole set of actors – including the Aymara segments of the wider *comunidad* who usually cared little about matters framed as "Afrobolivian" – was very eager to partake in the project, offered assistance, made claims and lobbied to receive their share of the benefits. For example, a recently founded local construction company with ties to community leaders in Cala Cala made great efforts to win the contract to build the infrastructure. The unionized taxi and minibus drivers claimed (exclusive) rights to bring the expected tourists directly to the *comunidad*. Families positioned themselves as possible hosts for tourists, hoping they would receive funds to build additional rooms for their houses and generate income from hosting, feeding and guiding tourists through the *comunidad*. In sum, talk of the project was widespread in the community and people were staking their claims to the promised benefits of the endeavor.

My aim in this chapter is to trace the planning, construction and eventual completion of the project *Casa Cultural Afro Cala Cala* from its beginning in the initial planning stages throughout the years 2014 and 2015 to its near completion in 2017. I discuss this example at length because it shows how different actors negotiate competing ideas of Afrobolivianity and how these ideas interact in practice. What I want to flesh out in the context of the project are the concrete negotiations originating from the encounter between the plurinational perspective on community and culture, and the lifestyles of the community. The former rely on ethnically defined and clearly bounded collectives and furthermore highlight Afrobolivianity as the collective identification most consequential for social differentiation. The latter, however, are marked by far-reaching entanglements and integration across ethnoracial boundaries. The project brought to the fore many latent conflicts, contradictions and frictions within the community, but also served as a starting point for forging new alliances, taking advantage of new opportunities and (re-)envisioning Cala Cala as a community. I will show how the period of envisioning and planning the project brought the people involved in this process into contact with specific technical, legal and political logics; I will then sketch how the very practical and material process of building the infrastructure put the premises laid out in the planning process to the test, and I will finally address some points related to the envisaged functioning of the project in the future. On the way, I will introduce both the political and institutional actors involved in the process, as well as account for community and individual responses to the frameworks and procedures proposed by those actors.

On a conceptual level, I want to problematize the concepts of community, culture and identity propagated by the project's financial and technical sponsors by juxtaposing them with what local people understand by these terms. Furthermore, I will show the subtle but pervasive influence of legal and technical categories that circulate among the people involved in the project. As will become clear through my discussion, the crucial question is whether and to what extent the notion of Afrobolivianity articulated according to these categories and logics (Clifford 2013) – and the ethnicized or indigenized subjectivities this engenders (Restrepo 2004) – can be brought into dialogue with the ways social relations are handled in practice and in local settings. My analysis in this chapter intends to explore the possibilities and limitations of "legalizing identities" (French 2009) (i.e. the processes by which social identities are re-shaped in response to legal provisions based on specific categories), as well as examine a concrete instance of ethnicized "group-making" (Brubaker 2002). I approach the collective identifications relevant in this context as "we-group processes" (Elwert 2002), where group boundaries may be widened, narrowed, re-drawn or re-conceptualized to a certain extent. Yet, as this case also shows, collective identities and boundaries between groups are not entirely flexible and have to make sense within the conceptual spaces of the societies in which they are embedded (Schlee 2004).

Origins and background of the project

The fact that the *Casa Cultural Afro Cala Cala* was even built is the result of mere coincidence – at least from the perspective of the people mostly involved in its planning. Originally, as Roberto told me multiple times, he and Víctor, another Afrobolivian community leader from Cala Cala, approached the *Mancomunidad de Municipios de los Yungas de La Paz* – a regional association of the municipal governments of the Yungas – in order to inquire into the possibility of obtaining funding for the construction of a building in which Cala Cala's residents could gather on various occasions, for example when holding a community meeting. The representatives of the *Mancomunidad* had told them, Roberto recalls, that there were no funds available in the Association's budget, but that "just down the hall" in the same building, were the offices of the PNTC and that they could ask there since the PNTC had just obtained funding for projects through an Interamerican Development Bank (IDB) credit. So Roberto and his companion went and asked and were received with open arms. They were told that their community could definitely apply for funding for an infrastructure project within the framework of the IDB-funded program aimed at fostering community tourism in Bolivia.

Applying for funding under the umbrella of the PNTC, however, made it necessary to reframe Cala Cala's request and make it compatible with the program's goals and conceptual framework. It was decided, therefore, not to apply for a meeting place for the community, but to redirect the project to fit the framework proposed by the PNTC and adjust it to the needs of community tourism.[1] According to the IDB, the program is designed to

> "stimulate community-based tourism, where rural communities of rural or indigenous origins are responsible for the organization, administration and receipt of the benefits of tourism activity in its territories, with the purpose of generating real sustainable development alternatives which allow for the increase in their standard of living." (http://www.iadb.org/en/projects/project-description-title,1303.html?id=bo-l1039) [14/09/2017]

According to the IDB, this strategy is consistent with the institution's broader country strategy for Bolivia that aims at "providing [...] local *development with identity*, given that community-based tourism promotes the *living cultural heritage* (Interamerican Development Bank 2009:5 emphasis added by the author). Moreover, the program is also consistent with Bolivia's National Development Plan and its National Tourism Plan, and was designed in close cooperation with the Vice Ministry of Tourism *(Viceministerio de Turismo)* "through a broad participatory planning process". It departs from the very general premise that Bolivia

> "is one of the richest [countries] of the continent in living cultures. It has more than 36 ethnic groups, or aboriginal peoples, and owners of lands, where, in addition to their present-day culture, customs, and worldview, the important archaeological and historical heritage has on occasion been declared a World Heritage site by the United Nations Educational, Scientific and Cultural Organization."(Interamerican Development Bank 2009:2)

What is more, "the fact that they are rural sites and to a certain extent remote or isolated locations has allowed them to retain and preserve their natural and cultural wealth" (Interamerican Development Bank 2009:2).

When Roberto and Víctor returned from La Paz to Cala Cala, they took with them not only a fifty-page technical manual called the *"Reglamento Operativo de Co-*

1 The idea of engaging in tourism was not completely new to the community. For example, the *Plan de Desarrollo Municipal de Coripata (2001-2005)* already stated that *"la cultura y costumbres afrobolivianas en los sectores de Coscoma, Nogalani, Dorado Chico y Calacala, que permita promocionar el Etnoecoturismo como una vocación futura, aunque en el presente solo se constituye en una potencialidad"* (p.290).

financiamiento" (ROC) (Operative Manual for Co-Financing) establishing the technical and legal details of the application they had to prepare, but also the conceptual baggage of a program employing vocabulary like "development with identity," "living cultural heritage," "ethnic groups," "aboriginal peoples," "remote and isolated," "retain and preserve." This is not to say that people in Cala Cala are generally unfamiliar with such discourses or that these buzzwords do not resonate with many of their aspirations. In fact, the discourses of Afrobolivian organizations employ a similar vocabulary. However, in this very concrete case, leaders from Cala Cala entered an office building in La Paz with the intention of approaching an institution that is regional rather than ethnic or cultural in focus (in this case the *Mancomunidad de Municipios de los Yungas*) to ask for funding for a meeting place. They left with documents and ideas from the PNTC – an institution concerned with culture, tourism and cultural heritage – planning to apply for a community tourism project based on their culture and identity. This case, in a nutshell, thus serves as a vivid example of how a particular articulation of Afrobolivianity focused on ethnicity and culture can take center stage when Afrobolivian individuals or organizations approach government institutions or NGOs, as well as how this articulation relates to life in Cala Cala.

In what follows, I want to highlight two fundamental aspects of negotiating the relationship between a particular political and legal articulation of Afrobolivianity and community life in Cala Cala through an ethnography of the process of planning and building *La Casa Cultural Afro Cala Cala*. The first aspect is concerned with the question of how and through which categorical distinctions the boundaries of Cala Cala as a community should be drawn. The second aspect is concerned with defining what constitutes 'Afrobolivian culture' in Cala Cala (and elsewhere). For the people involved, these aspects crystallized in two very simple, practical questions: "Who should participate and what will we show the tourists?"

Who should participate? Or: ethnoracial particularities and the limits of Cala Cala as a community

In the days after the initial meeting with the PNTC, Roberto and Víctor discussed the idea of applying for funding from the PNTC with other individuals from Cala Cala. They introduced the assembled community members to the ideas of the Operative Manual (ROC) they had obtained from La Paz and went through the nine initial legal requirements listed in the document. The first and fundamental requirement is presenting *"Personería Jurídica"* (legal credentials) of the *"Emprendimiento Turístico Comunitario"* (Community Tourism Enterprise; ETC) that will administer the funds. In the case of Cala Cala's application, the ETC was supposed to be based on an *organización social* (social organization), defined as

> "an entity of individuals that in consideration of the territory they occupy and/or common activities and similar interests that they pursue, organizes and/or advances initiatives of common interest for its individual members [...]" (ROC, p.14, my translation).[2]

In light of the different horizons of community in Cala Cala that I have analyzed in previous chapters, the PNTC's definition of *organización social* presents the challenge of determining on what grounds and referring to which specific "common activities" and "similar interests" the community should be delimited.

There were two takes on this question, each emphasizing a different horizon of community. For Roberto, it was clear that the relevant entity in this case would be *"los Afros de Cala Cala."* He argued that since the project was based on Afrobolivian identity and culture, it was only logical that the line between those who should and should not participate ought to be drawn in ethnoracial terms. Dividing people along the boundary of *Afro*/non-*Afro* and including only the former left him with a list of about twenty people, since *"los Afros de Cala Cala"* in the strictest sense comprise only about two dozen adult Afrobolivian individuals that reside in the community. Due to the small number, he decided to extend his list by recurring to a broader definition of what *"los Afros de Cala Cala"* means, including relatives of the residents of the community, like his three daughters living in La Paz and Santa Cruz. This left him with a longer list, yet one consisting mainly of dispersed individuals only linked through kinship ties to Cala Cala. While compiling the list, Roberto seemed to have no doubts determining who would rightfully belong to the group he termed *"los Afros de Cala Cala,"* since it was mostly a matter of tracing kinship ties to and from Cala Cala for each individual. He also did not express any concerns with regard to the question of whether the translocal *"Afros de Cala Cala"* could possibly be considered a group of people with common interests and activities, as is suggested in the PNTC manual's definition. Finally, he also did not find it problematic that the few *"Afros de Cala Cala"* actually living in the community would eventually have to do all the work – although his list suggested to the PNTC that there were many people ready to participate in the project.

Víctor took a different angle on the subject: for him, the tourism project would not be able to flourish without the participation of the wider *comunidad* of Nogalani. He repeatedly challenged Roberto's approach by pointing not only to the formal necessity of including the *sindicato* from Nogalani for legal reasons, but also to the practical impossibility of advancing the project without more people. Víctor argued that Cala Cala not only needed Nogalani's credentials for the paperwork and the *sindicato's* backing for proving ownership of the land that the *Centro Cultural Afro*

---

2 *"El conjunto de personas que en atención al territorio que ocupan y/o actividades comunes e intereses afines que desarrollan, se organizan y/o impulsan iniciativas de interés común para sus componentes [...]"* (ROC, p. 14).

Cala Cala was to be built on. He urged Roberto to consider that – when the time of construction came – they would actually be obliged to provide a significant amount of manpower and monetary contributions that *"los Afros de Cala Cala"* could not possibly provide by themselves.[3] Finally, Víctor also made a point of emphasizing the close and ongoing relationships between Cala Cala and Nogalani in many aspects of economic, social, religious and political life. In short, he argued for regarding *"la comunidad cocalera"* (community of coca farmers) as the collective with common activities and interests that the PNTC proposed as the beneficiary of the project.

Roberto and Víctor's disagreement vividly exemplifies what is at stake when trying to determine what horizon of community ought to be the guiding principle for collective efforts. Whereas Roberto openly embraced discourses of Afrobolivian cultural particularity, Víctor paid more attention to local entanglements blurring the boundaries between allegedly homogenous cultural and ethnic collectives. Roberto's point was backed up by the PNTC's fundamental interest in 'Afrobolivian culture' and he could draw from the well-known discourses of Afrobolivian identity politics. To support his view, he also often cited the Bolivian Constitution and its method of presenting discrete *pueblos* as the fundamental units of social organization. Víctor's take on the subject, on the contrary, was more grounded in the local situation of close entanglements between Afrobolivian and non-Afrobolivian parts of the population. As such, his view resonated directly with the PNTC's aim to foster projects through collectives defined by territory and common activities and interests. The practical challenges Cala Cala's inhabitants were facing in those moments mirror one of the fundamental contradictions of Bolivia's current plurinational moment, namely the assumption that *el pueblo Afroboliviano* is an "entity" occupying a specific territory and sharing common activities and similar interests.

People in Cala Cala had to find a way to balance the PNTC's legal and conceptual requirements with local social practice while at the same time keeping the project within the control of a group that they considered the legitimate administrators of an "Afrobolivian" cultural center. In community meetings, it was decided to found a Tourism Association *(Asociación Turística)* that would serve as the ETC's representation vis-à-vis the PNTC and would organize the tasks the community's inhabitants had to fulfill in order for the project to be put into practice. People agreed that Roberto and Víctor, who had organized the first negotiations with the PNTC and who were considered 'Afrobolivian leaders,' should be named as members of the association's board of directors. As a third member of the board, people agreed to Celia, an Aymara women from Nogalani who at that time also served as a member of the municipal council of the nearby town of Coripata. Her appointment was mostly explained in strategic terms since she was said to have good connections in municipal

3 In total, the PNTC required the beneficiary community to make a contribution (in money and manpower) covering one third of the total cost of the project.

politics. Reservations against appointing an Aymara individual to the board were mitigated by the fact that she was considered by many people from Cala Cala to be "friendly" towards the claims of Afrobolivians (*"es una amiga de la comunidad"*). Including her secured the legal backing of the *sindicato* in the early stages of planning when the Tourism Association had not yet obtained legal credentials and Roberto and Víctor hoped it would also help them secure Nogalani's support in the future. In fact, Celia's presence on the board proved to be highly valuable, not only for her contacts in municipal politics, but also due to her personal experience with regard to the formalities of Bolivian legality. For example, Celia's expertise was crucial in documenting all the decisions that had been taken in informal gatherings in order to meet legal requirements. Celia's presence on the board, however, must also be considered an important concession to the *sindicato* of Nogalani, securing access to information and participation for the community beyond *"los Afros de Cala Cala."*

Cala Cala's application for funds was presented to the PNTC in April 2015. Beyond the documents testifying to the organizational structure and the legitimacy of the leadership of the Tourism Association, it included the signatures and photocopies of the identity documents of *"los Afros de Cala Cala"* that Roberto had compiled on his list. It was furthermore accompanied by a written promise from the *sindicato* in Nogalani to support the construction with manpower from all *comunarios*, plus a certificate that ensured that the *Asociación de Turismo* could provide the necessary land to build the *Casa Cultural* and take legal ownership of it. What is more, Cala Cala's leaders also obtained and included a statement of commitment from the mayor's office in Coripata to provide cement for the construction.

In order to make all this work, Cala Cala had to mobilize support through different channels, appealing to different but essentially entangled horizons of community. *"Los Afros de Cala Cala"* were, on paper, the beneficiaries of the project. Although territorially dispersed, they were present as a list of individuals backed by photocopies of their identity documents. The *cocalero* community contributed by way of offering the legal backing of the local *sindicato*, as well as a contribution of labor to Cala Cala's efforts. Finally, a regional political institution (the *Municipio de Coripata*) offered some assistance in providing cement. The task of assembling the network of support the project required challenged people in Cala Cala in various ways. Conceptually, it demanded that *Cala Caleños* imagine the organizational structure, purview and function of an organization based on an Afrobolivian ethnoracial collective. Secondly, it meant adjusting this organization to the requirements of the nationally organized tourism program. Moreover, it required obtaining support for the project among those people of Nogalani who had no direct attachment to the Afrobolivian cause, but who were nevertheless crucial for many practical aspects of the plan. In sum, it required *Cala Caleños* to develop an interpretation of their reality that would meet the requirements of plurinational identity politics filtered through the PNTC, while simultaneously being sensitive to local ways of defining and organizing community.

The balancing act of bridging the gap between the two horizons of community worked fairly well within the confines of the project. Roberto and Víctor, for instance, decided to put their different perspectives aside for the sake of the project and sought to combine concepts, discourses and organizational logics in a way that would help advance the project. However, beyond the specific context, in which everybody in the community was quite happy about the project due to the fact that the application had been successful, the initiative also sparked debate and uncovered latent conflict. For example, many people in Cala Cala did not interpret the composition of the directors (two people from Cala Cala and one from Nogalani) of the *Asociación de Turismo* in such a positive light. I have presented this as an instance of pragmatically reconciling local sensibilities with strategic and legal requirements, a view most people in Cala Cala shared. Others, however, argued that Aymara people from Nogalani had again managed to obtain a share of an organization and project that did not belong to them. In this context, people explicitly mentioned rivalries dating back to the land reform period in the 1950s. The explicit framing of the project as "Afrobolivian" emphasized divisions of 'us' and 'them,' of identity and difference, and gave these additional resonance (Eidson et al. 2017; Schlee 2008). Moreover, by granting the category "Afrobolivian" such a fundamental role in allocating significant material resources and thus raising the stakes significantly, stories of conflict and competition were provided with an updated reference and ethnic framing (Brubaker 2002:173). Unfair treatment, discrimination and inequality are often linked with ethnic stereotypes that are re-activated in such contexts. Alison Spedding (1994) describes intra-community rivalries and factionalism at length in her excellent ethnography of the Yungas. Comparing her findings to my data shows great similarities. What is decidedly different from her study and others (Léons 1978; Spedding 1994), however, is the fact that I have found ethnoracial categories to be explanatory features of these conflicts. Similar to the Brazilian case described by French (2009:13), the "experience of new or revised ethnoracial identities" – in this case filtered through the logics of the tourism project – transforms notions of community, belonging and the interpretation of past and present conflict.

What are we going to show the tourists? Or: cataloging culture and the conceptual space of Afrobolivianity in the Yungas

During my stay in Cala Cala, the tourism project became the most important context in which identity, difference and concepts of community were negotiated. On the one hand, Cala Cala's encounter *par excellence* with plurinationality meant that a focus on ethnoracial differences between clearly defined entities *(pueblos)* clashed with alternative visions of social relationships within the community. The project thus reflected the tendencies I have described with regard to the changing meanings of ethnoracial identifications in the context of Bolivia's plurinational re-founding in chapter 5. On the other hand, the project also highlighted another process, which I discussed in chapter 7 with regard to the elaboration of regionally specific school curricula *(currículos regionalizados)*. Not only did the project propagate the salience of exclusive ethnoracial identifications and corresponding entities, it also inspired people in Cala Cala to compile a list of objective criteria for identifying those entities. Cala Cala's inhabitants engaged with the latter question when trying to determine what kind of activities for tourists they would offer as an 'Afrobolivian community.' Fundamental to the whole project was the idea that the *Casa Cultural* would be a shelter for tourists interested in getting to know *"la cultura Afroboliviana"* over the course of several days. So a question arose as to what the community could offer in order to entertain visitors for a number of days. With my participation and after some deliberation that also included the opinions of urban *Cala Caleños* (for example one of Roberto's daughters who had studied Tourism in Cochabamba for a few semesters), Cala Cala's tourism coordinators set out to elaborate a draft plan for hosting tourists. For this purpose, they set up a meeting with all the interested community members, invited me as an 'expert' and presented their plans for the tourism package. They had already been made familiar with the basics of the IDB's general strategy and major buzzwords like "development with identity," "living cultural heritage," "ethnic groups," "aboriginal peoples," "remote and isolated," "retain and preserve." Filtered through the PNTC and Bolivia's *Viceministerio de Turismo*, these basic assumptions concerning what the project was all about heavily influenced the way people set out to conceptualize their program. Following the PNTC's guidelines that highlight first and foremost the Yungas' "lush landscape" that resembles an "earthly paradise," as well as the region's particularities in terms of population ("Afro-Bolivians managed to establish themselves in this region [...] as a plus to the tourist attraction of the place" [Ministerio de Culturas y Turismo - Viceministerio de Turismo 2017]), the coordinators of the tourism association discussed the community's potential in terms of natural beauty and 'cultural traditions.'[4] The equation of cultural and natural assets was something I found highly problematic, yet the PNTC's assumption that landscape and culture are to some

4 Initially, also taking hints from the PNTC guidelines that prioritize *"Turismo de Aventura"* (mountain biking, canoeing, paragliding and the like) in the Yungas region, they thought about adding a sporting aspect to their package. Due to the lack of experience with any of the aforementioned activities and the lack of funding for, say, acquiring mountain bikes, the deliberations quickly focused on natural beauty and cultural traditions as the most important aspects of the program.

degree phenomena of the same order was never questioned in the meetings. The attendance of Cala Cala's residents was fairly limited and after the initial meeting it was mostly Roberto, Víctor and me (serving as a scribe since mine was the only computer available in the community) drafting the description of the project.

Roberto and Víctor quickly agreed on certain places that could be interesting for tourists, such as hiking paths, natural river basins and hills with nice panoramic views. In terms of defining appealing aspects of "Afrobolivian culture and tradition" the first element *(elemento cultural)* that people thought of was the Afrobolivian dance *saya*. This is not surprising given the central role of *saya* in the Afrobolivian cultural revitalization movement and in most representations of Afrobolivian culture, addressed in preceding chapters. However, and in spite of the repeated reference to *saya* as the most emblematic and most important cultural element of the Afrobolivian people of Cala Cala, *saya* hardly plays a role in Cala Cala's everyday life as an actual practice. When I left the community in mid-2017 after long stretches of fieldwork adding up to almost 12 months, I departed without ever having witnessed a *saya* performance by the community's residents. Nevertheless it was agreed that besides taking the tourists hiking and swimming, Cala Cala would offer visitors the opportunity to experience Afrobolivian culture and tradition through *saya*.

Another element people in Cala Cala considered suitable for touristic exploitation was *"el Matuasi,"* the ruins of the *casa de hacienda* (the landowner's mansion and administrative building prior to the 1952 Revolution) located in Cala Cala. Being an independent estate up until its integration into the larger *hacienda* of Nogalani around the end of the 19th century, Cala Cala had its own *casa de hacienda* located near the village church roughly at the geographic center of the settlement. Only ruins remain of the once grand mansion and the whole area is covered by thick vegetation. Yet *el Matuasi* is an important physical remnant of what *Cala Caleños* consider a particular aspect of their history. Interestingly, Roberto and Víctor both thought of it as a remnant of the past that said something about a specifically Afrobolivian part of history. Rather than representing common *Yungueño* rural history and the exploitation of *peones* (*hacienda* laborers) at the hands of the landowning elite, *el Matuasi* was framed as a reminder of "black slavery" *("esclavitud de los Afros")*. As I discussed in chapter 6, referring to narratives of slavery has become an increasingly important form of Afrobolivian engagement with diasporic frames of history and belonging. In Cala Cala, where connections to the wider African Diaspora are otherwise seldom made, the framing of *el Matuasi* as a reminder of "black slavery" situated *Cala Caleños* within a transnational framework of diasporic identity politics.[5]

As things turned out in the end, however, Cala Cala's efforts at making sense of their lifestyles by means of a tour for visitors were eclipsed by an unexpected change and the advent of a much larger project.

Interpreting Afrobolivian culture

Before even one tourist visited Cala Cala's *Casa Cultural Afro*, events took an unexpected turn that would change the course of the project significantly, exacerbate some of the underlying conflicts within the wider *comunidad* (and also in Cala Cala internally) and take the issue of compiling and adequately representing Afrobolivian culture to a completely different level. Cala Cala's very particular and small touristic endeavor, as I have described it in the sections above, already served to illuminate the workings and impacts of international cooperation, development discourse and categories and their interaction with local ways of belonging and organizing community relations. In 2017, in addition to overseeing the final preparations to start operating Cala Cala's *Casa Cultural Afro*, people had become involved in a much larger project. In an area located geographically between the settlements of Cala Cala and Nogalani that locals refer to as Bella Vista or Vaquería, a huge building had been erected in close proximity to the community school and soccer fields and I soon learnt that this was the *Centro de Interpretación de la Hoja de Coca, Café de Altura y Cultura Afroboliviana* (Center of Interpretation of the Coca Leaf, High Altitude Coffee and Afrobolivian Culture).[6] According to statements from employees

5 On notions of 'Africa,' the African Diaspora and transnational identity politics in Latin America see (Matory 2005; Rahier 2012a; Wade 2006b; Wade 2006a; Yelvington 2001; Yelvington 2006).

6 When I left Cala Cala in mid-2015 there was no talk of building this center in Bella Vista. During my occasional exchanges with people from the community during the year 2016, I heard no mention of the project and was puzzled to find the infrastructure almost completely finished in early 2017. Upon my return to Cala Cala, people were only waiting for the center's equipment to arrive. Originally, the center had been designed to be located in the nearby village of Coripata. As far as the story in Cala Cala goes, Nogalani *sindicato* leaders seized the opportunity to build the *Centro* in Bella Vista when they heard of problems concerning the property rights of the construction site in Coripata, and without having had any say in the initial design, concept or thematic focus of the project, were awarded the infrastructure. During my stay I was able to document several visits from technical commissions in La Paz, speak to the people in charge at the PNTC and the *Viceministerio de Turismo* (Vice Ministry of Tourism), as well as participate in the first official visit of the vice minister of tourism who arrived in April 2017 with a commission to oversee final preparations for the inauguration ceremony to be held in 2017 (see my description of the event in the introduction).

of both the PNTC and the *Viceministerio de Turismo*, a *Centro de Interpretación* is a museum whose concept is based on participatory engagement of the visitors with the topic of the exhibition and the objects displayed. The centers are designed to provide people with an interpretation of the topics in question through a combination of material exhibits, guided tours and interactive engagement with the contents. Since most people in Cala Cala most commonly referred to the *Centro de Interpreclación* as *"el museo,"* I asked people at the PNTC and at the *Viceministerio de Turismo* what distinguishes a *Centro de Interpretación* from a museum. Besides referring to the rulebook definition cited above, one PNTC representative told me that they decided to avoid the term "museum" since people would then expect to be able to see "important historical artefacts" *("artefactos hístoricos importantes")* which, in his view, most communities where such centers were built are not able to provide.

The center's concept is interesting for various reasons. The three topics the center singled out for "interpretation" (coca, coffee and Afrobolivian culture) and the way they are represented tell us a great deal about how the Yungas and their society and economy are viewed through the lens of plurinationality. Through the center's exhibition, *Afroboliviano* is singled out as the most salient and relevant culturally constituted category of difference in the Yungas. This is especially striking in contrast to earlier depictions of the region. The widespread opinion prevalent until well into the 1980s was that Afrobolivian culture was in fact on the verge of obliteration due to acculturation to the Aymara culture of the Yungas (Pizarroso Cuenca 1977). Nowadays, however, statements like this one from a tourism leaflet on the Yungas are ubiquitous: "In actuality, peasants [*campesinos*] and Afrobolivians live and work together for the productive development of the region."[7] As we can see, the logic and rhetoric of such statements separates Afrobolivians from the rest of society – juxtaposing the categories peasant and Afrobolivian. Aymara culture, on the other hand, is not seen as something playing a role in social differentiation in the Yungas by the initiators of the project. Afrobolivianity is thus granted a special place in the cultural geography of the Yungas and of plurinational Bolivia more generally.

When Roberto first showed me the center right after my arrival it was already equipped with the information panels on Afrobolivian culture, coffee and coca cultivation. When I asked him who had designed the panels he told me that *"el arquitecto"* had brought them and that he did not know who had written the text, selected the photos or compiled the information. He could not tell me how and by whom certain very important decisions regarding the exhibition were made. Neither he nor any individual from Cala Cala was involved in determining what topics would be addressed, nor in determining how they would be presented or what 'interpretation' of Afrobolivian Culture the center would provide. Some weeks later,

7 *"Actualmente tanto campesinos como Afrobolivianos viven y trabajan conjuntamente en el desarrollo productivo de la región."*

officials at the *Viceministerio de Turismo* told me that the panels, as well as the photographs and the entire *"guía museográfica,"* i.e. the basic concept of the exhibition, had been designed by an independent consultant. Even though the documentation I was able to consult at the *Viceministerio de Turismo* suggested that there ought to be workshops – first in order to compile information and then to present the *guía museográfica* to community members and discuss its adequacy – no such workshop had taken place in Cala Cala and the residents of the community first laid eyes on the content of the museum when everything was finished.

The exhibition features panels on Afrobolivian history in colonial times (entitled: *"de Potosí a los Yungas*), during the Republic and the National Revolution of 1953 *("Tiempos de hacienda")*. Furthermore, there are panels on Afrobolivian culture and religion *("La cultura Afroboliviana"* and *"La cultura, la religión Afroboliviana")*, Afrobolivian knowledge in medicine *("Saberes Afrobolivianas en medicina")*, Afrobolivian dress *("La vestimienta Afroboliviana")*, Afrobolivian hairstyles *("Las Pichicas y seques")*, Afrobolivian soccer players *("Afrobolivianos y la selección nacional, El legado de Ramiro Castillo")*, *saya* and its instruments *("La saya Afroboliviana," "La construcción de instrumentos musicales, instrumentos de la saya y su materia prima")*. Additionally, there are some photographs, mainly of *saya* dancers, ornamenting the walls of the center. The information included in the exhibition is very basic and provides a very general overview of what is considered important regarding Afrobolivians, and the panels hardly contain any information on local specificities. Since the *Centro de Interpretación* was a top-down project, it reflected basic notions of Afrobolivianity articulated in the national context, rather than locally grounded particularities important for *"los Afros de Cala Cala."*

According to the references on the panels, the information regarding 'Afrobolivian culture' was derived mainly from three written sources: The main thread of the exhibition follows the *Registro de Saberes y conocimientos del Pueblo Afroboliviano* (Registry of wisdom and knowledge of the Afrobolivian people) published by the *Minsterio de Educación* and elaborated under the supervision of the *Consejo Nacional Afroboliviano (CONAFRO)*, the *Instituto de Lengua y Cultura Afroboliviana (ILC-AFRO)* and the *Consejo Educativo del Pueblo Afroboliviano (CEPA)*. All of these institutions – CONAFRO, ILC-AFRO, and CEPA – are important actors shaping Afrobolivian interaction with the state and thus rely heavily on the articulated notion of Afrobolivianity circling around the idea of *pueblos*. The *Registro de Saberes y conocimientos del Pueblo Afroboliviano* is probably the most palpable representation of the pervasive tendency of cataloging, formalization and homogenization of Afrobolivian culture. This document serves as a guideline for government agencies, development actors and the general public when dealing with anything concerning *el pueblo Afroboliviano*. Thus the elements listed in this document also became the guiding principles of the exhibition. Besides taking cues for relevant topics and basic information from the *"Registro de Saberes,"* the exhibition draws on two additional sources, each problematic in their own way. Juan Angola's *"Raíces de un Pueblo"* (Angola Maconde 2000) is a book thoroughly grounded in Yungas ethnography, yet when addressing Afrobolivian cultural distinctiveness it remains largely speculative, establishing analogies with 'African cultures' that are dubious at least (Angola Maconde 2000: 17-23). In the same vein, Martín Ballivián's (Ballivián 2015) work on Afrobolivian culture, *saya* and the *hacienda* period sometimes sounds more like an invocation of African cultural roots than a substantiated analysis and is therefore, likewise, to be treated with caution as a source for an exhibition.

As for the *saya* pictures, I later found out just how these pictures came to figure so prominently in the exhibition. When I obtained the document containing all the information on the exhibition from the PNTC, it listed links to internet pages as the sources of the images. Indeed, a quick cross-check showed that almost all of the pictures I had seen on the panels in Cala Cala's *Centro de Interpretación* could be found on the first two result pages of a Google image search with the keywords *"saya afroboliviana."* Upon seeing those pictures on most of the panels and the photographs adorning the walls of the exhibition hall for the first time, people from Cala Cala immediately remarked that most of the photographs did not show Cala Cala's *saya*, but groups from Coroico, La Paz and Chicaloma. Given the importance of local variation in terms of *saya*, this was a serious issue and many people demanded that the pictures be taken down and replaced. In a similar vein, people complained about the *saya* outfits that the PNTC had brought from La Paz for exhibition on mannequins (see fig. 1 in the introduction). The garments had been styled according to photographs and thus looked very similar to outfits found among La Paz-based *saya* groups, rather than the less ostentatious outfits *Cala Caleños* are used to.

The fact that the planners of the exhibition had not consulted with people from Cala Cala before and during the designing of the center was heavily criticized on a number of occasions. Following the discussions and complaints, in internal meetings, informal conversations and in conversations with PNTC personnel, I got the impression that there was more at stake than the replacement of certain pictures and the correction of small errors. Woven into the criticism of those very obvious and superficial mistakes, people voiced their concerns over the general thread of the exhibition. The faults of many parts of the exhibition brought to the fore what was tacitly present: a certain unease many people felt when faced with an objectified image of what was considered their culture. For me, one of the decisive moments in the process of what it meant to deal with the *Centro de Interpretación* for people in Cala Cala was a meeting in which the architect responsible for the interior of the infrastructure explained to Roberto and Víctor how he wanted Cala Cala's *saya* drums to be part of the exhibition. He informed them they were required to deliver Cala Cala's *saya* drums *(cajas)* to the museum in order for them to be part of the exhibition. In exchange, the PNTC would provide the community with at least four brand new drums. Those new drums would serve for drumming in order to show the visitors how *saya* is played and could also be used by visitors to try drumming as part of their interactive experience in the *Centro*. "The old ones will not be played anymore," the architect concluded. The matter-of-fact tone and the complete lack of discussion of the issue struck me as quite remarkable. Although Roberto strongly opposed the idea that Cala Cala's *cajas* should rightfully belong to a museum, depriving the community of access to them, he did not object to the architect's plan on the spot. In conversations with me he repeatedly stated that he was absolutely sure that his opinion on the subject represented the majority within Cala Cala. Consequently, he was shocked find the *cajas* in the exhibition room on the day of an official visit by a delegation from La Paz, since he had even the night before stated that in his eyes there was absolutely no way the old *cajas* would end up on the wall of the center. It was Víctor – at whose house the drums were stored – who had brought the drums to the museum. Again, neither Roberto, nor any other *Cala Caleños* objected on the spot and Víctor's unilateral decision was not questioned. Later, Roberto remarked that he did not consider the issue of the drums resolved and that he would prefer that the original drums remain in the hands of the community, while equipping the museum only with newly crafted ones. It remains to be seen how the issue of the drums is resolved in practice. Yet it is undeniable that Cala Cala's Afrobolivian population is facing a powerful impetus towards objectifying their cultural practices and fixing them as 'tradition' and 'heritage.' While I have addressed this trend as part of my discussion of the pitfalls of folklorization in abstract terms, here we are talking of literally attaching the drums to the wall, removing them from cultural practice and reducing them to the role of representing Afrobolivian tradition in a museum.[8]

Reifying Afrobolivianity through infrastructure: the *Centro de Interpretación* as built identity politics

Whereas radio broadcasts on (indigenous) rights, the circulation of government leaflets highlighting cultural diversity, as well as the recurring references to *pueblos*, identity and culture in workshops and campaigns directed at Afrobolivians are often momentary and volatile in their outcomes, the *Centro de Interpretación* gives the plurinational perspective on diversity and culture a material expression and

8 In mid-2018, I was told by Roberto's eldest son that Roberto is busy making drums for the museum. This suggests to me that his perspective eventually prevailed and that he volunteered to craft the additional drums.

presence.[9] This presence goes beyond documents, action plans, and laws. If many of the examples of the pervasive presence of identity politics and the circulation of plurinational ideas regarding the functioning of Bolivian society I have discussed throughout this book largely remain in the realm of the discursive, the *Casa Cultural* and the *Centro de Interpretación* are almost excessively material results of the state's outlook on culture and society. The sheer size of the buildings and the somewhat out-of-place modernist design make them stand out in the Yungas landscape as beacons of the new plurinational age. This is certainly, at least in part, intended by the designers and planners of such infrastructure who wish to highlight their impact and activities for everybody to see. The question then is what these buildings represent and how they come to affect how people interpret their world and their position within that world. When once I was waiting for a car to take me from Arapata (a town located on the opposite mountain ridge) to Cala Cala, a woman approached me and asked me where I was going. When I told her that I was waiting for someone to take me to Cala Cala, she asked me if I knew what those orange buildings were that could be discerned even at considerable distance. I told her that it was the *Casa Cultural Afro Cala Cala*, a shelter and cultural center for tourists, to which she replied, smiling: *"Entonces han hecho construir eso con los Rubios"* ("So they built this with the Blondes"). *Los Rubios* (lit. the Blondes) is a common way to playfully refer to Afrobolivians, particularly among the non-Afrobolivian population of Coripata (see also Equipo CIPCA 1977:122). The *Casa Cultural* and the *Centro de Interpretación* thus inscribe plurinational logics into the territory for everybody to see. The mere presence of the building reminds the people in and around the *comunidad* of the presence of Afrobolivians and the alleged importance of Afrobolivian culture as a feature of social differentiation. Discourses on Afrobolivian cultural particularity have found material confirmation and reification through the presence of the buildings. Without even considering the details of the exhibitions, the *Centro de Interpretación* makes a powerful statement in terms of what the state considers relevant collective subjects and categories in the context of the Yungas. Most Afrobolivian inhabitants interpreted this statement in a very positive light. For most, it was empowering to be singled out, *"finalmente reconocidos"* ("finally recognized") and represented as a relevant cultural collective. The emphasis on Afrobolivian culture was generally seen as a timely recognition by the state that Afrobolivians 'exist' (i.e. recognized as a culturally distinct entity) and an important aspect of the recognition Afrobolivian organizations have so long been struggling for.

Recognition and representation comes at a price, however. What is represented in the exhibition is often not directly controlled by people from Cala Cala, and the Afrobolivianity depicted in the exhibition is a highly generic one, suffering from

9 The presence of anthropologists researching Afrobolivianity can be considered another momentary factor in this regard.

the general fallacies of the plurinational view of Bolivian reality and the homogenizing force of Afrobolivianity as a political and legal concept. Interestingly, and although the center is focused on Afrobolivian 'culture,' the exhibition also reifies racialized images and stereotypes about Afrobolivians. It features a statue that is intended to depict an Afrobolivian coffee cultivator (see fig. 1 in the introduction) which gives people a material phenotypical reference for how an Afrobolivian ought to look in the eyes of the planners. Given the complicated relationship between the denominations *negro* and *Afroboliviano* and with that the varying influence of phenotype, race and ethnicity for discourses on Afrobolivian identity, it is interesting that a *negro* is posited as most representative in this regard. This not only shows the continuing importance of phenotype, but also exemplifies the images of Afrobolivians circulating in Bolivia more generally. People did not generally comment on this statue and it received significantly less attention than the parts on 'culture' and 'tradition.' The only comment on it that I recall came from Roberto, who remarked that he would have chosen to make the nose flatter, since a "true *negro*" (*"un negro verdadero"*), in his view, doesn't have such a pointy nose.

Conclusion

Cala Cala's venturing into the world of community tourism catapulted its inhabitants into a web of relations including the Interamerican Development Bank, Bolivian central government institutions, regional political brokers and *sindicato* leaders. Their initial engagement with the PNTC led to a series of occasions where members of the community debated questions of culture, community, development, economic necessity and interethnic relations. The conceptual framework that they engaged through these encounters relies on an eclectic mixture of transnational development logics (efficiency, transparency and formalization), plurinational perspectives on cultural diversity, collective rights and discrete group boundaries. Local perspectives on collective identity and alternative ways of organizing social relations in the *comunidad* also shaped these encounters. At times, the logics of the tourism program clashed with perceptions of specific individuals in the community as well as causing difficulties with regard to practical issues of organizing the project.

Given the unexpected turn the engagement with tourism took through the construction of the *Centro de Interpretación*, the project shifted in focus and some frictions already present in the initial scheme were exacerbated. On the one hand, being largely a top-down project with little participation from within the community, the influence of the overarching conceptual framework of plurinationality increased. The exhibition's perspective on Afrobolivians is even more firmly grounded in plurinational ID-ology and a notion of Afrobolivianity articulated nationally.

Cala Cala's specificities are largely absent from the exhibition and the Afrobolivianity that is represented in the exhibition is highly generic. Its primary sources are documents and publications crafted under the influence of the plurinational goal of cataloging the culture of clearly bounded *pueblos*. I have analyzed the contradictions of this process at length in chapter 7. The *Centro de Interpretación* is thus a striking example of how those logics reach the local contexts and how they are engaged by people.

Moving beyond the aspects that the planners of the project associate with the idea of a *Centro de Interpretación* (i.e. a specific novel museological approach directed at the visitors) it is fruitful to inquire into the "interpretations" of the world the *Centro* and its exhibition proposes to the people in Cala Cala. First of all, its interpretation of the Yungas explicitly singles out three elements: coca, coffee and Afrobolivian culture.[10] Thus Afrobolivianity is marked as a consequential category of collective identification. In this context, what the exhibition does not explicitly name is also important: Aymara culture, which is not explicitly represented as salient or consequential in the Yungas context. Moreover, the exhibition specifically focuses on Afrobolivian 'culture,' thereby adhering to a very particular notion of Afrobolivianity that is not uncontested, as I have shown in chapter 6. What is more, the center offers an interpretation of what 'culture' is: a discrete list of elements (see chapter 7), mainly *saya*, represented through material objects (the drums), through photographs and through performances within the space of the museum. In a way, the project also highlights what the plurinational state thinks about the question of where 'culture' belongs. Although there are references to lived culture (*"culturas vivas"*), the fact that the architect expected people in Cala Cala to give their drums to the museum is quite telling. Cala Cala's most important material expression of Afrobolivian 'culture' should belong to the museum, where it is to be preserved as patrimony. Moreover, there are less explicit aspects and interpretations to be found in the museum. I have hinted at the racialized imagery of the Afrobolivian coffee cultivator and have also mentioned the dark-skinned mannequins (see the opening vignette in the introduction) that are used to display the *saya* outfits. Thus, although emphasizing culture in explicit terms, the exhibition also perpetuates racialized notions of Afrobolivianity through the absent (i.e. unnamed) material presence of race (Wade, Deister, et al. 2014).

Following James Clifford's (2013) approach to indigeneity as a process of becoming through articulation, performance and translation, I argue that the *Centro de Interpretación* is an important site of the articulation, performance and translation of Afrobolivianity in Cala Cala. The exhibition of the *Centro de Interpretación* provides us with a concise summary of many of the elements that I have described as

10 For reasons of space, I cannot discuss the first two aspects, but will focus only on 'Afrobolivian culture' (*"cultura Afroboliviana"*).

important in the process of articulating Afrobolivianity in contexts of cultural revitalization, political activism and plurinational recognition. The center also serves as a privileged site where this particular notion of Afrobolivianity is performed. Although the project focuses on the performances directed at tourists, the performances of Afrobolivianity in the context of the center also engage people from the *comunidad Nogalani* and *"los Afros de Cala Cala."* Finally, the element of translation is crucial. For people in Cala Cala, engaging with the *Centro de Interpretación* also means engaging with the apparent gap between local notions of what it means to be *Afro,* the Afrobolivianity the center depicts, as well as the expectations of experts and tourists. Recall the episode that I described in the ethnographic vignette in the introduction to this book. Prompted by the vice minister's visit, Roberto explained what the *saya* drums, representing Afrobolivianity, meant to him. His performance failed to meet the expectations of the experts, who took their view as representative of what visitors will expect. In that particular moment, the performative translation of Roberto's local, "intimate" Afrobolivianity into the plurinational idiom of the experts was not achieved.

This last aspect points us towards an important characteristic of articulations and the collective identifications they engender. Articulations are always contested, processual and unfinished (Clifford 2013:61–62). They can be made, unmade and adopted within the social, cultural, economic and legal contexts they are embedded in (Schlee 2004). The contested nature of articulations and the particular plurinational perspective on collective identification becomes most apparent in my discussion of the early stages of the project. When planning and conceptualizing the *Casa Cultural Afro Cala Cala,* people in Cala Cala had to find ways of accommodating the logics of the project within local perspectives and different horizons of community. The heated debates on delimiting the beneficiaries of the project ("Who should (be allowed to) participate?") among *"los Afros de Cala Cala"* point towards the contested nature of seemingly clear-cut boundaries of collectivity in Cala Cala. In the end, *Cala Caleños* resorted to translocal kinship ties (by including urban migrants from Cala Cala), as well as to broader overarching notions of collective belonging to *la comunidad Nogalani* (by relying on the support of the *sindicato*), in order to pursue the project. They thus simultaneously and interchangeably activated different frames of collective belonging. On the one hand, a frame based on kinship and ethnoracial identification, and on the other a frame based on crosscutting ties, integration and overarching similarities within Nogalani (Eidson et al. 2017; Elwert 2002; Schlee 2008).

I have analyzed the case of Cala Cala's *Casa Cultural Afro* and the *Centro de Interpretación* as a concrete example of the processes this study as a whole is concerned with. My discussion sheds light on a complex field of entangled practices and discourses. I have ethnographically explored how "legalized identities" (French 2009) influence "we-group processes" (Elwert 2002) on the local level. I have highlighted how local notions of Afrobolivianity interact with plurinational groupism (Brubaker 2002), most clearly expressed in the concept of *el pueblo Afroboliviano* and its related notions of 'culture.' Beyond collective ethnoracial identifications – local or plurinational – an alternative perspective on community and belonging, namely the overarching *comunidad cocalera* rooted in practice (*"cumplir función social,"* see chapter 4) also plays a crucial role. The outcomes of the negotiations those encounters engender cannot be prefigured. It must be noted, however, that if we perceive of articulation as a "process of social and cultural persistence [that] is political all the way" then we have to take into account that collective identifications are often negotiated "in power-charged, unequal situations" (Clifford 2013:61–62). Thus the agents of the plurinational machinery of ID-ology who are backed by law, as well as political and economic power and legitimized by technocratic knowledge, enjoy significant advantages when it comes to propagating their "interpretation" of Afrobolivianity. However, this does not preclude resistance and contestation. The evolving social and cultural practices of Afrobolivianity in Cala Cala constantly undermine and decenter the plurinational narrative of what it means to be *Afro* in contemporary Bolivia.

Conclusion: *"Eso de lo Afro, es un caminar"*

Shortly before I left Cala Cala for the last time in 2017, Roberto asked me if my stay had been "successful." He asked me if I "had found what I was looking for" (*"¿Encontraste lo que has buscado?"*). I told him that my time in Cala Cala had been enlightening in many ways and thanked him for his generous guidance, the time he and his family had shared with me, and their friendship. He then – just as he had innumerable times before – told me that he was exceptionally sad that I had not been able to witness a performance of *saya* in Cala Cala, despite the fact that we had talked so much about that topic. I told him that I would of course have liked to see him and the other *Cala Caleños* perform, but that he shouldn't worry. What I was interested in, I told him, was how people in Cala Cala live: how they spend their days, how they make a living, how they socialize and, ultimately, what they make of "being *Afro*." I reminded him of the many conversations we had had in the context of the tourism project during which he would always ask me what was "interesting," "unique" and "characteristic" about Cala Cala. Since on those occasions he expected strategic advice from me with regard to the Afrobolivian tourism project, I always told him that he should try to approach this question by focusing on the possible expectations of tourists, as well as on the things he and his fellow *comunarios* do in everyday contexts. On this occasion, however, I decided to tell him that – as an anthropologist – I do not share the expectations of tourists. Consequently, I neither came to Cala Cala expecting to see a performance of *saya*, nor did I think of "being *Afro*" as exclusively based on *saya*. What is more, I told him, my anthropological perspective on culture in general and on Afrobolivians in particular is decidedly different from what the Constitution states, what the 'experts' say or what the exhibition in the *Centro de Interpretación* portrays. He astutely captured the meaning of my improvised statement on Afrobolivianity and culture as contested, processual and inherently flexible phenomena, by replying: "So you're telling me that culture and *lo Afro* are like a journey [*un caminar*]."[1] I told him that

1 *"Me haces entender que eso de la cultura, de lo Afro, entonces es un caminar."* There is no single straightforward translation of his expression *"un caminar"* derived from the verb *"caminar"* meaning (to) walk, but also (to) wander and (to) travel. What he mainly wanted to express, I argue, was movement and process.

this is precisely what I meant, that culture, as well as "*lo Afro*" are not stable things or concepts but that they mean different things to different people in different places and contexts.

The aim of this study was to trace the changing and contested meanings of "*lo Afro*" in contemporary Bolivia and to analyze the significance of Afrobolivianity in processes of collective identity formation and social differentiation. As a key aspect of these processes, I have identified the tension between a specific articulation of Afrobolivianity, which I have termed plurinational Afrobolivianity, and the practices of people like Roberto and other individuals who self-identify as Afrobolivians. Approaching this key aspect as a tension, I do not wish to imply conflict or contradiction, since this tension is also productive, bridging different contexts of social and cultural practice and fostering exchange and interaction. I introduced my study by pointing out how this tension shaped the atmosphere during the inspection visit to the newly constructed *Centro de Interpretación* and detailed its local ramifications through my case study in the preceding chapter. Roberto's sadness with regard to the 'missing' *saya* performance in Cala Cala and his worries that this would make my stay in Cala Cala and my understanding of Afrobolivianity somehow incomplete, is another example of it. Further hints at the inherent discursive and practical multidimensionality of Afrobolivianity are the sometimes uneasy relationship between racialized images of Afrobolivians and the ubiquitous references to culture as constitutive of Afrobolivianity. Moreover, although current political and legal discourse incessantly propagate this perspective, 21st century Bolivian society cannot be conclusively described as characterized by the coexistence of discrete *pueblos*. In Cala Cala, "being *Afro*," is not the only modality of 'being' and consequently also not the only way of experiencing and expressing identity and belonging.

By focusing on this productive tension and through analyzing it in its different historical and ethnographic contexts, my study enriches the scholarship on Afrobolivians in decisive ways. The existing literature emphasizes either the national (mostly political) dimension of Afrobolivianity or focuses on Afrobolivians as part of the *comunidades cocaleras* in the Yungas. The former approach often uncritically adopts the concepts of political discourse and the rhetoric of activists and thus tends to overstate the salience of Afrobolivianity in local contexts. Proponents of the latter approach, in contrast, argue from the perspective of the *comunidad cocalera* in the Yungas. In their view, ethnic and/or indigenous identities are not salient in the Yungas, where identification as *cocaleros* prevails. Collective identifications as Afrobolivians are considered impositions from outside the local context. Afrobolivianity, to their eyes, is a matter of urban-based activists and their strategic use of identity politics and is of no further significance. The contributions of both perspectives thus remain partial and fail to holistically explain Afrobolivianity and its inherent multidimensionality.

I have approached collective identifications and how they are deployed in processes of social differentiation in Cala Cala by drawing on perspectives proposed by Schlee (1997; 2004; 2008), Elwert (1995; 2002) and Brubaker (2002; 2014; Brubaker and Cooper 2000).[2] As I have shown, being Afrobolivian in Cala Cala is not merely a physical characteristic just as inconsequential for social organization as being tall or fat. It is also, however, not simply a matter of objectified cultural difference. Belonging to *"los Afros de Cala Cala"* fundamentally means being part of a collective based on kinship ties in Cala Cala, as well as transcending the geographical boundaries of the community. The members of this collective furthermore ground their belonging in notions of shared local history and culture. Beyond Afrobolivianity, there are alternative frames for collective identification, mainly the processual notion of belonging to the *comunidad cocalera* by "performing a social function" (*"cumplir función social"*). I have argued that collective identifications as Afrobolivians and as *comunarios* are not only complementary but intertwined. It is possible to identify as a *comunario* and as Afrobolivian simultaneously or interchangeably. It would be misleading to analyze the entanglements of *Cala Caleños* with Nogalani merely as cooperation in economic (within the coca economy) and political terms (through the *sindicato*). Coca plays a fundamental role as a "total social fact" (Spedding 1997) beyond the economy in Cala Cala. Similarly, the *sindicato* is not only an institution of political mobilization: in a way "it is the community" (Conzelman 2007).

However, neither Afrobolivianity nor identification as *comunarios* are stable identities. Their meaning is contested and their relationship to each other changes. These changes have to do with local processes, as well as with national and international political and legal developments, and how they are experienced in local contexts. Besides pointing out changes in the local economy, namely the increased monetarization and individualization of the coca economy, my study focuses on the changing notions of Afrobolivianity that emerge in the context of Bolivia's plurinational conjuncture (Canessa 2012a; Farthing and Kohl 2014; Postero 2017; Schilling-Vacaflor, Brand, and Radhuber 2012). Drawing on James Clifford's (2007; 2013) suggestion to engage with indigeneity as an articulation, I have described the contested articulation of Afrobolivianity. As I was able to document, this articulation combines elements of indigenism (Niezen 2003) with influences stemming from the transnational discourses of the African Diaspora (Wade 2006b; Yelvington 2001; 2006) as well as the language of citizenship (Canessa 2012b; Yashar 2005; Van Cott 2000). It is furthermore shaped by processes similar to those Jan Hoffmann

2 For a recent attempt at synthesizing those approaches in order to develop a "comprehensive framework for the comparative analysis of collective identities and corresponding processes of identification" see Eidson et al. (2017).

French (2002; 2004; 2009) has described as "legalizing identities" in her study of a village in northeastern Brazil.

Following important contributions in the field of the anthropology of Afro-Latin America (Anderson 2007; 2009; Greene 2007a; 2007b; Ng'weno 2007; Restrepo 2004; 2007), as well as in the study of indigeneity in Latin America (de la Cadena 2008; de la Cadena and Starn 2007b; Canessa 2007; 2012c; 2018; Goodale 2006; Halbmayer 2011), I also inquired into the possible articulations and disjunctions of Afrobolivianity and indigeneity with regard to what Shane Greene (2007a) has described as Latin America's "Afro-Indigenous Multiculturalisms." Broadening my perspective beyond the commonplace association of indigenous people with ethnicity, culture and pre-Colombian roots and Afro-Latin Americans with race and a routed diasporic identity (Wade 2010) made it possible to flesh out the discursive entanglements of the idioms of indigeneity and autochthony, as well as the idiom of diaspora in the articulation of Afrobolivianity. However, I would not go as far as Mark Anderson, who coined the terms "Black Indigeneity" and "Indigenous Blackness" in his study of Garifuna communities in Honduras (Anderson 2009). Although the discursive articulation of Afrobolivianity owes at least as much to indigeneity as it does to diaspora and blackness, and the legal status and political positioning of Afrobolivians is strikingly similar to that of indigenous people in Bolivia, Afrobolivianity and indigeneity continue to be imagined as clearly separate modalities of belonging. If anything, the legalization (French 2009) of Afrobolivian and indigenous identities in Bolivia has led to an even sharper distinction between the two categories. The constant denial of being in any way "like indigenous people" by Afrobolivian activists, as well as the widespread avoidance of terms like *"Afro-Aymara"* are a clear indicator of this. This has to do with the plurinational logics of recognition and representation that rely on the concept of *pueblos*, conceptualized as bounded, discrete, culturally homogenous and mutually exclusive entities.

The influence of these logics is most clear in the political discourses of Afrobolivian organizations, but also shapes notions of collectivity and culture more generally, especially since legal recognition has fueled efforts at cataloging and categorizing Afrobolivian culture. In order to benefit from the plurinational politics of recognition, activists positioned Afrobolivianity according to specific logics. It is important to note that those logics are not entirely new, despite the continuing insistence on the revolutionary character of the "process of change" *("el proceso de cambio")* and the groundbreaking importance of Bolivia's re-founding as a plurinational state in 2009 (Escobar 2010; García Linera 2008; 2009). Their conceptual roots date back to indigenous mobilizations beginning in the 1970s, Bolivia's engagement with multiculturalism in the 1990s and the transnational political and legal discourse on indigenous people and indigenous rights.[3]

Starting out as a movement of Afrobolivian cultural revival based on the dance *saya*, the *Movimiento Afro* set in motion an important set of processes that have to be taken into consideration for the contemporary plurinational articulations of Afrobolivianity. The very term *Afroboliviano* emerged from those efforts, as did the idea that Afrobolivianity was to be approached as a phenomenon beyond skin color. Racialized *negros* and *negras* were fundamentally repositioned as *Afrobolivianos/as* in Bolivia's "structures of alterity" (Wade 2010). This culturalization of Afrobolivianity initially emerged from urban Afrobolivians. It went hand in hand with the establishment of a politicized Afrobolivianity. As a result of these processes, the contexts of expressing and experiencing Afrobolivianity also changed. For the growing urban Afrobolivian population, Afrobolivianity was no longer rooted in village settings and in everyday practices in local contexts. *Saya* as cultural performance (Cohen 1993; Guss 2000; Parkin, Caplan, and Fisher 1996) and workshops as spaces for the articulation of collective identification became the primary contexts in which an increasingly "lite" Afrobolivianity (Canessa 2018; Grisaffi 2010) – relying more on key symbols and formal recognition of Afrobolivianity than on everyday cultural practice – was experienced and expressed. Recent developments include the judicialization of Afrobolivian activism and political rhetoric (Couso, Huneeus, and Sieder 2010; Sieder, Schjolden, and Angell 2005b; de Sousa Santos and César A Rodríguez-Garavito 2005), most clearly expressed in the proliferation of "rights talk" (Merry 2003). Moreover, I have described a process that I have termed the *pueblo*-ization of Afrobolivianity. Similar to the processes described as an "ethnicization of blackness" in Colombia (Ng'weno 2007; Restrepo 2004; Wade 1995), notions of Afrobolivianity were fashioned according to the plurinational logics of *pueblos*. The *pueblo*-ization of Afrobolivianity inspired the foundation of a novel type of Afrobolivian organization, the *Consejo Nacional Afroboliviano (CONAFRO)*, designed according to the logics of indigenous mobilization in Bolivia. *Pueblo*-ization is not limited to the political and legal context, however. It increasingly shapes Afrobolivian subjectivities and notions of Afrobolivian culture, as I have shown in the context of cataloging and codifying Afrobolivian culture.

In the last chapter I analyzed a concrete case from Cala Cala, where local notions of community and belonging interact with broader conceptualizations of Afrobolivianity that were shaped by Afrobolivian activism and plurinational ID-ology. In the context of these interactions, "*los Afros de Cala Cala*" are drawn into national

3 As has been observed, for example, by Robert Albro (2010a), the definition of "*naciones y pueblos indígena originario campesinos*" in the Plurinational Constitution of 2009 is heavily influenced by the "United Nations Declaration on the Rights of Indigenous Peoples," as well as by ILO 169.

and transnational spaces of identity politics, legal recognition and cultural performance. Consequently, local processes of collective identification and social relations are transformed. From cases like this, we can develop a better understanding of the phenomenon of collective identities and corresponding processes of identification by not only focusing on "re-identification," that is, "alterations in the actor[s'] orientation, attitude, and behavior with reference to selected categories of identification," but simultaneously taking into consideration what has been referred to as the "redefinition of categories of identity" (Eidson et al. 2017:342). The redefinition of categories of identity involves multiple processes such as strategic repositioning, changing political and legal circumstances, but also "largely unintended effects of the combined actions of multiple actors over several generations" (Eidson et al. 2017:342). In order to grasp the processes of redefinition and show how they are intertwined with processes of re-identification in social practice, I have proposed drawing on articulation theory (Clarke 2015; Clifford 2013; Hall 1985) and combining it with actor-centered approaches to collective identifications (Eidson et al. 2017; Schlee 2004; 2008).

This study fills an ethnographic lacuna by documenting and analyzing the cultural practices and political discourses of Afrobolivians in a comprehensive manner, a topic that is underrepresented in anthropological writing on Bolivia. It also contributes to discussions of Bolivia's plurinational conjuncture by adding a fresh perspective on the political and legal transformations in the country, transcending the focus on indigenous groups as the prototypical 'others.' In a broader comparative framework, my analysis of Afrobolivianity engages with the anthropology of Afro-Latin America, where the Bolivian case has not been systematically taken into consideration in debates on race and ethnicity, as well as with regard to the transformations of *Afro*/black identities in the context of transnational diaspora politics and Latin America's Afro-indigenous multiculturalisms. Finally, my study suggests that combining actor-centered approaches to collective identification with theories of articulation can be a fruitful way to approach the subject of collective identities in Bolivia and Latin America, as well as on a global scale.

Bibliography

Acosta, Alberto. 2015. *Buen vivir: Vom Recht auf ein gutes Leben*. München: oekom verlag.

Aillón Soria, Esther. 2005. "La Afro-Andinización de Los Esclavos Negros En Las Viñas de Cinti (Chuquisaca) Siglos XVIII-XIX." *Raíces. Revista Boliviana de La Fundación de Afro Descendientes* 2: 10–11.

Albiez-Wieck, Sarah. 2017. "Indigenous Migrants Negotiating Belonging: Peticiones de Cambio de Fuero in Cajamarca, Peru, 17th–18th Centuries." *Colonial Latin American Review* 26 (4): 483–508.

Albó, Xavier. 2008. "The 'Long Memory' of Ethnicity in Bolivia and Some Temporary Oscillations." In *John Crabtree and Laurence Whitehead (Eds.): Unresolved Tensions: Bolivia Past and Present*, 13–34. Pittsburgh: University of Pittsburgh Press.

———. 2016. "La Paradoja Aymara o Desafíos de La Solidaridad Aymara." In *Xavier Albó: Obras Selectas. Tomo II 1974-1977*, 371–499. La Paz, Bolivia: Fundación Xavier Albó.

Albro, Robert. 2005. "The Indigenous in the Plural in Bolivian Oppositional Politics." *Bulletin of Latin American Research* 24 (4): 433–453.

———. 2006. "Actualidades: Bolivia's 'Evo Phenomenon': From Identity to What?" *Journal of Latin American Anthropology* 11 (2): 408–428.

———. 2007. "Indigenous Politics In Bolivia's Evo Era: Clientelism, Llunkerío, And The Problem of Stigma." *Urban Anthropology and Studies of Cultural Systems and World Economic Development* 36 (3): 281–320.

———. 2010a. "Confounding Cultural Citizenship and Constitutional Reform in Bolivia." *Latin American Perspectives* 37 (3): 71–90. https://doi.org/10.1177/0094582X10364034.

———. 2010b. *Roosters at Midnight: Indigenous Signs and Stigma in Local Bolivian Politics*. Santa Fe: SAR Press.

Anderson, Benedict. 2006. *Imagined Communities: Reflections on the Origin and Spread of Nationalism*. Revised edition. London; New York: Verso.

Anderson, Mark. 2007. "When Afro Becomes (like) Indigenous: Garifuna and Afro-Indigenous Politics in Honduras." *The Journal of Latin American and Caribbean Anthropology* 12 (2): 384–413.

———. 2009. *Black and Indigenous: Garifuna Activism and Consumer Culture in Honduras*. Minneapolis: University of Minnesota Press.

Andrews, George Reid. 2004. *Afro-Latin America, 1800-2000*. Oxford, New York: Oxford University Press.

Angola Maconde, Juan. 2000. *Raíces de Un Pueblo: Cultura Afroboliviana*. La Paz: Producciones CIMA; Embajada de España; Cooperación Española.

———. 2001. "El Afrodescendiente En La Historia de Bolivia." In *XIV Reunión Anual de Etnología*, 1:496–505. Anales de La Reunión Anual de Etnología. La Paz: MUSEF.

———. 2003. "Los Yungas. Enclave Africano." *Raíces. Revista Boliviana de La Fundación de Afro Descendientes* 1: 3–9.

———. 2007. "Los Afrodescendientes Bolivianos." *The Journal of Latin American and Caribbean Anthropology* 12 (1): 246–53.

———. 2008. *Comunidad Dorado Chico. Nuestra Historia*. La Paz: FUNDAFRO.

———. 2010. "Las Raíces Africanas En La Historia de Bolivia." In *Sheila S. Walker (Ed.): Conocimiento Desde Adentro: Los Afrosudamericanos Hablan de Sus Pueblos y Sus Historias*, Vol. 1:145–221. La Paz: PIEB.

———. 2012. *El Habla Afroyungueña. Cho, Así Jay Hablamu, Más Vale Qui Oté Nuay Olvidá*. La Paz: FUNDAFRO.

Arnold, Denise Y., ed. 2009. *Indígenas u Obreros?: La Construcción Política de Identidades En El Altiplano Boliviano*. Identidades Regionales de Bolivia. La Paz: UNIR.

Ballivián, Martín Miguel. 2014. *La Saya Afroboliviana: Conociendo "Desde Casa Adentro y Casa Afuera" Nuestra Historiografía y Saberes Ancestrales"*. Cochabamba: INIAM, Fundación Intercultural Martin Luther King.

———. 2015. *Somos Afrobolivianas Afrobolivianos. Historía, Testimonios, Tiempo de Hacienda, Futbol, e Imagenes de Mi Cultura*. La Paz, Bolivia: Fundación Martin Luther King/Ministerio de Culturas y Turismo/Unidad de Industrias Culturales.

Benda-Beckmann, Franz von, Keebet von Benda-Beckmann, and Julia Eckert, eds. 2009. *Rules of Law and Laws of Ruling: On the Governance of Law*. Farnham; Burlington: Ashgate.

Benda-Beckmann, Franz von, Keebet von Benda-Beckmann, and Anne Griffiths, eds. 2005. *Mobile People, Mobile Law: Expanding Legal Relations in a Contracting World*. Aldershot; Burlington: Ashgate.

———., eds. 2009. *The Power of Law in a Transnational World: Anthropological Enquiries*. Oxford; New York: Berghahn Books.

Bigenho, Michelle. 2002. *Sounding Indigenous: Authenticity in Bolivian Music Performance*. New York: Palgrave Macmillan.

Bridikhina, Eugenia. 1995a. *La Mujer Negra En Bolivia*. La Paz: Ministerio de Desarrollo Humano.

———. 1995b. "La Vida Urbana de Los Negros En La Paz En El Siglo XVIII." In *Reunión Anual de Etnología 1994*, 23–32. Anales de La Reunión Anual de Etnología. La Paz: MUSEF.

———. 1997. "Coca, Dinero o Jornales. La Situación Económico Social de Los Ex-Esclavos Negros En Yungas Del Norte, Segunda Mitad Del Siglo XIX." In *Rossana Barragán and Seemin Qayum (Eds.): El Siglo XIX: Bolivia y América Latina*, Nueva edición [en línea], 463–74. Lima: IFEA. http://books.openedition.org/ifea/7381.

Brubaker, Rogers. 2002. "Ethnicity without Groups." *Archives Européennes de Sociologie* XLIII.2: 163–89.

———. 2009. "Ethnicity, Race, and Nationalism." *Annual Review of Sociology* 35 (1): 21–42. https://doi.org/10.1146/annurev-soc-070308-115916.

———. 2014. "Beyond Ethnicity." *Ethnic and Racial Studies* 37 (5): 804–808. https://doi.org/10.1080/01419870.2013.871311.

Brubaker, Rogers, and Frederick Cooper. 2000. "Beyond 'Identity.'" *Theory and Society* 29 (1): 1–47.

Busdiecker, Sara. 2003. "Negros En Bolivia: Imágenes Existentes, Silencios Significativos, y La Construcción Discursiva Del Afro-Boliviano." In *XV Reunión Anual de Etnología*, Tomo II:105–13. Anales de La Reunión Anual de Etnología. La Paz: MUSEF.

———. 2007. "We Are Bolivians Too: The Experience and Meaning of Blackness in Bolivia. PhD Thesis." University of Michigan.

———. 2009a. "The Emergence and Evolving Character of Contemporary Afro-Bolivian Mobilization: From the Performative to the Political." In *Leith Mullings (Ed.): New Social Movements in the African Diaspora. Challenging Global Apartheid.*, 121–37. New York: Palgrave Macmillan.

———. 2009b. "Where Blackness Resides: Afro-Bolivians and the Spatializing and Racializing of the African Diaspora." *Radical History Review* 2009 (103): 105–16.

———. 2019a. "Crowning Afro-descendant Memory and Visibility in an Indian/Mestizo Country." *Transition* No. 127, Afro-Latin America Rising: 191-215. DOI: 10.2979/transition.127.1.19.

———. 2019b. "The promises and limits of Bolivia's anti-racism law for Afro-Bolivians: tundiqui, the National Afro-Bolivian Council, and the battle against blackface." *Latin American and Caribbean Ethnic Studies.* Published online 12 Sep 2019. DOI: 10.1080/17442222.2019.1664722.

Cadena, Marisol de la. 2000. *Indigenous Mestizos: The Politics of Race and Culture in Cuzco, Peru, 1919–1991*. Durham, London: Duke University Press.

———. 2005. "Are Mestizos Hybrids? The Conceptual Politics of Andean Identities." *Journal of Latin American Studies* 37 (2): 259–284.

———. 2008. "Alternative Indigeneities: Conceptual Proposals." *Latin American and Caribbean Ethnic Studies* 3 (3): 341–49.

Cadena, Marisol de la, and Orin Starn, eds. 2007a. *Indigenous Experience Today*. Oxford: Berg.

———. 2007b. "Introduction." In *Marisol de La Cadena and Orin Starn (Eds.): Indigenous Experience Today*, 1–32. Oxford: Berg.

Canessa, Andrew, ed. 2005. *Natives Making Nation: Gender, Indigeneity, and the State in the Andes*. Tucson: University of Arizona Press.

———. 2007. "Who Is Indigenous? Self-Identification, Indigeneity, and Claims to Justice in Contemporary Bolivia." *Urban Anthropology* 36 (3): 195–237.

———. 2012a. *Conflict, Claim and Contradiction in the New Indigenous State of Bolivia*. desiguALdades. net Working Paper Series, No.22, Berlin: desiguALdades.net Research Network on Interdependent Inequalities in Latin America.

———. 2012b. "New Indigenous Citizenship in Bolivia: Challenging the Liberal Model of the State and Its Subjects." *Latin American and Caribbean Ethnic Studies* 7 (2): 201–221.

———. 2012c. *Intimate Indigeneities: Race, Sex, and History in the Small Spaces of Andean Life*. Durham, London: Duke University Press.

———. 2018. "Indigenous Conflict in Bolivia Explored through an African Lens: Towards a Comparative Analysis of Indigeneity." *Comparative Studies in Society and History* 60 (2).

Carsten, Janet. 2000. "Introduction: Cultures of Relatedness." In *Janet Carsten (Ed.): Cultures of Relatedness: New Approaches to the Study of Kinship*, 1–36. Cambridge: Cambridge University Press.

Centro Pedagógico y Cultural "Simón I. Patiño." 1998a. *El Tambor Mayor: Música y Cantos de Las Comunidades Negras de Bolivia*. Série: Littératures et Cultures Latino-Américaines: Literaturas y Culturas Latinoamericanas 43. Cochabamba: Fundación Simón I. Patiño.

———. 1998b. "'Tiempo Para Contestar Las Palabras. Testimonio Del Abuelo Manuel Barra. Tokaña.'" In *Centro Pedagógico y Cultural "Simón I. Patiño": El Tambor Mayor. Musica y Cantos de Las Comunidades Negras de Bolivia.*, 89–115. Série: Littératures et Cultures Latino-Américaines: Literaturas y Culturas Latinoamericanas 43. Cochabamba: Fundación Simón I. Patiño.

Céspedes, Gilka Wara. 1993. "'Huayño,' 'Saya,' and 'Chuntunqui': Bolivian Identity in the Music of 'Los Kjarkas.'" *Latin American Music Review/Revista de Música Latinoamericana* 14 (1): 52–101.

Ceuppens, Bambi, and Peter Geschiere. 2005. "Autochthony: Local or Global? New Modes in the Struggle over Citizenship and Belonging in Africa and Europe." *Annual Review of Anthropology* 34: 385–407.

Clarke, John. 2015. "Stuart Hall and the Theory and Practice of Articulation." *Discourse: Studies in the Cultural Politics of Education* 36 (2): 275–86. https://doi.org/10.1080/01596306.2015.1013247.

Clifford, James. 2007. "Varieties of Indigenous Experience: Diasporas, Homelands, Sovereignties." In *Marisol de La Cadena and Orin Starn (Eds.): Indigenous Experience Today*, 197–223. Oxford: Berg.

———. 2013. *Returns: Becoming Indigenous in the Twenty-First Century*. Cambridge, Massachusetts: Harvard University Press.

Cohen, Abner. 1993. *Masquerade Politics. Explorations in the Structure of Urban Cultural Movements*. Oxford: Berg.

Collier, Jane F., Bill Maurer, and Liliana Suarez-Navaz. 1996. "Sanctioned Identities: Legal Constructions of Modern Personhood." *Identities* 2 (1–2): 1–27.

Comaroff, Jean, and John L. Comaroff. 2003. "Reflections on Liberalism, Policulturalism, and ID-Ology: Citizenship and Difference in South Africa." *Social Identities* 9 (4): 445–73.

———. 2012. *Theory from the South: Or, How Euro-America Is Evolving Toward Africa*. Boulder: Routledge.

Comaroff, John L., and Jean Comaroff. 2006. "Law and Disorder in the Postcolony: An Introduction." In *Jean Comaroff and John L. Comaroff (Eds.): Law and Disorder in the Postcolony*, 1–56. Chicago; London: University of Chicago Press.

———. 2009. "Reflections on the Anthropology of Law, Governance and Sovereignty." In *Franz von Benda-Beckmann, Keebet von Benda Beckmann and Julia Eckert (Eds.): Rules of Law and Laws of Ruling: On the Governance of Law*, 31–60. Farnham; Burlington: Ashgate.

Conzelman, Caroline Sommer. 2007. "Coca Leaf and Sindicato Democracy in the Bolivian Yungas: The Andeanization of Western Political Models and the Rise of the New Left. PhD Thesis." Department of Anthropology, Boulder: University of Colorado at Boulder.

Course, Magnus. 2011. *Becoming Mapuche: Person and Ritual in Indigenous Chile*. Urbana, Chicago and Springfiled: University of Illinois Press.

Couso, Javier, Alexandra Huneeus, and Rachel Sieder, eds. 2010. *Cultures of Legality: Judicialization and Political Activism in Latin America*. Cambridge: Cambridge University Press.

Crabtree, John, and Laurence Whitehead, eds. 2008. *Unresolved Tensions: Bolivia Past and Present*. Pitt Latin American Series. Pittsburgh, Pa: University of Pittsburgh Press.

Crespo R., Alberto. 1977. *Esclavos Negros En Bolivia*. 2da edición. La Paz: Librería Editorial Juventud.

Cunha, Manuela Carneiro da, and Mauro W.B. de Almeida. 2000. "Indigenous People, Traditional People, and Conservation in the Amazon." *Daedalus* 129 (2): 315–338.

Dixon, Kwame, and John Burdick, eds. 2012. *Comparative Perspectives on Afro-Latin America*. Gainesville, Fla.: University Press of Florida.

Downey, Greg. 2005. *Learning Capoeira: Lessons in Cunning from an Afro-Brazilian Art.* Oxford; New York: Oxford University Press.

Dunkerley, James. 1984. *Rebellion in the Veins: Political Struggle in Bolivia, 1952-82.* London: Verso.

Eckert, Julia. 2006. "From Subjects to Citizens: Legalism from below and the Homogenisation of the Legal Sphere." *The Journal of Legal Pluralism and Unofficial Law* 38 (53–54): 45–75.

———. 2012. "Rumours of Rights." In *Julia Eckert, Brian Donahoe, Christian Strümpell and Zerrin Özlem Biner (Eds.): Law against the State. Ethnographic Forays into Law's Transformations*, 147–70. Cambridge: Cambridge Univ. Press.

Eidson, John R., Dereje Feyissa, Veronika Fuest, Markus V. Hoehne, Boris Nieswand, Günther Schlee, and Olaf Zenker. 2017. "From Identification to Framing and Alignment: A New Approach to the Comparative Analysis of Collective Identities." *Current Anthropology* 58 (3): 340–59. https://doi.org/10.1086/691970.

Elwert, Georg. 1995. "Boundaries, Cohesion and Switching. On We-groups in Ethnic, National and Religious Forms." *Bulletin de l'APAD*, no. 10 (December). http://journals.openedition.org/apad/1111.

———. 2002. "Switching Identity Discourses: Primordial Emotions and the Social Construction of We-Groups." In *Günther Schlee (Ed.): Imagined Differences: Hatred and the Construction of Social Identities*, 33–54. Münster, Hamburg: LIT.

Equipo CIPCA. 1976. *Yungas: Los "Otros Aymaras": Diagnóstico Económico-Socio-Cultural de Sud Yungas*. La Paz, Bolivia: CIPCA.

———. 1977. *Coripata. Tierra de Angustias y Cocales*. La Paz, Bolivia: CIPCA.

Eriksen, Thomas Hylland. 2010. *Ethnicity and Nationalism: Anthropological Perspectives*. 3rd edition. London: Pluto Press.

Escobar, Arturo. 2010. "Latin America at a Crossroads: Alternative Modernizations, Post-Liberalism, or Post-Development?" *Cultural Studies* 24 (1): 1–65.

Fabian, Johannes. 2002. *Time and the Other: How Anthropology Makes Its Object*. New Edition. New York: Columbia University Press.

Farthing, Linda C., and Benjamin H. Kohl. 2014. *Evo's Bolivia: Continuity and Change*. Austin, TX: University of Texas Press.

Foster, George M. 1953. "Cofradia and Compadrazgo in Spain and Spanish America." *Southwestern Journal of Anthropology* 9 (1): 1–28.

French, Jan Hoffman. 2002. "Dancing for Land: Law-Making and Cultural Performance in Northeastern Brazil." *PoLAR: Political and Legal Anthropology Review* 25 (1): 19–36. https://doi.org/10.1525/pol.2002.25.1.19.

———. 2004. "Mestizaje and Law Making in Indigenous Identity Formation in Northeastern Brazil: 'After the Conflict Came the History.'" *American Anthropologist* 106 (4): 663–74.

———. 2009. *Legalizing Identities: Becoming Black or Indian in Brazil's Northeast.* Chapel Hill: The University of North Carolina Press.

Friedemann, Nina S. de. 1984. "Estudios de Negros En La Antropología Colombiana: Presencia e Invisiblidad." In *Jaime Arocha y Nina S. de Friedeman (Eds.): Un Siglo de Investigación Social: Antropología En Colombia.*, 507–72. Bogotá: Editorial Etno.

García Linera, Álvaro. 2008. "Los Tres Pilares de La Nueva Constitución Política Del Estado. Estado Plurinacional, Economía Estatal y Estado Autonómico. Discurso Del Vicepresidente de La República Ciudadano Álvaro García Linera En La Sede de La Confederación Sindical Única de Trabajadores Campesinos de Bolivia. 4 de Noviembre de 2008." Vicepresidencia del Estado Plurinacional.

———. 2009. "El Estado Plurinacional. Discurso Del Ciudadano Vicepresidente Del Estado Plurinacional Álvaro García Linera En La Escuela de Fortalecimiento y Formación Política "Evo Morales Ayma". IV Seminario Taller 'La Nueva Bolivia'. La Paz, 10 de Marzo de 2009." Vicepresidencia del Estado Plurinacional.

Geschiere, Peter. 2009. *The Perils of Belonging: Autochthony, Citizenship, and Exclusion in Africa and Europe.* Chicago: University of Chicago Press.

Geschiere, Peter, and Stephen Jackson. 2006. "Autochthony and the Crisis of Citizenship: Democratization, Decentralization, and the Politics of Belonging." *African Studies Review* 49 (2): 1–7.

Geschiere, Peter, and Francis Nyamnjoh. 2000. "Capitalism and Autochthony: The Seesaw of Mobility and Belonging." *Public Culture* 12 (2): 423–52. https://doi.org/10.1215/08992363-12-2-423.

Gill, Lesley. 2000. *Teetering on the Rim: Global Restructuring, Daily Life, and the Armed Retreat of the Bolivian State.* New York: Columbia University Press.

Gilroy, Paul. 1993. *The Black Atlantic: Modernity and Double Consciousness.* Cambridge, Mass.: Harvard University Press.

Golash-Boza, Tanya Maria. 2012. *Yo Soy Negro: Blackness in Peru.* Gainesville, Fla.: University Press of Florida.

Goodale, Mark. 2006. "Reclaiming Modernity: Indigenous Cosmopolitanism and the Coming of the Second Revolution in Bolivia." *American Ethnologist* 33 (4): 634–649. https://doi.org/10.1525/ae.2006.33.4.634.

———. 2007. "The Power of Right(s): Tracking Empires of Law and New Modes of Social Resistance in Bolivia (and Elsewhere)." In *Mark Goodale and Sally Engle Merry (Eds.): The Practice of Human Rights: Tracking Law Between the Global and the Local*, 130–162. Cambridge, Mass.: Cambridge University Press.

———. 2009. *Dilemmas of Modernity: Bolivian Encounters with Law and Liberalism.* Stanford, Ca: Stanford University Press.

Goodale, Mark, and Nancy Grey Postero, eds. 2013. *Neoliberalism, Interrupted: Social Change and Contested Governance in Contemporary Latin America.* Stanford, Ca: Stanford University Press.

Gotkowitz, Laura. 2008. *A Revolution for Our Rights: Indigenous Struggles for Land and Justice in Bolivia, 1880–1952*. Durham: Duke University Press.

Greene, Shane. 2007a. "Entre Lo Indio, Lo Negro, y Lo Incaico: The Spatial Hierarchies of Difference in Multicultural Peru." *The Journal of Latin American and Caribbean Anthropology* 12 (2): 441–74. https://doi.org/10.1525/jlat.2007.12.2.441.

———. 2007b. "Introduction: On Race, Roots/Routes, and Sovereignty in Latin America's Afro-Indigenous Multiculturalisms." *The Journal of Latin American and Caribbean Anthropology* 12 (2): 329–55.

———. 2009. *Customizing Indigeneity: Paths to a Visionary Politics in Peru*. Stanford, Ca: Stanford University Press.

Grisaffi, Thomas. 2010. "We Are Originarios …'We Just Aren't from Here': Coca Leaf and Identity Politics in the Chapare, Bolivia." *Bulletin of Latin American Research* 29 (4): 425–39. https://doi.org/10.1111/j.1470-9856.2010.00385.x.

Gruzinksi, Serge. 2002. *The Mestizo Mind: The Intellectual Dynamics of Colonization and Globalization*. London: Routledge.

Guss, David M. 2000. *The Festive State. Race, Ethnicity, and Nationalism as Cultural Performance*. Berkeley: University of California Press.

Gustafson, Bret. 2009. "Manipulating Cartographies: Plurinationalism, Autonomy, and Indigenous Resurgence in Bolivia." *Anthropological Quarterly* 82(4): 985-1016.

Gutiérrez Brockington, Lolita. 2000. "The African Diaspora in the Eastern Andes: Adaptation, Agency, and Fugitive Action, 1573-1677." *The Americas* 57 (2): 207–224.

———. 2006. *Blacks, Indians, and Spaniards in the Eastern Andes: Reclaiming the Forgotten in Colonial Mizque, 1550-1782*. Lincoln: University of Nebraska Press.

Halbmayer, Ernst. 2011. "Indigene Kreolisierung, Kosmopolitismus Und Millenaristische Diskurse." In *Eva Gugenberger, Kathrin Sartingen (Eds..) Hybridität – Transkulturalität – Kreolisierung. Innovation Und Wandel in Kultur, Sprache Und Literatur Lateinamerikas.*, 51–71. Atención. Jahrbuch Des Österreichischen Lateinamerika-Instituts. Bd. 14. Wien, Berlin: LIT.

Hale, Charles R. 1996. "Introduction." *Journal of Latin American Anthropology* 2 (1): 2–3. https://doi.org/10.1525/jlca.1996.2.1.2.

———. 2008. "Neoliberal Multiculturalism: The Remaking of Cultural Rights and Racial Dominance in Central America." *PoLAR: Political and Legal Anthropology Review* 28 (1): 10–19.

Hale, Tamara. 2014. "Mixing and Its Challenges: An Ethnography of Race, Kinship and History in a Village of Afro-Indigenous Descent in Coastal Peru." PhD Thesis, The London School of Economics and Political Science (LSE). http://etheses.lse.ac.uk/1075/.

———. 2015. "A Non-Essentialist Theory of Race: The Case of an Afro-Indigenous Village in Northern Peru." *Social Anthropology* 23 (2): 135–51. https://doi.org/10.1111/1469-8676.12123.

Hall, Stuart. 1985. "Signification, Representation, Ideology: Althusser and the Post-structuralist Debates." *Critical Studies in Mass Communication* 2 (2): 91–114. https://doi.org/10.1080/15295038509360070.

———. 1986. "On Postmodernism and Articulation: An Interview with Stuart Hall." *Journal of Communication Inquiry* 10 (2): 131–50.

———. 1997. "Old and New Identities, Old and New Ethnicities." In *Anthony D. King (Ed.): Culture, Globalization and the World System: Contemporary Conditions for the Representation of Identity*, 41–68. Minneapolis: University of Minnesota Press.

Handler, Joel F. 1979. *Social Movements and the Legal System: A Theory of Law Reform and Social Change*. London: Academic Press.

Hart, Gillian. 2001. "Development Critiques in the 1990s: Culs de Sac and Promising Paths." *Progress in Human Geography* 25 (4): 649–58.

Healy, Kevin, and Susan Paulson. 2000. "Political Economies of Identity in Bolivia 1952-1998." *Journal of Latin American Anthropology* 5 (2): 2–29. https://doi.org/10.1525/jlca.2000.5.2.2.

Heath, Dwight B. 1972. "New Patrons for Old: Changing Patron-Client Relationships in the Bolivian Yungas." In *Arnold Stricken and Sidney M. Greenfield (Eds.): Structure and Process in Latin America: Patronage, Clientage, and Power Systems*, 101–38. Santa Fe: SAR Press.

Herskovits, Melville J. 1990. *The Myth of the Negro Past*. New edition. Boston: Beacon Press.

Hodgson, Dorothy Louise. 2002. "Introduction: Comparative Perspectives on the Indigenous Rights Movement in Africa and the Americas." *American Anthropologist* 104 (4): 1037–49.

———. 2009. "Becoming Indigenous in Africa." *African Studies Review* 52 (3): 1–32.

———. 2011. *Being Maasai, Becoming Indigenous. Postcolonial Politics in a Neoliberal World*. Bloomington, Ind.: Indiana University Press.

Hooker, Juliet. 2005. "Indigenous Inclusion/Black Exclusion: Race, Ethnicity and Multicultural Citizenship in Latin America." *Journal of Latin American Studies* 37 (2): 285–310.

———. 2008. "Afro-Descendant Struggles for Collective Rights in Latin America: Between Race and Culture." *Souls* 10 (3): 279–91.

Huneeus, Alexandra, Javier Couso, and Rachel Sieder. 2010. "Cultures of Legality: Judicialization and Political Activism in Contemporary Latin America." In *Javier Couso, Alexandra Huneeus and Rachel Sieder (Eds.): Cultures of Legality: Judicialization and Political Activism in Latin America*, 3–21. Cambridge: Cambridge Univerity Press.

Jackson, Jean E. 1991. "Being and Becoming an Indian in the Vaupés." In *Greg Urban and Joel Sherzer (Eds.:): Nation States and Indians in Latin America*, 131–55. Austin: University of Texas Press.

———. 1995. "Culture, Genuine and Spurious: The Politics of Indianness in the Vaupés, Colombia." *American Ethnologist* 22 (1): 3–27. https://doi.org/10.2307/646044.

Jackson, Jean E., and Kay B. Warren. 2005. "Indigenous Movements in Latin America, 1992-2004: Controversies, Ironies, New Directions." *Annual Review of Anthropology* 34: 549–573.

Jenkins, Richard. 2000. "Categorization: Identity, Social Process and Epistemology." *Current Sociology* 48 (3): 7–25.

———. 2008. *Rethinking Ethnicity*. 2nd edition. Los Angeles: SAGE Publications Ltd.

———. 2014. *Social Identity*. 4th Revised edition. New York: Routledge.

Kelley, Jonathan, and Herbert S. Klein. 1981. *Revolution and the Rebirth of Inequality: A Theory of Inequality and Inherited Privilege Applied to the Bolivian National Revolution*. Berkeley: University of California Press.

Kent, Allison D. 2001. "La Identidad Afroboliviana En Chicaloma, Sud Yungas." In *XIV Reunión Anual de Etnología*, 1:483–92. Anales de La Reuníon Anual de Etnología. La Paz: MUSEF.

Klein, Herbert S. 2011. *A Concise History of Bolivia*. 2nd edition. Cambridge: Cambridge University Press.

Kohl, Benjamin, and Linda C. Farthing. 2006. *Impasse in Bolivia: Neoliberal Hegemony and Popular Resistance*. London; New York: Zed Books.

Komadina, George, and Pablo Regalsky. 2016. *La Política de La Saya. El Movimiento Afroboliviano*. La Paz: Plural/AJWS.

Kuper, Adam. 2003. "The Return of the Native." *Current Anthropology* 44 (3): 389–402.

Kymlicka, Will, and Wayne Norman. 2000. "Citizenship in Culturally Diverse Societies: Issues, Contexts, Concepts." In *Will Kymlicka and Wayne Norman (Eds.): Citizenship in Diverse Societies*, 1–41. Oxford: Oxford University Press.

Lacroix, Laurent. 2012. "Indigenous Territoriality and Political Agenda in Bolivia (1970-2010)." *HAL. Archive Ouverte En Sciences de l'Homme et de La Société*. https://halshs.archives-ouvertes.fr/halshs-00738479.

Larson, Brooke. 2004. *Trials of Nation Making: Liberalism, Race, and Ethnicity in the Andes, 1810-1910*. Cambridge, Mass.: Cambridge University Press.

Lazar, Sian. 2008. *El Alto, Rebel City: Self and Citizenship in Andean Bolivia*. Durham, London: Duke Univeristy Press.

Lentz, Carola. 2006. *Ethnicity and the Making of History in Northern Ghana*. Edinburgh: Edinburgh University Press.

Léons, Madeline Barbara. 1966. *Changing Patterns of Social Stratification in an Emergent Bolivian Community*. PhD Thesis, University of California at Los Angeles.

———. 1967. "Land Reform in the Bolivian Yungas." *America Indígena* XXVII (4): 689–713.

———. 1978. "Race, Ethnicity, and Political Mobilization in the Andes." *American Ethnologist* 5 (3): 484–494.

———. 1998. "Stratification and Pluralism in the Bolivian Yungas." In *Norman E. Whitten, Jr. and Arlene Torres (Eds.): Blackness in Latin America and the Caribbean: Social Dynamics and Cultural Transformations. Vol 1. Central America and Western South America*, 1:335–56. Bloomington: Indiana University Press.

Léons, Madeline Barbara, and William Léons. 1971. "Land Reform and Economic Change in the Yungas." In *James M. Malloy and Richard Thorn (Eds.):Beyond the Revolution: Bolivia since 1952*, 269–99. Pittsburgh: University of Pittsburgh Press.

Léons, Madeline Barbara, and Harry Sanabria, eds. 1997. *Coca, Cocaine, and the Bolivian Reality*. Albany: SUNY Press.

Léons, William. 1972. "Dimensions of Pluralism in a Changing Bolivian Community." PhD Thesis Anthropology, Pennsylvania State University.

———. 1974. "Las Relaciones Etnicas de Una Comunidad Multi-Racial En Los Yungas Bolivianos." *Estudios Andinos* Año 4, Vol. IV (No.2): 161–77.

Levi, Jerome M., and Biorn Maybury-Lewis. 2012. "Becoming Indigenous: Identity and Heterogeneity in a Global Movement." In *Gillette G. Hall and Harry Anthony Patrinos (Eds.): Indigenous Peoples, Poverty, and Development*, 73–117. Cambridge: Cambridge University Press.

Li, Tania Murray. 2000. "Articulating Indigenous Identity in Indonesia: Resource Politics and the Tribal Slot." *Comparative Studies in Society and History* 42 (1): 149–179.

Lipski, John M. 2007. "Afro-Yungueno Speech: The Long-Lost" Black Spanish"." *Spanish in Context* 4 (1): 1–43.

———. 2008. *Afro-Bolivian Spanish*. Madrid: Iberoamericana Vervuert.

———. 2012. "Africanisms in Afro-Bolivian Spanish." www.personal.psu.edu/jml34/afrobolbt w.pdf.

Lisocka-Jaegermann, Bogumila. 2010. "Los Afrodescendientes En Los Países Andinos. El Caso de Bolivia." *Revista Del CESLA* Vol. 1 (13): 317–29.

Loza, H., and M. Méndez. 1981. *Apuntes Sobre Colonización. Parte II. La Colonización En Alto Beni*. La Paz, Bolivia: Editorial Crítica.

Luykx, Aurolyn. 1999. *The Citizen Factory: Schooling and Cultural Production in Bolivia*. New York: SUNY Press.

Mallon, Florencia E. 1996. "Constructing Mestizaje in Latin America: Authenticity, Marginality, and Gender in the Claiming of Ethnic Identities." *Journal of Latin American Anthropology* 2 (1): 170–181. https://doi.org/10.1525/jlca.1996.2.1.170.

Malloy, James M., and Richard Thorn, eds. 1971. *Beyond the Revolution: Bolivia since 1952*. Pittsburgh: University of Pittsburgh Press.

Marcus, George E. 1995. "Ethnography in/of the World System: The Emergence of Multi-Sited Ethnography." *Annual Review of Anthropology* 24 (1): 95–117. https://doi.org/10.1146/annurev.an.24.100195.000523.

Matory, J. Lorand. 2005. *Black Atlantic Religion: Tradition, Transnationalism, and Matriarchy in the Afro-Brazilian Candomble*. Princeton, NJ: Princeton University Press.

McCann, Michael W. 1994. *Rights at Work: Pay Equity Reform and the Politics of Legal Mobilization*. Chicago: University of Chicago Press.

McEwen, William J. 1975. *Changing Rural Society: Study of Communities in Bolivia*. New York: Oxford University Press.

Mendoza Salazar, David. 1992. *El Negro No Es Un Color, Es Una Saya*. La Paz: Gobierno Municipal de La Paz.

Merry, Sally Engle. 2003. "Rights Talk and the Experience of Law: Implementing Women's Human Rights to Protection from Violence." *Human Rights Quarterly* 25 (2): 343–81.

———. 2006. "Transnational Human Rights and Local Activism: Mapping the Middle." *American Anthropologist* 108 (1): 38–51.

Mesa, José de, Teresa Gisbert, and Carlos Mesa Gisbert. 2008. *Historia de Bolivia*. 7. edición actualizada y aumentada. La Paz: Editorial Gisbert.

Miller, Marilyn Grace. 2004. *Rise and Fall of the Cosmic Race: The Cult of Mestizaje in Latin America*. 1st edition. Austin: University of Texas Press.

Ministerio de Culturas y Turismo - Viceministerio de Turismo. 2017. *Guía Turística. Emprendimientos Comunitarios*.

Minority Rights Group. 1995. *No Longer Invisible: Afro-Latin Americans Today*. London: Minority Rights Publications.

Mintz, Sidney W., and Eric R. Wolf. 1950. "An Analysis of Ritual Co-Parenthood (Compadrazgo)." *Southwestern Journal of Anthropology* 6 (4): 341–68.

Montaño, Sonia. 2016. "Diálogo. Violencia Contra La Mujer En Bolivia: Leyes Que No Se Cumplen." *T'inkazos* 19 (39): 9–26.

Muratorio, Blanca. 1969. "Participación Social y Política de Los Campesinos de Nor Yungas, Bolivia." *Revista Mexicana de Sociología* 31 (4): 909–45. https://doi.org/10.2307/3538925.

Nader, Laura. 2002. *The Life of the Law: Anthropological Projects*. Berkeley: University of California Press.

Ng'weno, Bettina. 2007. "Can Ethnicity Replace Race? Afro-Colombians, Indigeneity and the Colombian Multicultural State." *The Journal of Latin American and Caribbean Anthropology* 12 (2): 414–40. https://doi.org/10.1525/jlat.2007.12.2.414.

Niezen, Ronald. 2003. *The Origins of Indigenism. Human Rights and the Politics of Identity*. Berkeley: University of California Press.

Nolte, Detlef, and Almut Schilling-Vacaflor, eds. 2012. *New Constitutionalism in Latin America. Promises and Practices*. Farnham, Surrey; Burlington, VT: Ashgate.

O'Toole, Rachel Sarah. 2012. *Bound Lives. Africans, Indians, and the Making of Race in Colonial Peru*. Pittsburgh: University of Pittsburgh Press.

Parkin, David J., Lionel Caplan, and Humphrey J. Fisher, eds. 1996. *The Politics of Cultural Performance*. New York: Berghahn Books.

Pearse, Andrew. 1972. "Peasants and Revolution: The Case of Bolivia." *Economy and Society* 1 (4): 399–424. https://doi.org/10.1080/03085147200000022.

Pelican, Michaela. 2009. "Complexities of Indigeneity and Autochthony: An African Example." *American Ethnologist* 36 (1): 52–65.

———. 2015. *Masks and Staffs: Identity Politics in the Cameroon Grassfields*. New York: Berghahn Books.

Pellegrini Calderón, Alessandra. 2016. *Beyond Indigeneity: Coca Growing and the Emergence of a New Middle Class in Bolivia*. Tucson: University of Arizona Press.

Pérez Inofuentes, Danae. 2010. "Polvadera Se Levanta. Las Estrategias Reivindicativas de La Comunidad Afroboliviana." *LARevista, Bolletin, Société Suisse Des Americanistes*, No. 72: 49–57.

———. 2015. "Traces of Portuguese in Afro-Yungueño Spanish?" *Journal of Pidgin and Creole Languages* 30 (2): 307–43. https://doi.org/10.1075/jpcl.30.2.04per.

Pizarroso Cuenca, Arturo. 1977. *La Cultura Negra En Bolivia*. La Paz: Ediciones ISLA.

Portugal Ortiz, Max. 1977. *La Esclavitud Negra En Las Épocas Colonial y Nacional de Bolivia*. La Paz: Instituto Boliviano de Cultura.

Postero, Nancy Grey. 2006. *Now We Are Citizens: Indigenous Politics in Post-Multicultural Bolivia*. Stanford, Ca: Stanford University Press.

———. 2013. "Introduction: Negotiating Indigeneity." *Latin American and Caribbean Ethnic Studies* 8 (2): 107–21. https://doi.org/10.1080/17442222.2013.810013.

———. 2017. *The Indigenous State. Race, Politics, and Performance in Plurinational Bolivia*. Oakland: University of California Press.

Postero, Nancy Grey, and León Zamosc, eds. 2004. *The Struggle For Indigenous Rights In Latin America*. Eastbourne: Sussex Academic Press.

Quispe, Filemón. 1994. "Historía y Tradición: La Música Afroboliviana." In *Reunión Anual de Etnología 1993*, Tomo II:155–84. Anales de La Reunión Anual de Etnología. La Paz: MUSEF.

Rahier, Jean Muteba. 2008. "Soccer and the (Tri-) Color of the Ecuadorian Nation: Visual and Ideological (Dis-) Continuities of Black Otherness from Monocultural Mestizaje to Multiculturalism." *Visual Anthropology Review* 24 (2): 148–182.

———., ed. 2012a. *Black Social Movements in Latin America: From Monocultural Mestizaje to Multiculturalism*. New York: Palgrave Macmillan.

———. 2012b. "Introduction. Black Social Movements in Latin America: From Monocultural Mestizaje and 'Invisibility' to Multiculturalism and State Corporatism/Co-Optation." In *Jean Muteba Rahier (Ed.): Black Social Movements in Latin America: From Monocultural Mestizaje to Multiculturalism*, 1–14. New York: Palgrave Macmillan.

———. 2014. *Blackness in the Andes: Ethnographic Vignettes of Cultural Politics in the Time of Multiculturalism*. New York: Palgrave Macmillan.

Rajagopal, Balakrishnan. 2003. *International Law from Below: Development, Social Movements and Third World Resistance*. Cambridge, U.K.; New York: Cambridge University Press.

Rappaport, Joanne. 2014. *The Disappearing Mestizo: Configuring Difference in the Colonial New Kingdom of Granada*. Durham: Duke University Press Books.

Restall, Matthew, ed. 2005. *Beyond Black and Red: African-Native Relations in Colonial Latin America*. Albuquerque: University of New Mexico Press.

———. 2009. *The Black Middle: Africans, Mayas, and Spaniards in Colonial Yucatan*. Stanford, Ca: Stanford University Press.

Restrepo, Eduardo. 2004. "Ethnicization of Blackness in Colombia." *Cultural Studies* 18 (5): 698–753.

———. 2007. "Commentary: El 'Giro Al Multiculturalismo' Desde Un Encuadre Afro-Indígena." *The Journal of Latin American and Caribbean Anthropology* 12 (2): 475–486.

———. 2009. "Eventalizing Blackness in Colombia. PhD Thesis." Chapel Hill: University of North Carolina at Chapel Hill.

Revilla Orías, Paola. 2011. "'Mi Esclava, La Negra María, Está Inquieta Desde Que Escuchó Al Indio Francisco Tocar El Harpa': Gestos, Miradas y Afectos Ignorados, Charcas (1632-1822)"." In *Historias de Mujeres. Mujeres, Familias, Historias. Anales Del Encuentro MUSEF, Sucre 2010*, 19–34. Santa Cruz, Bolivia: El País.

———. 2013a. "Bailando Memorias Negras: La Crítica Afroboliviana a Su Representación." In *María de Lourdes Ghidoli y Juan Francisco Martinez Peria (Eds.): Estudios Afrolatinoamericanos: Nuevos Enfoques Multidisciplinarios: Actas de Las Terceras Jornadas Del GEALA*, 149–62. Buenos Aires: Ediciones del CCC Centro Cultural de la Cooperación Floreal Gorini.

———. 2013b. "'Manuel de La Cruz Dice Ser Casi Negro y No Indio': Estrategias de Negociación Identitaria de La Población Afrodescendiente Ante La Justicia Charqueña (Siglos XVII-XVIII)." *Anuario de La Sociedad Boliviana de Historia Del Derecho* 1 (1): 233–52.

———. 2014a. "De Coronaciones y Otras Memorias. Afrobolivianos y Estado Plurinacional." *T'inkazos* 17 (36): 121–31.

———. 2014b. "¡Morir Antes Que Esclavos Vivir!: República Libertaria y Esclavitud En Bolivia Decimonónica." In *Nicholas Robins and Rosario Barahona (Eds.): Mitos Expuestos: Falsas Leyendas de Bolivia*. Cochabamba: Kipus.

———. 2015. "'Yo Hijo Mío, Haré Cuanto Pueda Por Vos...De Esclavos Que Deciden No Estar a La Merced de Sus Amos (Charcas, Siglo XVIII).'" *Historia y Cultura. Revista de La Sociedad Boliviana de La Historia*, no. 38–39: 85–103.

Revilla Orías, Paola, and Fernando Cajías de la Vega. 2017. "Balance Historiográfico Sobre Afrodescendencia En Bolivia (Siglos Xvi-Xxi)." *Historia y Cultura*, no. 40: 37–57.

Rey, Mónica. 1998. *La Saya Como Medio de Comunicación y Expresión Cultural En La Comunidad Afroboliviana. Tesis Para Optar Al Título de Licenciatura En Comunicación Social*. La Paz: UMSA.

Rocha Torrez, Eveline. 2007. "Tanz Im Spiegel von Anerkennung Und Macht Oder Aus „schwarz' Mach „weiß'..." *Die Maske. Zeitschrift Für Kultur- Und Sozialanthropologie*, no. 1 (Juni 2007): 59–61.

Rodríguez-Carmona, Antonio. 2008. *El Proyectorado: Bolivia Tras 20 Años de Ayuda Externa*. La Paz, Bolivia: Intermón Oxfam.

———. 2009. *Rompiendo Con El Proyectorado: El Gobierno Del MAS En Bolivia*. La Paz, Bolivia: Plural/Itaca.

Rosaldo, Renato. 1994. "Cultural Citizenship in San Jose, California." *PoLAR: Political and Legal Anthropology Review* 17 (2): 57–64.

Rossbach de Olmos, Lioba. 2007. "Expresiones Controvertidas: Afrobolivianos y Su Cultura Entre Presentaciones y Representaciones." *Indiana* 24: 173–90.

———. 2009. "¿Qué Pasa Con El Pacífico Negro En El Atlántico Negro? El Atlántico Negro de Paul Gilroy Frente a Los Acontecimientos (Afro)Colombianos." *Memorias. Revista Semestral de Historia y Arqueologia Del Caribe.*, Uninorte. Barranquilla, Colombia, No.11. http://rcientificas.uninorte.edu.co/index.php/memorias/article/viewArticle/519/5112.

———. 2011. "Dinámicas Controvertidas Entre Expresión Étnica-Cultural y Articulación Política." *Memorias. Revista Semestral de Historia y Arqueologia Del Caribe.*, Uninorte. Barranquilla, Colombia, No. 15. http://rcientificas.uninorte.edu. co/index.php/memorias/article/viewArticle/2122.

Rossbach de Olmos, Lioba, and Heike Drotbohm. 2009. "Einleitung: Ethnologie in der Diaspora – Gestern und Heute." In *Heike Drotbohm and Lioba Rossbach de Olmos (Eds.): Kontrapunkte. Theoretische Transitionen Und Empirischer Transfer in Der Afroamerikaforschung. Beiträge Der Regionalgruppe Afroamerika Auf Der Tagung Der Deutschen Gesellschaft Für Völkerkunde in Halle (Saale) 2007.*, 7–24. Marburg: Curupira.

Rycroft, Daniel J, and Sangeeta Dasgupta, eds. 2011. *The Politics of Belonging in India: Becoming Adivasi*. New York: Routledge.

Sánchez Canedo, Walter. 2010. "Sin Purezas y Con Mezclas. Las Cambiantes Identidades Sonoras Negro-Africanas En Bolivia." In *Albert Recasens Barberà (Ed.): A Tres Bandas: Mestizaje, Sincretismo e Hibridación En El Espacio Sonoro Iberoamericano*, 115–23. Madrid: Sociedad Estatal Para La Acción Cultural Exterior/Ediciones Akal.

———. 2011. "Identidades Sonoras de Los Afro-Descendientes de Bolivia." *Traspatios*, no. 2, Marzo: 145–71.

Schavelzon, Salvador. 2012. *El Nacimiento Del Estado Plurinacional de Bolivia. Etnografía de Una Asamblea Constituyente*. La Paz: Plural.

Scheingold, Stuart A. 2004. *The Politics of Rights: Lawyers, Public Policy, and Political Change*. 2nd edition. Ann Arbor: University of Michigan Press.

Scheuzger, Stephan. 2007. "Die Re-Ethnisierung Gesellschaftlicher Beziehungen. Neuere Indigene Bewegungen." In *Bernecker, Walther; Kaller-Dietrich, Martina;*

Potthast, Barbara et. Al. (Eds.):Lateinamerika 1870-2000. Geschichte Und Gesellschaft, 191–211. Wien: Promedia.

Schilling-Vacaflor, Almut. 2010. *Recht Als Umkämpftes Terrain: Die Neue Verfassung Und Indigene Völker in Bolivien*. Studien Zu Lateinamerika. Baden-Baden: Nomos.

Schilling-Vacaflor, Almut, Ulrich Brand, and Isabella Radhuber, eds. 2012. *Plurinationale Demokratie in Bolivien. Gesellschaftliche Und Staatliche Transformationen*. Münster: Verlag Westfälisches Dampfboot.

Schlee, Günther. 1997. "Cross-Cutting Ties and Interethnic Conflict: The Example of Gabbra Oromo and Rendille." In *Katsuyoshi Fukui, Eisei Kurimoto and Masayoshi Shigeta (Eds.): Ethiopia in Broader Perspective: Papers of 13th International Conference of Ethiopian Studies, Vol. II.*, 577–96. Kyoto: Shokado.

———. 2004. "Taking Sides and Constructing Identities: Reflections on Conflict Theory." *The Journal of the Royal Anthropological Institute* 10 (1): 135–56.

———. 2008. *How Enemies Are Made: Towards a Theory of Ethnic and Religious Conflict*. New York: Berghahn Books.

Scott, James C. 1998. *Seeing like a State: How Certain Schemes to Improve the Human Condition Have Failed*. New Haven: Yale University Press.

Sessarego, Sandro. 2011a. *Introducción Al Idioma Afroboliviano. Una Conversación Con El Awicho Manuel Barra*. La Paz: Plural.

———. 2011b. "On the Status of Afro-Bolivian Spanish Features: Decreolization or Vernacular Universals?" In *Jim Michnowicz and Robin Dodsworth (Eds.): Selected Proceedings of the 5th Workshop on Spanish Sociolinguistics*, 125–41. Somerville, MA: Cascadilla Proceedings Project.

———. 2014. *The Afro-Bolivian Spanish Determiner Phrase: A Microparametric Account*. Columbus: Ohio State University Press.

Shakow, Miriam. 2014. *Along the Bolivian Highway. Social Mobility and Political Culture in a New Middle Class*. Philadelphia: University of Pennsylvania Press.

Shultz, Jim, and Melissa Crane Draper, eds. 2009. *Dignity and Defiance: Stories from Bolivia's Challenge to Globalization*. Berkeley: University of California Press.

Sieder, Rachel. 2010. "Legal Cultures in the (Un) Rule of Law: Indigenous Rights and Juridification in Guatemala." In *Javier Couso, Alexandra Huneeus and Rachel Sieder (Eds.): Cultures of Legality: Judicialization and Political Activism in Latin America*, 161–81. Cambridge: Cambridge University Press.

Sieder, Rachel, Line Schjolden, and Alan Angell. 2005a. "Introduction." In *Rachel Sieder, Line Schjolden, and Alan Angell (Eds.): The Judicialization of Politics in Latin America*, 1–20. New York: Palgrave Macmillan.

———., eds. 2005b. *The Judicialization of Politics in Latin America*. New York: Palgrave Macmillan.

Sigl, Eveline, and David Mendoza Salazar. 2012. *No Se Baila Así No Más...* Vol. I: género, poder, política, etnicidad, clase, religión y biodiversidad en las danzas del altiplano boliviano. II vols. La Paz, Bolivia: Greco SRL.

Soruco Sologruen, Ximena. 2012. “Coloquio. Mestizajes y Ascenso Social En Bolivia.” *T'inkazos* 15 (31): 9–24.

Sousa Santos, Boaventura de. 2002. *Toward a New Legal Common Sense: Law, Globalization, and Emancipation*. Cambridge: Cambridge University Press.

Sousa Santos, Boaventura de, and César A Rodríguez-Garavito, eds. 2005a. *Law and Globalization from below: Towards a Cosmopolitan Legality*. Cambridge: Cambridge University Press.

Sousa Santos, Boaventura de, and Cesar A. Rodríguez-Garavito. 2005b. “Law, Politics, and the Subalten in Counter-Hegemonic Globalization.” In *Boaventura de Sousa Santos and Cesar A. Rodríguez-Garavito (Eds.): Law and Globalization from below: Towards a Cosmopolitan Legality*, 1–26. Cambridge: Cambridge University Press.

Soux, María Luisa. 1993. *La Coca Liberal: Producción y Circulación a Principios Del Siglo XX*. La Paz, Bolivia: Misión de Cooperación Técnica Holandesa.

Spedding, Alison. 1994. *Wachu Wachu: Cultivo De Coca e Identidad En Los Yunkas De La Paz*. La Paz, Bolivia: Hisbol - Cipca.

———. 1995. “Bolivia.” In *Minority Rights Group: No Longer Invisible: Afro-Latin Americans Today*, 319–31. London: Minority Rights Group.

———. 1996. “Morir En Yungas.” *Revista Del Museo Nacional de Etnografía y Folklore*, no. Número Doble 7-8: 75–146.

———. 1997. “The Coca Field as a Total Social Fact.” In *Madeline Barbara Léons and Harry Sanabria (Eds.): Coca, Cocaine, and the Bolivian Reality*, 47–70. Albany: SUNY Press.

———. 2004. *Kawsachun Coca. Economía Campesina Cocalera En Los Yungas y El Chapare*. La Paz, Bolivia: Fundación PIEB.

———. 2009. “Los Yungas y El Norte de La Paz: Cocaleros, Colonizadores y Afrobolivianos.” In *Denise Y. Arnold (Ed.): Indígenas u Obreros? La Construcción de Identidades En El Altiplano Boliviano*, 429–70. La Paz: Fundación UNIR.

———. 2013. *Chulumani Flor de Clavel. Transformaciones Urbanas y Rurales, 1998-2012*. La Paz, Bolivia: Fundación PIEB.

———. 2014. “Almas, Anchanchus y Alaridos En La Noche: El Paisaje Vivificado de Un Valle Yungueño.” In *Silvia Arze, Rossana Barragán, Laura Escobari and Ximena Medinaceli (Eds.): Etnicidad, Economía y Simbolismo En Los Andes. II Congreso Internacional de Etnohistoria. Coroico*, 229–330. Lima: Institut français d'études andines. https://books.openedition.org/ifea/2312.

Spedding, Alison, and Abraham Colque. 2003. *Nosotros Los Yungueños: Testimonios de Los Yungueños Del Siglo XX*. La Paz Bolivia: PIEB, Mama Huaco.

Spedding, Alison, and David Llanos. 1999. *“No Hay Ley Para La Cosecha”. Un Estudio Comparativo Del Sistema Productivo y Las Relcaiones Sociales En Chari (Provinicia Bautista Saavedra) y Chulumani (Provincia Sud Yungas), La Paz*. La Paz, Bolivia: PIEB.

Spitzer, Steven. 1983. "Marxist Perspectives in the Sociology of Law." *Annual Review of Sociology* 9 (January): 103–24.

Stefanoni, Pablo. 2010. *"Qué Hacer Con Los Indios…" y Otros Traumas Irresueltos de La Colonialidad*. La Paz, Bolivia: Plural.

Ströbele-Gregor, Juliana, Bert Hoffman, and Andrew Holmes. 1994. "From Indio to Mestizo… to Indio: New Indianist Movements in Bolivia." *Latin American Perspectives* 21 (2): 106–23. https://doi.org/10.1177/0094582X9402100207.

Sturtevant, Charles Carter. 2013. "I Was Born Here: Community and Belonging in an Afro-Bolivian Town." Thesis MPhil in Ethnographic Documentary. The University of Manchester.https://www.escholar.manchester.ac.uk/item/?pid=uk-ac-man-scw:208089.

———. 2017. "Claiming belonging, constructing social spaces: Citizenship practices in an Afro-Bolivian town." *Critique of Anthropology*. 37(1): 3-26. DOI: 10.1177/0308275 X16671789.

Stutzman, Ronald. 1981. "El Mestizaje: An All-Inclusive Ideology of Exclusion." In *Norman E. Whitten, Jr. (Ed.): Cultural Transformations and Ethnicity in Modern Ecuador*, 45–94. Urbana: University of Illinois Press.

Templeman, Robert W. 1995. "Renacimiento de La Saya: El Rol Que Juega La Música En El Movimiento Negro En Bolivia." In *Reunión Anual de Etnología 1995*, 89–94. La Paz: Banco Central de Bolivia.

———. 1998. "We Are the People of the Yungas, We Are the Saya Race." In *Norman E. Whitten, Jr. and Arlene Torres (Eds.): Blackness in Latin America and the Caribbean: Social Dynamics and Cultural Transformations. Vol 1. Central America and Western South America*, 426–44. Bloomington: Indiana University Press.

Torrez, Yuri F., and María Teresa Zegada. 2008. *Movimientos Sociales En Tiempos de Poder. Articulaciones y Campos de Conflicto En El Gobierno Del MAS (2006-2007)*. La Paz: Centro Cuarto Intermedio/Plural Editores.

Tyson, Adam D. 2010. *Decentralization and Adat Revivalism in Indonesia: The Politics of Becoming Indigenous*. New York: Routledge.

Van Cott, Donna Lee. 2000. *The Friendly Liquidation of the Past. The Politics of Diversity in Latin America*. Pittsburgh: University of Pittsburgh Press.

———. 2005. *From Movements to Parties in Latin America: The Evolution of Ethnic Politics*. Cambridge: Cambridge University Press.

Van Vleet, Krista E. 2008. *Performing Kinship: Narrative, Gender, and the Intimacies of Power in the Andes*. Austin: University of Texas Press.

Wade, Peter. 1993. *Blackness and Race Mixture. The Dynamics of Racial Identity in Colombia*. Baltimore and London: The Johns Hopkins University Press.

———. 1995. "The Cultural Politics of Blackness in Colombia." *American Ethnologist* 22 (2): 341–357.

———. 1999. "Working Culture: Making Cultural Identities in Cali, Colombia." *Current Anthropology* 40 (4): 449–72. https://doi.org/10.1086/200045.

———. 2004. "Human Nature and Race." *Anthropological Theory* 4 (2): 157–72.

———. 2005. "Rethinking Mestizaje: Ideology and Lived Experience." *Journal of Latin American Studies* 37 (02): 239–257.

———. 2006a. "Afro-Latin Studies. Reflections on the Field." *Latin American and Caribbean Ethnic Studies* Vol. 1 (1): 105–124.

———. 2006b. "Understanding 'Africa' and 'Blackness' in Colombia. Music and the Politics of Culture." In *Kevin A. Yelvington (Ed.): Afro-Atlantic Dialogues: Anthropology in the Diaspora*, 351–78. Santa Fe: School of American Research Press.

———. 2008. "Race in Latin America." In *Deborah Poole (Ed.): A Companion to Latin American Anthropology*, 177–92. London: Wiley-Blackwell.

———. 2009a. *Race and Sex in Latin America*. London: Pluto Press.

———. 2009b. *Race, Ethnicity and Nation: Perspectives from Kinship and Genetics*. New York: Berghan Books.

———. 2009c. "Defining Blackness in Colombia." *Journal de La Société Des Américanistes* 95 (95–1): 165–84. https://doi.org/10.4000/jsa.10783.

———. 2010. *Race and Ethnicity in Latin America*. 2nd Edition. London and Chicago: Pluto Press.

———. 2013. "Blackness, Indigeneity, Multiculturalism and Genomics in Brazil, Colombia and Mexico." *Journal of Latin American Studies* 45 (2): 205–233.

———. 2015. *Race: An Introduction*. Cambridge: Cambridge University Press.

———. 2017. *Degrees of Mixture, Degrees of Freedom: Genomics, Multiculturalism, and Race in Latin America*. Durham: Duke University Press Books.

Wade, Peter, Carlos López Beltrán, Eduardo Restrepo, and Ricardo Ventura Santos, eds. 2014. *Mestizo Genomics: Race Mixture, Nation, and Science in Latin America*. Durham: Duke University Press Books.

Wade, Peter, Vivette García Deister, Michael Kent, María Fernanda Olarte Sierra, and Adriana Díaz del Castillo Hernández. 2014. "Nation and the Absent Presence of Race in Latin American Genomics." *Current Anthropology* 55 (5): 497–522. https://doi.org/10.1086/677945.

Walsh, Catherine, and Edizon León. 2006. "Afro-Andean Thought and Diasporic Ancestrality." In *Marina Paola Banchetti-Robino and Clevis Ronald Headley (Eds.): Shifting the Geography of Reason: Gender, Science and Religion.*, 211–24. Newcastle: Cambridge Scholars Press.

Weismantel, Mary. 2001. *Cholas and Pishtacos: Stories of Race and Sex in the Andes*. Chicago: University Of Chicago Press.

Whitten, Norman E., Jr. 2007. "The Longue Durée of Racial Fixity and the Transformative Conjunctures of Racial Blending." *The Journal of Latin American and Caribbean Anthropology* 12 (2): 356–383. https://doi.org/10.1525/jlat.2007.12.2.356.

Whitten, Norman E., Jr., and Arlene Torres, eds. 1998. *Blackness in Latin America and the Caribbean: Social Dynamics and Cultural Transformations. Vol 1. Central America and Western South America*. Bloomington: Indiana University Press.

Wolff, Inge. 1964. "'Negersklaverei Und Negerhandel in Hochperu 1545-1640.'" *Jahrbuch Für Geschichte Und Staat, Wirtschaft Und Gesellschaft Lateinamerikas (Köln)* 1: 157–86.

Yashar, Deborah J. 2005. *Contesting Citizenship in Latin America: The Rise of Indigenous Movements and the Postliberal Challenge*. Cambridge: Cambridge University Press.

Yelvington, Kevin A. 2001. "The Anthropology of Afro-Latin America and the Caribbean: Diasporic Dimensions." *Annual Review of Anthropology* 30 (1): 227–60. https://doi.org/10.1146/annurev.anthro.30.1.227.

———. , ed. 2006. *Afro-Atlantic Dialogues: Anthropology in the Diaspora*. Santa Fe: School of American Research Press.

Zambrana B., Amilcar, ed. 2014. *El Pueblo Afroboliviano. Historia, Cultura y Economía*. Cochabamba/ La Paz: FUNPROEIB Andes/CONAFRO.

Zenker, Olaf. 2011. "Autochthony, Ethnicity, Indigeneity and Nationalism: Time-Honouring and State-Oriented Modes of Rooting Individual-Territory-Group Triads in a Globalizing World." *Critique of Anthropology* 31 (1): 63–81. https://doi.org/10.1177/0308275X10393438.

Newspaper articles

BBC News 2009: "Hidden kingdom of the Afro-Bolivians", http://news.bbc.co.uk/2/hi/americas/7958783.stm [26/09/2018].

El Cambio 2012: Çongreso afroboliviano debatirá sobre justicia y discriminación", http://www.cambio.bo/sociedad/20120907/congreso_afroboliviano_debatira_sobre_justicia_y_discriminacion_78884.htm [18/01/2013].

El País 2016: "The last king of the Americas", https://elpais.com/elpais/2016/11/11/inenglish/1478859420_050367.html [26/09/2018].

The Guardian 2007: "Bolivia's African king", https://www.theguardian.com/world/2007/dec/10/bolivia-senegal [26/09/2018].

Laws and documents

Bolivian Laws (available at the homepage of the *Gaceta Oficial del Estado Plurinacional de Bolivia:* www.gacetaoficialdebolivia.gob.bo)

Constitución Política del Estado Plurinacional de Bolivia 2009

Constitución Política del Estado 1967 (reformed in 1994)

Ley No. 045 del 8 de Octubre de 2010: Ley contra el Racismo y toda forma de discriminación

Ley No. 070 del 20 de Diciembre de 2010: Ley de la Educación "AVELINO SIÑANI - ELIZARDO PÉREZ"

Ley No. 138 del 14 de Junio de 2011: Declárase Patrimonio Histórico Cultural e Inmaterial del Estado Plurinacional de Bolivia a la expresión artística cultural viva "Saya Afroboliviana" perteneciente al Pueblo Afroboliviano.

Ley No. 906 del 8 de Marzo de 2017: Ley General de la Coca

Ley No. 1008 del 19 de Julio de 1988: Ley del Régimen de la Coca y Sustancias Controladas

Ley No. 1551 del 20 de Abril de 1994: Ley de Participación Popular

Ley No. 1565 del 7 de Julio de 1994: Ley de la Reforma Educativa

Ley No. 1715 del 18 de Octubre de 1996: Ley de Servicio Nacional de Reforma Agraria

Ley de la Reforma Agraria del 2 de Agosto de 1953

Reglamento Operativo de Cofinanciamiento, Programa Nacional de Turismo Comunitario (PNTC)

International conventions, declarations and documents

ILO Convention 169 concerning Indigenous and Tribal Peoples in Independent Countries 1989 (www ilo org/dyn/normlex/en/f?p=NORMLEX-PUB: 12100:0::NO::P12100_ILO_CODE:C169)

Interamerican Development Bank Project BO-L1039: Programa Nacional de Turismo Comunitario 2009 (http://idbdocs.iadb.org/wsdocs/getdocument.aspx?docnum=2258669)

United Nations Declaration on the Rights of Indigenous Peoples 2007 (https://www.un.org/development/desa/indigenouspeoples/declaration-on-the-rights-of-indigenous-peoples.html)

Cultural Studies

Elisa Ganivet
Border Wall Aesthetics
Artworks in Border Spaces

2019, 250 p., hardcover, ill.
79,99 € (DE), 978-3-8376-4777-8
E-Book: 79,99 € (DE), ISBN 978-3-8394-4777-2

Jocelyne Porcher, Jean Estebanez (eds.)
Animal Labor
A New Perspective on Human-Animal Relations

2019, 182 p., hardcover
99,99 € (DE), 978-3-8376-4364-0
E-Book: 99,99 € (DE), ISBN 978-3-8394-4364-4

Andreas Sudmann (ed.)
The Democratization of Artificial Intelligence
Net Politics in the Era of Learning Algorithms

2019, 334 p., pb., col. ill.
49,99 € (DE), 978-3-8376-4719-8
E-Book: 49,99 € (DE), ISBN 978-3-8394-4719-2

All print, e-book and open access versions of the titles in our list are available in our online shop www.transcript-verlag.de/en!